CONTENTS

Table of Cases		*xi*
Table of Legislation		*xiii*
Preface		*xxvii*
1.	**Introduction and Background**	**1**
	Development of data protection law in the United Kingdom	3
	Other areas of law protecting personal data	7
	Summary	9
2.	**The Data Protection Directive**	**12**
	Introduction	12
	General approach to data protection set out in the Directive	13
	General provisions	15
	General rules on the lawfulness of processing	16
	Judicial remedies, liabilities and sanctions	19
	Transfers to third countries	19
	Codes of conduct	21
	Supervisory authorities and the Working Party	21
	Community implementing measures and final provisions	22
3.	**Outline of the Data Protection Act 1998**	**24**
	Introduction	24
	Mechanism of Data Protection under the 1998 Act	25
	Some perspectives on the Act	27
	The data controller	27
	The data subject	30
	The data processor	34
	Third parties	36
	Summary of changes brought in by the Data Protection Act 1998	37
4.	**The Definitions**	**40**
	Basic definitions	40
	Data	40
	Relevant filing system	42

Accessible records   45
Personal data   46
Sensitive personal data   50
Processing   51
Processing for the special purposes   54
Actors (persons affected)   55
Application of Act   57
Definitions relevant to the transitional provisions   58

5.   The Data Protection Principles   60
The Data Protection Principles   60
Interpretation of the Principles   62
    First Principle   62
    Second Principle   63
    Third Principle   64
    Fourth Principle   64
    Fifth Principle   66
    Sixth Principle   66
    Seventh Principle   66
    Eighth Principle   69
Summary   70

6.   Notification   72
Notification   73
    Duty to notify changes   78
The Register   79
    Exemptions from notification   80
Assessable processing   83
Data Protection Supervisors   85
Duty to make information available   86
Notification Regulations and the Commissioner   87

7.   Constraints on Processing   88
Conditions for processing   89
    Non-sensitive personal data and Schedule 2   89
    Sensitive data and Schedule 3   96
Further conditions for processing sensitive personal data   104
Transfers to third countries   106

8.   Rights of Data Subjects   116
Introduction   116
Transparency   118
    Providing information to data subjects   119
    Disproportionate effort   124
        Subject access   127
        Subject access where another individual would be identified 133
        Credit reference   138

Enforced subject access   140
Subject access fees   142
Control over processing activity   143
  Right to prevent processing likely to cause substantial
        damage or substantial distress   143
  Impact on the laws of defamation and passing off   145
  Right to prevent processing for direct marketing   147
  Rights in relation to automated decision-taking   149
  Requirements for individuals' consent   152
  Compensation   154
  Rights in relation to inaccurate data, etc.   156
  Jurisdiction and procedure   158

9.   Exemptions and Transitional Provisions   160
Exemptions   160
  National security   164
  Crime and taxation   166
  Health, education and social work   170
     Health   170
     Education   175
     Social work   176
  Regulatory activity   178
  Special purposes – journalism, literature and art   180
  Research, history and statistics   184
  Manual data held by public authorities   185
  Information available to the public   186
  Disclosures required by law etc.   187
  Domestic purposes   189
  Schedule 7 exemptions   190
     Confidential references   190
     Armed forces   ·   191
     Judicial appointments and honours   192
     Crown employment etc   192
     Management forecasts   193
     Corporate finance   193
     Negotiations   195
     Examination marks   195
     Examination scripts   196
     Legal professional privilege   197
     Self-incrimination   197
     Miscellaneous subject access exemptions   197
The Transitional Provisions   198
  Introduction   198
  The first transitional period   200
     Manual data   200

Eligible automated data – general exemption   200
Eligible automated data – particular exemptions   202
The second transitional period   203
Processing for historical research (partial derogation)   204
Assessable processing   206

10. Enforcement and Criminal Offences   207
Introduction   207
System of notices   208
  Enforcement notice   209
  Information notice   210
  Special information notice   211
  Processing for the special purposes – restrictions on notices and
    determinations   212
  Appeals   212
Requests for assessment   213
Offences   214
  Offences related to notification   215
  Offences related to notices served by the Commissioner   217
  Obtaining, disclosing, procuring and selling offences   218
  Obstructing or failing to give assistance in respect of overseas
    information systems   219
  Enforced subject access   219
  Miscellaneous offences   220
  Liability of employees, senior officers etc.   222
  Mode of trial and penalties   222
Powers of entry and inspection   223
Forfeiture, etc.   226

**11. The Information Commissioner and the Information
Tribunal   227**
Introduction   227
The Information Commissioner   228
  The office of Information Commissioner   228
  Functions of the Information Commissioner   230
    Good practice and compliance   230
    Dissemination of information   231
    Codes of practice   231
    Dissemination of Community findings in relation to transfers to
      third countries   232
    Assessing processing with consent of data controllers   233
    Laying reports and codes of practice before each House of
      Parliament   234
    Assisting individuals where processing is for the special
      purposes   234
    International co-operation   235

Co-operation under the Data Protection Convention   235
Co-operation with the European Commission and other
    supervisory authorities   237
Co-operation in relation to transfers to third countries   239
Other potential functions   239
Power to inspect overseas information systems   239
Information provided to the Commissioner or Tribunal   240
The Information Tribunal   240
    Constitution   241
    Jurisdiction   242
    Procedure   243
        Notice of appeal and reply by Commissioner   243
        Amendment, application for striking out, withdrawal and
            consolidation   245
        Directions and inspection   246
        Power to determine without a hearing   248
        The hearing   248
        Determination and costs   250
    Procedure – national security   251
        Constitution and general duty of the Tribunal   252
        Bringing appeal, acknowledgement and reply   252
        Pre-hearing   254
        The hearing   255

12. **The First Report of the Commission on the Implementation
     of the Data Protection Directive   256**
Introduction   256
No amendment of the Directive   256
On-line survey   257
Main findings in the Report   258
    General disparities in implementation   258
    Applicable law   259
    Transfers to third countries   260
    Sound and image data   261
Summary and conclusions   261

13. **Processing Personal Data and the Community
     Institutions   263**
Introduction   263
Definitions and scope   264
Principles relating to data quality   264
Lawfulness of processing and special categories of data   265
Informing data subjects of their rights   266
Confidentiality of processing   267
Data protection officers   269
Transfers of personal data   271

Transfers within or between Community institutions or bodies   271
Transfers to recipients subject to the Directive   271
Transfers to recipients not subject to the Directive   272
Remaining provisions   273

14.   Privacy in Electronic Communications   276
Introduction   276
Relationship with the Data Protection Directive and Data Protection
    Act 1998   277
Security and confidentiality   278
Traffic data and itemised billing   278
Calling or connected line identification   280
Location data   281
Malicious or nuisance calls   282
Emergency calls   282
Automatic call forwarding   282
Directories of subscribers   283
Automated calling systems   284
Direct marketing purposes   284
Exemptions   286
Compensation etc.   286
Other provisions   287

Appendix 1

Directive 95/46/EC of the European Parliament and of the Council of 24
October 1995   289

Index   xx

TABLE OF CASES

A v B plc [2003] QB 195 117

A v X [2004] EWHC 447 (QB) 96

Amp Inc v *Utilux Pty Ltd* [1972] RPC 103 95

Anderson v *Halifax plc* [2000] NI 1 188

Ashcroft, Lord v *Attorney General* [2002] EWHC 1122 QB.....................7, 28, 61

Attorney-General v *Guardian Newspapers (No 2)* [1990] 1 AC 109 102

British Gas Trading Ltd v *Data Protection Registrar*, 24 March 1998 ....62, 120

Campbell, Naomi v *Mirror Group Newspapers Ltd* [2002]
    EWHC 499 (QB)...42, 54, 155, 182

Campbell, Naomi v *Mirror Group Newspapers Ltd* [2003] QB 633 ....54, 155, 182

Campbell, Naomi v *MGN Limited* [2004] 2 All ER 995 ....8, 54, 117, 155, 183

CCN Systems Ltd v *Data Protection Registrar*, 15 February 1991 131

Charleston v *News Group Newspapers* [1995] 2 AC 65 145

Clark, Alan Kenneth McKenzie v *Associated Newspapers Ltd* [1998] RPC 261 145

Coco v *A N Clark (Engineers) Ltd* [1969] RPC 41 102

Commission for the European Communities v *Grand Duchy of Luxembourg*,
    4 October 2001 24

Data Protection Registrar v *Amnesty International (British Section)*,
    23 November 1994 4

Data Protection Registrar v *Griffin* (unreported) 22 February 1993 189

Davidoff & Cie v *Gofkid Ltd* [2003] FSR 28 20

Douglas, Michael v *Hello! Limited* [2003] EMLR 585 ....8, 42, 117

Douglas, Michael v *Hello! Ltd* [2003] 3 All ER 996 ....154, 183

Douglas, Michael v *Hello! Limited* [2004] EMLR 13 154

Durant v *Financial Services Authority* [2003]
    EWCA Civ 1746..10, 33, 40, 43, 130, 135

Equifax Europe Ltd v *Data Protection Registrar*, 28 February 1992 ....131, 138

Farrer v *Secretary of State* [2002] EWHC 1917 (Admin) 69

Gaskin v *United Kingdom* [1989] ECHR 13 ....3, 33, 92, 120, 133
Guyer v *Walton (Inspector of Taxes)* [2001] STC (SCD) 75 187

Halifax Building Society, Agreement in the Enforcement Action against,
   6 January 1992...166
Hannover, von v *Germany*, 24 June 2004..8

Infolink Ltd v *Data Protection Registrar*, 28 February 1992 131
Information Commission v *Islington Borough Council* [2002]
   EWHC 1036 (Admin) 64
Innovations v *Data Protection Registrar*, 29 September 1993 ....27, 62, 120

Johnston v *Ireland* [1986] ECHR 17 120
Johnson v *Medical Defence Union Ltd* [2004] EWHC 2509 (Ch) 158

Lindqvist, Bodil, 6 November 2003...18, 47, 108, 262
Linguaphone Institute Ltd v *Data Protection Registrar*, 14 July 1995........120, 126

Martin's, James, Application for Judicial Review, 20 December 2002 167
M G v *United Kingdom* [2002] ECHR 627 ....3, 120, 135, 156
McGinley & Egan v *United Kingdom* [1998] ECHR 51 192
McGinley & Egan v *United Kingdom* [2000] ECHR 44 192
Midlands Electricity plc v *Data Protection Registrar*, 7 May 1999 ....9, 62
Morning Star Cooperative Society Ltd v *Express Newspapers Ltd* [1979]
   FSR 113 145

Ogle v *Chief Constable of Thames Valley Police [2001] EWCA*
   Civ 598..2, 65, 155

Peck v *United Kingdom* [2003] EHCR 44 168
Pelling v *Families Need Fathers Ltd* [2002] 2 All ER 440 188
Philips Electronics NV v *Remington Consumer Products* [1998] RPC 283 96

R v *Brentwood Borough Council, ex parte Peck* [1998] EMLR 697 168
R v *Brown* [1996] 1 AC 543...4, 53, 67
R v *Caldwell* [1982] AC 341 ....4, 217
R v *Chief Constable of 'B' ex parte R*, 24 November 1997 140
R v *Chief Constables of C and D ex parte A, The Times*, 7 November 2000 167
R v *Department of Health ex parte Source Informatics Ltd* [1999] 4 All ER 185 101
R v *Department of Health ex parte Source Informatics Ltd* [2001]
   QB 424 ....7, 49, 103, 184
R v *G* [2003] UKHL 50 217
R v *Gold* [1988] 2WLR 984 108
R v *Lawrence* [1982] AC 510 ....4, 217

R v *Mid-Glamorgan Family Health Services, ex parte Martin* [1995] 1
    All ER 356 174
R v *Ministry of Agriculture, Fisheries and Food, ex parte Fisher* [2000]
    ECR I-6751...17, 95
R *(on application of Alan Lord)* v *Secretary of State for the Home Department*
    [2003] EWHC 2073 (Admin)......................................129, 136, 138, 158
R *(on application of Ellis)* v *Chief Constable of Essex Police* [2003] EWHC 1321
    (Admin) 169
R *(on application of S and another)* v *Chief Constable of South Yorkshire* [2003] 1
    All ER 148 169
R *(Robinson)* v *Wakefield Metropolitan District Council* [2002] QB 1052 148
R v *Wozencroft* [2002] EWHC 1724 (Fam) 138
Re Ewing (unreported) 20 December 2002...166, 252
Rechnungshof v *Österreichischer Rundfunk and Others* [2003] ECR I-4989 ..18,91
Rhondda BC v *Data Protection Registrar* (unreported) 11 October 1991 64
Rowley v *Liverpool City Council* (unreported) 26 October 1989 187
RTE & ITP v *Commission* [1995] FSR 530 8

Sidaway v *Board of Governors of the Bethlem Royal Hospital* [1985] AC 871 ..174
Sim v *Stretch* [1936] 2 All ER 1237 145
Spring v *Guardian Assurance plc* [1995] 2 AC 296 190

Tournier v *National Provincial* [1924] 1 KB 461..7, 139

X v *Chief Constable of Greater Manchester* [2004] EWHC 262 (QB) 155

Z v *Finland* (1988) 25 EHRR 371 2

TABLE OF LEGISLATION

Page No.

Acts of Parliament

Access to Health Records Act 1990 ....30, 41, 131
Access to Personal Files Act 1987..3, 30, 41, 200
Adoption Act 1976...198
Banking Act 1987 ....44, 55, 82–85
Child Support Act 1991 171
Child Support Act 1995 171
Children Act 1989
s 24D...180
s 26 180
s 26ZA...180
s 26ZB 180
s 41 177
Communications Act 2003 280
s 56(5)...283
s 151 278
Companies Act 1985
s 356(6)..188
Competition Act 1998
s 18 8
Computer Misuse Act 1990
s 1 77
s 2 77
Consumer Credit Act 1974 130
s 158 ....31, 38, 138
s 159 ....138, 200, 229
Contempt of Court Act 1981
s 14(1)...221
Contracts (Rights of Third Parties) Act 1999 112
Copyright, Designs and Patents Act 1988
s 17(6)...108
s 47 113
s 84 147

Crime (International Co-operation) Act 2003...239
s 81 219
Criminal Justice and Public Order Act 1994
s 161 218
s 163 168
Courts and Legal Services Act 1990
s 71 241
Data Protection Act 1984..4, 26, 30, 33, 37, 71, 116, 140
s 5(1)..133
s 5(2)...53, 103
s 5(2)(b) and (d) 217
s 5(6)..133, 218
s 5(7)..133, 218
s 7(6)...77
s 21 140
s 23 7
s 26(4)...140
s 32(2)...187
s 33(2) to (5)...203
s 34(4)...203
s 34(5)...187
Data Protection Act 1998...6, 25
s 1 16
s 1(1)...40, 44, 46, 143, 146, 199
s 1(1)(a)...41, 58, 73, 142
s 1(1)(b) 41, 58, 73, 142
s 1(1)(c)...41
s 1(1)(d) 41
s 1(1)(e)...41
s 1(3)..53
s 2 ....50, 97, 100
s 3 ....54, 105, 144
s 4(4) 55, 61, 73,165
s 5 57
s 5(1)..238
s 6(2)..227
s 6(5)..241
s 6(6)..241
ss 7 to 9 127
s 7 ....44, 66, 138, 158, 160, 162, 166, 170, 186, 197, 200, 221
s 7(1)..127
s 7(1)(b) to (d) 177
s 7(1)(c)(i) 142
s 7(3)..133
s 7(4) to (6)...159

s 7(4)..133, 136, 138, 176
s 7(4)(b) 135
s 7(4)(c) 174
s 7(5)...134
s 7(6)..77, 134, 136
s 7(9)..................................44, 133, 137, 159, 174, 176, 180
s 7(12)...176
s 8 127
s 8(2)...128
s 8(2)(a) 129,137
s 8(3)...129
s 8(5)...132
s 9 ....127, 130, 138, 200
ss 10 to 14 47
s 10 ....161, 163, 186
s 10(1)..66, 143, 145
s 10(3)...66
s 10(4)...180
s 11 ....148, 284
s 11(1)..66
s 11(2)...148
s 12 ....66, 150,163, 186
s 12(1)...150
s 12(2)(a)..151
s 12(2)(b) 151
s 12(3)...151
s 12(5) to (7)..150
s 12(7)...150
s 12(8)...180
s 12A...23, 158, 200
s 12A(3) 180, 234
s 13 ....7, 61, 154, 156, 159, 182, 186
s 14 ....61, 138, 156, 159, 180
s 14(1) to (3)..161, 163, 186, 203
s 14(1)...157
s 14(2)...157
s 14(3)...157
s 15 158
s 15(2)...158
s 16(1)..74, 216
s 17(1)...73
s 19(1)...79
s 19(2)...79
s 19(4)...77
s 19(6)...80

s 19(7)...80
s 20 78
s 20(1)...78
s 20(2)...78
s 21(1)...74, 215, 226
s 21(2)..215, 226
s 21(3)...215
s 22 ....83, 206, 226
s 22(6)..216, 226
s 22(7)...85
s 23 85
s 24 ....75, 77, 86
s 24(4)...216
s 24(5)...216
s 25 87
s 27 160
s 27(5)...161
s 28 ....88, 105, 162, 164, 225, 242, 251
s 28(2)..165, 243
s 28(4)...241, 243, 251
s 28(6)...243, 251, 253
s 29 ....94, 105, 162, 166
s 29(1)...166
s 29(2)...167
s 29(3)...167
s 29(4)...170
s 29(5)...170
s 30 ....161, 162, 170
s 31 ....163, 178
s 31(2)...178
s 31(4)...179
s 31(4A) 179
s 31(5)...179
s 31(6)...179
s 32 ....88, 105, 163, 211
s 32(1) to (3)..182
s 32(2)..144, 180
s 32(3)..181, 232
s 32(4)...180, 182, 211
s 32(5)..180, 182
s 32(6)...181
s 33 ....23, 105, 163, 204
s 33(1)..184, 204
s 33(2)...185
s 33(3)...185

s 33(4)..185
s 33(5)..185, 205
s 33A..163, 185
s 34..163, 186
s 35..163, 187
s 35(1)..188
s 36...80, 87, 88, 105, 164, 189
s 37..190
s 38(1)...161, 170, 175, 197
s 38(2)..161
s 40..209
s 41..210
s 42...150, 207, 211, 213, 236
s 43..210
ss 44 to 46 287
s 44..211
s 45..180, 182, 210, 212, 223, 243
s 45(1)..212
s 46..212
s 46(3)..210
s 47..208
s 47(1)..217, 226
s 47(2)..217
s 47(3)..217
s 48..210, 212, 242
s 48(1)..245, 249
s 48(3)..242, 245, 248
ss 51 to 54 228
s 51..229, 230
s 51(1)..230
s 51(2)..231
s 51(3)..231, 234
s 51(4)..231
s 51(6)..232
s 51(7)..229, 232
s 51(8)..234
s 52(1)..234
s 52(3)..234
s 53..234
s 54..57, 235
s 54(1)..235
s 54(2)..236
s 54(3)..237
s 54(4)..239
s 54(5)..239

s 54(6)..239
s 54(7)..239
s 54A..219, 239
s 54A(6) 219
s 55 ....162, 164, 186, 189, 218, 222, 226, 251
s 55(1)..208, 218
s 55(2)..218
s 55(4)..218
s 55(5)..218
s 56 ....24, 32, 141, 165, 219, 222, 226
s 56(1)..219
s 56(2)..219
s 56(3)..220
s 57 142
s 58 240
s 59 ....77, 215, 220
s 59(2)..220
s 60(1)..215
s 60(2)..223
s 60(3).............................:..221
s 60(4)..226
s 61 ....215, 222
s 62 138
s 62(2) to (4)..229
s 67(2)..197
s 67(3)..232
s 68 41
s 68(1)...45
s 68(2)..45, 142
s 69 ....45, 101, 142, 171
s 70 ....16, 56
s 70(1)..221
s 70(2)..156
s 75(4)..141
Sch 1 ....24, 35, 60
Part I 61
Part II 62
paras 2 to 4 63
para 2 ....124, 160
para 2(1) 121
para 2(2) 122
para 2(3) 121, 124
para 3(1) 125
para 3(2) 125
para 5 ....121, 124

para 7 157
para 10 214
para 11 214
para 13 232
para 15 111
para 15(2) 232
Sch 2 ....17, 50, 61, 89, 144, 152, 160
Sch 3 ....17, 50, 61, 89, 96, 152, 160
para 2(2) 99
para 3 106
para 4 101
para 4(a)(ii)...101
para 9(2) 99
para 10 ....99, 104
Sch 4...70, 110
para 2 ....112, 153
para 3 ....112, 153
para 5 92
para 8 ....153, 239
para 9 239
Sch 5 ....228, 241
para 1(2) 228
para 2 228
para 3 228
para 4 228
para 6 229
para 7 229
para 8 229
para 9 229
para 10 229
Sch 6...213, 242
para 3 252
Sch 7...24
para 1 ....164, 190
para 2 ....164, 191
para 3 ....164, 192
para 4 ....161, 164
para 5 ....164, 193
para 6 ....164, 193
para 7 ....161, 164, 195
para 8 ....164, 195
para 9 164
para 10 ....94, 164, 197
para 11 164
Sch 8..58, 198

para 1 198
para 5 202
para 6 202
para 13 201
para 19 206
Sch 9 ....221, 223
para 12 221
Sch 10 235
Sch 11 ....45, 132
para 4(a) 176
para 4(b) 176
Sch 12 46
Sch 13 23
para 1 ....158, 200
Sch 14 ....77, 198
para 2(1) 77
para 2(3) 77, 198
Education Act 1996
s 6(2) 45, 175
s 576(1) 175
s 579(1) 132
Employer's Liability (Compulsory Insurance) Act 1969 229
Financial Services Act 1986 194
Financial Services and Markets Act 2000
s 233 179
Forgery and Counterfeiting Act 1980 108
Freedom of Information Act 2000 ....6, 8, 34, 77, 185, 190, 220, 227, 240
s 1 221
s 3(2) 41
s 6 41
s 23(2) 241
s 23(3) 241
s 60(1) 241
s 77 ....221, 226
Sch 1 41
Sch 3 226
Health and Social Care (Community Health and Standards) Act 2003
s 113(1) 179
s 113(2) 179
s 114(1) 179
s 114(3) 179
Human Fertilisation and Embryology Act 1990 198
Human Rights Act 1998 ....43, 116, 191
Jobseekers Act 1995 141
Judicial Pensions and Retirement Act 1993 242

Local Government Act 1972
s 111 168
Office of Communications Act 2002
s 1 280
Police Act 1997..219
Part V 141, 220
Police and Criminal Evidence Act 1984
s 64(1A) 169
Police and Criminal Justice Act 2001 169
Powers of Criminal Courts (Sentencing) Act 2000
s 92 141
Prison Act 1952 141
Rehabilitation of Offenders Act 1974 140
Registered Designs Act 1949 95
Social Security Administration Act 1992...141
Social Security Contributions and Benefits Act 1992 141
Supreme Court Act 1981
s 42 ....166, 241
Taxes Management Act 1970
s 19A 188
Trade Union and Labour Relations (Consolidation) Act 1992
s 296 80

Statutory Instruments
Data Protection Act 1998 (Commencement Order) 2000...........................141
Data Protection (Conditions under Paragraph 3 of Part II of Schedule 1)
    Order 2000 122,125
Art 4 125
Art 5 125
Data Protection (Corporate Finance Exemption) Order 2000 164,194
Data Protection (Crown Appointments) Order 2000 ....164, 193
Data Protection (Designated Codes of Practice) (No 2) Order 2000 ....181, 232
Data Protection (Fees under section 19(7)) Regulations 2000.......................80
Data Protection (Functions of Designated Authority) Order 2000 235
Data Protection (International Co-operation) Order 2000 237
Art 3 237
Art 4 237
Art 4(2) 237
Art 5 238
Art 7 238
Data Protection (Miscellaneous Subject Access Exemptions) (Amendment)
    Order 2000...39
Data Protection (Miscellaneous Subject Access Exemptions)
    Order 2000...39, 197
Data Protection (Notification and Notification Fees) (Amendment)
    Regulations 2001 77

Data Protection (Notification and Notification Fees)
 Regulations 2000 ....39, 74, 120, 187, 201
Reg 3...80
Reg 4...75
Reg 5...76
Reg 6...76
Reg 8...74
Reg 11...78
Reg 12(2) 79, 215
Reg 13...78
Data Protection (Processing of Sensitive Personal Data) (Elected
 Representatives) Order 2002 106
Data Protection (Processing of Sensitive Personal Data)
 Order 2000...51, 97, 104, 168
Data Protection (Subject Access) (Fees and Miscellaneous Provisions)
 (Amendment) Regulations 2001 ....130, 142
Data Protection (Subject Access) (Fees and Miscellaneous Provisions)
 Regulations 2000 ....128, 130
Reg 3...142
Reg 4...133
Reg 5...142
Data Protection (Subject Access Modification) (Education)
 Order 2000...164, 175
Art 5(1) 175
Art 7 176
Data Protection (Subject Access Modification) (Health) Order 2000 ..164, 170
Art 4 171
Art 5(1) 173
Art 5(2) 171
Art 6(1) 171
Art 6(2) 171
Art 7 172
Art 8 174
Data Protection (Subject Access Modification) (Social Work)
 Order 2000...164, 176
Art 5(1) 177
Sch 176, 178
Data Protection Tribunal (Enforcement Appeals) Rules 2000 ....243, 250
Rule 4 243
Rule 27 246
Data Protection Tribunal (National Security Appeals) Rules 2000 251
Education (Special Educational Needs) Regulations 1994..........................198
Family Proceedings Courts (Children Act 1989) Rules 1991 171,198
Family Proceedings Rules 1991 198
Information Tribunal (Enforcement Appeals) (Amendment) Rules 2002....240

Investment Services Regulations 1995..194
Sch 1..194
Health and Social Services Trust under the Children (Northern Ireland)
    Order 1995..93
Magistrates' Courts (Children and Young Persons) Rules 1992 175
Parental Orders (Human Fertilisation and Embryology) Regulations 1994 198
Pensions Appeals Tribunals (Scotland) Rules 1981
Rule 6 192
Privacy and Electronic Communications (EC Directive) (Amendment)
    Regulations 2004 277
Privacy and Electronic Communications (EC Directive)
    Regulations 2003 ....227, 277
Reg 2(2) 277
Reg 2(3) 277
Reg 4..277
Reg 5..278
Reg 6..278
Reg 7..279
Reg 8..279
Reg 9..280
Reg 10..280
Reg 11..280
Reg 12..281
Reg 13..281
Reg 14..281
Reg 15..282
Reg 16..282
Reg 18..283
Reg 19..284
Reg 20..284
Reg 21..285
Reg 22..285
Reg 23..285
Reg 24..286
Reg 26..285
Reg 27..287
Reg 28..286
Reg 29..286
Reg 30..286
Reg 31..287
Representation of the People (England and Wales) (Amendment)
    Regulations 2002 149
Telecommunications (Data Protection and Privacy)
    Regulations 1999 ....227, 276

Telecommunications (Data Protection and Privacy) (Amendment)
   Regulations 2000 276

European Community Legislation

Treaties
EC Treaty (Treaty of Rome)
Art 81 8
Art 82 8
Art 226 ....259, 262
Art 234 10
Art 288 ....263, 274

Regulations
Regulation (EC) 45/2001 on the protection of individuals with regard to the
processing of personal data by the Community institutions and bodies and
on the free movement of such data, OJ L 8, 12.01.2001, p.1 263
Art 2 264
Art 3 264
Art 4 ....264, 271
Art 5 265
Art 6 ....265, 271
Art 7 271
Art 8 271
Art 9 272
Art 9(6) 272
Art 9(7) 273
Art 10 ....265, 271
Art 11 266
Art 12 267
Art 13 267
Art 15 267
Art 22(2) 268
Art 24 269
Art 27 269
Arts 28 to 31...273
Art 32 274
Art 33 275
Art 41 273
Arts 46 to 48...274

Directives
First Council Directive 89/104/EEC of 21 December 1988 to approximate the
laws of the Member States relating to trade marks, OJ L 40, 11.02.1989, p.1
Art 5(2) 20

Directive 95/46/EC of the European Parliament and of the Council of
  24 October 1995 on the protection of individuals with regard to the
  processing of personal data and on the free movement of such data,
  OJ L 281, 23.11.1995, p.31 3
Art 1 13
Art 1(1) 12,17
Art 2...51,90
Art 2(a) 146
Art 2(b) 15
Art 2(h)..16, 152
Art 3 16
Art 3(2) 88, 161, 189
Art 4 ....16, 257, 259
Art 5 16
Art 6 ....14, 17, 23
Art 6(1) 92
Art 7 ....17, 23, 89, 92
Art 7(c) 92
Art 7(e) 89, 92
Art 7(f) 94, 259
Art 8 ....17, 23, 92, 96, 100, 257
Art 8(5) 97
Art 9 ....18, 54, 180
Art 10 ....18, 262
Art 11 18
Art 11(1) 123
Art 11(2) 120, 122
Art 12 ....18, 257
Art 12(a) 141
Art 13 ....18, 162, 196
Art 13(1) 162
Art 13(1)(g)..162
Art 14 18
Art 14(b)..148
Art 15 ....18, 149
Art 15(1) 131
Art 16 19
Art 17 19
Arts 18 to 21...19
Art 18 257
Art 19 ....29, 260
Art 20 83
Art 22 19
Art 23 19
Art 24 19

Art 25 ....19, 111, 153, 257
Art 25(1) 108, 260
Art 25(2) 111, 232
Art 25(4) 70
Art 25(6) 70, 260
Art 26 ....20, 110, 153, 257
Art 26(1) 153
Art 26(2) 237, 239
Art 26(3) 22, 233
Art 26(4) 22, 233, 260
Art 27 21
Art 28 21
Art 28(3) 238
Art 29 ....21, 111, 262
Art 30 22
Art 30(1) 111
Art 31 22
Art 31(2) 70, 111, 232, 239
Art 32 23
Art 32(2) 52
Art 33 ....256, 261
Directive 97/66/EC of 15 December 1997 concerning the processing of
    personal data and the protection of privacy in the telecommunications
    sector, OJ L 24, 30.01.1998, p.1 276
Directive 2002/58/EC of the European Parliament and of the Council of
    12 July 2002 concerning the processing of personal data and the
    protection of privacy in the electronic communications sector,
    OJ L 201, 31.07.2002, p.37 277
Art 19 ....273, 277

Decisions
Commission Decision 2001/497/EC of 15 June 2001 on standard contractual
    clauses for the transfer of personal data to third countries, under Directive
    95/46/EC, OJ L 181, 04.07.2001, p.19...114
Commission Decision 2002/16/EC of 27 December 2001 on standard
    contractual clauses for the transfer of personal data to processors
    established in third countries, under Directive 95/46/EC, OJ L 6,
    10.01.2002, p. 52...114
Decision 2004/55/EC of the European Parliament and of the Council of 22
    December 2003 appointing the independent supervisory body as
    provided under Article 286 of the EC Treaty (European Data Protection
    Supervisor), OJ L 12, 17.01.2004, p.47 ....263, 274

Conventions
Council of Europe Convention for the Protection of Human Rights and
    Fundamental Freedoms...34

Art 8 ....1, 43, 117, 134, 154, 156, 168, 192, 196
Art 8(1) 169, 188
Art 8(2) 169, 188
Art 10 ....1, 54, 117
Art 13 168
Council of Europe Convention for the Protection of Individuals with regard
    to Automatic Processing of Personal Data of 1981 ....14, 116
Art 1 2
Art 5 14
Art 7 14
Art 8 ....128, 236
art 13 235
Art 14(3) 236
Protocol 14

PREFACE

There have been many developments since the first edition of this book was published in 2000. The Data Protection Act 1998 has undergone a number of changes and there have been numerous important cases which have helped clarify some of the more obscure parts of data protection law. What has become even clearer is that data protection law is intertwined with the Council of Europe Convention for the Protection of Human Rights and Fundamental Freedoms. This Convention informs data protection law and helps in understanding and balancing the right of respect for private and family life and the right of freedom of expression. The law of breach of confidence has also been influenced by this Convention and also overlaps with data protection law. It is not unusual for litigation to involve the Convention rights, issues of confidence and data protection law.

The Freedom of Information Act 2000 also has implications for data protection law as much information held by public authorities will contain or constitute personal data. Indeed, the definition of 'data' in the Data Protection Act 1998 has been extended to include unstructured files held by public authorities. However, where the data are personal data, they fall to be dealt with under the Data Protection Act 1998.

The European Commission has completed its first Report on the working of data protection law, somewhat late as a result of the delays in implementing the Directive in a number of member states, including the United Kingdom. The latest date for transposing the Directive into national law was 24 October 1998. The United Kingdom's Act (plus a host of secondary legislation) came into force on 1 March 2000. This resulted in more complex transitional provisions than would otherwise have been the case. The European Commission's report shows that there are a number of concerns about data protection law and, unfortunately, some disparities between the different implementations of it. However, it was thought too early to change the Directive at this stage but some of the concerns are bound to be of a continuing nature and it would not be surprising if the next report proposes modification to the Directive.

One area where the Directive is particularly weak is in respect of the internet. The European Court of Justice held that placing personal data on a webpage did not involve a transfer of data to third countries. This finding has serious implications for the protection of personal data but shows how information technology has moved on since the Directive was drafted.

A parallel area of concern is the use of personal data in telecommunications and electronic networks. The European Commission had to act quickly to catch up with technological change and the original privacy in telecommunications Directive of 1997 was replaced by a Directive on privacy in electronic communications in 2002. This was implemented in the United Kingdom by the Privacy and Electronic Communications (EC Directive) Regulations 2003 and forms the subject matter of the final chapter of this book.

My aim in writing this second edition has been to describe and explain the data protection law, including all the developments subsequent to the Act at Royal Assent, in a practical and accessible manner from the perspectives of both data controllers and data subjects. The first two chapters give an introduction to data protection law and the Directive. Chapter 3 gives an outline of the Act and its underlying mechanism and logic whilst Chapter 4 looks closely at the definitions in the Act. These definitions are central to the scope and reach of data protection law. The data protection principles are then examined in Chapter 5. These are at the root of data protection law. They originally derive, at least in large part, from the Council of Europe Convention on the Protection of Individuals with regard to Automatic Processing of Personal Data. The following two chapters look at data protection law specifically from the perspective of data controllers in relation to the requirements for notification of processing activities and the constraints on processing, such as the conditions for processing and the situation regarding transfers of personal data to third countries, being countries outside the European Economic Area. In view of the growing internationalisation of data processing these latter provisions are of some importance. International transfers to third countries is also an area attracting some criticism by the European Commission.

Chapter 8 covers the rights of data subjects, which are more extensive than under the previous law though their exercise appears to be somewhat variable. Lack of awareness may be a problem, though it seems that individuals in the United Kingdom have a better awareness than in some other Member States. The exemptions and transitional provisions are contained in Chapter 9. The exemptions are particularly extensive and case law has usefully clarified the scope of some of them. Chapters 10 and 11 relate to the Information Commissioner and enforcement of data protection law and the criminal offences under the Act. The role of the Information

Tribunal is also covered as are the duties and powers of the Information Commissioner in relation to data protection law. Chapter 12 contains a summary of the European Commission's first report on the implementation of data protection law and Chapter 13 looks at the appointment and role of the recently appointed European Data Protection Commissioner, charged with ensuring compliance with a data protection Regulation that applies to Community institutions and bodies. The final chapter, as noted above, deals with privacy in electronic communications, which can be seen as a form of data protection law tailored to the particular risks to privacy posed by traditional telephones, mobile telephony and communications via the internet.

I would like to thank those that have helped and encouraged me, in particular, my wife Lorraine and Andrew Griffin. I have endeavoured to state the law as it was on 1 January 2005.

David Bainbridge
1 January 2005

CHAPTER 1
INTRODUCTION AND BACKGROUND

Data protection law affects us all. We are all data subjects and numerous organisations and individuals are processing personal data relating to each and every one of us. Everyone is affected by data processing activities where personal information is involved and it is in all our interests that such activities are regulated. However, regulation cannot be too restrictive otherwise this can have consequences for the right of freedom of expression and would also impose heavy organisational and financial costs on those who process personal data. A balance has to be struck and this is one of the aims of data protection law – to reconcile privacy and freedom of expression. This itself is a reflection of the Council of Europe Convention for the Protection of Human Rights and Fundamental Freedoms 1950 ("the Human Rights Convention") with its right to respect for private and family life under Article 8 and the right of freedom of expression under Article 10.

Changes to society and technology have increased the dangers associated with inadequate controls on processing activities. The use of computer technology and the ability to transfer and publish information all over the world, the processing of sensitive data (for example, relating to medical conditions, criminal convictions or DNA profiles), offender naming schemes, the use of CCTV and the ability to locate an individual carrying a mobile telephone are just some of the things that could give rise to concerns if not properly regulated. In one case, a man was caught on CCTV carrying a large knife. He later slashed his wrists in a failed suicide attempt. The footage was broadcast and stills from the footage were published. Although an attempt was made to hide his identity, some people recognised him. Another problem is where inaccurate personal data are processed or disclosed to others. A man who was driving was stopped by the police and arrested because the police national computer incorrectly recorded him as being disqualified from driving. That information should have been entered against another person who had a similar name. The man lost his job and his car was impounded. It took him four months to trace the person to whom the conviction related before he could clear his name and have the entry corrected.[1]

---

[1] (1990) *The Times*, 8 May p.4.

In a similar case, a man had been disqualified from driving for four years and this was recorded on the police national computer. His appeal was successful to the extent that the period of disqualification was reduced to two years but the computer entry did not properly reflect this and 21 months after his two-year ban ended he was arrested on suspicion of driving whilst disqualified and detained by the police for over two hours before being released.[2] Other processing activities can give rise to concerns, for example, the use of information relating to a person's financial status or credit rating or where a person is denied an opportunity because a previous occupant of the person's house or flat happened to have been in default of a loan. An evil of lesser degree, though still of some nuisance value, is the sending of 'junk mail' and unwanted emails ("spam").

This book is not only concerned with data protection law from the perspective of individuals, it also addresses the position of those who process personal data and have to comply with data protection law. Hardly any organisation in the private and public sector does not fall within the realms of data protection law and the same applies to sole traders, partnerships and even private individuals, though the latter are exempt from much of data protection law if the processing is carried out purely for personal or household purposes.

Data protection law derives originally from the Council of Europe Convention for the Protection of Individuals with regard to Automatic Processing of Personal Data 1981 ("the Data Protection Convention"). That Convention is itself influenced by the Human Rights Convention; Article 1 states that its purpose is to secure respect for "... *rights and fundamental freedoms, and in particular [the] right to privacy, with regard to automatic processing of personal data* ...". The link between data protection law and human rights was seen in *Z v Finland*[3], where the European Court of Human Rights stated (at para 95):

> "... *the court will take into account that the protection of personal data, not least medical data, is of fundamental importance to a person's enjoyment of his or her right to respect for private and family life as guaranteed by article 8 of the Convention. Respecting the confidentiality of health data is a vital principle in the legal systems of all the contracting parties to the Convention. It is crucial not only to respect the sense of privacy of a patient but also to preserve his or her confidence in the medical profession and in the health services in general.*"

Article 8 of the Human Rights Convention provides for a right of respect for private and family life. This may impose a positive duty to give access to

---

[2] *Ogle v Chief Constable of Thames Valley Police* [2001] EWCA Civ 598.
[3] (1988) 25 EHRR 371.

personal data which mirrors the right of access under data protection law. In *MG v United Kingdom*,[4] European Court of Human Rights, a person sought access to social service records relating to his time in care as a child. The records were created before 1 April 1989. Limited access was given but this was held to breach Article 8 up to 1 March 2000. That date is significant. It is the date that the Data Protection Act 1998 came into force which provided for appeals against a refusal to provide access to some or all of the data requested, no matter when the data were created (apart from some transitional provisions). As the person had not exercised his right of appeal under the 1998 Act, he could not show that there had been a failure of the positive duty to provide the information he sought. Before 1 March 2000, the Access to Personal Files Act 1987 applied to social records and gave a right to appeal but only in respect of records created on or after 1 April 1989, the date the 1987 Act and Regulations made under it came into force. The Data Protection Act 1998 sought to include the effect of an earlier case on subject access[5], to deal with subject access requests where other persons might be identified or where the person creating the relevant data objected to its release. Cases such as these show clearly how the Human Rights Convention provides the touchstone for the most important elements of data protection law.

The Data Protection Convention remains the principal source of data protection law and the rights and freedoms set out in the Convention are given substance and are amplified by Directive 95/46/EC of the European Parliament and of the Council of 24 October 1995 on the protection of individuals with regard to the processing of personal data and on the free movement of such data.[6] The Directive is the basis for the Data Protection Act 1998.

The previous Act of the United Kingdom, the Data Protection Act 1984 was a response to the Data Protection Convention and, like the Convention, only applied to automatic processing of personal data and not manual processing of personal data. The Data Protection Act 1998 subsequently extended data protection law to some forms of manual processing and made other sweeping changes to data protection law.

DEVELOPMENT OF DATA PROTECTION LAW IN THE UNITED KINGDOM

In the United Kingdom there have been concerns expressed about automatic processing of personal data from as early as 1961 resulting in a number of

---

[4] [2002] ECHR 627.
[5] *Gaskin v United Kingdom* [1989] ECHR 13.
[6] OJ L 281, 23.11.1995, p.31 (see recital 11 to the Directive).

Parliamentary Bills, Reports and White Papers concerning privacy and data protection. The watershed report was the *Lindop Report*.[7] Following the European Convention on data protection, and delayed for a year because of an impending general election, the Data Protection Act 1984 received Royal Assent on 12 July 1984. George Orwell would have been impressed with the timing. The Act was brought into force in a number of stages, the last of which concerned individuals' rights of access and which came into force on 11 November 1987. There were quite a number of cases under the Act, most of which were heard by the Data Protection Tribunal (set up under the Act and now called the Information Tribunal) or otherwise unreported though one case in which the meaning of using personal data was at issue did make it to the House of Lords.[8] A narrow view was taken by their lordships (by a 3:2 majority) but, because of the much wider definitions in the 1998 Act, this case is of historical interest only. Nevertheless, some cases under the 1984 Act still have relevance today and are useful in interpreting the current law. In particular, cases on what constitutes fair processing of personal data are still enlightening. Another case in the Queen's Bench Division involving Amnesty International[9] even helped explain the meaning of recklessness, reconciling the distinction between Lord Diplock's judgments on recklessness delivered on the same day in *R* v *Caldwell*[10] and *R* v *Lawrence*.[11] Incredibly, this case was never included in the recognised formal law reports, even though *Caldwell* and *Lawrence* had attracted considerable interest amongst law students and academic lawyers for many years.

Just as those persons and organisations affected by the 1984 Act, the Office of the Data Protection Registrar (which had been established under the Act) and the courts were coming to terms with the implications of this strange new law, things were developing in Europe. Data protection law varied across the European Community and some member states were without a formal data protection law. The European Commission recognised that this posed dangers in two ways. First, it could prejudice the rights and freedoms of individuals in some member states and, secondly, it could result in barriers to the free flow of personal data being erected within the Community. For example, a Member State with strong data protection law, such as Germany, might object to the transfer of personal data from Germany to another Member State such as Greece which did not, at the time, have specific data protection laws in place.

The way forward was simple in its conception. By implementing a strong data protection law throughout the Community, freedom of movement of

---

[7] Report of the Committee on Data Protection, Cmnd. 7341, HMSO, 1978.
[8] *R* v *Brown* [1996] 1 AC 543.
[9] *Data Protection Registrar* v *Amnesty International (British Section)*, 23 November 1994.
[10] [1982] AC 341.
[11] [1982] AC 510.

personal data throughout the Community could be assured. The difficulty was how to achieve that in practice and it proved to be a difficulty which appeared at one time almost insurmountable. Cries of over-regulation and dispropor- tionate costs of compliance came from some governments and many organi- sations processing personal data. This was particularly so in the United Kingdom and the Netherlands. In respect of the United Kingdom, the prin- ciple of self-regulation was then in vogue.

The first proposed Directive came out of Brussels in 1990[12] and, with its twin track approach for the public sector and the private sector, it looked very unwieldy. The next proposal[13] managed to attract outright hostility. A survey commissioned by the Home Office in 1994 and carried out by the CBI indi- cated that the cost of compliance with the proposed new law would, for the 625 organisations included in the survey, be in the order of £2.3bn in the first year alone. The NHS considered that all individuals would have to be asked for their express permission for personal data relating to them to be processed and that this would cost in excess of £1bn. Around 70 per cent of the anticipated costs in the Home Office survey were associated with the extension of data protection law to manual files.

During 1994, a team from Aston Business School (including the author of this book) together with colleagues from the University of Leiden carried out an in-depth study of the implementation and recurring costs for data controllers in complying with the proposed new data protection law for the European Commission. This study, which looked at compliance and on-going costs in a number of organisations of different sizes and in different sectors in the United Kingdom and the Netherlands showed that the above figures were greatly exaggerated and the costs would be much less in practice. Some of the requirements of the new law such as having proper security measures, ensuring personal data were accurate and up to date and not retaining data longer than necessary, simply reflected good practice in information systems. Other requirements, particularly in respect of manual data seemed more onerous but, especially as the new law was implemented, have proved not to be as burdensome as might have been anticipated. As Mr Ulf Bruhann of the European Commission told us during one of our meetings at the Commission "A cake is not so hot in the eating as it is in the oven".[14]

The Directive was adopted towards the end of 1995, with the United Kingdom abstaining (previously the United Kingdom had intimated that it would vote the Directive down). Although the Directive as adopted was similar in many respects to the text of the 1992 proposal, there had been a number of changes,

---

[12] OJ C 277, 5.11.1990, p.3.
[13] OJ C 311, 27.11.1992, p.38.
[14] I quote from memory but, hopefully, accurately.

some of which could be said to reflect some of the concerns being shown about the financial impact of the new law.

The new data protection law was required to be implemented by 24 October 1998 at the latest. Given the breadth and complexity of data protection law (the Act at Royal Assent contained some 75 sections and 16 Schedules and 17 statutory instruments were made under the Act, not including the Commencement Order), it is not surprising that it was not transposed into United Kingdom law at that time. Eventually, the deadline was set at 1 March 2000, partly because of the amount of delegated legislation that needed to be drafted. So far as the costs of implementation were concerned the financial memorandum to the Bill as laid before Parliament contained the following estimates:

Sector	Start-up costs £m	Annual recurring costs £m
Central Government	90	46
Local Government	104	29
Private Sector	836	630
Voluntary Sector	120	37

It will be noted that these estimates are considerably less than those arrived at in the Home Office survey.

It is fairly clear that the Bill was a hurried piece of draftsmanship and there were some significant amendments in Parliament. Even then there were defects that had to be cured by statutory instruments. For example, the Act provided exemption from some of its provisions in relation to processing for research purposes but, if the data were sensitive personal data, the Act in its original form did not permit processing sensitive personal data for research purposes. An amendment to the Bill allowed processing of sensitive personal data relating to racial or ethnic origin for the purposes of equal opportunity monitoring but equivalent processing of personal data relating to religious beliefs or disability was missed. Amongst other things, this had to be remedied by statutory instrument.

Since the 1998 Act came into force, there have been numerous amendments to the Act and delegated legislation. There have also been some important cases on data protection law, including cases before the House of Lords and the European Court of Justice. Further, the Act has had to cope with the impact of the Freedom of Information Act 2000 and other legislation. It seems amazing that a Directive containing only 34 Articles has generated, and will continue to generate, so much domestic legislation.

It is important to note just how different the 1998 Act is compared to its predecessor. Apart from the wider reach of data protection law which now applies to structured manual files and some forms of unstructured manual files, the rights of individuals have been significantly enhanced and improved. An example is afforded by the case of *Lord Ashcroft* v *Attorney General*[15] in which Gray J confirmed that the Data Protection Act 1984 only gave rise to a private claim in damages for a breach of section 23. This section provided a right to compensation, *inter alia*, for disclosure of personal data not authorised by the data controller (termed the data user under the 1984 Act). The data protection principles did not give rise to a private law right to damages but was a matter only for the Data Protection Registrar. The 1998 Act is completely different in this respect and any breach of the Act, including a breach of the principles, can give rise to a private action for damages. Section 13 of the 1998 Act makes this explicit.

OTHER AREAS OF LAW PROTECTING PERSONAL DATA

Of course, data protection law is not the only area of law that is relevant to the processing of personal data and individuals may exercise control over the use of personal data in other ways. Depending on the circumstances, the law of breach of confidence may also play a part. However, this is unlikely to be helpful in all cases, for example, where the data have been rendered anonymous prior to disclosure, as in *R* v *Department of Health ex parte Source Informatics Ltd*[16] discussed in Chapter 7. Other exceptions in the context of banking were set out long ago in *Tournier* v *National Provincial*[17] for the purposes of defeating fraud, though this case must now be read as subject to the Data Protection Act 1998. In other cases, the law of copyright may be relevant where, for example, the personal data have been derived from the individual concerned and are substantial enough to be considered to be a work of copyright. This could be the case where an individual provides another person with a photograph of himself or a lengthy curriculum vitae. The law of defamation could be relevant where the personal data are inaccurate and have been disclosed in such a manner or to such a person as to amount to a defamatory statement.

As noted above, data protection law has its root in human rights law and the twin rights of privacy and freedom of expression provided by the Human Rights Convention. It can be seen as a particular example of those rights set in the context of processing personal data. That being so, in many cases where

---

[15] [2002] EWHC 1122 QB.
[16] [2001] QB 424.
[17] [1924] 1 KB 461.

data protection law is engaged, the Convention right to privacy will also be relevant and it is becoming increasingly common to see a claim for a breach under the Data Protection Act 1998 coupled with a claim under the Convention rights see, for example, *Naomi Campbell v MGN Limited*[18] concerning reportage of Naomi Campbell and treatment for drug addiction. An alternative is the claim under the law of breach of confidence which, in some respects, can be seen as a fortuitous English pre-emption of the right of privacy. An example is given by *Michael Douglas v Hello! Limited*[19] where surreptitious photographs were taken at the reception following the marriage of Michael Douglas and Catherine Zeta-Jones. Sometimes it may be simpler to base the claim on human rights law only, as in *von Hannover v Germany*[20] in which Princess Caroline of Monaco complained about intrusive paparazzi photography. All these cases and many other recent cases on or associated with data protection law are discussed in more detail in this book.

Another piece of legislation relevant to data protection law is the Freedom of Information Act 2002. This provides for a right of access to information held by public authorities and this could cover any type of information, not just personal information relating to individuals. For example, it could apply with respect to planning matters (transport, education, health, internal decision-making procedures, spending plans, policies) where such information has not been published. However, certain information will be exempt where it is reasonably accessible in other ways, for example, under the Data Protection Act 1998. Freedom of information law could be seen, therefore, as being complementary to data protection law but there may be issues where the exemptions under each law do not match. Even so, the Data Protection Act 1998 has been modified to incorporate the effects of the Freedom of Information Act 2000 where the latter involves personal data.

The Competition Act 1998, which also came into force on 1 March 2000, brings competition law in the United Kingdom much closer to that which applies under the EC Treaty, being based on Articles 81 and 82 of that Treaty. It may be important in peripheral cases, for example, where the data controller has a massive data warehouse comprising personal data not readily available from any other source. The data controller could thus be in a dominant position and be accused on an abuse of that dominant position contrary to section 18 of the Competition Act 1998. We have seen the possibility of an abuse of a dominant position in relation to information in the European Court of Justice in the television listing case of *RTE & ITP v Commission 19*[21].

---

[18] [2004] 2 All ER 995.
[19] [2003] EMLR 585.
[20] European Court of Human Rights, 24 June 2004.
[21] [1995] FSR 530.

One feature of data protection law in the United Kingdom has been the changing terminology used. Data protection law was originally administered and enforced by the Data Protection Registrar. Following the implementation of the Directive, the post was called the Data Protection Commissioner. Overseeing the Freedom of Information Act 2000 also came under the auspices of that person and, consequently, the title became the Information Commissioner. The Data Protection Tribunal is now known as the Information Tribunal. In the light of other areas of law such as the law of breach of confidence and human rights law, it might be cynical to suggest that the United Kingdom's approach to data protection law has been disproportionate in its complexity and its relentless evolution. Nevertheless, those processing personal data must know how data protection law impacts on data processing and what compliance means in practice. Data subjects need to know what rights they have under data protection law and how they can exercise those rights. Those processing personal data should ensure that their processing operations comply with data protection law (and other relevant laws) and consider how they can set up systems, procedures and strategies to comply. An example of the difficulties of a lack of awareness of the practical consequences of data protection law was where a large public utility provider, since privatised, failed to foresee the importance of including an opt-out field in its database of customers.[22]

SUMMARY

The changes to data protection law brought by the Data Protection Act 1998 heralded what seemed to be a stricter and more onerous regime for persons and organisations processing personal data. It gave improved rights for individuals and reflected concerns over privacy issues and the growing use of information technology in what is now an information rich society. In the United Kingdom the impact of data protection law under the 1984 Act could be seen as relatively benign, with relatively few prosecutions and no more than a handful of enforcement cases each year. In spite of the raft of legislation implementing the Data Protection Directive and consequently modifying data protection law, enforcement orders and prosecutions remain at very low levels. This approach could be seen as weakening the impact of data protection although many organisations have adopted a self-regulation approach and have examined and modified their processing activities in response to data protection. Nevertheless, significant confusion exists and we have seen the serious consequences of misunderstandings of the workings of the law under the 1998 Act. The two prime examples were the erasure by Humberside Police of data concerning previous allegations of sexual offences

---

[22] *Midlands Electricity plc* v *Data Protection Registrar* (unreported) 7 May 1999.

by Ian Huntley, the Soham murderer, and the deaths of two pensioners after British Gas cut off the gas supply to their home. British Gas claimed that the Data Protection Act did not allow it to inform social services of the action it had taken. In both cases, the decisions taken as to the workings of data protection law were erroneous, as will be shown in the relevant parts of this book.

If the application of data protection law has been patchy, it may have been significantly weakened in its scope by a recent controversial case in the Court of Appeal which has shown that data protection law is of much more limited scope than was the general view and reflected on the nature of manual processing covered by data protection law and what sort of data falls within the meaning of personal data.[23] It is astonishing that the Court of Appeal did not refer this case to the European Court of Justice for a preliminary ruling under Article 234 of the EC Treaty. The decision seriously undermines individuals' right of access to personal data relating to them.

Some would-be litigants considering suing for negligence have realised that they can get access to evidence by virtue of their right of access under the Data Protection Act. This can be much quicker and cheaper than commencing legal proceedings and going through the usual legal process of discovery. This could be seen as an abuse of data protection law. Other abuses include requiring job applicants to disclose whether they have a criminal record by insisting that they exercise their right of access to personal data held by the police before confirming a job offer.

Although data protection law does not stand in isolation, its importance lies in raising public awareness of the need to regulate processing of personal data and imposing obligations on those processing personal data (data controllers). The benefits of compliance are not always appreciated by data controllers. Improvements in data processing efficiency are inevitable when issues raised by data protection law are raised, such as security, accuracy of data and for how long data ought to be kept before being erased. In many respects, compliance with data protection law simply reflects good practice in data processing.

Although the data protection law imposes an increased regulatory framework on the processing of personal data, it is not all bad news for those processing personal data. For example, real efforts have been made by the Information Commissioner to reduce the burden of notification of processing activity by making it easier, even to the extent that the Commissioner's Office will partially complete the necessary forms following telephone contact from the

---

[23] *Durant v Financial Services Authority* [2003] EWCA Civ 1746.

person or organisation seeking to notify processing activity. Notification via the internet is also a possibility.

Those processing personal data, nevertheless, have expressed serious concerns about the law under the 1998 Act. These concerns included:

- the extension of data protection law to certain structured manual files;

- the fact that processing may only take place if one or more conditions are satisfied;

- the requirement for prior checking of processing posing specific risks before such processing can commence;

- that automated individual decisions are controlled and may be prevented by individuals in some cases;

- the increased obligations to inform individuals on collection of personal data and in other cases, particularly where a subsequent disclosure to a third party is envisaged;

- the enhanced and extended rights of individuals, including the absolute right to prevent processing for direct marketing and the right to prevent processing likely to cause substantial damage or substantial distress;

- the possibility of potential constraints and restrictions on transfers of personal data to countries and territories outside the European Economic Area which are deemed, by European standards, not to have adequate protection for personal data.

The extent to which these concerns have been realised is addressed by this book. Some were overstated and reflect differences between the present law and the old law, and were at least, to some extent, a reaction to change. The fact that data protection law now more closely mirrors the twin rights of privacy and freedom of expression under the Human Rights Convention can only be seen as a welcome step, particularly as the compliance costs of data protection law have not proved to be disproportionately onerous. Part of the reason for this is that the United Kingdom has taken advantage of the derogations and options set out in the Directive.

CHAPTER 2
THE DATA PROTECTION DIRECTIVE

INTRODUCTION

Directive 95/46/EC of the European Parliament and the Council on the protection of individuals with regard to the processing of personal data and on the free movement of such data[1] provided a fresh and welcome opportunity to review and strengthen data protection law. This Directive went much further than the Data Protection Act 1984 and had a greater emphasis on privacy and freedoms. Article 1(1) of the Directive is the key to its underlying philosophy and required Member States to:

> protect the fundamental rights and freedoms of natural persons, and in particular their right to privacy with respect to the processing of personal data.

Recital 2 to the Directive reinforced this emphasis and stated that data processing systems must ...

> whatever the nationality or residence of natural persons, respect their fundamental rights and freedoms, notably the right to privacy, and contribute to economic and social progress, trade expansion and the well-being of individuals.

Thus, the Data Protection Directive extended the principle of freedom of movement within the Community to the freedom of movement of personal data. Fuelled by concerns that intra-Community flows of personal data could be impeded by unequal levels of protection for personal data throughout the Community, the Directive sought to establish a good level of protection of personal data, thereby reinforcing individuals' rights to privacy in respect of such data, so as to prevent the erection of barriers to free movement of

---

[1] OJ L281, 23.11.95, p.31 – "the Data Protection Directive".

personal data within the Community. Though expressed in the Directive in terms of the Community, this now applies to all Members States of the European Economic Area (EEA).

The route to the adoption of the Directive was not an easy one. A proposal was published in 1990[2] and proposed a twin-track approach differentiating between the public and private sector. However, a much-revised further proposal was published in 1992[3] but this raised serious concerns in a number of member states, notably the United Kingdom, about the likely costs of compliance for organisations and persons processing personal data. A particular objection was in relation to the extension of data protection law to certain types of manual filing systems and the obligations to inform data subjects. Other concerns were in respect of the rights of data subjects to prevent processing in some cases and the perceived need to seek the consent of individuals to the processing of personal data relating to them.

In 1994, a survey was commissioned by the Home Office and was carried out by the CBI. It suggested that the cost of compliance for the 625 organisations surveyed would be in the region of £2.3 bn.[4] An estimate by the Department of Health was that it would cost over £1 bn to obtain the consent of the population of the United Kingdom to the Department's use of their personal data. From then until the time the Directive was adopted, a number of changes were made to the detail of the text of the Directive though not to its substance. An in-depth study for the European Commission in 1994 indicated that the concerns over costs of compliance had been exaggerated. Consequently, the Data Protection Directive was adopted in July 1995 and required implementation by 24 October 1998 at the latest. Needless to say the United Kingdom, in common with a number of other Member States, did not achieve this deadline. One of the reasons was the complexity and broad scope of the new law, requiring a significant piece of primary legislation and numerous statutory instruments to implement it.

GENERAL APPROACH TO DATA PROTECTION SET OUT IN THE DIRECTIVE

Article 1 of the Directive neatly and succinctly sets out its main thrust. It is as follows:

---

[2] COM (90) 314 final – SYN 287, OJ C 277, 05.11.1990, p.3.
[3] COM(92) 24 final – SYN 393, OJ C 311, 27.11.1992, p.38.
[4] Home Office, *Costs of implementing the Data Protection Directive: Paper by the United Kingdom*, 1994.

1. *In accordance with this Directive, Member States shall protect the fundamental rights and freedoms of natural persons, and in particular their right of privacy, with respect to the processing of personal data.*

2. *Member States shall neither restrict nor prohibit the free flow of personal data between Member States for reasons connected with the protection afforded under paragraph 1.*

Therefore, because Member States have agreed to implement data protection laws in accordance with the Directive, no Member State can object to the freedom of movement of personal data throughout the Community on the basis of data protection law. Although the language of the Directive is in terms of the European Community, the other Member States of the European Economic Area are also participating in the new data protection law on the basis of the Directive.

The Data Protection Directive sets out a data protection law that is more extensive than that under the Data Protection Act 1984 and at first sight it looks quite different but it has common foundations with the prior law as both are based on the Council of Europe Convention for the Protection of Individuals with regard to Automatic Processing of Personal Data 1981. The data protection principles in the 1998 Act are based on those in the Directive which, in turn, are closely modelled on those in the Convention. The Directive follows the arrangement of the principles in the Convention. Article 5 of the Convention contains the requirements for the quality of personal data and Article 6 of the Directive is the equivalent with some changes in language and with additional provisions relating to processing of data for historical, statistical or scientific purposes. Data security is separately provided for in Article 7 of the Convention and there are provisions concerning trans-border data flows from within the EEA to other countries.

The Data Protection Acts of 1984 and 1998 collect the principles together but there is no principle dealing specifically with transfers to countries outside the EEA without an adequate level of protection in the 1984 Act. It would simply be a matter for the Registrar as to whether proposed transfers were likely to conform with the data protection principles in that Act, particularly the first, on fair and lawful obtaining and processing and the eighth, on security measures. The Directive develops the provisions in the Convention on transfers to third countries or territories to a significant extent. Although the Data Protection Convention did not have any provisions relating specifically to transborder data flows, the Protocol to the Convention, dated 8 November 2001 does have such a provision. The Preamble to the Protocol states, *inter alia*:

Considering that, with the increase in exchanges of personal data across national borders, it is necessary to ensure the effective protection of human rights and fundamental freedoms, and in particular the right to privacy, in relation to such exchanges of personal data.

The Data Protection Directive is structured into subdivisions on general provisions, rules on the lawfulness of processing (the most substantial part of the text), judicial remedies, liabilities and sanctions, transfers to third countries, codes of conduct, supervisory authorities and the working party established under the Directive, Community implementing measures and final provisions which permit a number of derogations in terms of the application of the new law to processing already underway. Each of those subdivisions (chapters in the Directive) is described briefly below. It is not the author's intention to give an exhaustive description of all the provisions, particularly those adequately dealt with in the following chapters. Rather, the description of the Directive is intended to give the reader a feel for its underlying rationale and the philosophy of data protection law to set the scene for the remainder of the book. A more in-depth analysis of the Directive can be found in *EC Data Protection Directive* (Bainbridge) Butterworths, 1996.

GENERAL PROVISIONS

Chapter 1 of the Directive includes the objective of the Directive, as mentioned above, the definitions, scope and applicable law. The definitions are notable for their width compared to equivalent definitions under the Data Protection Act 1984. In particular the definition of processing in Article 2(b) is extremely wide and even covers simply being in possession of personal data as the definition includes operations involving storage. Therefore, simply placing personal data in a store, for example, by placing structured files in an archive appears to fall within the definition. All manner of access and use appears to be catered for, as does obtaining personal data and destroying them. When reading the recitals to the Directive it is also clear that the Directive is not restricted to personal data represented by text (digital or printed) but also extends to voice and image data in so much as the individual concerned can be identified from those data.

In addition to data processed or intended to be processed by automatic means, the Directive also applies to certain types of manual files, defined as "personal data filing systems" which are structured sets of data accessible by specific criteria. It matters not if the set of data is dispersed and not held in one file or one geographic location.

There are then definitions of the various actors involved in (or persons affected by) data protection law – the controller (referred to as "the data controller" in the 1998 Act and equivalent to "the data user" under the 1984 Act), processors (who process on behalf of the controller, referred to in the 1998 Act as "the data processor" and much wider than the definition of computer bureau under the 1984 Act, especially because of the wide definition of processing), third parties and recipients. The 1998 Act contains the equivalent definitions in section 1 of the Act and, in the case of third parties and recipients, in section 70 (supplementary definitions).

Individuals about whom personal data relate are, as before, data subjects. Article 2(h) indicates that the consent of a data subject must be freely given, specific and informed consent. The meaning of the definitions of the various persons involved is important especially in terms of notification (there must be a description of recipients or categories of recipients) and in providing information to data subjects (a duty to do so may be triggered by disclosures of personal data to third parties).

The scope of the Directive is given in Article 3 and apart from stating that it applies to processing wholly or partly by automatic means and to other processing where the data form part of a relevant filing system, it confirms that the Directive does not apply to activities outside the scope of Community law, including public and State security, defence and the activities of the State in relation to criminal law (that does not prevent Member States in providing for criminal offences in respect of breaches of data protection law, of course). Nor does the Directive apply to processing by a natural person in the course of a purely personal or household activity.

The applicable law provisions are contained in Article 4. Basically, the applicable law is that of the Member State in which the processor is established rather than the location at which the processing is carried out. However, if a controller in one Member State uses a processor established in that other Member State, there are provisions for co-operation between the supervisory authorities in those Member States. If a controller is established in more than one Member State, for example, in the case of wholly owned subsidiary companies established in other Member States, the controller will be subject to the domestic law in each of those States as appropriate. The provisions confirm, *inter alia*, that where a controller is not established in a Member State but uses equipment for processing situated in a Member State, the controller will be subject to that Member State's domestic data protection law unless the equipment is used only for the purposes of transit through the territory of the Community. An example of the latter case is where a controller established in America transmits personal data to equipment situated in England purely for onward transmission to Japan. In that case, the controller will not be subject to United Kingdom data protection law, regardless of the nationality of the data subjects.

GENERAL RULES ON THE LAWFULNESS OF PROCESSING

This part of the Directive sets out the bulk of the model of data protection law under the Directive as it impacts on the various actors involved. First, Article 5 requires Member States to be more precise in determining the conditions under which processing is lawful within the limits of this part of the Directive. Article 6 then sets out the principles relating to data quality which are similar to those under the Data Protection Convention. Articles 7 and 8 set out conditions for processing to be permitted. Article 7 relates to "non-sensitive" data and Article 8 applies in respect of "sensitive" data, described as being "special categories" of data. One of the conditions in Article 7 must be met if processing is to be lawful and, in the case of sensitive data, one of the conditions in Article 8 must also be met. Personal data cannot be processed otherwise. These provisions find their equivalent in Schedules 2 and 3 of the Data Protection Act 1998. Many data controllers were very concerned when they saw these conditions as, if none applied to their processing they would not be permitted to carry out such processing. In the event, though, it would be extremely rare for none of them to apply. What the conditions do, in reality, is provide more specificity to what constitutes fair and lawful processing than was the case under the prior law. In the vast majority of cases, data controllers should have little trouble in relying on one or more of the conditions.

One of the conditions for processing in Article 7 is that the processing is necessary for the purposes of the legitimate interests pursued by the controller or by the third party or parties to whom the data are disclosed, except where such interests are overridden by the interests for fundamental rights and freedoms of the data subject which require protection under Article 1(1) (being the fundamental rights and freedoms of natural persons, and in particular their right to privacy with respect to the processing of personal data). Whether processing falls within this "legitimate interests" condition requires a balancing of the data controller's legitimate interests with the data subject's rights. The Ministry of Agriculture, Fisheries and Food refused to disclose information relating to what crops had been grown on a farm to a new farmer, so as to enable the new farmer to make official returns. On a reference to the European Court of Justice, the Court stressed the need to balance legitimate interests with the possible prejudice to the previous farmers. Having such information certainly fell within the legitimate interests of the new farmer and the prejudice to the rights and freedoms of the previous farmers was negligible. The new farmer could be liable for criminal penalties if he failed to provide such information in the official return.[5]

Placing information relating to an injury on a website (the fact that a friend of the person in charge of the website was working part-time because of a foot injury) was processing personal data that fell within the meaning of sensitive data and, as she had not asked consent of the individuals mentioned on the

---

[5] *R v Ministry of Agriculture, Fisheries and Food, ex parte Fisher* [2000] ECR I-6751.

website, this was a breach of data protection law as none of the other conditions for processing sensitive personal applied.[6]

National legislation may make specific provision for the collection and disclosure of personal data. This may result in a potential conflict between such legislation and Articles 6, 7 or 8 of the Directive. That conflict may be an issue to be resolved by national courts though a person aggrieved by such national law may rely on those provisions in the Directive, being directly applicable, to oust national laws apparently in conflict with those provisions.[7]

A further provision is contained in Article 9 and which is intended to balance the right of freedom of expression with the right to privacy and which requires Member States to implement exemptions for such processing but only if necessary to reconcile these potentially conflicting rights.

Articles 10 and 11 cover the requirements for data controllers to provide information to data subjects. Article 10 applies when the data in question are first collected from the data subject and Article 11 applies when the data have not been obtained directly from the data subject, such as where the data are first recorded or are disclosed to a third party. This is particularly important where a data controller makes his customer details available to another data controller, for example, for the purposes of direct marketing. However, it is not limited to such disclosure. An important aspect is that the information need not be given if the data subject already has it, such as where he has been informed of a potential disclosure and, in the case of Article 11, where to provide the information would be impossible or would require a disproportionate effort.

Data subjects' rights are covered by Articles 12, 14 and 15. Article 12 is the right of access which includes rights to have, for example, incorrect, out of date or excessive data rectified, erased or blocked. Article 14 gives rights to object to processing. One is where there are "compelling legitimate grounds" (the 1998 Act describes this in terms of where the processing is likely to cause substantial damage or substantial distress to the data subject or some other person). The other right to object is in respect of processing for the purposes of direct marketing. Article 15 contains provisions dealing with automated decision-taking and includes, in some cases, a right to object. Article 13 contains the basis for exemptions from some of the provisions of the Directive, permitting Member States to grant exemption from the data quality requirements, the need to inform data subjects, rights of access and certain requirements as to notification.

---

[6] Case C-101/01 *Bodil Lindqvist*, 6 November 2003, European Court of Justice.
[7] It was so held in Joined Cases C-465/00, C-138/01 and C-139/01 *Rechnungshof* v *Österreichischer Rundfunk and Others* [2003] ECR I-4989.

Articles 16 and 17 are concerned with confidentiality and security of processing. An important aspect is that where a processor is used, the processor must give security guarantees and the processing must be under a contract or legal act binding on the processor imposing equivalent security obligations as those required of the controller. Articles 18 to 21 are concerned with notification. The Directive allows exemption from or simplification of the notification requirements in cases where individuals' rights and freedoms are unlikely to be adversely affected. Further exemptions from notification are allowed, for example, where the data are contained in a public register. In terms of manual processing, the wording suggests that there is a presumption that notification is not required unless Member States stipulate otherwise. A new concept is the arrangements for prior checking (described as preliminary assessment in the 1998 Act). This is where the supervisory authority checks processing operations which are likely to present specific risks to rights and freedoms of data subjects. Processing cannot commence until after checking. A further possibility in the Directive is for the appointment of "in-house" data protection officials. This aspect has not been implemented as yet in the United Kingdom and would need a statutory instrument to bring it into force.

JUDICIAL REMEDIES, LIABILITIES AND SANCTIONS

Under Article 22, Member States must provide judicial remedies in respect of any breach of individuals' rights under the Directive. Thus, under the 1998 Act, data subjects can enforce their other rights by application to a county court or to the High Court. Under Article 22 this is without prejudice to enforcement by the supervisory authority. Article 23 requires that provision is made for individuals to have a right to compensation for damage resulting from unlawful processing or other contravention of the national data protection law, subject to a defence if the controller can prove lack of responsibility for the relevant event (the due diligence defence under the 1998 Act). Article 24 simply requires the imposition of sanctions for infringements to ensure full compliance.

TRANSFERS TO THIRD COUNTRIES

One of the most difficult areas in data protection law is the position regarding transfers of personal data to countries outside the EEA which do not have adequate protection for personal data. There is something of a dilemma here as it is recognised that preventing such transfers altogether could seriously hamper the activities of EEA-based data controllers, especially given the globalisation of information processing and data flows. Thus, although Article 25 lays down the basic rule (and provisions for co-operation between Member States and the Commission in terms of transfers to third countries and for

Member States to comply with Commission findings as to whether a third country does or does not have adequate protection), Article 26 contains derogations, so allowing controllers to transfer the personal data notwithstanding lack of adequate protection. Such transfers may still take place if one of a number of conditions applies, for example, where the data subject has given consent or where the transfer is related to a contract involving the controller. Transfers may also be allowed where sufficient safeguards are adduced by the controller or on the basis of approved contractual terms.

The Directive was adopted at a time when the internet, although it had been around for some time, had not become the force it is today. The internet has immense implications in the context of transborder data flows, for example, where personal data are placed on a website or an organisation based in Europe makes its database containing personal data available for access in other countries. Another example is where businesses transfer data for processing outside the EEA. In *Bodil Lindqvist*, 6 November 2003, European Court of Justice, it was held that placing personal data on a website did not constitute a transfer of personal data to a country outside the EEA even if persons outside the EEA accessed the website. The Court of Justice said (at para 68):

> Given, first, the state of development of the internet at the time Directive 95/46 was drawn up and, second, the absence, in Chapter IV, of criteria applicable to use of the internet, one cannot presume that the Community legislature intended the expression transfer [of data] to a third country to cover the loading, by an individual in Mrs Lindqvist's position, of data onto an internet page, even if those data are thereby made accessible to persons in third countries with the technical means to access them.

It is true that the Directive did not deal with the internet expressly (a fact pointed out to the European Commission by the author during the study for the Commission). However, given the spirit of the Directive and the potential risks to the right to privacy posed by the internet, this decision is unsupportable. In cases in other areas, the Court has been only too willing to interpret the language of Articles in Directives in line with its perceived spirit, notwithstanding clear words to the contrary. An excellent example is provided by the trade mark case of *Davidoff & Cie v Gofkid Ltd*[8] where the Court held that the phrase "... goods or services which are not similar ..." in Article 5(2) of the Trade Marks Directive included identical and similar goods or services also.

---

[8] [2003] FSR 28 p.490.

CODES OF CONDUCT

Under Article 27, Member States and the European Commission are to encourage the drawing up of codes of practice and are to allow codes drafted by trade associations and the like to be submitted for the opinion of the national authority. Where appropriate, data subjects or representatives of data subjects will have an opportunity to give their views on the draft codes so submitted. Draft Community codes may be submitted to the Working Party established under the Directive. The European Federation of Direct Marketing code of conduct on the use of personal data in direct marketing is an example of a code approved by the Working Party.[9] It took seven years of negotiations before approval was finally given.

The Working Party, set up under Article 29, also gives opinions about particular processing activities and publishes annual reports and working documents.

SUPERVISORY AUTHORITIES AND THE WORKING PARTY

Article 28 requires that one or more public authorities (supervisory authorities) are to be responsible for the monitoring of data protection law. These authorities (in the United Kingdom there is only one, headed by the Information Commissioner) are to be consulted as to the measures taken to implement or regulate data protection law and are to be given powers of investigation, intervention and participation in legal proceedings. A right of appeal to the courts against decisions of supervisory authorities is required. Other requirements are for co-operation between supervisory authorities. They are also responsible for prior checking and drawing up a report at regular intervals. Members and staff of supervisory authorities must remain subject to a duty of confidence even after their employment has ended.

Article 29 establishes the Working Party which comprises a representative of each Member State's supervisory authority or authorities (a joint representative shall be appointed if there is more than one authority in a Member State) and a representative of such authorities established for Community institutions (a joint representative if more than one) and a representative of the Commission. The Working Party elects a chairman for two years and voting is by simple majority. The Working Party adopts its own rules of procedure. Items may be placed on the agenda by the chairman on his own initiative, following a request from a representative of the supervisory authorities or at the Commission's request.

---

[9] 10066/03/EN final, WP177, 13 June 2003.

The remit of the Working Party is set out in Article 30. It shall:

- examine any question on the application of national measures taken with the aim of contributing to a uniform application of those measures;

- give the Commission its opinion on the level of protection in the Community or third countries;

- advise the Commission on proposed amendments of the Directive or additional or specific measures to safeguard rights and freedoms of data subjects;

- give its opinion on codes of conduct drawn up at Community level;

- inform the Commission on divergences in equivalence of protection within the Community.

Furthermore, the Working Party may, on its own initiative, make recommendations on all matters relating to data protection within the Community. Opinions and recommendations are forwarded to the Commission and the Committee established under Article 31. The Commission then informs the Working Party on action to be taken in response in a report, a copy of which is also forwarded to the European Parliament and the Council. Areas of current concern to the Working Party are airline passenger name records, genetic data and video surveillance. Working Party publications are available through the EUROPA data protection site at: *http://europa.eu.int/comm/internal_market/ privacy/index_en.htm*

The Committee was set up under Article 31 to assist the Commission. The Committee comprises representatives of the Member States and is chaired by the representative of the Commission. Draft measures to be taken are submitted to the Committee which delivers its opinion on those measures. The Committee votes by a qualified majority, the chairman not voting. The Commission is to adopt measures which apply immediately. However, if these measures are not in accordance with the opinion of the Committee, the Commission must communicate this to the Council and the application of the measures must be deferred for three months and the Council, acting by a qualified majority, may make a different decision within that three month period. Draft measures include measures where a Member State or the Commission objects to an authorisation granted by one Member State in respect of transfers to third countries and in respect of standard contractual clauses offering sufficient safeguards in respect of transfers to third countries not having an adequate level of protection for personal data under Article 26(3) and (4).

COMMUNITY IMPLEMENTING MEASURES AND FINAL PROVISIONS

This part of the Directive contains the usual provisions such as the time the Directive must be implemented nationally and communication of the texts of domestic laws adopted by the Commission. There is also a requirement that the Commission reports to the Council and European Parliament at regular intervals starting no later than three years after 24 October 1998 on the implementation of the Directive together, if necessary, with proposals for amendment.

The Directive was required to be implemented nationally no later than 24 October 1998 but there are a number of derogations in Article 32. There are two particular derogations which delayed the application of the new law. The first applies in respect of processing already underway "on the date the national provisions ... enter into force". The United Kingdom has wisely chosen the starting point for these derogations as the date the Directive ought to have been implemented, not the date the 1998 Act came into force. Such processing was brought into conformity within the three years permitted by the Directive, that is, by 24 October 2001.

Where data was already held in manual filing systems on the date of entry of the new law (again the United Kingdom has chosen the date 24 October 1998), processing of such data does not need to conform with Articles 6, 7 and 8 until 12 years from the *date of adoption* of the Directive: that is, 24 October 2007. Those Articles concern data quality and the conditions for processing. To compensate for this, data subjects are given a specific right of rectification, erasure or blocking of data which are incomplete or "stored in a way incompatible with legitimate purposes pursued by the controller". This was given effect in the Data Protection Act 1988 by section 12A (inserted by Schedule 13, a self-repealing provision which lasts until 24 October 2007).

There is a further derogation from the effect of Articles 6, 7 and 8 in respect of data kept for the sole purpose of historical research. If this derogation is included in domestic legislation (as it is in the United Kingdom), suitable safeguards must be provided. The primary safeguard provided in the 1998 Act is in section 33, requiring that the data are not processed to support measures or decisions with respect to particular individuals and are not processed in such a way that substantial damage or substantial distress is, or is likely to be caused, to any data subject.

CHAPTER 3
OUTLINE OF THE DATA
PROTECTION ACT 1998

INTRODUCTION

The Data Protection Act 1998 came into force on 1 March 2000, around 16 months later than required under the Directive. The United Kingdom was not the last Member State to do so and a declaration of failure to implement the Directive was made by the European Court of Justice in respect of Luxembourg.[1] The complexity of the United Kingdom's implementation of data protection law is probably the main reason for the delay in implementing the Directive which was further compounded by the transitional provisions which themselves were made more complex as a result of the delay. The Act is structured in a curious way with some of the most important provisions and derogations tucked away in Schedules, of which there were no less than 16 in its initial form. The data protection principles, which are at the very heart of data protection law, are set out in Schedule 1 together with some provisions on interpretation of the principles. The principles were also contained in a Schedule in the 1984 Act. Some of the exemptions from parts of the Act are contained in the main body of the Act whilst others are contained in Schedule 7. The only part of the Act not in force is section 56 which makes enforced subject access an offence. This will apply, for example, where an employer requires a job applicant to make a subject access request to confirm that the applicant has no convictions or police cautions. Bringing this section into force now looks some way off. In relation to some types of work, such as where someone is employed in the care of young or vulnerable people, it is important that information showing a previous record or allegations of relevant offences is available to the employer.

The Data Protection Directive contained a number of options and deroga-tions. For example, Member States could delay some of the provisions of data protection law in respect of processing already underway before 24 October

---

[1] See Case C-450/00 *Commission for the European Communities* v *Grand Duchy of Luxembourg*, 4 October 2001.

1998, the latest date for implementation of the Directive. Exemption or simplification from the notification requirements was also possible under the Directive, for example, in cases where the processing carried little risk to the rights and freedoms of individuals or where processing was carried out by a not for profit organisation. Member States could also choose whether to require the notification of all or some manual processing. All these different possibilities required decisions which further explain the delay in implementing the new data protection law. The United Kingdom's approach has been, generally, to take advantage of derogations and to choose options which carry the least burden for those who process personal data. (A data controller is a person who determines the purposes and manner of processing and a data processor is a person who process personal data on behalf of the data controller.) An example of the United Kingdom's approach is that notification of manual processing is not required. However, this does not prevent a data controller choosing to notify manual processing, as this may carry advantages as will be seen in Chapter 6.

Before looking at the Act from a variety of perspectives, it will be helpful to reflect on the mechanism of data protection law as set out in the Act.

MECHANISM OF DATA PROTECTION UNDER THE 1998 ACT

The basic mechanism within which data protection law under the 1998 Act operates is shown in Figure 3.1. This is, of course, a simplification but serves to indicate the main obligations and duties under the Act. The data controller, the person (or persons, jointly or in common) who decide(s) upon the purpose and means of processing, notifies the processing activity and other information related to that activity to the Information Commissioner. There are some exemptions from notification but, in the majority of cases, the data controller must notify before processing can commence. The Information Commissioner will add the details to the data protection register if all the relevant information is furnished and the fee is paid. There is one exception and this is a general description of security measures which must be notified but is not placed on the register which is available to the public. Failure to notify, unless exempt, is a criminal offence of strict liability. The Commissioner has a number of powers, including the power to investigate processing activity and powers of enforcement, for example, where a breach of the data protection principles is occurring or has occurred.

In some cases, the data controller must inform the data subject (the person to whom the personal data relate) at least of his identity, for example, when collecting the data from the data subject or in other cases, such as where the data are to be disclosed to a third party. Further information may need to be given such as the purposes of the processing and other information to ensure

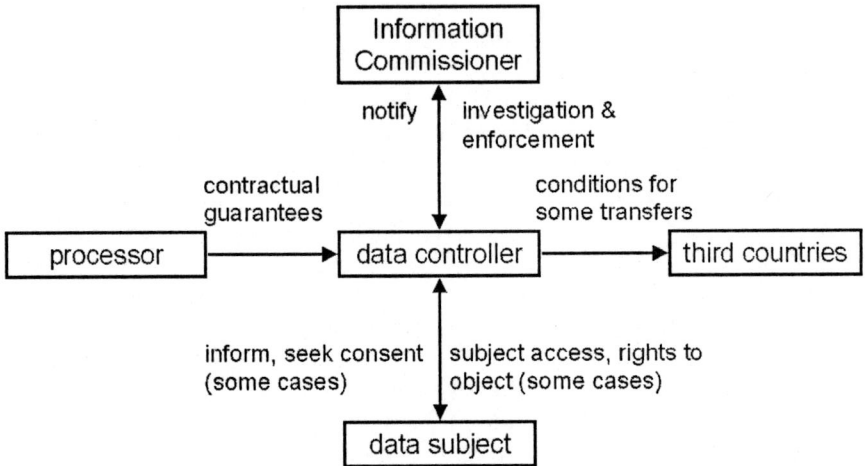

Figure 3.1 Basic mechanism of data protection under the Data Protection Act 1998.

that the processing is fair. For example, in line with case law under the 1984 Act, the data controller should inform the data subject, (the individual to whom the personal data relate) of non-obvious uses of the data such as where the data controller intends to pass on the data to a third party to enable the latter to send marketing material to the data subject. The data subject has the right to object to processing in specific cases, such as where it is likely to cause substantial damage or substantial distress or where it is to be used for direct marketing. In a number of cases, the data subject must consent to the processing. Consent may be implied, for example, by failure to tick a box on a form. Where the personal data fall within the meaning of "sensitive personal data" or where transfers to a third country with inadequate protection is envisaged, the data subject's informed and express consent must be obtained. It is better also to obtain express consent when obtaining personal data on the internet, for example, by requiring the individual to click on a box indicating that that person has no objection to receiving marketing material, whether by email or otherwise.

Data subjects also have a right of access to personal data relating to them. This right existed under the 1984 Act but is enhanced in terms of the amount of information to be made available to the data subject in addition to access to the personal data themselves. Subject access has been something of a bone of contention in some fields. For example, access to health data, including X-rays, can prove expensive to health authorities. Charges may be made for access up to specified limits. In most cases the limit is £10. A lower limit applies in respect of requests made to credit reference agencies and higher levels apply to health and educational data.

Where a data controller makes use of a data processor, (a person processing personal data on behalf of the data controller) there must be contractual security guarantees provided by the processor which are made or evidenced in writing. Transfers to third countries which do not have adequate levels of data protection in specific cases may only be made if one of a number of conditions governing the transfer is satisfied. This may range from the data subject's consent to the inclusion of specific contractual terms governing the transfer.

SOME PERSPECTIVES ON THE ACT

THE DATA CONTROLLER

From the perspective of the data controller (the person who decides the purposes and means of processing, alone, jointly or in common with others) the Data Protection Act 1998 appears at first sight to impose a regulatory straightjacket on the processing of personal data. As before, there is a duty to keep processing activity within the data protection principles but there are a number of features of the 1998 Act which caused concern to data controllers, being that:

- processing can only proceed, unless otherwise exempt, if one of a set of specified conditions for processing is present (if the data are sensitive data, there must also be present a further condition from another set of conditions);

- there are specific obligations to inform data subjects when data are collected from them and in other cases, such as where the data are disclosed to a third party (however, case law under the 1984 Act required that the data subject be informed of non-obvious uses at the time the data were obtained from the data subject);[2]

- data subjects are given rights to object to processing if it is likely to cause substantial damage or substantial distress to themselves or to others and an absolute right to object to processing for the purposes of direct marketing;

- data subjects are given rights in relation to automatic decision-taking, for example, in some cases, data subjects can require that the decision in question is not taken by automatic means or is re-taken by other means: in other cases, they have a right to make representations;

---

[2] See *Innovations* v *Data Protection Registrar*, (Case DA/92 31/49/1) 29 September 1993, Data Protection Tribunal.

- the extension of data protection law to certain manual files; and

- the requirement for particular safeguards in some cases where personal data are transferred to a country outside the European Economic Area which does not have an adequate level of protection in relation to processing of the type involved.

Other issues include the requirement for security guarantees from processors which must be imposed contractually and made or evidenced in writing. This could catch a number of data controllers out as the definition of processing is very wide and even holding personal data (the term in the Directive is "storage") is within the meaning of processing. Therefore, a data controller who has archived data, whether stored digitally or in structured manual files, has to consider the impact of data protection law on such data, including subject access, accuracy, excessiveness and so on. As data that were in existence before the coming into force of the Act are within its scope, this could be very worrying. Some data controllers may take the view that they have to trawl through all this old data to check for compliance. However, this is not required in all cases, for example, where to do so would prove impossible or would impose disproportionate costs.

There were further concerns about the scope of the transitional provisions, whereby the full force of the new law was not to be felt until 24 October 2001 (pre-existing automated and manual data) or, in some cases, will not be felt until 24 October 2007 (pre-existing manual data, that is, in existence before 24 October 1998). Apart from data subjects' enhanced rights of access and other new rights, their right to compensation applies in respect of any breach of the Act. Before, it was much more limited. For example, a breach of a data protection principle did not, *per se*, give rise to a private right of action, unlike the case under the 1998 Act.[3]

Although many data controllers initially viewed the Data Protection Act 1998 with some trepidation, it was not all bad news for them. One of the primary aims of the Directive was to encourage freedom of movement of personal data throughout the European Community (now extended to the European Economic Area, which comprises the EC Member States, Norway, Iceland and Liechtenstein). If data protection law had not been harmonised at a reasonably high level in terms of individuals' rights of privacy in respect of personal data, some Member States could have been tempted to erect barriers to such freedom of movement. With the new regime of data protection in place, that should not happen. The notification procedure is not onerous and the Office of the Information Commissioner have made notification relatively easy with the adoption of standard descriptors (for example, of sources, recip-

---

[3] See, for example, *Lord Ashcroft* v *Attorney General* [2002] EWHC 1122 QB, per Gray J at para 29.

ients and purposes of processing). Standard "templates" are available for different types of data controller. A significant part of the notification process can be undertaken online or even over the telephone. Article 19 of the Directive requires notification details to include, *inter alia*, identification of "the recipients *or categories of recipient* to whom the data might be disclosed" (emphasis added). The United Kingdom has taken the sensible approach of accepting generic descriptions of recipients. If each and every potential recipient had to be identified by name, this could be incredibly onerous with the added difficulty of trying to predict new recipients during the forthcoming notification period. Notification itself lasts for 12 months and costs £35. Renewal is a simple matter unless processing activities have changed significantly compared with the previous notification.

There were numerous exemptions from various provisions of the 1984 Act and many of these exemptions continue, although in some cases with modification. There are some new exemptions also, such as in the case of confidential references and management forecasts. An important feature of the exemptions is that, generally, a data controller may only avail himself of an appropriate exemption to the extent that compliance with an exempted provision would prejudice the objective of the exemption. Examples are the exemptions in relation to crime, taxation, discharging statutory functions and regulatory activities. An example of the latter is where subject access is refused on the basis of the exemption because this would be likely to alert a person suspected of dishonesty or malpractice in the context of banking, insurance or investment business that he was under suspicion. However, if complying with the subject access request would not alert the person to this, the data controller must comply and cannot rely on the exemption. Another example in the same context is where personal data relating to such a person are disclosed to the police or FSA. The exemption applies to remove the obligation to inform the individual that his data have been disclosed.

The transitional provisions diluted the immediate impact of the new law as noted above. In particular, these provisions provided exemptions in respect of personal data in existence before 24 October 1998 so that, in effect, the old law continued to apply to such data until 24 October 2001. A further transitional period remains until 24 October 2007 and applies to manual data in existence prior to 24 October 1998. This is by no means a blanket exemption and only provides exemption from some of the principles, effectively giving the data controller a breathing space before manual data has to fully comply. In particular, the right of access applies as do the obligations concerning security measures.

One important benefit of data protection law is that it encourages good practice in terms of information processing (whether computer or paper based). By adopting and monitoring effective procedures for processing, more

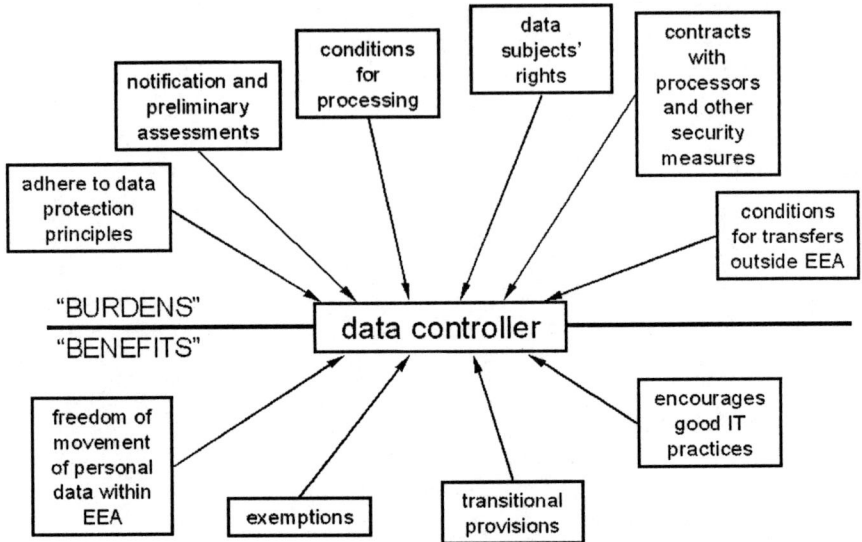

Figure 3.2 Benefits and burdens from the data controller's perspective

efficient use can be made of personal data. For example, efforts to verify the accuracy of data are encouraged as is the avoidance of retaining excessive data or data which are out of date and of no potential future use. It may even encourage some data controllers to investigate the greater use of information technology for their information processing activities. They may decide to examine their paper files and store relevant information on computer and destroy the remainder. The importance of good security is also vital and data controllers are under a duty to take appropriate technical and organisational measures in this respect. Finally, by requiring security guarantees from data processors and, in some cases, requiring the use of contractual terms to regulate the transfers of personal data to countries outside the European Economic Area, relationships between data controllers, data processors and others will be better regulated and formalised. Figure 3.2 indicates the benefits and burdens of the new data protection law from the data controller's perspective.

THE DATA SUBJECT

The Data Protection Act 1984, together with other legislation granting rights of access to personal data such as the Access to Personal Files Act 1987 and the Access to Health Records Act 1990, brought valuable new rights to individuals, such as a right of access to personal data relating to them and a right to have inaccurate data rectified. The 1984 Act was also important from the point of view of individuals in that it imposed a regulatory framework controlling the processing of personal data and keeping it within acceptable boundaries. Although no figures have yet been published, the volume of data subject access requests appears to have been relatively light. This may be because the data user could charge up to £10 for complying with subject access. A further problem is that, apart from obvious data users (now "data controllers"), such as an employer, bank or building society, health service providers and insurance companies, it has not always been an easy matter for individuals to determine the identity of all the other data users that may have been processing personal data relating to them. One type of organisation that did experience significant requests from individuals for access has been credit reference agencies, but access in this case was available through section 158 of the Consumer Credit Act 1974 and the fee payable was £2 (originally only £1).

Some measure of the concerns of individuals in respect of processing personal data may be gleaned from figures published in the Annual Reports of the Information Commissioner (previously Data Protection Registrar and then Data Protection Commissioner). The number of complaints received under the 1984 Act by the then Registrar from individuals has consistently stood at a few thousand each year, as indicated in Figure 3.3. The highest number of complaints was 4,590 during 1992/93 which was probably influenced by an advertising campaign to alert individuals to their rights under the Data Protection Act 1984. Numbers of complaints (strictly speaking they are now called requests for assessment) have risen significantly under the 1998 Act as indicated in Figure 3.3. Also note that the Information Commissioner has responsibilities in respect of data protection and privacy telecommunications complaints (now electronic communications) and these are also indicated in the figures from the Year 1999/2000.

The Data Protection Act 1998 makes significant improvements to the rights of data subjects. The rights that existed under the 1984 Act are improved and some new rights were introduced, such as rights to object to processing. It should be noted that an overriding objective implicit in the Data Protection Directive is that data processing should be transparent. That is, that individuals should be in a better position to know what is happening to personal data relating to them. That explains the obligation to inform data subjects, for example, of the identity of the data controller and the purposes of processing. The rights to object to processing are threefold. First, there is a right to object to processing where it is likely to cause substantial damage or substantial distress to the data subject or another person. Another is the right to object to processing for the purposes of direct marketing. This is an absolute right and the data controller must comply within a reasonable time after receiving written notice from the data subject. The perceived dangers of automated decision-taking are addressed by giving specific rights to individuals, to prevent it in some cases or, if the individual has not exercised that right, a right to require that the decision is reconsidered. In some cases, particularly in

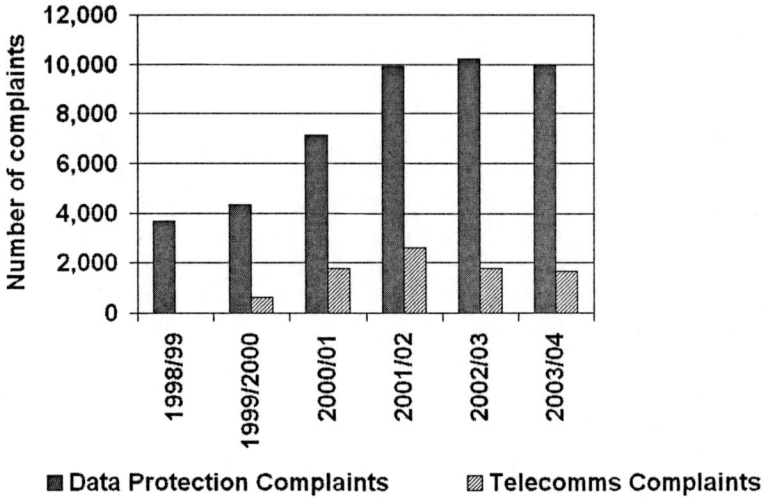

Figure 3.3 Complaints from individuals received by the Information Commissioner
(Source: Information Commissioner Annual Report and Accounts July 2004: London, Stationery Office, 2004, HC669)

the context of a contract between the data controller and the data subject, other steps must be taken by the data controller to safeguard the legitimate interests of the individual. This could mean that the individuals have a right to make representations if the decision is contrary to the individual's wishes. Under the 1984 Act, individuals had no rights whatsoever to object to processing providing such processing was registered and complied with the registration and the data protection principles. Nevertheless, if the processing was contrary to the principles, a complaint by the data subject to the then Data Protection Registrar could result in an enforcement notice or even a criminal prosecution, effectively putting an end to the processing activity objected to. The new rights to object are, however, much simpler and more direct. Even so, if the data controller does not comply with the data subject's request, the data subject may have to commence court proceedings to enforce the right or, alternatively, apply to the Information Commissioner for an assessment.

An activity which troubled the Data Protection Registrar for some time under the 1984 Act was enforced subject access. This may occur, typically, where an applicant for employment is required to carry out a subject access request by the prospective employer in order to confirm that the individual does not have previous criminal convictions. In some cases, requiring an individual to request a data subject access will be made a criminal offence, if and when section 56 is brought into force. There are also controls in respect of enforced subject access to health records. These latter provisions were brought into force with the rest of the Act on 1 March 2000. There are no criminal offences associated with these controls.

Individuals' rights are further enhanced by the application of data protection law to certain manual files, requiring them to conform to the data protection principles and giving individuals a right of access to personal data which relate to them in such files. One problem that existed under the 1984 Act was what should be done if a subject access request disclosed data relating to other individuals, as in *Gaskin* v *United Kingdom*.[4] If the other individual is the person who provided the information, in some cases the data controller may have to make a value judgment as to whether such information may be disclosed even if the other person is identified and even if that other person objects. An important aspect is that the decision as to whether to disclose information which identifies another person is subject to review. An application can be made to the court to enforce proper compliance with the subject access provisions. Of course, it may be possible to suppress or conceal those data that identify the other person. This is usually referred to as a process of redaction, the dictionary meaning of which includes editing for publication. An example of this is given in *Durant* v *Financial Services Authority*[5] discussed in Chapter 8 in this context.

Subject access requests require the data controller to provide more information than previously under the 1984 Act and the rights of rectification of inaccurate data and compensation are improved and extended. Individuals may make requests to the Commissioner for an assessment as to whether any processing activity which the individual believes directly affects him is in compliance with the Act (loosely equivalent to the mechanism for dealing with complaints under the 1984 Act). Where the individual is an actual or potential party to legal proceedings, that person may ask the Commissioner for assistance. This could result in legal advice or representation being made available where the matter is seen to be one of public importance.

Another feature of the law under the Data Protection Act 1998 is that, in some cases (though in practice it may not be that many), the individual who is the subject of the personal data must give his consent for the processing of his personal data to proceed. This could apply particularly in respect of the processing of sensitive personal data (for example, data relating to the individual's health, political or religious beliefs or the fact of his membership of a trade union) or where data are to be transferred to a country outside the European Economic Area which does not provide an adequate level of data protection in a particular case. The data subject's consent is one of the

---

[4] [1989] ECHR 13.
[5] [2003] EWCA Civ 1746.

conditions for processing which should be informed consent where the data are sensitive personal data, for example, if they relate to the health of the data subject. In many cases, however, other conditions for processing will be satisfied and the data subject's consent will not be required. Even so, consent will be a necessary pre-requisite for processing in some cases.

In spite of the new and enhanced rights, there does not seem to be a great deal of evidence of data subjects flexing their muscles and exercising these rights, apart perhaps from subject access. It is likely that individuals still prefer to seek the help of the Information Commissioner. The increase in requests for assessment bears this out. It is, of course, virtually impossible to assess the extent to which individuals directly exercise their rights under the Act. The only clue is the public's awareness of individuals' rights under data protection law. According to the Information Commissioner's surveys in 2003/4 it was only 74%, although this is a significant improvement compared to awareness under the 1984 Act.[6] Awareness of the equivalent rights under the Freedom of Information Act 2000 stands at just over half.

Individuals also have parallel rights in relation to the Human Rights Convention which are more extensive and in addition there are the rights of individuals to obtain information from public bodies under the Freedom of Information Act 2000. From having an erratic and patchy general law of privacy, the United Kingdom can now claim to have a far-reaching right of privacy and this is a very welcome step, especially in relation to processing personal data and the significant risks and dangers posed by information processing. That is reason enough to have specific and targeted regulation of processing of personal data. Whether the law has done this effectively without imposing disproportionate burdens on data controllers will be explored further in subsequent chapters of this book.

THE DATA PROCESSOR

There was no direct equivalent to the term "data processor" under the 1984 Act. As well as data users (now known as "data controllers") computer bureaux were required to register under the 1984 Act. Essentially, a computer bureau was someone who processed data on behalf of the data user or provided the data user with equipment for the processing activity. Processing was relatively narrowly defined but, under the 1998 Act, the definition of processing is much wider and so "data processors" now include far more types of person than simply computer bureaux. The difference is important. Under the 1984 Act, computer bureaux had to register but this was relatively straightforward

---

[6] *Information Commissioner Annual Report and Accounts*: London, The Stationery Office, 2004, HC669, p.88.

and the only data protection principle with which they had to comply was the one concerning security. Under the 1998 Act, data processors are not required to notify their processing activity but, instead, must be made subject to security obligations. In effect, processors have to provide the same level of security as that provided by the data controller and the imposition of this duty must be guaranteed by contractual means and must be in, or evidenced in, writing. Apart from imposing the security provisions in the Act, the data processor must carry out the processing only under the data controller's instructions. Again this must be imposed contractually.

The new definition of processing includes activities such as collecting personal data, holding them (the Directive uses the term "storage" and it is clear that simply being in possession of the data is enough) and any one or more of numerous descriptions which include retrieval, use, disclosure and destruction. Thus, an independent contractor engaged to collect personal data from individuals will be a processor, as will any person having access to the data and anyone engaged to provide back-up facilities or any person engaged to destroy or modify the data. Such persons must be under contractual obligations as regards security of the data equivalent to that owed by the data controller. Employees of the data controller are not deemed to be processors but any agent, self-employed consultant or contractor engaged by the data controller will be data processors if they process data on behalf of the data controller.

In practice, it should be relatively straightforward to draft appropriate contractual clauses to be included in contracts with data processors, probably the easiest way being to refer to the security obligations in the Data Protection Act 1998, contained in Schedule 1. The only problem is that, because of the very wide definition of processing (discussed in the following chapter), some data controllers might not be aware that a particular agent or contractor is a data processor for the purposes of the Act. It is also incumbent on data processors to make themselves aware of the security requirements of the Act (in particular, the eighth data protection principle) and they should also make themselves aware of any guidance issued by the Information Commissioner or trade associations and relevant codes of practice. Reference to the appropriate International and British Standards relevant to information processing may also prove useful.

Notwithstanding the security obligations imposed on data processors, data controllers have overall responsibility for any failure to meet the requirements of the eighth data protection principle to take appropriate technical and organisation measures. The rationale behind imposing equivalent duties on data processors is twofold. Firstly, it will focus their minds on the importance of security and, secondly, the data controller is likely to require an appropriate indemnity from the data processor to reinforce this. A final factor is that the data controller cannot simply delegate the responsibility for security on the data processor as the data controller must still satisfy himself that the requirements are being complied with. This will usually mean some form of checking and monitoring.

THIRD PARTIES

Third parties to whom data are disclosed will, in the vast majority of cases, also be data controllers in their own right and should, unless exempt, notify their processing activity. However, unlike the position under the 1984 Act, notification does not require details to be given of the source or sources of the data. This is not so under the 1998 Act but, instead, the provisions for informing data subjects may require more specific information to be given directly to the individuals concerned. Unless it involves a disproportionate effort, the data subject must be given certain information, the bare minimum being the identity of the data controller and the purposes of processing (unless this has been notified to the Information Commissioner and is on the public register). Other information may have to given in certain cases to ensure that the processing is fair. The third party will not have to provide the information if it is readily available to the data subject. Thus, where the data controller disclosing personal data to a third party has already given the relevant information to the data subject, the third party will be excused from doing so. The main implication of this is that data controllers disclosing personal data to each other should decide between them who is in the best position to give the appropriate information. For example, if a data controller collects personal data from an individual and, at that time, informs the individual that the data will be disclosed to another, identified, data controller within a certain period of time, the second data controller may be excused. This could be important as it may be much easier for the first data controller to provide the information than might be the case if the second data controller had to provide it.

Although information may have to be provided to the data subject on a transfer to a third party, the identity of third parties (or categories of third parties) is not required to be notified to the Information Commissioner. However, the identity of recipients or categories of recipients is required to be notified and, in many cases third parties will also be recipients. Whilst there is a specific exception to the meaning of recipient, as a consequence of the manner in which the notification requirements have been applied in practice, this exception is of little consequence.

SUMMARY OF CHANGES BROUGHT IN BY THE DATA PROTECTION ACT 1998

The major changes brought about by the 1998 Act can be gleaned from an inspection of the transitional provisions. To those familiar with the regime of data protection under the 1984 Act, this is perhaps the best way to identify the differences in the extent of the new law and the changes to the exemptions. The changes are (in general terms only):

- the application of data protection law to certain manual files;

- processing not by reference to the data subject now falls within the meaning of processing (previously this was expressly excluded and was intended, primarily to exclude the preparation of the text of documents, for example word processing, from the scope of data protection law);

- the requirements to provide information to data subjects on collection or in other cases;

- the conditions for processing (normal and sensitive data);

- the requirement for data processors to be under a contractual obligation in respect of security;

- the constraints on transfers to countries outside the European Economic Area not having an adequate level of protection for personal data;

- the requirement to provide more information in response to a subject access request than was the case under the 1984 Act (including information as to the logic involved in certain automated decision-taking, unless or to the extent that the logic constitutes a trade secret);

- data subjects' new rights:
    - to object to processing likely to cause substantial damage or substantial distress,
    - to prevent processing for the purposes of direct marketing,
    - in respect of certain forms of automated decision-taking;

- data subjects' rights to compensation are extended to cover any contravention of the Act (previously limited to inaccurate data, unauthorised disclosure, loss or destruction of data). However, the right to compensation for distress is immediately available if the processing is for the special purposes, that is, journalism, artistic and literary purposes.

Some of the old exemptions under data protection law disappear (but is some cases, similar, though not identical, exemptions have been provided for in regulations made under the Data Protection Act 1998). Those 1984 Act exemptions were:

- the exemption of processing for the purposes of payroll and accounts (such processing was exempt from the registration and supervision provisions and the rights of data subjects under the 1984 Act);

- the exemption of processing by an unincorporated members' club or for the purposes of mailing lists (these forms of processing were exempt from the registration and supervision provisions and the rights of data subjects under the 1984 Act);

- the exemption for back-up data from subject access; and

- specific exemption where the data subject could make a request under section 158 of the Consumer Credit Act 1974 (to a credit reference agency) – this is now brought under the auspices of the 1998 Act and, thus, the exemption is no longer required.

There are also some new exemptions introduced by the 1998 Act, being:

- the pre-existing exemption from subject access for health and social work is extended to education and, in all cases, is to include the provision of information to the data subject (implemented by statutory instruments under the new Act);

- wide-ranging exemptions in respect of processing for the special purposes with a view to publication, having regard to the public interest in freedom of expression;

- in certain cases exemptions for processing for the purposes of research (exemption from the second principle – processing only for one or more lawful and specified purposes – and the fifth principle – allowing retention of the data indefinitely. A pre-existing exemption from the subject access provisions, where the identities of data subjects are not made known, remains);

- confidential references are exempt from the subject access provisions;

- a specific exemption from subject access and the provision of information to the data subject where these rights could prejudice the combat-effectiveness of the Crown; and

- processing for management forecasts or management planning is exempt from subject access and the provision of information to the data subject.

Other exemptions cover corporate finance, negotiations with the data subject and examination scripts. It should be noted that, in some cases, the exemption applies only to the extent that the relevant activity would be likely to be prejudiced without the exemption.

Some further exemptions from subject access have been granted by virtue of the Data Protection (Miscellaneous Subject Access Exemptions) Order 2000. They include information relating to human fertilisation and embryology, adoption records and reports. Because of a mistake, this had to be amended by the Data Protection (Miscellaneous Subject Access Exemptions) (Amendment) Order 2000. This was because the reference to adoption agencies in the original SI did not extend to any such agency which was not a local authority.

Exemptions from notification were provided for by the Data Protection (Notification and Notification Fees) Regulations 2000. These apply, *inter alia*, to processing for staff administration, accounts and advertising and marketing. Further changes to the Act have been made. For example, the definition of data has been extended to include data covered by the Freedom of Information Act 2000. The Data Protection Act 1998, the secondary legislation under it and amendments to the legislation are described in the next few chapters. The following chapter looks at the definitions contained in the Act. These are central to an understanding of the reach of data protection law under the Act.

CHAPTER 4
THE DEFINITIONS

The definitions are of such importance to understanding the reach and scope of the new law that they are deserving of a separate chapter. Whilst some of the definitions are similar to those under the 1984 Act, some are new and others are breathtakingly wide compared to their equivalent under the 1984 Act. A decision in the Court of Appeal[1] has taken a fairly restrictive view of the meaning of personal data and relevant filing system. These two definitions are very important to data protection law and any narrowing of them is of considerable interest. The decision was controversial to say the least and, in the circumstances, a reference to the European Court of Justice might have been expected but this was not forthcoming. It also seems that an appeal to the House of Lords is unlikely, leaving determination of the scope of data protection law in the United Kingdom in an unsatisfactory state for the time being. The decision is discussed in relation to the two definitions below.

BASIC DEFINITIONS

The basic definitions are fundamental to data protection law. Unless data are within the meaning of personal data, the Data Protection Act 1998 cannot apply to them. This definition is made in two stages: first, data are defined and this is followed by a definition of personal data. Another vital definition is that of processing. Like the definitions of data and personal data it is a wide definition. Other definitions are also quite wide, increasing the extent and spread of data protection law. First, the definition of data is considered.

DATA

The most important definitions are contained in section 1(1) and key to these is the meaning of data which is as follows:

---

[1] *Durant* v *Financial Services Authority* [2003] EWCA Civ 1746.

"data" means information which–

(a) *is being processed by means of equipment operating automatically in response to instructions given for that purpose,*

(b) *is recorded with the intention that it should be processed by means of such equipment,*

(c) *is recorded as part of a relevant filing system or with the intention that it should form part of a relevant filing system,*

(d) *does not fall within paragraph (a), (b) or (c) but forms part of an accessible record as defined by section 68, or*

(e) *is recorded information held by a public authority and does not fall in any of the paragraphs (a) to (d).*

The fourth meaning, information forming part of an accessible record covers certain health, educational and public records which are not processed or intended to be processed automatically and which are not relevant filing systems. In other words, this covers such information held in unstructured manual files. These records used to be subject to the Access to Health Records Act 1990 and the Access to Personal Files Act 1987 but have been brought within the ambit of the Data Protection Act 1998 (parts of the 1990 Act and the whole of the 1987 Act were repealed by the Data Protection Act 1998). The final meaning of data, public authority information, was inserted by the Freedom of Information Act 2000. It relates to unstructured manual personal data held by or on behalf of public authorities. Under that Act, individuals' right of access to information commenced on 1 January 2005. "Public authority" has the same meaning as in the Freedom of Information Act (being listed in Schedule 1 to that Act or is a publicly-owned company as defined in section 6, not to be confused with a plc). Data is "held" by a public authority if it is held by the authority other than on behalf of another person or is held by another person on behalf of the authority.[2] Limitations that apply in relation to information subject to that Act also apply in relation to data held by public authorities for the purposes of (e) above.

The definition of data is not specific and is more to do with how the data are to be processed or how they are structured (as will be seen later when the definition of "relevant filing system" is examined), although certain forms of unstructured data are within definitions (d) and (e). "Data" is simply described as "information". Neither "data" nor "information" is further defined as a "term" of art. The *Oxford Concise Dictionary* (9th edition) defines "data" as:

1. *known facts or things used as a basis for inference or reckoning;*

---

[2] Section 3(2) of the Freedom of Information Act 2000.

2.   quantities or characters operated on by a computer.

The word "information" has a number of meanings but an appropriate dictionary definition is:

"something told, knowledge, items of knowledge".

It must be noted that none of these definitions give a real clue to the width of meaning intended. Of course, textual data such as words, letters and numerals (however represented or stored) may fall within the meaning of data, provided otherwise the data fall within one of the limbs of the definition. But the Directive is quite specific and recital 14 thereto states that the Directive should apply to the processing of sound and image data relating to natural persons. (There is an exception in the case of video surveillance carried out for specific purposes such as national or public security.) Thus, images stored on videotape and all manner of information stored on magnetic media, CD-ROM or DVD will fall within the meaning of data if it falls within any one of the four limbs of the definition of data. Also caught will be conventional photographs. The key to the scope of data protection law in relation to such data is the definition of "personal data".

It was accepted by Lindsay J that image data in the form of photographs are included within the definition of data in *Michael Douglas v Hello! Ltd*[3] and also appears to have been implicitly accepted, at first instance, in *Naomi Campbell v Mirror Group Newspapers Ltd*[4]. In subsequent appeals and other applications in these cases, nothing has been said to the contrary, indeed the matter seems so clear that it no longer seems to be worth a mention.

The definition of data processed by equipment operating automatically should be wide enough to cover not only information processed by computers as such but also where information is transmitted electronically, such as by telecommunications systems or over the internet, or stored digitally, for example, by taking a photograph using a digital camera or even a camera using conventional film. Recording on videotape, CD or DVD should also be covered.

RELEVANT FILING SYSTEM

The meaning of relevant filing system is of considerable importance and marked a considerable extension of data protection law in respect of manual filing systems.

---

[3] [2003] EMLR 585.
[4] [2002] EWHC 499 (QB).

"relevant filing system" means any set of information relating to individuals to the extent that, although the information is not processed by means of equipment operating automatically in response to instructions given for that purpose, the set is structured, either by reference to individuals or by reference to criteria relating to individuals, in such a way that specific information relating to a particular individual is readily accessible.[5]

Recital 15 of the Data Protection Directive makes it clear that what is important in determining whether a manual filing system is within data protection law is that ease of access to personal data is facilitated by virtue of the structured nature of the system. A card index system containing information relating to employees is certainly within the meaning of "relevant filing system", where it is set out in a standardised order, where each employee has his or her own card containing information about that employee and the card bears the name of the employee clearly visible on the card, the cards being kept in alphabetic order. Another example is where a filing system contains application forms (having an internal structure) which are arranged in name order. The nature of the system is such as to enable information to be accessed easily and quickly in relation to a particular individual or individuals. So, for example, if a person wanted to know someone's date of birth, they could retrieve that information from the filing system quickly. A general correspondence file is not a relevant filing system as there is no structure allowing quick access to particular data. It is at least arguable that the risks to privacy associated with the ability to find details relating to individuals are not so great if it takes some time and effort to access those details. But, if the data are particularly sensitive and are being painstakingly extracted for some purpose which prejudices the interests or right of privacy of the data subject, the dangers still exist. Though, in such cases, the Human Rights Act 1998 may provide a remedy, on the basis of Article 8 of the Council of Europe Convention for the Protection of Human Rights and Fundamental Freedoms 1950 (the 'Human Rights Convention'). By virtue of that Act, which came into force on 2 October 2000, the Convention has direct effect in the United Kingdom and has been used on a number of occasions in conjunction with data protection law. Other areas of law could also be relevant such as the law of breach of confidence or breach of fiduciary duty and if the information is untrue, the law of defamation may provide remedies for the individual concerned.

The meaning of "relevant filing system" was considered by the Court of Appeal in *Durant* v *Financial Services Authority*.[6] The appellant, Mr Durant, was a customer of Barclays Bank and had been involved in legal proceedings with

---

[5] Recital 15 of the Data Protection Directive.
[6] [2003] EWCA Civ 1746.

the bank which he had lost. He asked the Financial Services Authority ("the FSA") to assist him and it carried out an investigation but did not disclose the outcome to Mr Durant as it was under a duty of confidentiality pursuant to sections 82 to 85 of the Banking Act 1987. Mr Durant later made subject access requests to the FSA, under section 7 of the Data Protection Act 1998 to obtain disclosure of personal data held in electronic and manual files. Material held on computer was disclosed but some of the documents had been redacted to conceal the names of other persons. However, the FSA refused the whole of Mr Durant's request for information held in manual files on the ground that that the information sought was not "personal" within the definition of "personal data" in section 1(1) of the Data Protection Act 1998 (see below) and, even if it was personal data, it was not part of a "relevant filing system". Disclosure was refused in relation to four categories of file. One was arranged in date order and related to the systems and controls that Barclays Bank was required to maintain, another was a complaints file with dividers arranged by names of individuals alphabetically. Behind the divider marked Mr Durant there were a number of documents arranged by date order. The third file was the FSA's regulatory enforcement department's file organised by reference to cases or issues concerning Barclays Bank though not necessarily arranged by reference to individuals but which contained a sub-file marked Mr Durant but, otherwise, neither the file nor sub-file was indexed in any way. The final file, the Company Secretariat papers contained a sheaf of papers relating to Mr Durant's complaints about the FSA's refusal to give further disclosure and the outcome of the investigation into his complaints against Barclays Bank. This file was not organised by date or otherwise. All the files contained information in which Mr Durant featured. Mr Durant sought a court order for disclosure under section 7(9) of the Data Protection Act 1998 but this was refused. Eventually, he appealed to the Court of Appeal.

Auld LJ (with whom Mummery and Buxton LLJ agreed) noted that the definitions in the Data Protection Directive and the recitals to the Directive make it clear that the main focus is on computerised processing of personal data and that manual filing systems are caught only if they are sufficiently sophisticated to be broadly equivalent to computerised systems by virtue of their structure giving ready access to information constituting personal data. It is not enough that a manual file has an individual's name on it if the person carrying out a subject access request has to leaf through documents to see if there are any references to the data subject in a time-consuming and costly manner. Not only must files be indexed by name or unique identifier but also the files must have some internal structure permitting quick and easy access to specific data. A narrow meaning must be given to "relevant filing system" such that it is limited to:

1.   *a filing system in which the constituent files are structured or referenced in such a way so as to make it clear at the beginning of a search for*

personal data whether personal data relating to an individual carrying out a subject access request is held within the system and, if that is so, in which file or files they are held; and

2. *a filing system that has, as part of its own structure or referencing system, a method, sufficiently sophisticated and detailed, to readily indicate whether and where in an individual file or files, specific criteria or information about the data subject can be readily located.*

Auld LJ thought that it was clear that the FSA's manual filing systems were unstructured and did not contain indexing mechanisms to enable location of particular documents and personal data concerning the claimant. Therefore, the FSA was entitled to refuse access to its manual files.

This is a sensible decision as regards the meaning of "relevant filing system" and in line with the spirit of the Directive (though that part of the decision on the meaning of personal data is controversial, see below). Of course, the Act has to be interpreted in line with the Directive and this was the approach Auld LJ took. A wider approach to what constitutes a relevant filing system would be contrary to the clear intention of the Directive to only catch filing systems indexed by reference to individuals or criteria relating to individuals and which are structured in such a way as to permit easy access to personal data concerning them. None of the files in question could be so described. If access to personal data in manual files such as those held by the FSA were granted this would significantly increase the burden of complying with subject access requests directed towards manual files.

ACCESSIBLE RECORDS

Under section 68(1) of the Data Protection Act 1998, an accessible record is:

(a)   *a health record as defined by subsection (2),*

(b)   *an educational record as defined by Schedule 11, or*

(c)   *an accessible public record as defined by Schedule 12.*

Section 68(2) defines a health record as any record which consists of information relating to the physical or mental health or condition of an individual and has been made by a health professional in connection with the care of that individual. "Health professional" is itself widely defined in section 69.

Educational records are defined in Schedule 11 and, in England and Wales are records of information processed by or on behalf of the governing body of, or a teacher at, a local education authority maintained school or a special school within the meaning of section 6(2) of the Education Act 1996. The information must relate to any person who is or has been a pupil at the school. It must also have originated from or have been supplied by or on behalf of employees of local education authorities, teachers or employees at special schools, the pupil to whom the record relates or a parent of that pupil. Schedule 12 covers local authority housing and social services records.

PERSONAL DATA

The Act only applies to personal data. The Directive talks in terms of "natural persons" (to exclude artificial legal persons such as companies) but the United Kingdom approach is to limit this to living individuals and to exclude deceased persons. The Directive is not entirely clear on this point but it could be argued that a deceased person is no longer a natural person, though he or she may be supernatural! However, one dictionary definition is that the word means having a physical existence, as opposed to a spiritual one. Under section 1(1),

"personal data" means data which relate to a living individual who can be identified–

(a) *from those data, or*

(b) *from those data and other information which is in the possession of, or likely to come into the possession of, the data controller, and includes any expression of opinion about the individual and any indication of the intentions of the data controller or any other person in respect of the individual.*

The acid test should be whether a person could be identified from the data in question (or from those data and other information which may supplement them). One feature of data protection law is that it could give individuals rights over recordings of their images and of their speech or singing. However, there are significant exemptions to some of the provisions of the Act and constraints over the powers of the Information Commissioner where processing is for the "special purposes" listed, which includes journalism. In many, but by no means all situations, the data controller may be able to use the special purposes exemption as a shield which may at least allow publication. One important exception is the rights of data subjects to prevent processing likely to cause substantial damage or substantial distress. However, even where the processing is for the special purposes, the data subject's rights to compensation are untouched and compensation for distress only is available. The special purposes are examined in more detail below.

Under the 1984 Act, indications of intention were excluded from the meaning of personal data and were outside the scope of the Act. Now, however within data protection law, such information may be withheld from the data subject under some of the exemptions to the subject access provisions.

One would think that the meaning of personal data as defined above would give a right of access to any information which relates to the person making the request for access, assuming that it falls within one of the categories of data for the purposes of the Act and the obligation to provide access is not exempted under the Act. That would seem to be the only sensible interpretation. The Directive defines personal data as any information relating to an identified or identifiable natural person and the right of access is to data relating to the person making the request. It would be natural to expect a wide meaning so as to extend to, for example, information pertaining to a person's attributes, characteristics or personality and to information written or expressed by or about an individual (hence the inclusion of expressions of opinion and indications of intention). In Case C-101/01 *Bodil Lindqvist*, 6 November 2003, the European Court of Justice, accepted that information about a named person's telephone number, occupation, hobbies and medical condition undoubtedly fell within the meaning of personal data. Unfortunately, the Court did not explore this further.

In *Durant v Financial Services Authority*[7] a narrow meaning was taken. It was a matter concerning whether the information was relevant to a person's right of privacy, bearing in mind that this is one of the pillars of data protection law. In the Court of Appeal, Auld LJ, with whom the other two judges agreed, looked at the purpose of the subject access provisions and said that it was to give an individual access to information in the form of his personal data so that he could verify that the processing of those data did not unlawfully infringe his privacy. If it did, then he could make use of the provisions in sections 10 to 14 of the Act to protect his privacy. The purpose was not to permit the individual to obtain discovery of documents in contemplation of legal proceedings or complaints against third parties. He went on to say that the focus of the Directive and the Act was on ready accessibility, and, in most cases, only information that names, or which directly refers to the individual will qualify as personal data. However, although ready accessibility is important, it is not the starting point and not all information that can be retrieved, for example, by a computer search against an individual's name or unique identifier, will be personal data for the purposes of the Act. The mere mention of the data subject does not necessarily amount to his personal data. Auld LJ suggested two factors that may assist in determining whether information constitutes personal data to which an individual is entitled to access.

- Whether the information is biographic in a significant sense, going beyond the recording of the individual's involvement in a matter or event that has no personal connotations – a life event in respect of which his privacy could not be said to be compromised.

---

[7] [2003] EWCA Civ 1746.

- Focus – the information should have the data subject as its focus rather than someone else with whom he may have been involved or some event in which he may have had an involvement or interest.

This narrow interpretation of personal data was, in the opinion of Auld LJ, supported by the inclusion of expressions of opinion and statements of intention in the definition of personal data in section 1(1) of the Act and by the definition of sensitive personal data and the provisions relating to the conditions for processing personal data. He considered that most of the further information sought by Mr Durant was not personal data within the meaning of the Act but was information about his complaints, the FSA and Barclays Bank and the mere fact that a document was retrievable by using his name did not entitle him to a copy of that document. Buxton LJ stressed the guiding principle of data protection law, being to protect an individual's privacy. In the present case, the claimant's letters of complaint and the FSA's investigation of the complaint did not relate to him but to his complaint. He said the Act would be engaged only if the FSA had expressed an opinion about the claimant. The definition of personal data requires that (i) the data relate to a living individual who (ii) can be identified from those data alone or in conjunction with other information. Buxton LJ said that much of the argument on behalf of the claimant focused on the second part of that definition without consideration of the first part of it. In other words, it is essential that the data relate to the individual, first and foremost.

This narrow construction can be criticised on a number of grounds. Coming to the definition from the perspective of the purpose of the subject access provisions is mistaken. The definition of personal data is fundamental to data protection law and feeds into all the other provisions of the Act, many of which have other purposes. It is like trying to give a generic description of a ball by saying it is spherical, small, white and has dimples on its surface. In any case, the purpose of subject access is to enable an individual to verify the accuracy of the data and the lawfulness of the processing.[8] This is not quite the same as that given by Auld LJ (though it will overlap in the vast majority of cases). It should also be noted that subject access is not restricted to providing access to the data themselves but requires other information to be given, such as a description of the purposes of processing, recipients or classes of recipients and the logic involved in any automated decision-taking. It may be that a data controller is in breach of the Act because he has failed to notify the identity of a country outside the European Economic Area to which he intends to transfer personal data but in respect of which all the individuals concerned have given their express consent to the transfer. In such a situation, those individuals' right of privacy cannot be said to be engaged.

---

[8] Recital 41 of the Directive.

Speaking of whether the mere mention of an individual in a document amounts to his personal data, Auld LJ said (at para 28):

"Whether it does so in any particular instance depends on where it falls in a continuum of relevance or proximity to the data subject as distinct, say, from transactions or matters in which he may have been involved to a greater or lesser degree."

Apart from cases where it is clear that the information is personal data, such as in *Lindqvist*, this will require the data controller to make a judgment as to whether subject access extends to all the information he has which to a greater or lesser extent relate to the data subject. It is likely that some data controllers will seize on this view and withhold more information than they might have done otherwise. In any case, the fact that a person has made a complaint surely is personal data as, if it were widely known, this could give others the impression that the person was a nuisance or vexatious. Of course, one can agree that not all the information concerning his complaint and the subsequent investigation was personal data but where Mr Durant was named, it may well have been. Although Auld LJ said that the purpose of subject access was not to obtain discovery of documents that may help a person in litigation, a person making a subject access request is not required to state the reasons he is making the request.

The point about the meaning of personal data being a narrow one because of the inclusion of expressions of opinion and indications of intention is not convincing. The reason is that these terms are a throwback to the 1984 Act which expressly included in the definition of personal data, expressions of opinion and expressly excluded indications of intention. It is likely that both were included in the definition in the 1998 Act simply for the avoidance of doubt. Neither term, nor any equivalent term, is to be found in the Directive. Finally, Auld LJ focused on name as the identifier (as it was the predominant identifier in the case). It should be noted, however, that the Directive mentions, in particular, identity number or one or more factors specific to physical, physiological, mental, economic, cultural or social identity. The use of the term "in particular" shows that this is not intended to be an exhaustive list.

Where personal data have been stripped of any information that can identify particular individuals, they cease to be personal data, unless the identifiers can be re-associated with the relevant data. So it was held by the Court of Appeal in *R v Department of Health, ex parte Source Informatics Ltd*[9] which was predominantly concerned a breach of confidence. Source Informatics tried to persuade general practitioners and pharmacists to disclose data relating to the

9 [2001] QB 424.

prescribing habits. It was intended that the data would be made anonymous before being supplied to the data company which considered the data would be valuable to drug companies and would provide useful data to monitor prescribing patterns. The intention was that general practitioners and pharmacists, for payment, would download onto disks details of the quantity and identity of drugs prescribed. The Department of Health issued a policy document warning of the complex legal and policy issues and advising against such disclosures. The Court of Appeal said that as a matter of common sense the data once rendered anonymous were outside the scope of the Data Protection Directive. The Court also held that the activity would involve no breach of confidence and, in particular, that the patients had no property rights in the information concerning the items they had been prescribed.

SENSITIVE PERSONAL DATA

For processing to be permitted, the data controller must satisfy one of the conditions in Schedule 2 to the Act. In most cases, the data controller will find it easy to identify one or more of these conditions on which he can rely. However, in view of the fact that processing certain types of personal data may pose greater threats to individuals (for example, in relation to disclosures to third parties), there is a further set of conditions in Schedule 3 to the Act which apply to processing sensitive personal data. Where such data are processed, the data controller must also fall within one of these conditions which are generally of more limited scope compared to the list in Schedule 2. It is therefore important to be able to determine the meaning of such data and section 2 defines sensitive personal data as

personal data consisting of information as to–

(a) *the racial or ethnic origin of the data subject,*
(b) *his political opinions,*
(c) *his religious or other beliefs of a similar nature,*
(d) *whether he is a member of a trade union (within the meaning of the Trade Union and Labour Relations (Consolidation) Act 1992),*
(e) *his physical or mental health or condition,*
(f) *his sexual life,*
(g) *the commission or alleged commission by him of any offence, or*
(h) *any proceedings for any offence committed or alleged to have been committed by him, the disposal of such proceedings or the sentence of any court in such proceedings.*

The Directive required personal data relating to offences and convictions to be processed only under the control of official authority but it did allow derogation, subject to suitable safeguards, providing a complete register of convictions was only to be kept under the control of official authority. The Act provided for no such derogation but the Data Protection (Processing of Sensitive Personal Data) Order 2000, *inter alia,* allows processing of sensitive data if necessary for the prevention of crime or any unlawful act (or omission) which must be carried out without explicit consent of the data subject if not to prejudice those purposes, if such processing is in the substantial public interest. This may allay concerns amongst organisations vulnerable to fraud.

It would appear that processing by organisations of information relating to civil judgments can be processed, not being sensitive data, provided one of the conditions in Schedule 2 is met, the most appropriate one being processing for the legitimate interests of the data controller or a third party to whom the data are disclosed. The Directive allowed Member States, optionally, to require the processing of information relating to civil judgments to be carried out only under the control of official authority. The United Kingdom has declined to adopt this approach. The conditions for processing for both normal and sensitive personal data are described in full in Chapter 7. Satisfying the requirements of Schedule 2 and, if appropriate, Schedule 3 are an essential pre-requisite for processing. A number of additional conditions have been added to the Schedule 3.

PROCESSING

The definition of "processing" is significantly wider than that in the 1984 Act which was relatively narrow, being "amending, augmenting, deleting or re-arranging the data or extracting the information constituting the data" and, in the case of personal data, meant performing any of those operations by reference to the data subject. Under the 1998 Act the definition, which is clearly not an exhaustive one, is as follows.

> *"processing", in relation to information or data, means obtaining, recording or holding the information or data or carrying out any operation or set of operations on the information or data, including–*
> *(a) organisation, adaptation or alteration of the information or data,*
> *(b) retrieval, consultation or use of the information or data,*
> *(b) disclosure of the information or data by transmission, dissemination or otherwise making available, or*
> *(c) alignment, combination, blocking, erasure or destruction of the information or data.*

Almost any activity that could be perceived in relation to data processing is covered by this definition. Even simply having personal data is within the meaning. "Holding" information or data must mean being in possession of it. The Directive, in its definition of processing in Article 2, uses the word "storage" instead (a sole noun amongst a collection of verbs). Further clues in the Directive indicate that simply being in possession of data is to be considered within the meaning of processing. For example, Article 32(2) gives the opportunity for providing further transitional arrangements in respect of manual filing systems providing the data subject is given a right to subject access and other rights in respect of data which are "incomplete, inaccurate or *stored* in a way incompatible with the legitimate interests pursued by the controller" (emphasis added).

The scope of "processing" can be illustrated by way of an example.

- *obtaining* – ARTEMUS ACTIVITY HOLIDAYS LTD decided to run a survey as part of a marketing campaign. The survey is carried out by DATA PROCUREMENT LTD, a company specialising in surveys carried out in busy shopping centres. Employees of DATA PROCUREMENT stop passers-by and ask them a number of questions about their preferences for food and wine and leisure activities. They are also asked if they own their own homes.

- *recording and holding* – the names and addresses of individuals prepared to participate and their answers are entered on proformas which are collected together and sent to COMPU-ASSIST LTD, engaged by ARTEMUS to process the data, which keeps them in a store for a while until enough have been collected to make it worthwhile entering the information on computer (a second act of recording).

- *organisation, alteration, consultation or use, etc* – COMPU-ASSIST's employees check the data for obvious errors and then carry out a number of operations to produce statistical information and to create profiles on individuals and how likely they are to be interested in ARTEMUS's holiday offers. Mailshots are then sent to these persons advertising "special offer" holiday package deals. The database of individuals contains a further piece of information to record the fact that some of the persons inter-viewed expressed a desire not to have information relating to them passed onto organisations other than ARTEMUS ACTIVITY HOLIDAYS (*blocking*). The database is then sent to and installed on ARTEMUS's computer (recording again).

- *retrieval, consultation, alteration and use* – some of the individuals go to ARTEMUS's premises and choose holidays – the relevant details of these persons are retrieved on screen and those that ask for credit have to wait a short time whilst a check is made at a credit reference agency – the operator also checks whether the person concerned is a home owner – further details are added relating to the particular customer (choice of holiday destination, dates of holiday, etc.).

- *adaptation and disclosure* – some information, for example, the fact of home ownership is disclosed to credit reference agencies (this results in a database which omits other details). A copy of the report of individuals' profiles of preferences together with their names and addresses is given to DIRECT INDEMNITY PLC, a company offering insurance services (apart from those individuals who expressed a wish that their data should not be disclosed in this way).

- *alignment and combination* – ARTEMUS obtained a list of customers from ELEGANT FASHIONS LTD and combined this database with its own. In many cases the amount of useful information is significantly enhanced and, the next holiday season, ARTEMUS thinks its marketing efforts will be better targeted.

- *holding, erasure and destruction, recording* – some time later, ARTEMUS bought a rival company's assets and discovered that its database of potential customers was much more sophisticated than its own. ARTEMUS decided to erase its own database and to destroy all the printed reports obtained from it, many of which had been stored away or archived. ARTEMUS engaged the services of DROSS DESPATCH LTD to remove and destroy the old printed reports. The new database is loaded onto ARTEMUS's computer.

The special significance of the wide definition is that a whole range of persons who carry out processing activities on behalf of the data controller will be deemed to be data processors and subject to the security requirements of the Act. Thus, in the example, above, even DATA PROCUREMENT, which obtains and records on proformas information from passers-by, and DROSS DESPATCH, which disposes of the old printed reports, will be data processors for the purposes of the Act.

Under the 1984 Act, there was a problem with one of the offences (in section 5(2) of that Act) where it was held by the House of Lords that simply retrieving data was not using those data – something further needed to be done with the data after they had been retrieved.[10] The offence was using personal data other than for a purpose or purposes described in the register entry. However, there is no direct equivalent offence contained in the 1998 Act and that narrow and unsatisfactory decision (it was a 3: 2 majority decision) is no longer of any relevance to data protection law.

Under section 1(3) of the Data Protection Act 1998, obtaining, recording, using or disclosing data extends to the information contained within the data. It is immaterial if the intention is that the processing or inclusion in a relevant filing system takes place outside the European Economic Area (EEA). This latter provision is not worded to extend to accessible records.

---

[10] *R* v *Brown* [1996] 1 AC 543.

PROCESSING FOR THE SPECIAL PURPOSES

Recital 17 of the Directive provides that the principles of the Directive should apply in a restricted manner to the processing of sound and image data for the purposes of journalism or literary or artistic expression, in particular in the audiovisual field. Recital 37 mentions that specific exemption will be available, as set out in Article 9, to "processing of personal data for purposes of journalism of [sic] for purposes of literary or artistic expression, in particular in the audiovisual field ...". Article 9 simply leaves it to Member States to implement exemptions or derogations only if necessary to reconcile the right to privacy with the rules governing freedom of expression (an oblique and implied reference to the right under Article 10 of the Human Rights Convention). As implemented in the United Kingdom, there is a wide-ranging exemption where processing is with a view to publication in cases where that publication would be in the public interest. This applies to processing for the "special purposes" which are defined in section 3 as any one or more of the following–

(a)   *the purposes of journalism,*
(b)   *artistic purposes, and*
(c)   *literary purposes.*

One might question why the Act did not use the exact wording of the Directive and whether literary or artistic purposes are the same as purposes of literary or artistic expression. The special purposes are not further defined in the Act and there is no attempt at limiting the exemption to the audiovisual field, nor any mention of such a field (Article 9 of the Directive does not mention this field either despite the clear references to it in the recitals, although Recital 37 does not altogether exclude other fields). In *Naomi Campbell* v *Mirror Group Newspapers Ltd*[11] the special purposes were relevant not only to a photograph of the model but also covered textual information published in the defendant's newspaper giving details of the model's treatment by Narcotics Anonymous for her drug addiction. There was no attempt to limit the special purposes to the audiovisual field. However, the judge in the High Court held that the defence only applied up to the time of publication, though this was reversed in the Court of Appeal[12] which accepted that it applied post-publication and the Court of Appeal also held that there was no breach of confidence. Ms Campbell's appeal to the House of Lords[13] was successful on the breach of confidence aspect by a 3: 2 majority. Their Lordships did not feel the need to explore the data protection point at length,

---

[11] [2002] EWHC 499 (QB).
[12] [2003] QB 633.
[13] [2004] 2 All ER 995.

on the basis that it was agreed that the result would be the same as the breach of confidence issue.

In terms of reconciling privacy with freedom of expression, it could be argued that the Data Protection Act 1998 has come down on the side of freedom of expression, especially as the exemption applies where the data controller reasonably believes publication to be in the public interest. However, this subjective approach is tempered by the fact that the reasonableness of the belief must be viewed in the context of any applicable code of practice, such as that published by the Press Complaints Commission. Furthermore, individuals' rights to compensation still apply notwithstanding the exemption.

ACTORS (PERSONS AFFECTED)

The persons identified by the new law are data controllers, data subjects, data processors, recipients and third parties to whom the data are disclosed.

> *"data controller" means ... a person who (either alone or jointly or in common with other persons) determines the purposes for which and the manner in which any personal data are, or are to be, processed.*

Under the 1984 Act, the equivalent term was "data user" being the person who controls the contents and use of the data. It is the data controller who is subjected to the vast majority of the controls set out in the 1998 Act and, under section 4(4) of the Act, the data controller has a duty to comply with the data protection principles, unless covered by any of the exemptions. This is irrespective of whether the data controller has to notify all or any of his processing activities.

The significance of whether data controllers operate jointly or in common simply means that, for data controllers to operate jointly, they are working to the same design and purposes and share all the processing activities. An example of data controllers acting in common is where one data controller has created a database and uses it for a specific purpose and another data controller, by agreement, is allowed to use the database for a different purpose.

One problem is that it may be difficult to determine whether a provider of IT facilities management services is a data controller or data processor (defined below) or both in respect of the provision of those services. To some extent this difficulty stems from the definition of data controller as the person who determines the purposes *and* the manner of processing. Where an IT facilities management service provider is engaged it could be argued that the client determines the purposes whilst the service provider determines the manner. Alternatively, it could be said that the determination of the manner of processing is a task which, although delegated to the service provider, remains the responsibility of the client.

Where processing is required by law under an enactment, the person under the obligation to process the data will be the data controller for the purposes of the Act.

"data subject" means an individual who is the subject of personal data.

This simply restates the definition under the 1984 Act. We are all data subjects – there can be very few people that have managed to escape others having personal data relating to them. Even a long-term vagrant is likely to have had some contact with authorities, or others, such as providers of health care. Therefore, with very few exceptions, the Data Protection Act 1998 affects us all.

"data processor", in relation to personal data, means any person (other than an employee of the data controller) who processes data on behalf of the data controller.

As noted above, the wide definition of "processing" means that a great many organisations and individuals are data processors under the Act.

Further definitions of other various persons involved are contained in section 70 (supplementary definitions). They are as follows.

"recipient", in relation to any personal data, means any person to whom the data are disclosed, including any person (such as an employee or agent of the data controller, a data processor or an employee or agent of a data processor) to whom they are disclosed in the course of processing the data for the data controller, but does not include any person to whom disclosure is or may be made as a result of, or with a view to, a particular inquiry by or on behalf of that person made in the exercise of any power conferred by law.

The significance of this definition is that descriptions of recipients or categories of recipients must be included in the notification of processing activity. As generic descriptions tend to be used, the last part of the definition is not really important. It was included as an amendment to the Bill to ease fears of some data controllers such as local authorities which were worried that they might not be able to predict in advance all their potential recipients.

"third party", in relation to personal data, means any person other than–

(a) the data subject,
(b) the data controller, or

*(c) any data processor or other person authorised to process data for the
     data controller or processor.*

Note that third parties to whom personal data are disclosed will also be recipients, subject only to the specific exception in the definition of recipient. The
importance of the definition of third parties is that disclosures to third parties
may trigger an obligation to inform data subjects. There may also be requirements to notify third parties to whom the data have been disclosed of any
inaccuracy in the data.

APPLICATION OF ACT

By section 5 of the Data Protection Act 1998, except as otherwise provided for
by or under section 54 (for example, the Commissioner carrying out designated functions to enable the government to give effect to any international
obligations of the United Kingdom), the Act applies to a data controller in
respect of any data only if –

*(a) the data controller is established in the United Kingdom and the data
     are processed in the context of that establishment, or*
*(b) the data controller is established neither in the United Kingdom nor in
     any European Economic Area State but uses equipment in the United
     Kingdom for processing the data otherwise than for transit through the
     United Kingdom – such a data controller must nominate a represen-
     tative established in the United Kingdom.*

The meaning of "established" in the United Kingdom covers:

(a) an individual ordinarily resident in the United Kingdom,
*(b) a body incorporated under the law of the United Kingdom or any part of
     it,*
*(c) a partnership or unincorporated association formed under the law of
     any part of the United Kingdom, and*
*(d) any other person, not included above, who maintains in the United
     Kingdom an office, branch or agency through which he carries on any
     activity or a regular practice.*

Any reference to an establishment in any other EEA State has a corresponding
meaning. This is all fairly self-explanatory. For example, an English company
processing personal data relating to its employees based in England will obviously be subject to the United Kingdom Act. An American company which
uses a Scots company to process data on its behalf will be subject to the United
Kingdom Act and must nominate a representative – most likely the Scots
company. A German company operating as an employment agency for
construction companies in Germany but which sets up a recruitment office in

Wales, will be subject to the German Act in relation to its processing in Germany and the United Kingdom Act in respect of its processing in Wales. In this latter case, there is no requirement for the German company to nominate a representative. Unless exempt, the German company must notify under the United Kingdom Act.

As the final meaning of establishment refers to any activity or regular practice, it is potentially quite wide-ranging. Of course, companies operating in a number of countries usually have subsidiary companies set up in those countries under their appropriate laws. Thus, where a company incorporated in Northern Ireland is a wholly owned subsidiary of an Italian company, it will be the Northern Ireland company which will be subject to the United Kingdom Act.

DEFINITIONS RELEVANT TO THE TRANSITIONAL PROVISIONS

The transitional provisions were important because they gave data controllers a breathing space in respect of processing already under way on 24 October 1998 (the date the new law should have been transposed into national law). The intention was to reduce the impact of the new law in respect of such processing. "Eligible data" benefited, and in some cases continue to benefit, from the transitional provisions and there are significant differences depending on whether the data are "automated" or "manual". There were also two transitional periods. The relevant definitions are set out in Schedule 8 to the Act.

> *personal data are "eligible data" at any time if, and to the extent that, they are at that time subject to processing which was already under way immediately before 24th October 1998.*

This is a puzzling definition but it seems that personal data are within the meaning if in existence before that date. But they remain eligible only in respect of pre-existing processing activities. For example, new personal data subsequently added after 23 October 1998 would not be eligible data. Furthermore, if a new form of processing was subsequently used in connection with pre-existing data, this would not have been able to benefit from the transitional provisions. Another problem was what the situation was with respect to pre-existing personal data which had been processed in a certain manner some time before the above date but were no longer being processed in such a manner at that date. The full significance of the meaning of eligible data is discussed in Chapter 9.

Eligible automated data are eligible data within section 1(1)(a) and (b), that is data which are being or are intended to be processed by automatic means and eligible manual data are eligible data that are not within section 1(1)(a) and (b), that is relevant filing systems, accessible records and unstructured manual data held by public authorities.

The first transitional period was the period beginning with the date of commencement of Schedule 8, containing the transitional provisions, ending with 23 October 2001. That is, three years from the date the Directive should have been implemented. The second transitional period is from 24 October 2001 ending with 23 October 2007. The second transitional period applies only to eligible manual data. However, there are further exemptions which run from 24 October 2001 indefinitely where processing is for historical research. These provisions apply to both eligible manual data and eligible automated data though with some differences.

CHAPTER 5

THE DATA PROTECTION PRINCIPLES

The data protection principles originally derive from the Council of Europe Convention of 28 January 1981 for the Protection of Individuals with regard to Automatic Processing of Personal Data. By Recital 11 of the Data Protection Directive, these principles are given substance and amplified by the Directive. The principles in the Convention were also implemented in the Data Protection Act 1984 and, consequently, the data protection principles contained in that Act and those in the Data Protection Act 1998 appear to be very similar. There are some notable differences however. One example is the eighth principle concerning transfers to countries or territories outside the European Economic Area (EEA). Further differences result from the increased provisions on the interpretation of the data protection principles, reflecting some of the important changes brought about by implementing the Data Protection Directive. As under the previous legislation, the data protection principles and the interpretation of those principles are contained in Schedule 1 to the Data Protection Act. First, it will be useful to set out the principles as they appear in the Act.

THE DATA PROTECTION PRINCIPLES

1. *Personal data shall be processed fairly and lawfully and, in particular, shall not be processed unless -*
    (a) at least one of the conditions in Schedule 2 is met, and
    (b) in the case of sensitive personal data, at least one of the conditions in Schedule 3 is also met.

2. *Personal data shall be obtained only for one or more specified and lawful purposes and shall not be further processed in any manner incompatible with that purpose or those purposes.*

3. *Personal data shall be adequate, relevant and not excessive in relation to the purpose or purposes for which they are processed.*

4. *Personal data shall be accurate and, where necessary, kept up to date.*

5. *Personal data processed for any purpose or purposes shall not be kept for longer than is necessary for that purpose or those purposes.*

6. *Personal data shall be processed in accordance with the rights of data subjects under this Act.*

7. *Appropriate technical and organisational measures shall be taken against unauthorised or unlawful processing of personal data and against accidental loss or destruction of, or damage to, personal data.*

8. *Personal data shall not be transferred to a country or territory outside the European Economic Area unless that country or territory ensures an adequate level of protection for the rights and freedoms of data subjects in relation to the processing of personal data.*

Schedules 2 and 3 set out conditions for processing and will be examined in more detail in Chapter 7. Basically, a data controller needs to satisfy one of the conditions in Schedule 2 but, where the data are sensitive as defined in section 2 of the Act, an additional condition from Schedule 3 must also be satisfied. In terms of normal data, the vast majority of data controllers will have no difficulty in meeting at least one of the conditions in Schedule 2. Generally, Schedule 3 is more restrictive and seeks to limit the processing of sensitive data.

It should be noted that data subjects have a right to compensation if they have suffered damage for any contravention of the requirements of the Data Protection Act 1998 and this includes a breach of the data protection principles. Similarly, a right to compensation for distress is also available where the data subject has suffered damage or where the processing is for the special purposes, resulting from any contravention of the requirements of the Act. This is unlike the position under the 1984 Act where the right to compensation was available only under a number of specific circumstances, such as the loss or unauthorised destruction of personal data or because of any inaccuracy of the data; see *Lord Ashcroft* v *Attorney General*[1] where Gray J said (at para 29):

"The position under the 1998 Act is entirely different: there is a free-standing duty on data processors under section 4(4) to comply with the principles which are set out in Schedule 1B part I. By section 13 breach of those principles does sound in damages, as does breach of any of the requirements of the 1998 Act. Section 14 confers a right to rectification, blocking, erasure

---

[1] [2002] EWHC 1122 (QB).

or destruction of personal data. Although enforcing compliance with the principles is for the Commissioner, it is clear that her jurisdiction is non-exclusive so far as claims for damages by data subjects are concerned."

It might assist in determining whether there has been a breach of the data protection principles to consider whether the activity in question conforms with a code of practice approved by the Working Party established under the Data Protection Directive, such as the European Code of Practice for the use of personal data in direct marketing published by the Federation of European Direct Marketing.

INTERPRETATION OF THE PRINCIPLES

Part II of Schedule 1 gives guidance as to the interpretation of each of the principles. Some of the key aspects of the Data Protection Directive are given effect in the provisions on interpretation, such as the requirements to provide individuals with information on collection of personal data from them and in other cases.

FIRST PRINCIPLE

In determining whether processing is fair, regard is to be had to the method by which the data were obtained. This includes, in particular, whether any person from whom the data were obtained was deceived or misled as to the purposes of the processing. If personal data are obtained from either the data subject or another person by means of a trick, then the processing will be unfair. In some cases, this might amount to the criminal offence of procuring the disclosure of personal data. But fairness goes further than this. Fair processing should also require that the data subject is informed of any non-obvious uses to which the data controller intends to put the data at the time the data are collected. Cases before the Information Tribunal (then named the Data Protection Tribunal)[2] confirmed that individuals should be informed of marketing uses of personal data at the outset and given a simple means of opting out there and then, for example, by use of the ubiquitous "tick box".

Data comprising information obtained from a person who was authorised by or under any enactment to supply such information are treated as fairly obtained as are data comprising information obtained from a person who was required to supply it by or under any enactment or convention or other

---

[2] Such as *Innovations v Data Protection Registrar* (Case DA/92 31/49/1) 29 September 1993; *British Gas Trading Ltd v Data Protection Registrar*, 24 March 1998 and *Midlands Electricity plc v Data Protection Registrar*, 7 May 1999.

instrument imposing an international obligation on the United Kingdom. In many cases, this will apply to personal information in documents which are made available to the public, for example, patent specifications, birth certificates and information disclosed in connection with extradition proceedings. However, the requirements to provide information to the data subject still apply in such cases.

Where personal data contain a general identifier (such as a number or code forming part of a set of similar identifiers of general application) the Secretary of State may lay down conditions to be complied with, otherwise the processing will not be treated as being fair and lawful. This is intended to allow for additional safeguards if a system of national identification numbers is introduced into the United Kingdom.

Paragraphs 2 to 4 of Part II of Schedule 1 set out the requirements for providing information to data subjects on collection and in other cases. Where the data have not been obtained directly from the data subject, the data controller may be excused from providing information to the data subject where to do so would require a disproportionate effort and the data subject has not notified the data controller that he requires to be informed. The implications of these provisions are discussed more fully in Chapter 8. However, at this stage it should be noted that, apart from case law to the effect that non-obvious uses should be indicated to the data subject at the time data are collected from the data subject, there was no equivalent requirement under the 1984 Act. Of course, "fair processing" is quite a wide concept and the provision of information to the data subject could have been required in other cases. The rationale for providing individuals with information is so as to make processing activity more transparent so that individuals can at least be in a better position to know who is processing personal data relating to them and what the purposes of that processing are. In practice, the amount of information to be given will, in many cases, simply be the identity of the data controller, especially where the purposes are included in the data controller's entry on the data protection register. However, to ensure processing is fair, additional information may need to be given in some cases.

SECOND PRINCIPLE

This principle restricts processing to one or more specified and lawful purposes. Where processing is notified, the purposes of processing must be described in the notification. Where processing is not notified, for example, in the case of manual processing (although some data controllers may take the view that notification of manual processing is desirable), a description of the purposes of processing is part of the information which must be supplied to any person making a request in writing.

Where information has to be given to the data subject, this must include the purposes of processing unless the processing has been notified to the Commissioner. The register of persons giving notification is available for inspection by the public and all information, except a general description of security measures to be taken by the data controller in order to comply with the seventh data protection principle, may be inspected by members of the public. By consulting the register, data subjects can discover the purposes of processing. Thus, notification obviates the need for providing data subjects with information as to the purposes when data are collected from the data subject and in other cases.

To determine whether disclosures are compatible with the purposes for which personal data are obtained, regard is to be had to the purposes of processing intended by any person to whom the data are disclosed. For example, if an employer discloses personal data he obtained from employees for the purpose of calculating employees' salaries to a company intending to use the data for marketing activities; this would be unlikely to be compatible with the employer's purposes for obtaining the data in the first place. The purposes intended by any person to whom the data are disclosed will probably have to be similar or analogous to the purposes for which the personal data were obtained by the person now disclosing the data to another person.

As with the other principles, breach of the second principle gives rise to a private right of action. Under the 1984 Act, it could also attract criminal penalties where the holding of personal data was for purposes other than those noted on the register providing the person responsible knew or was reckless as to this fact; see *Information Commission* v *Islington Borough Council*.[3] Being in breach of the principles no longer is an offence under the 1998 Act.

THIRD PRINCIPLE

There are no interpretative provisions for this principle, which is fairly self-explanatory. Prior case law under the 1984 Act gives some help. For example, in *Rhondda BC* v *Data Protection Registrar*,[4] a local authority was collecting data which it did not need in relation to purposes of processing.

FOURTH PRINCIPLE

This principle requires that personal data are accurate and also imposes a duty to keep them up to date. As far as accuracy is concerned, in some circumstances, the data may be inaccurate and yet the data controller will not be in

---

[3] [2002] EWHC 1036 (Admin).
[4] (unreported) 11 October 1991.

breach of the fourth principle. This is where the inaccuracy accurately records information provided by the data subject or a third party. The data controller must have taken reasonable steps to ensure accuracy in the light of the purposes for which the data were obtained and further processed. This will mean that what constitutes "reasonable care" may vary from case to case. For example, if the processing constitutes some degree of risk if the data are inaccurate, the data controller should consider putting effective verification systems in place. Even if the data controller has taken reasonable steps, if the data subject has expressed his view that the data are inaccurate, the data must indicate that fact.

Where a data subject has informed the data controller that the data are inaccurate, in most cases, the data controller will simply make appropriate amendments. If, for whatever reason, the data controller does not intend to rectify such inaccuracies, this could have implications for the design of databases of personal data requiring, for example, the addition of an extra data field to record data subjects' views on inaccuracies. Of course, most data controllers will want to ensure as best as they can that the data are accurate. One case where a data controller might want to retain the inaccuracy is where the information came from a data subject who is suspected of being engaged in fraudulent or other dishonest activity and has tried to change details relating to him, for example, home ownership, outstanding loans, marital status, postal address, etc.

The retention of inaccurate data without being in breach of the fourth principle is important for data controllers as, without that protection, a data subject might be able to claim compensation in respect of the inaccuracy even if the source of the inaccuracy is the data subject himself.

Where data are inaccurate and someone suffers damage as a result, an action for compensation under data protection law may be more appropriate, and easier to bring, than an action in negligence. For example, all that is required under data protection law is to prove the breach and the causal link between the breach and the damage sustained by the individual. In *Ogle v Chief Constable of Thames Valley Police*[5] the Court of Appeal said that an action for compensation (albeit under the 1984 Act) was more appropriate than an action in negligence. The claimant had been arrested and held in police custody for over two hours as a result of an inaccuracy on the Police National Computer which failed to show that his disqualification from driving had expired.

---

[5] [2001] EWCA Civ 598.

FIFTH PRINCIPLE

There are no interpretative provisions for the fifth principle which simply requires that personal data shall not be kept longer than is necessary for the purposes for which they were processed. There is a specific exemption from the fifth principle which applies to data processed for research (statistical or historical) purposes and, under certain conditions, such data may be kept indefinitely, notwithstanding the fifth principle.

SIXTH PRINCIPLE

Breach of the sixth principle (processing only in accordance with the rights of data subjects) occurs only in specified cases even though data subjects have additional rights. Breach of the sixth principle concentrates on a failure by the data controller to comply with a subject access request or a failure to comply with, give or respond to notices as set out below:

- failure to supply information in response to a subject access request under section 7;

- to the extent that the notice is justified, failure to comply with a notice from a data subject under section 10(1) requiring the data controller to cease or not begin processing activity likely to cause substantial damage or substantial distress to the data subject or another and where that damage or distress is unwarranted;

- failure under section 10(3) to respond by giving a written notice to a data subject who has served a section 10(1) notice on the data controller;

- failing to comply with a notice under section 11(1) whereby a data subject requires a data controller to cease or not begin processing for the purposes of direct marketing;

- failing to comply with a data subject notice in respect of automated decision-taking or failing to notify a data subject in respect of such decision-taking as required under section 12.

Data subjects' rights are more extensive and other rights may be enforced even though there is no breach of the sixth principle. Other rights include a right to compensation, which can apply to any contravention of the Act, and a right to have inaccurate data rectified, blocked, erased or destroyed.

SEVENTH PRINCIPLE

The seventh principle is concerned with security measures against unauthorised or unlawful processing of personal data and against accidental loss or destruction of, or damage to, personal data. Relevant factors in determining the level of security are:

- the state of technical development;
- the costs of implementation;
- the harm which might result; and
- the nature of the data.

The last factor is probably redundant as, in assessing the harm likely to result from unauthorised processing, etc, the nature of the data will be all important. Where the data are particularly sensitive and the possibility of harm correspondingly greater, the better the security measures should be. Another point is that security should be reviewed at appropriate intervals to take account of improvements in security technology and changing costs. At the end of the day, data controllers will have to take a view of what is required though it will be in the interests of data controllers generally to have good security. As the Act also applies to some forms of manual files, security should not be overlooked here. It may be that structured paper files and other paper files caught by the Act should be kept in locked cabinets or locked rooms and only made available to those having a legitimate need to consult them. Computers should be kept secure and appropriate efforts should be made to prevent computers and computer storage media being stolen. This also applies to persons using notebook or portable computers as these are especially vulnerable. In the past, concern was expressed about general practitioners' security arrangements following a number of thefts of computers from doctors' surgeries.

The data controller must take reasonable steps to ensure the reliability of employees having access to personal data and it is probably employees that present the greatest threats to security. The Audit Commission study on computer misuse[6] found that 85 per cent of incidents disclosed in the survey were perpetrated by internal staff.

Unauthorised processing may come about by employees using their employer's computer facilities for their own purposes, such as where a policeman made use of the Police National Computer to try to discover the identity of the owner of a vehicle for purposes unconnected with police work.[7] Accidental loss, destruction or damage should be less of a problem with computer data, providing appropriate back-up facilities are in place, including the use of fireproof safes for storage of back-up data (or storage off-site). More

---

[6] *Ghost in the Machine: An Analysis of IT Fraud and Abuse* (February 1998).
[7] *R v Brown* [1996] 1 AC 543.

troublesome is manual data, particularly in the case of fire damage. Consideration may have to be given to the installation of sprinkler systems or other precautions.

There are special provisions which apply where processing is carried out on behalf of the data controller by a data processor. These are particularly important given the wide definition of processing together with the fact that, if the requirements are not met, the data controller will automatically be in breach of the seventh principle. There are four things the data controller must do, being that:

- he must choose a data processor who can provide sufficient guarantees in respect of security measures (technical and organisational);

- he must take reasonable steps to ensure that the data processor complies with those measures – this means that the data controller should satisfy himself that the data processor is complying (in some cases, where the potential for harm is significant, the data controller may need to police the processing activities to ensure compliance is taking place in fact and is continuing);

- the processing must be carried out under a contract made or evidenced in writing, and which requires the data processor only to act on instructions from the data controller; and

- the contract must require that the data processor complies with obligations equivalent to those imposed on the data controller by the seventh principle.

The insistence on contractually enforceable obligations will not be onerous in most cases and a written note, memorandum or schedule to the main agreement under which the processing is carried out will suffice if it states that the data processor is to act only on the instructions of the data controller and incorporates or refers to the seventh principle and the interpretation of it. However, in some cases, these requirements could be troublesome where the processing is not carried out under a contract, for example, where voluntary workers obtain personal data for a charity. Taking the interpretation to the seventh principle at face value, there must be a contract. Therefore, in such a case, a contract will have to be executed – either by deed or at nominal consideration.

Some local authorities and magistrates' courts make use of intermediaries to make enquiries with DVLA (Driver and Vehicle Licensing Agency) in respect of ownership of vehicles to enable the authorities to execute warrants of distraint against goods. Access to DVLA is provided to these intermediaries under a contract which mentioned the Data Protection Act (although it was the 1984 Act mentioned in the contract) and which imposed responsibility on the intermediary for preventing unauthorised disclosure, controlling access by passwords and user IDs, reporting any unauthorised use and all aspects of security of data. A system of checking for compliance (including spot checks) was in place and the contract pointed out the seriousness of a breach of the obligations and the fact that any abuse or misuse would result in termination of the contract and would be reported to the Commissioner. This system was held not to be unreasonable by the court in *Farrer* v *Secretary of State*.[8] It is difficult to think of a better example of complying with the seventh data protection principle though it is notable that this was not simply a case of imposing the obligations by contractual means, as it included a proactive system of checking to ensure that the processor complied with the obligations in practice.

EIGHTH PRINCIPLE

Transfers of personal data to countries or territories outside the European Economic Area (EEA) could be hindered or even prevented in some cases. The concept of adequacy of protection is something which is likely to be variable in many cases as a number of factors must be taken into account in any particular case. A transfer to a particular country of certain types of data (for example, non-sensitive data) may be quite acceptable but transfers of other personal data may not be. Bearing in mind that data processing activities may be severely hindered if some transfers are banned outright, transfers may still be permitted in certain circumstances even if the country or territory of destination does not provide adequate protection for personal data. However, where this is so, the Data Protection Act 1998, in line with the Directive, seeks to build in additional safeguards.

The factors used to determine whether a country or territory has an adequate level of protection are as follows:·

- the nature of the data (obviously the more sensitive the data the more likely some countries will be deemed not to have adequate protection);

- the country or territory of origin of the information contained in the data;

- the country or territory of final destination of that information (origin and destination should be considered together – if the country of origin has weak data protection law that probably will not be too much of a problem if that country is also the country of final destination, say after non-sensitive processing in the EEA);

---

[8] [2002] EWHC 1917 (Admin).

- the intended purposes and duration of processing;

- the law in force, international obligations, relevant codes of conduct or other enforceable rules in the country or territory in question;

- any security measures taken in respect of the data in the country or territory in question.

In any proceedings under the Act, where the question of adequacy of protection in a third country arises and there has been a Community finding relating to transfers of the kind in question, that question is to be determined in accordance with that finding. Under Article 25(4) of the Data Protection Directive, on the basis of the procedure set out in Article 31(2), the Commission may find that a third country does not have an adequate level of protection and, if so, Member States are to take measures to prevent transfers of the same type. Under Article 25(6), the Commission may also find that a third country does have an adequate level of protection. Such findings will be disseminated in the United Kingdom by the Information Commissioner. Up to the time of writing, the Commission has confirmed Switzerland, Canada, Argentina, Guernsey, Isle of Man and the transfer of Air Passenger Name Records to the United States' Bureau of Customs and Border Protection as providing adequate protection (although there had been some particular concerns about the provision of detailed passenger information by airlines to countries such as the United States).

Personal data may also be transferred to companies in the United States that have signed up to a "Safe Harbor" arrangement made with the Commission. Not surprisingly, a very large number of companies have signed up to this.

Even if a country or territory does not have an adequate level of protection in respect of transfers of a particular kind, by way of derogation, transfers may still take place providing the transfer falls within Schedule 4 to the Data Protection Act 1998. These will be discussed in more detail in Chapter 7 but suffice it to say at this stage that examples are where the data subject has given his consent, where the transfer is necessary in respect of a contract between the data controller and the data subject or where the transfer is made on terms which have been approved as ensuring adequate safeguards for the rights and freedoms of data subjects. Model approved contracts and contract terms are now available.

SUMMARY

The data protection principles lie at the very root of data protection law and it could be said that all else flows from them. Indeed, it could be claimed that the first principle, fair and lawful processing, is the very root of all data protection law and the remainder of the principles and the other legal provisions simply give detailed expression to that principle. Whilst many of the principles are similar or even identical to those under the 1984 Act, the eighth principle (transfers to third countries) is new. Even though most of the other principles look very familiar, the interpretative provisions have been significantly expanded and include a number of new concepts such as informing data subjects and requiring one or more conditions to be met for processing to proceed. The requirements for data processors to be under contractually imposed security obligations is also new though, under the 1984 Act, computer bureaux were required to register and were subject to the eighth principle (which then related to security measures). The provisions dealing with transfers to third countries have caused some controversy, particularly with respect to the United States but now, thanks to the Safe Harbor arrangements this is less of a problem. Effectively, by signing up to the Safe Harbor arrangements, companies agree to respect the privacy of personal data in line with the underlying principles in the Data Protection Directive.

CHAPTER 6
NOTIFICATION

Taking advantage of the possibility in the Data Protection Directive of exempting some forms of processing unlikely to adversely affect the rights and freedoms of data subjects, the United Kingdom has adopted an approach whereby automated processing is, subject to some sweeping exemptions, notifiable but manual processing is not required to be notified. Even though manual processing and some forms of automatic processing are exempt from notification, data controllers may consider it expedient to notify such processing. This is because there is an obligation, backed by criminal sanction, to supply most of the information required for notification within 21 days to any person making a written request. This is not limited to requests made by individuals in respect of whom the data controller is processing personal data. Anyone can submit a request for this information. A further factor is that it may reduce the amount of information a data controller has to provide to a data subject on collection of personal data or otherwise.

The Data Protection Act 1998 follows previous practice in making failure to notify a criminal offence of strict liability. However, unlike the previous law, the 1998 Act makes no provision generally for the Commissioner to consider whether the details supplied in the notification indicate that the processing is likely to involve a breach of any of the data protection principles. One exception is where processing falls within the meaning of "assessable processing" and, in such a case, the Information Commissioner must consider whether the processing in question would or would not comply with the provisions of the Act. Evaluating assessable processing will be triggered when notification is received or when the data controller notifies changes to the information supplied under notification. As preliminary assessments by the Commissioner depend on notification, they cannot apply to manual processing or exempt automatic processing unless the notification requirements are extended to such processing and it has been declared assessable processing by the Secretary of State. There is no immediate prohibition on processing where it is assessable processing after receiving an unfavourable notice from the Information Commissioner or, in the absence of a notice, after expiry of the time limit for serving such a notice. Of course, a data controller who decides to process after receiving an unfavourable notice would risk an

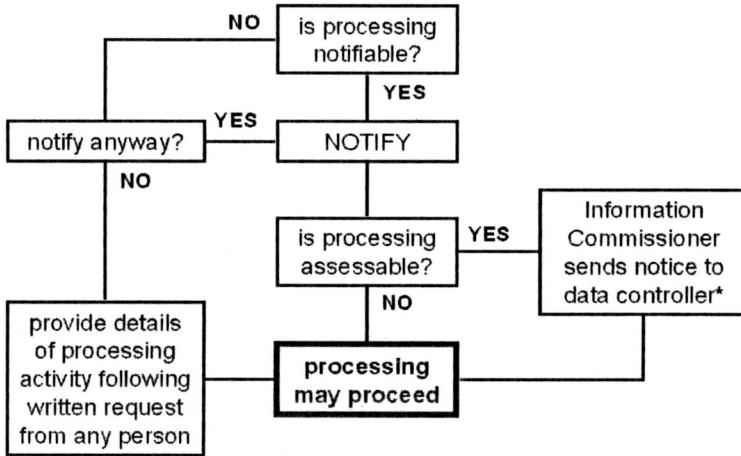

* If notice unfavourable, data controller may take view on whether or not to proceed.

Figure 6.1 Notification

enforcement notice in addition to potential exposure to private actions by individuals for compensation. No processing has been classified as assessable processing as yet.

The Act also allows for the appointment of data protection supervisors. These will be in-house persons, appointed by the data controller, who will be responsible for ensuring that the Act is complied with. They will be expected to carry out their duties in an independent manner. However, data protection supervisors cannot be appointed until such time as the Secretary of State provides for them by order. At the time of writing no such order has been made.

Whether or not a data controller is exempt from notification in whole or in part, under section 4(4), he or she must comply with the data protection principles, subject to any relevant exemptions. Before looking at the notification and related provisions in more detail, the general scheme for these provisions is set out in Figure 6.1.

NOTIFICATION

Section 17(1) of the Act imposes a general requirement not to process unless the data controller has an entry in the register maintained by the Commissioner. This applies to processing of personal data by automatic means (including personal data intended to be processed by automatic means) within section 1(1)(a) and (b). It does not apply to manual processing (although it may be subject to the provisions relating to assessable processing) nor to processing for which exemption from notification is given. Notification is not required in respect of processing carried out for the sole purpose of maintaining a public register and exemptions from notification have been granted to certain types of processing "unlikely to prejudice the rights and freedoms of data subjects" by virtue of the Data Protection (Notification and Notification Fees) Regulations 2000, being in relation to staff administration, advertising, marketing and public relations, accounts and records and by non-profit-making organisations. These are discussed later in this chapter.

An entry on the register is achieved through notification. The applicant must provide the "registrable particulars" (which will be placed on the register and available to the public) together with a general description of measures to be taken to comply with the seventh principle on security of personal data (this is not available to the public) and, in practice, will be a bland confirmation that basic security requirements are complied with. The above Regulations provide for the time as from which an entry on the register is to be treated as having been made. Allowing for a deemed registration date may reduce the period of time before processing can commence (except in the case of assessable processing) to compensate for any time delay at the Office of the Information Commissioner caused by the time it takes to process notifications. In practice, regulation 8 of the Data Protection (Notification and Notification Fees) Regulations 2000 treats the date of entry in the register as being the date notification by registered post or recorded delivery is received for dispatch by the Post Office. In other cases, it is the date the notification is received by the Commissioner.

In cases where notification is required, processing without an appropriate entry on the register, where this is required, is a criminal offence of strict liability, under section 21(1).

The registrable particulars are set out in section 16(1), being in relation to a data controller:

(a) *his name and address;*

(b) *if he has nominated a representative for the purposes of the Act, the name and address of the representative (where the data controller is established outside the European Economic Area but uses equipment in the United Kingdom for processing otherwise than for transit through the United Kingdom, he must nominate a representative established in the United Kingdom);*

(c) *a description of the personal data being or to be processed by or on behalf of the data controller and of the category or categories of data subject to which they relate;*

(d) a description of the purpose or purposes for which the data are being or are to be processed;

(e) a description of any recipient or recipients to whom the data controller intends or may wish to disclose the data;

(f) the names, or a description of, any countries or territories outside the European Economic Area to which the data controller directly or indirectly transfers, or intends or may wish directly or indirectly to transfer, the data; and

(g) in any case where-
   (i) personal data are being, or are intended to be, processed in circumstances [such that they are non-notifiable manual data or specifically exempted from notification (that is where either section 17(2) and (3) applies)], and
   (ii) the notification does not extend to those data, a statement of that fact.

The statement in (g) is intended to alert persons consulting the register that other, non-notifiable processing, is being carried on by the data controller. Any person wanting to find out details of such processing, as in (a) to (f) above, can apply in writing to the data controller who must provide the relevant information within 21 days under section 24. This obligation does not apply in respect of processing whose sole purpose is the maintenance of a public register.

The degree of specificity required is dependent upon notification regulations made under the Act. Under regulation 4 of the Data Protection (Notification and Notification Fees) Regulations 2000, these allow the Commissioner to determine the form in which the registrable particulars and the general description of security measures are to be specified, including in particular, the detail required for (c), (d), (e) and (f) of the registrable particulars above. The reality is that, typically, generic descriptions suffice and notification may be initiated through the internet using prepared templates, which may be modified in individual cases. An example of one template, "General Business", gives purposes such as accounts and records and advertising, marketing and public relations. For the accounts and records purpose, data subjects are suppliers, customers and clients and complainants, correspondents and enquirers. For this purpose, classes of data include personal details, financial details and goods or services provided whilst recipients are:

- suppliers, providers of goods or services;
- other companies in the same group;

- financial organisations and advisers;

- employees and agents of the data controller;

- debt collection and tracing agencies;

- credit reference agencies;

- central government; and

- business associates and other professional advisers.

Although such general descriptions may ease the burden of notification, it is questionable whether this compromises the principle of transparency. However, it must be said that to specifically identify actual recipients at the notification stage would be almost impossible to achieve. This is in line with the Directive which allows descriptions of categories of data subjects and recipients. Transparency is redeemed to some extent because there is a requirement to identify third parties to whom personal data are disclosed unless this proves impossible or requires a disproportionate effort. Notification may also be carried out by use of the telephone which will result in a draft notification being sent to the data controller who can then modify it as appropriate. It seems clear that the Information Commissioner has been mindful of the burdens placed on data controllers by the notification process and has done as much as possible, within the spirit of the Directive, to minimise those burdens.

The requirement to provide a general description of security measures may be complied with relatively easily by simply ticking boxes against statements such as "Have you taken any measures to comply with the requirement to maintain appropriate security?", "Have you adopted an information security policy?" and "Do you train your staff on security systems and procedures?". It may be that some sensitive processing will require more detail and this may also apply in respect of preliminary assessments.

Regulation 5 of the Data Protection (Notification and Notification Fees) Regulations 2000 allows partnerships to notify in the name of the firm and regulation 6 allows joint notification for the head teacher and governing body of a school, unlike the position under the 1984 Act.

Although general descriptions will normally suffice for the purposes of notification, more detailed information may be required to be given to data subjects, under the obligations to inform data subjects or in response to a subject access request to ensure that the processing is fair within the first data protection principle.

As regards the general description of security measures required, following publication of the 1992 text of the then proposed Directive, concerns were expressed by some data controllers about giving too much detail to the Commissioner. Even though the information is not available to the public, the Commissioner's staff has access to it. Apart from the possibility of unauthorised access to such information by a member of the Commissioner's staff or an agent of the Commissioner, committing offences under sections 1 and 2 of the Computer Misuse Act 1990, making an unauthorised disclosure of such information is covered by a specific offence under section 59 of the Data Protection Act 1998. This offence requires that such a disclosure is made knowingly or recklessly.

Under section 19(4), no entry will be retained on the register for more than 12 months (this period can be modified and different periods may be prescribed for different cases) except on payment of the fee specified in the regulations which is £35. In its White Paper which preceded the Act, the government proposed that notification would be simpler than registration under the 1984 Act and that all data controllers would be required to do, following first notification under the 1998 Act, was to pay an annual renewal fee unless they had to notify changes. It was the intention also to allow data controllers to notify processing not required to be notified. These proposals have been implemented by the new law. In particular, notifying processing exempt from the notification requirements is permitted and may be advantageous thereby removing the requirement to provide information about processing under section 24 to any person within 21 days of receipt of a written request for such information.

The Act contained transitional provisions concerning notification of changes in respect of subsisting registered entries made under the 1984 Act[1] and there were also some transitional provisions relating to registration under the 1984 Act set out in Schedule 14 of the Act. By paragraph 2(1), processing covered by existing registrations (or treated as accepted by section 7(6) of the 1984 Act) was exempt from notification under the 1998 Act until the end of the registration period or 24 October 2001, if earlier. The reference to 24 October 2001 was deleted by the Freedom of Information Act 2000 with effect from 30 November 2000. An equivalent change to section 19(4) of the Data Protection Act 1998 was made by the Data Protection (Notification and Notification Fees) (Amendment) Regulations 2001, with effect from 23 October 2001. Therefore, registration under the 1984 Act continued until such time as it would normally expire, bearing in mind that registration under that Act lasted for up to three years. Furthermore, by paragraph 2(3) applications for registration made before commencement of notification provisions in the 1998 Act were assessed in accordance with the 1984 Act. There were further provisions dealing with, for example, appeals against refusal of registration under the

---

[1] Regulation 13 of the Data Protection (Notification and Notification Fees) Regulations 2000.

1984 Act and the effect of applying to notify under the 1998 Act when exempt because of a valid 1984 registration. These provisions are now only of historic interest. The transitional provisions are considered in more detail in Chapter 9. Some of these provisions, dealing with manual data and processing for historical research, are still relevant.

Regulation 11 of the Data Protection (Notification and Notification Fees) Regulations 2000 allows the Commissioner to include further information in a register entry, being:

- a registration number issued by the Commissioner;

- the date the entry is treated as having been made (as noted above, if sent by registered post or recorded delivery it is the day after receipt for dispatch by the Post Office or, in other cases, the day it is received by the Commissioner);

- the date the entry falls or may fall to be removed;

- additional information to assist persons to consult the register to communicate with any data controller (an example might be an address for service of data subject access requests if different to the registered address).

Duty to notify changes

The data controller has a duty, imposed by section 20(1), to notify changes in the registrable particulars or in the general description of measures taken to comply with the seventh principle (security measures). The purpose of notifying changes is set out in section 20(2), being that the entries in the register contain current names and addresses and describe current practice or intentions of the data controller and that the Commissioner is provided with a general description of security measures currently being taken.

Failure to notify changes is a criminal offence subject to a due diligence defence, that is, where the person charged with the offence had exercised all due diligence to comply with the duty. This should be satisfied if, in spite of the failure, the data controller had adopted reasonable systems and procedures for alerting the data controller of changes, for example, to processing activities, and for notifying those changes in a timely manner to the Information Commissioner. The fact of the matter is that it is often the case that individuals responsible for or engaged in data processing activities may not appreciate the need to notify changes. Educating employees, contractors and others involved in processing decisions of the importance of notifying changes should go a long way to prevent liability under section 20.

Unlike the case for notification generally, there is no mention of the possibility of allowing for deemed changes to the register entry to compensate for any delays in processing the information and modifying the register. However, the duty imposed on the data controller is simply to notify the changes and, providing this is done, the criminal offence of failing to notify changes does not apply. It would seem that as soon as the notification of changes is received by the Commissioner, it is effective. Thus, if a data controller notifies changes to the purposes of processing, it would seem that those changes can be put into effect by the data controller as soon as the Commissioner receives the relevant information in the requisite form (or the day following receipt for dispatch by the Post Office if sent by registered post or recorded delivery). In reality, in many cases, it will usually only be after the changes have been implemented that the data controller will notify those changes. There are likely to be many other issues of concern to the data controller relating to changes to processing, such as implementing a new system to deal with a new commercial venture. Nonetheless, this could leave the data controller exposed to liability. A sensible approach would be to involve a person within the data controller's organisation (given responsibility for data protection compliance) in the planning and development of new or modified processing activities. To reflect the fact that notification of changes may not be made until after the changes have been implemented, regulation 12(2) of the Data Protection (Notification and Notification Fees) Regulations 2000 allows a 28-day period of grace.

THE REGISTER

Under section 19(1), the Commissioner has a duty to maintain a register of persons notifying and to make entries in the register in respect of notifications received from persons who were not already on the register as data controllers. The intention was to have only one entry per data controller unlike the practice under the 1984 Act where many data users had multiple entries. Section 19(2) requires that each entry shall consist of the registrable particulars, as amended following notification of changes if appropriate, and such other information as may be authorised or required by notification regulations.

No entry can be retained on the register for more than the relevant period except on payment of the prescribed fee. This period may be modified by order and different periods may be prescribed for different cases. The Data Protection (Notification and Notification Fees) Regulations set the fee for notification at £35 (zero-rated for VAT purposes) as it remains at the time of writing. The fee for renewal is also £35. There is no fee for notifying changes. The basis of the fee is that it should be set at such a level to cover the expenses of the Commissioner and Tribunal and related expenses incurred by the

Secretary of State. Any deficit incurred will also be taken into account as will be superannuation payments made to the officer or staff of the Commissioner.

The Commissioner must make the register available for inspection in visible and legible form by members of the public at reasonable hours and free of charge and provide other facilities for making the information available to the public free of charge.[2] Under the 1984 Act, the register was available for inspection at the Offices of the Data Protection Registrar. Now, it is available online at the Information Commissioner's website, the address of which is: *http: //www.informationcommissioner.gov.uk/*

By virtue of section 19(7), certified copies in writing of register entries must be provided by the Commissioner on request for the payment of a prescribed fee which is set at £2 by the Data Protection (Fees under section 19(7)) Regulations 2000.

Exemptions from notification

Some of the exemptions contained in the Act relate to notification. Thus, an individual is exempt from the notification provisions where the processing is only for the purposes of that individual's personal, family or household affairs.[3] Further exemptions from notification are contained in the Data Protection (Notification and Notification Fees) Regulations 2000. These exemptions are granted on the basis that the processing activity appears to the Secretary of State to be unlikely to prejudice the rights and freedoms of data subjects.[4] Under the Regulations, the exemptions are in relation to processing in the following contexts:

- staff administration;

- advertising, marketing and public relations;

- accounts and records;

- non-profit-making organisations.

The first three are sometimes referred to as core business activities. These exemptions from notification are not absolute and only relate to certain purposes, classes of data subject and types of personal data.

In respect of the first exemption, "staff" includes employees or office holders, workers within the meaning of section 296 of the Trade Union and Labour

---

[2] Section 19(6).
[3] Section 36.
[4] Regulation 3.

Relations (Consolidation) Act 1972, persons working under any contract for services and volunteers. Note that persons working under a contract for services are also within the definition, for example, a self-employed person engaged to perform a particular service or services, such as writing new computer software. For this exemption, the purposes are appointment and removal, pay, discipline, superannuation, work management or other personnel matters in relation to the data controller. Data subjects may be past, existing or prospective members of staff and any other person the processing of whose personal data is necessary for the above purposes. The types of personal data which may be processed under the exemption are name, address and other identifiers and information as to qualifications, work experience or pay or other matters the processing of which is necessary for the exempt purposes.

For this and the other exemptions in the regulations, disclosures to third parties are not permitted (but see below) except with the consent of the data subject or where necessary for the exempt purposes. The personal data must not be kept longer than is necessary for the exempt purposes after termination of the relationship between the data subject and the data controller. The retention of personal data after termination of employment should be given special attention. It may be required for the purposes of giving references or in respect of legal proceedings, such as a claim for unfair dismissal or negligence. As far as giving references is concerned, it would not appear that this falls within the exempt purposes as it is not a personnel matter *in relation to the data controller*. Rather it is in relation to a prospective employer or client. One would expect data to be kept for as long as legal exposure to claims from ex-employees are possible, being based on limitation of actions periods (bearing in mind the court has a discretion to extend the periods). However, it is not clear that the exempt purposes extend to this type of situation and, where there is any doubt, it is advisable that notification should be made.

The advertising, marketing and public relations exemption applies to the following purposes, data subjects and types of personal data:

exempt purposes:

- advertising or marketing the data controller's business activity, goods or services, and

- promoting public relations in connection with that business, activity, goods or services;

personal data:

- past, existing or prospective customer or supplier, or

- any person the processing of whose personal data is necessary for the exempt purposes;

types of personal data:

- name, address, other identifiers, or

- information as to other matters the processing of which is necessary for the exempt purposes.

The accounts and records exemption applies as follows:

exempt purposes:

- keeping accounts relating to the business or other activity carried on by the data controller,

- in the context of deciding whether to accept any person as a customer or supplier,

- keeping records of purchases, sales or other, transactions for ensuring the requisite payments and deliveries are made,

- services provided by or to the data controller in respect of such transactions, or

- making financial or management forecasts to assist the data controller in the conduct of any such business or activity;

personal data:

- past, existing or prospective customer or supplier, or

- any person the processing of whose personal data is necessary for the exempt purposes;

types of personal data:

- name, address, other identifiers,

- information as to financial standing, or

- other matters the processing of which is necessary for the exempt purposes (but this does not extend to personal data processed by or obtained from a credit reference agency).

The non-profit-making organisation exemption applies in respect of processing carried out by a data controller which is a body or association not established or conducted for profit and is as follows:

exempt purposes:

- establishing or maintaining membership or support for the organisation, or

- providing or administering activities of individuals who are members or have regular contact with the organisation;

personal data:

- past, existing or prospective member,

- any person who has regular contact with the organisation in connection with the exempt purposes, or

- any person the processing òf whose personal data is necessary for the exempt purposes;

types of personal data:

- name, address, other identifiers,

- information as to eligibility for membership, or

- other matters the processing of which is necessary for the exempt purposes.

For all the above exemptions, notwithstanding the fact that disclosures are only permitted with the data subject's consent or where necessary for the exempt purposes, the exemption from notification is not lost if the disclosure is required by or under any enactment, by any rule of law or by order of a court or by virtue of the non-disclosure provisions in Part IV of the Act.

ASSESSABLE PROCESSING

The Data Protection Directive contained provisions for prior checking of processing operations likely to present specific risks to the rights and freedoms of individuals. Article 20 required that such processing operations be examined before processing could commence. The approach in the Data Protection Act 1998, under section 22, is to allow the Secretary of State to designate certain descriptions of processing as assessable processing, where it appears to be particularly likely:

- to cause substantial damage or substantial distress to data subjects; or

- otherwise to significantly prejudice the rights and freedoms of data subjects.

Needless to say, no forms of processing have been so designated at the time of writing. The following discussion is, therefore, academic at this stage.

When notification is made (or notification of changes is made) in respect of assessable processing, the Commissioner has to consider whether the processing in question is likely to comply with the provisions of the Act (preliminary assessment). The government, in its White Paper, made it clear that preliminary assessment would be required in relatively few cases, giving as examples, processing involving data matching (where data from more than one source relating to any given individual is checked for inconsistencies), genetic data and private investigation activities. Under the current notification provisions, this can only apply to notifiable processing so it cannot apply to manual processing unless the notification provisions are extended to include some forms of manual processing. The same applies in respect of automated processing presently exempt from the notification provisions.

The provisions for assessable processing are contained in section 22 and are indicated in Figure 6.2. If the Commissioner considers any of the processing to which a particular notification relates is assessable processing, he has to determine whether that processing is likely to comply with the Act within a period of time. The basic period of time is 28 days from the date of receipt of notification from the data controller, though this may be extended by up to a further 14 days if the Commissioner believes there are special circumstances, by giving notice of such extension to the data controller before the end of the 28-day period. At the end of the period (or period as extended) or when the data controller receives a notice from the Commissioner setting out his views on whether the processing is likely to comply with the Act, whichever is the sooner, processing may commence. This is so even if the Commissioner's notice is unfavourable. Of course, if it is and the data controller decides to go ahead with the processing, the Commissioner may exercise his powers of enforcement to prevent it continuing.

Processing before expiry of the period (or period as extended) or receipt of the Commissioner's notice regarding likely compliance, if sooner, will be a criminal offence of strict liability. It is notable that the wide definition of processing, which includes mere "possession" (that is, holding or, under the Directive, storage) may significantly increase the reach of criminal liability should some forms of processing be declared assessable processing.

The maximum period for an extension for consideration by the Commissioner is 14 days. It does not have to be 14 days and, in any particular case where special circumstances exist, the Commissioner may choose a shorter period for an extension. There is no guidance in the Act as to what constitutes "special circumstances". Presumably it is intended that extensions to the period for a preliminary assessment should be available in cases of

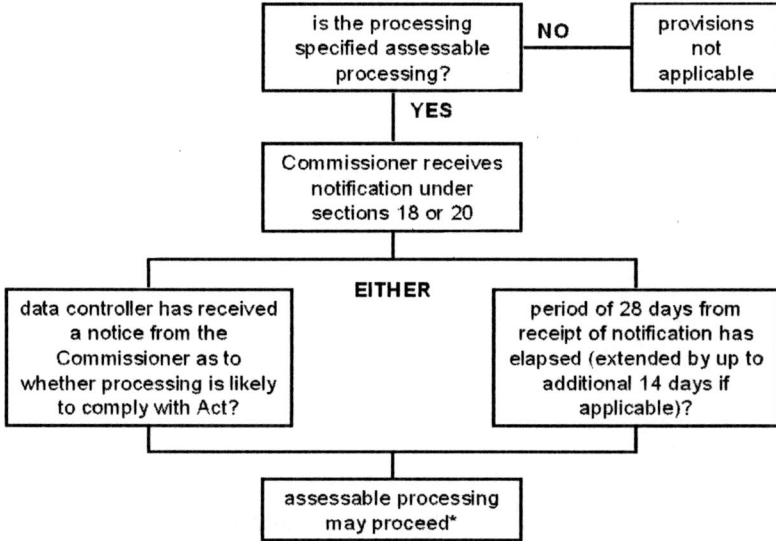

Processing may still contravene Act – it simply means that an offence is not committed under s 22(5) & (6).

Figure 6.2 Commencement of Assessable Processing

complexity rather than simply being because of a heavy workload at the Office of the Information Commissioner. Under section 22(7), the Secretary of State may, by order, amend the time periods.

DATA PROTECTION SUPERVISORS

Another provision in the Act yet to be given effect to is the power given to the Secretary of State to make orders for a system of personal data supervisors under section 23. Although appointed by the data controller they are to be responsible in particular for monitoring, in an independent manner, the data controller's compliance with the provisions of the Act. Any order made may make exemptions or modification to the provisions on notification in the Act where a data controller appoints a data protection supervisor. For example, it may be that preliminary assessments, where required, will be carried out by data protection supervisors rather than the Information Commissioner. Further exemption from the requirement to notify, or in the amount or detail of information to be given, is another possibility.

Duties owed to the Commissioner may be imposed on data protection supervisors and functions may be conferred on the Commissioner in relation to data protection supervisors. In other words, the Commissioner may have powers to supervise the supervisors.

In its White Paper, the government, although noting some interest in the concept of data protection supervisors, indicated that it may be some time before this system is introduced. If and when provision is made for data protection supervisors, they are likely to prove popular in the public sector, at least initially. How workable such a scheme is likely to be in the United Kingdom remains to be seen. There may be many conflicts of interests to be resolved, for example, where the data controller who employs the data protection supervisor takes one view on whether a particular processing operation complies with the Act (perhaps after taking legal advice) and the supervisor, perhaps acting under guidelines issued by the Commissioner, takes the opposite view.

DUTY TO MAKE INFORMATION AVAILABLE

Where processing is not required to be notified, such as most descriptions of manual processing (if still within the scope of the Act) and the data controller has elected not to notify then under section 24, the data controller is still under a duty to provide certain information to anyone making a written request.

The purpose of this duty is to ensure transparency of processing even though not formally notified. Of course, many data controllers who have processing which they are required to notify may take the view that it is desirable to notify all their processing, including that not required to be subject to formal notification.

The information to be provided, described as the "relevant particulars" is as set out in the registrable particulars with the exception of the statement that other processing which has not been notified is taking place, such statement being completely meaningless in the present context. A data controller must respond within 21 days of receipt of a written notice from any person. No charge can be made for supplying this information and failure to respond within that period is a criminal offence. There is a defence where the data controller has exercised all due diligence to comply with the duty.

A great many data controllers will be subject to this duty, ranging from a sole trader newsagent, with a card index system containing details of persons to whom he delivers newspapers, to large corporations which have chosen not to notify those processing activities not required to be notified. It would seem sensible for data controllers subject to this duty to prepare a statement containing the relevant particulars so that it is ready to supply as and when asked for. The Act makes no provision for ambiguous or unclear requests and this could be a problem where a request is not specifically targeted at the relevant particulars, for example, a written request to be supplied with details of the data controller's data protection policies. There is no requirement for a data controller to provide information relating to policy, *per se*, but it would seem sensible to respond with the relevant particulars, if appropriate.

It should be noted that a request under section 24 can be made by any person and is not limited to individuals who are the subject of personal data processed by the data controller. There is a danger that a data controller operating in some controversial field could find himself inundated with "nuisance" requests. This should be borne in mind when preparing the statement to give in response.

Where a data controller is exempt from the notification provisions, such as where personal data are processed only for domestic purposes as defined in section 36, the duty under section 24 does not arise.

NOTIFICATIONS REGULATIONS AND THE COMMISSIONER

Section 25 sets out the functions of the Commissioner with respect to the notification regulations made under the Act. They are as follows:

- to submit proposals as to the regulations to the Secretary of State as soon as practicable after the passing of the Act;

- to keep the working of the notification regulations under review;

- to submit proposals for amendments from time to time (this is discretionary – obviously if the notification process is working satisfactorily there will be no need to do this);

- to submit proposals for amendments if required to do so by the Secretary of State.

The Commissioner must be consulted by the Secretary of State before notification regulations are made and he must also consider any proposals made by the Commissioner in respect of the regulations or amendment thereof.

CHAPTER 7
CONSTRAINTS ON PROCESSING

This chapter looks at the various constraints on processing activity imposed by the Data Protection Act 1998, in particular from the perspective of the data controller. Other areas of law may also be relevant such as the law of confidence and the impact of this area of equity was seen in *R* v *Department of Health ex parte Source Informatics Ltd* [1999] 4 All ER 185, though the decision was overturned on appeal (see later). In comparison to the Data Protection Act 1984, the 1998 Act contains a more tightly regulated regime. As under the previous law, processing must be in accordance with the data protection principles, but there are some differences between those under the 1984 Act and those under the 1998 Act, not only in relation to the principles themselves but also as regards the interpretation of them.

Of particular concern to data controllers are the conditions for processing. Unless a data controller can process within one of these (or two, in the case of sensitive data) he simply cannot carry out the processing envisaged, unless exempt from the first data protection principle in as much as it requires the conditions for processing to apply. (There are only two such exemptions being in relation to national security, under section 28, and journalism, literature and art under section 32. A third exemption, processing for domestic purposes, under section 36, is exempt not only from the conditions for processing but, effectively from data protection law altogether in line with the Data Protection Directive – see Article 3(2).) Other concerns raised by data controllers focused on potential prohibitions or restrictions on transfers of personal data to third countries (being countries outside the European Economic Area) and the data subjects' rights, enhanced and extended under the 1998 Act. These include rights to more information and to object to processing and, in some cases, to prevent processing altogether. Furthermore, data subjects' consent might be required in a number of cases. Although the rights of data subjects are the subject matter of the following chapter, they will be mentioned and outlined as appropriate in this chapter. Figure 7.1 shows the main potential constraints on processing activity.

First, the conditions for processing are examined. They are not as restrictive as might at first appear, especially in relation to the processing of non-sensitive personal data.

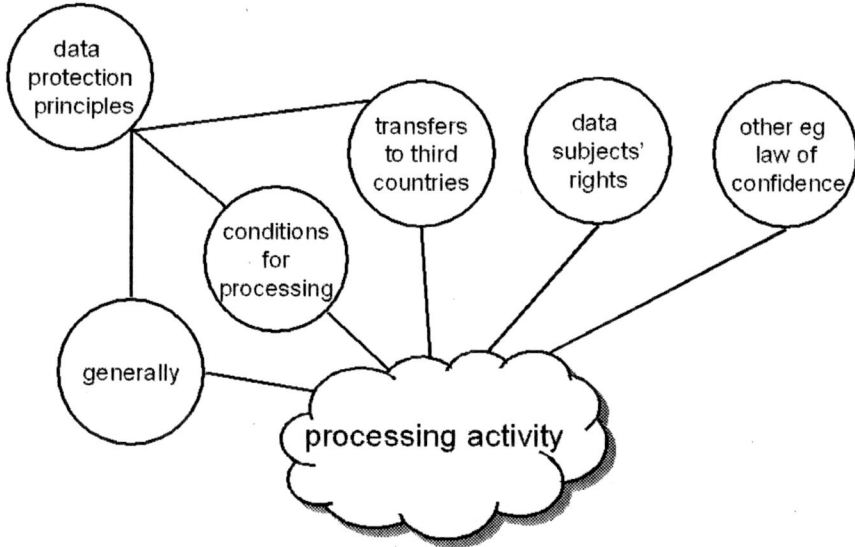

Figure 7.1 Constraints on Processing Activity

CONDITIONS FOR PROCESSING

Where personal data are not within the definition of sensitive data given in section 2, one of the conditions in Schedule 2 to the Data Protection Act 1998 must be met. Where processing involves sensitive personal data as so defined, one of the conditions in Schedule 2 must be met together with one of the conditions set out in Schedule 3. The requirement to meet a condition in Schedule 2 or, in the case of sensitive data, also in Schedule 3, is a result of the first data protection principle and is a requirement for the processing to be fair and lawful. That does not mean to say that meeting the condition or conditions automatically classifies the processing as fair and lawful and other issues may be relevant such as whether information given to the data subject is such as to make the processing fair in relation to the data subject. For example, fairness, as under previous case law, may require that the data controller makes explicit any non-obvious uses to which he intends to put the personal data when collecting them from the data subject.

NON-SENSITIVE PERSONAL DATA AND SCHEDULE 2

Schedule 2 is based on Article 7 of the Data Protection Directive and follows the Directive fairly closely, with some useful interpretation of Article 7(e) (public interest or official authority – see para 5 below). The conditions are that:

1. *The data subject has given his consent to the processing.*

2. *The processing is necessary-*
    (a) for the performance of a contract to which the data subject is a party, or
    (b) for the taking steps at the request of the data subject with a view to entering into a contract.

3. *The processing is necessary for compliance with any legal obligation to which the data controller is subject, other than an obligation imposed by contract.*

4. *The processing is necessary in order to protect the vital interests of the data subject.*

5. *The processing is necessary-*
    (a) for the administration of justice,
    (b) for the exercise of any functions conferred on any person by or under any enactment,
    (c) for the exercise of any functions of the Crown, a Minister of the Crown or a government department, or
    (d) for the exercise of any other functions of a public nature exercised in the public interest by any person.

6. *(1) The processing is necessary for the purposes of legitimate interests pursued by the data controller or by the third party or parties to whom the data are disclosed, except where the processing is unwarranted in any particular case by reason of prejudice to the rights and freedoms or legitimate interests of the data subject.*

    (2) The Secretary of State may by order specify particular circumstances in which this condition is, or is not, to be taken to be satisfied.

In terms of the first condition (the data subject's consent) it would seem that acquiescence might be sufficient such as where an individual completing a form fails to tick the ubiquitous box to declare lack of consent. This is because consent in Schedule 3 is described as explicit. It therefore seems reasonable to suggest that implicit consent is acceptable for the purposes of Schedule 2. However, the Data Protection Directive is couched in terms of the data subject's unambiguous consent (Article 7) and the definitions in Article 2 state that the data subject's consent means any freely given specific and informed consent or indication of wishes signifying agreement to the processing in question. Nevertheless, this could still be satisfied by failing to tick a box if the form provides the necessary information and the individual concerned signs the form. Basic principles of the English law of contract ought to prevail in such a case, such as the *non est factum* rule. But there must be a proviso to this in relation to data processing. If information about potential uses (such as marketing) is presented in very small type and is unlikely to be noticed or read by the data subject, it is very questionable whether this will satisfy the requirement of fairness under the first data protection principle.

There are good reasons why a data controller, as a potential party to a contract, needs to process personal data relating to the data subject. The second limb is stated in terms of the data subject requesting the taking of steps with a view to entering a contract. It is not necessary that a contract comes into existence. It may be that the data subject wants credit and, after processing (for example, by retrieving data concerning the data subject's credit record), the data controller may decline. In such a case, it is probable that the sixth condition, "legitimate interests", will apply also in relation to both a credit reference agency and the data controller who is a potential party to the contract. It may also be the case that a data controller needs to verify that his goods or services are appropriate or suitable for the data subject. As regards the performance of a contract, the data controller may need to know information such as the data subject's preferences (for colour, accessories, etc.) and even his address for delivery. Another item of information could be something such as shoe size, if it is recorded and processed within the meaning of the Act. Of course, most information of this nature will be obtained directly from the data subject and can be said to have been obtained with consent which will apply to the processing in question if that processing is obvious to the data subject.

The third condition could apply, for example, where the data controller is making official returns as required by a government department. Processing under an enactment was considered in Case C-465/00 *Rechnungshof* v *Österreichisher Rundfunk and Others*[1] which concerned the disclosure to public bodies of payments over a certain level made to employees and pensioners to the Rechnungshof (Court of Audit) for preparation of an annual report submitted to the Austrian Parliament and subsequently published. Disclosure of payments and names of recipients was required by domestic Austrian law. The aim was to try to keep salaries paid to persons working for public bodies within reasonable limits.

The Court of Justice held that it was for the national court to determine whether publishing individuals' names was proportionate to the aim of keeping salaries of public officials within reasonable limits. The interference with the right of privacy by publishing names must be necessary and appropriate to the aim of keeping salaries to reasonable levels. If the national court

---

[1] [2003] ECR I-4989.

finds that national legislation requiring disclosure and publication of names was incompatible with the right of privacy under Article 8 of the Council of Europe Convention for the Protection of Human Rights and Fundamental Freedoms, then it would also fail to satisfy the requirement of proportionality under Articles 6(1) and 7(c) or (e) of the Data Protection Directive. Furthermore, the Court of Justice held that those provisions in the Directive were also of direct effect and could be relied upon by individuals to challenge national legislation.

Article 6(1) sets out most of the data protection principles. Article 7(c) is equivalent to paragraph 3 in Schedule 2 above and Article 7(e) is broadly equivalent to paragraph 5. Although the Court of Justice did not comment, it would seem that the other conditions in Article 7 should be of direct effect and, in combination with Article 6(1), could also be used to challenge domestic legislation. One effect of *Rechnungshof* is that it would seem that the conditions in Article 7 (or at least the ones in issue in that case) are subordinate to the data protection principles.

The fourth condition – processing necessary for the vital interests of the data subject – may be more likely to apply in relation to sensitive data and there is an appropriate though slightly wider condition in Schedule 3. This can also apply to persons other than the data subject and there are more safeguards built in. The Directive does not give much help in determining what are vital interests in relation to non-sensitive personal data. Recital 31 to the Directive states that processing must be regarded as lawful "where it is carried out in order to protect an interest which is essential for the data subject's life". However, Article 7 (and Article 8 on the conditions for processing sensitive personal data) is in terms of protecting the vital interests of the data subject (including some other person in Article 8). Whether vital interests processing is restricted to life-threatening situations or can include the best interests of the data subject is not entirely clear and it is uncertain whether this condition would apply, for example, to the disclosure or other processing of personal data to assist in tracing beneficiaries of a will. The phrase "essential to the data subject's life" suggests a narrow interpretation, especially if the word essential is taken in a strong sense. However, the case of *Gaskin* v *United Kingdom*[2] suggests that vital interests may be wider than being a matter of life or death. In that case, the European Court of Human Rights held (at para 49) that a vital interest could be in the context of:

> "... *receiving the information necessary to know and to understand their childhood and early development.*"

---

[2] [1989] ECHR 13.

On the basis of this high authority, it seems reasonable to assume that vital interests extend to anything of importance concerning the life of the data subject. *Gaskin* was concerned with details of Gaskin's treatment and record of care as a child. Vital interests may also extend to information relating to the adoption of a person or record of fostering. As will be seen in the next chapter, there may be issues where the processing involves disclosure of information under a subject access request where a person other than the data subject will be identified when complying with that request.

Recital 31 does not differentiate between sensitive and non-sensitive data. One example where it could apply to non-sensitive data is where the new address of a data subject who has recently changed address is disclosed to a health practitioner after it has been discovered that a medical test undergone by the data subject was defective. The personal data disclosed, the address, is not sensitive data. Another example is the disclosure of location data by a telecommunications company to rescue services (tracing the whereabouts of a person carrying a mobile telephone) where a data subject is ill or injured and his exact location is not known. A further example may be to discover details of the care given to an individual as a child which may not include sensitive personal data.

Apart from the above, a reason for the inclusion of the fourth condition is to give effect to the equivalent condition in Schedule 3 (though different in scope as it can also apply to the vital interests of a person other than the data subject). The simple explanation is that, for the processing of sensitive personal data, one of the conditions in Schedule 2 must also be present. The fourth condition therefore underpins, at least to some extent, the equivalent condition in Schedule 3.

The fifth condition is really self-explanatory, subject to what has been said in relation to *Rechnungshof* above. There is an equivalent provision in Schedule 3 with the exception of processing necessary for any other function of a public nature exercised in the public interest by any person. However, in Schedule 3, the Secretary of State can exclude such processing in specific cases, thereby adding a further safeguard.

Condition 5(b) of Schedule 2 (and also the equivalent provision 7(b) in Schedule 3) were considered in relation to disclosures by a Health and Social Services Trust under the Children (Northern Ireland) Order 1995 which allows, *inter alia*, such a Trust to take action to safeguard a child's welfare where there is reasonable cause to suspect that the child was likely to suffer significant harm. In *James Martin's Application for Judicial Review*, 20 December 2002, the applicant sought judicial review of a decision by the Trust in question to inform his new partner, who had three children, that allegations had been made about him in the past for physical and sexual abuse of children of a former partner. Although investigations had been made by the police, no charges had been brought against him. In the event, he agreed to inform his new partner of the allegations in the presence of a social worker. Soon after, the applicant and his new partner separated.

It was held, in the Queen's Bench Division, that the exemption under section 29 of the Data Protection Act 1998 applied (prevention of crime) and that the disclosure was required by law under condition 5(b) (and condition 7(b) in Schedule 3). Weatherup J also accepted that the disclosure was necessary for the purposes of the exercise of the respondent's statutory functions.

Schedule 2 does not contain an equivalent to that in Schedule 3 in relation to legal proceedings, legal advice, etc., ensuring that the process of discovery of documents, for example, is not hindered. Of course, such processing is subject to the rules on legal professional privilege as confirmed in paragraph 10 of Schedule 7 (miscellaneous exemptions). Where the data are not sensitive data, the data controller will have to find another condition in Schedule 2 which can apply and the obvious one, perhaps the most wide-ranging condition, is the sixth one – legitimate interests of the data controller or a third party to whom the data are disclosed.

The sixth condition will apply in a great many cases and will be relied upon by many data controllers and third parties to whom data are disclosed. It is somewhat regrettable that the term is vague. Just what are legitimate interests? In terms of a corporation or other body, are they interests relating to any purpose which is *intra vires*, including ancillary or associated purposes, or does it go further than this? Does it simply mean lawful purposes, that is, not illegal? Perhaps the best approach is to look at the context within which the processing is taking place. In terms of organisations, it would seem sensible to consider processing carried out in the normal course of that organisation's activities, making reasonable allowance for the fact that those activities may change over time. Where the data controller is an individual, such as a sole trader, the same sentiments ought to apply. To give some flexibility to the concept of purposes of legitimate interests, the Secretary of State may, by order, specify particular circumstances in which the condition is or is not to be taken to be satisfied.

The Act seeks to reach a balance between legitimate interests and rights and freedoms of individuals. The processing cannot fall within the sixth condition if it is "unwarranted". It may be difficult to determine when processing is unwarranted. Schedule 2 uses the phrase "unwarranted in any particular case by reason of prejudice to rights and freedoms or legitimate interests of the data subject". The data subject also has legitimate interests. However, the Directive uses a different phrase in Article 7(f) being

"... except where such interests are overridden by the interests for fundamental rights and freedoms of data subjects which require protection under Article 1(1)".

That being so, the Data Protection Act 1998 seems a little more restrictive than the Directive. "Unwarranted" means unauthorised or unjustified, "overridden" implies having precedence or superiority over. The Directive seems to require a balance between the processing and rights and freedoms whereas the Act suggests the condition cannot be met if there is any prejudice or, at least, less prejudice than the Directive might allow.

The application of Article 7(f) was considered by the Court of Justice in Case C-369/98 *R* v *Minister for Agriculture, Fisheries and Food, ex parte Fisher.*[3] This involved an application by farmers who had acquired farms, to the Ministry ("MAFF") for disclosure of information relating to crops previously grown on those farms, for the purposes of applying for Community aid. MAFF controlled a database of information concerning crops grown on farms but the farmers had been unable to obtain the necessary information elsewhere. Eventually, MAFF released some basic information but refused to disclose information as to the cropping history of the farms on the basis of data protection law. Consequently, the farmers did not have all the information they needed and had to make decisions as to which crops to plant in the absence of the relevant information . When the farmers submitted the forms they were required to submit to MAFF, they were informed that, because of the cropping history of the farms, they would not be entitled to payments and penalties were imposed. MAFF argued that it could not disclose the information because of obligations to the previous farmer, who had been declared bankrupt, and the receiver. The Court of Justice stressed the importance of balancing the interests of the individuals concerned. After such a balancing exercise, the information sought may be disclosed to a new farmer who needs such information to be able to submit a claim for payment under Community Regulations. If, after balancing the interests of the individuals, the information is withheld, penalties could not be imposed on the farmers on the basis of information which had been so withheld.

Apart from the first condition in Schedule 2, the data subject's consent, all the others require that the processing is necessary for the condition to apply. It is reasonable to assume that the word is not used in a particularly strong sense. The processing should be reasonably necessary rather than essential to the purpose. There is a useful House of Lords authority in *Amp Inc* v *Utilux Pty Ltd*[4] a registered design case under the Registered Designs Act 1949. The word in question, which related to an exception from design protection, was "dictated". It was held that the word should not be interpreted in a strong

---

[3] [2000] ECR I-6751.
[4] [1972] RPC 103.

sense otherwise the particular provision would be reduced "almost to vanishing point". Very few features of shape or configuration are completely dictated by function. The vast majority of designs permit at least a small amount of design freedom. Although in a different field, there is no reason to suspect that the same principle should not apply. More recently, in another registered design case, Jacob J adopted a similar approach in construing the word "necessary".[5] However, in *A* v *X*[6] Morland J noted that the word necessary is used in CPR 31.17, Article 8 and in the Data Protection Act 1998. CPR 31.17 deals with applications for disclosure by a person not party to the proceedings and requires, *inter alia*, that the disclosure is necessary in order to fairly dispose of the claim. Morland J said (at para 14)

"... only in a very exceptional factual situation would a court be justified in civil proceedings in ordering disclosure of a non-party's confidential medical data".

This latter decision suggests that, again, the interests of the persons involved must be subject to a balancing exercise. The greater the risk to the right of privacy, the less likely that the processing will be deemed to be "necessary". Of course, the disclosure of confidential medical data in the context of a civil action not involving the data subject is a very serious matter and will inform the court's decision as to whether to order disclosure, which would be very rarely granted. This can be contrasted with the *MAFF* case above, where the potential risk to privacy was relatively low and where the data were not sensitive personal data. In conclusion it can be said that the word "necessary" must have some elasticity about it and whether it is taken in a strong or weak sense must depend on the circumstances.

SENSITIVE DATA AND SCHEDULE 3

Schedule 3 derives from Article 8 of the Data Protection Directive, paragraph 1 of which contains a blanket prohibition on the processing of personal data revealing racial or ethnic origin, political opinions, religious or philosophical beliefs, trade-union membership and the processing of data concerning health or sex life. However, the remainder of Article 8 contains a number of cases in which the prohibition does not apply and also allows the possibility of Member States further derogating from the prohibition. The overall effect is to allow processing of sensitive data only in specific cases and there is no equivalent in Schedule 3 to the "legitimate interests" processing for non-sensitive personal data in Schedule 2. Of course, as noted earlier, for processing sensitive personal data, one condition must be met from Schedule 2 in addition to one condition from Schedule 3. Recital 33 to the Directive indi-

---

5 *Philips Electronics NV v Remington Consumer Products* [1998] RPC 283.
6 [2004] EWHC 447 (QB).

cates the importance of tightly controlling the processing of sensitive personal data which are described as data "which are capable by their nature of infringing fundamental freedoms or privacy".

Schedule 3 applies to sensitive personal data which are defined in section 2 of the Data Protection Act 1998. It goes further than the Directive in that it also extends to data relating to criminal offences, including the commission of any offence, criminal proceedings for any offence committed or alleged to have been committed, the disposal of such proceedings or the sentence of any court in such proceedings. Article 8(5) of the Data Protection Directive covers such data and requires that it is only carried out under the control of official authority but allows derogation from this subject to suitable safeguards. However, a complete register of criminal convictions may only be kept under the control of official authority. The difficulties faced by commercial organisations not being able to process data relating to criminal offences and the like was cured by the Data Protection (Processing of Sensitive Personal Data) Order 2000 which adds to the conditions for processing sensitive personal data to allow processing of such data in the substantial public interest where it is necessary for the prevention or detection of any unlawful act. This allows processing by, for example, credit reference agencies of such data, as discussed below.

Schedule 3 is set out below (this does not include further circumstances under which sensitive personal data can be processed under the Data Protection (Processing of Sensitive Personal Data) Order 2000, the effect of which is set out in the following section of this chapter).

1. The data subject has given his explicit consent to the processing of the personal data.

2. (1) The processing is necessary for the purposes of exercising or performing any right or obligation which is conferred or imposed by law on the data controller in connection with employment.
    (2) The Secretary of State may by order -
    (a) exclude the application of sub-paragraph (1) in such cases as may be specified, or
    (b) provide that, in such cases as may be specified, the condition in sub-paragraph (1) is not to be regarded as satisfied unless such further conditions as may be specified in the order are also satisfied.

3. The processing is necessary –
    (a) in order to protect the vital interests of the data subject or another person, in a case where -
        (i)   consent cannot be given by or on behalf of the data subject, or
        (ii) the data controller cannot reasonably be expected to obtain the consent of the data subject, or

(b) in order to protect the vital interests of another person, in a case where consent by or on behalf of the data subject has been unreasonably withheld.

4. The processing –
   (a) is carried out in the course of its legitimate activities by any body or association which -
       (i) is not established or conducted for profit, and
       (ii) exists for political, philosophical, religious or trade-union purposes,
   (b) is carried out with appropriate safeguards for the rights and freedoms of data subjects,
   (c) relates only to individuals who either are members of the body or association or have regular contact with it in connection with its purposes, and
   (d) does not involve disclosure of the personal data to a third party without the consent of the data subject.

5. The information contained in the personal data has been made public as a result of steps deliberately taken by the data subject.

6. The processing -
   (a) is necessary for the purpose of, or in connection with, any legal proceedings (including prospective legal proceedings),
   (b) is necessary for the purpose of obtaining legal advice, or
   (c) is otherwise necessary for the purposes of establishing, exercising or defending legal rights.

7. (1) The processing is necessary -
       (a) for the administration of justice,
       (b) for the exercise of any functions conferred on any person by or under an enactment, or
       (c) for the exercise of any functions of the Crown, a Minister of the Crown or a government department.
   (2) The Secretary of State may by order -
       (a) exclude the application of sub-paragraph (1) in such cases as may be specified, or
       (b) provide that, in such cases as may be specified, the condition in sub-paragraph (1) is not to be regarded as satisfied unless such further conditions as may be specified in the order are also satisfied.

8. (1) The processing is necessary for medical purposes and is undertaken by -
       (a) a health professional, or
       (b) a person who in the circumstances owes a duty of confidentiality which is equivalent to that which would arise if that person were a health professional.
   (2) In this paragraph "medical purposes" includes the purposes of preventative medicine, medical diagnosis, medical research, the provision of care and treatment and the management of healthcare services.

9. (1) The processing -
(a) is of sensitive personal data consisting of information as to racial or ethnic origin,
(b) is necessary for the purpose of identifying or keeping under review the existence or absence of equality of opportunity or treatment between persons of different racial or ethnic origins, with a view to enabling such equality to be promoted or maintained, and
(c) is carried out with appropriate safeguards for the rights and freedoms of data subjects.

(2) The Secretary of State may by order specify circumstances in which processing falling within sub-paragraph (1)(a) and (b) is, or is not, to be taken for the purposes of sub-paragraph (1)(c) to be carried out with appropriate safeguards for the rights and freedoms of data subjects.

10. The personal data are processed in circumstances specified in an order made by the Secretary of State for the purposes of this paragraph.

At the time of writing, no orders have been made under paragraphs 2(2) or 9(2) but two have been made under paragraph 10 which are described later in this chapter.

The first condition, the data subject's explicit consent, would seem to require that the consent is express and informed consent, simply failing to tick a box on a form would not seem to suffice. An acceptable manner of obtaining such consent would be by adding a statement describing the processing activity or activities contemplated to a form which is signed by the data subject. Even this might not be enough unless the presence of the statement is indicated to the data subject who is asked to read it, making it clear that, by signing the form, the individual will be taken to assent to the processing. The Data Protection Directive allows Member States to override the data subject's consent as a condition of processing, for example, by enacting a law to the effect that the data subject's consent is not a condition for processing sensitive data in particular cases. The provisions in the Data Protection Act 1998 on enforced subject access can be seen as an example of this though not yet in force.

Processing for the purpose of employment law rights or obligations conferred or imposed by law is permitted subject to exclusion or the imposition of further conditions by order of the Secretary of State (no order has been made thus far). Processing under this head could cover purposes such as making official returns or calculating redundancy payments.

The "vital interests" condition is wider than the equivalent in relation to non-sensitive data. Here it is the vital interests of the data subject or another where consent cannot be obtained or the data controller cannot be reasonably expected to obtain the data controller's consent. Another case is where the vital interests of another are in need of protection and the consent of the data subject is being unreasonably withheld. An example might be where a relative of the data subject is seriously ill and data relating to the data subject's medical history could be important in the treatment given but the data subject has objected to processing such data. As mentioned in the case of non-sensitive data, a vital interest should be one which is essential for the data subject's life (see recital 31 of the Data Protection Directive).

It would appear that the reason a "vital interests" condition appears in Schedule 2 is to support the equivalent under Schedule 3 but it is not clear why the condition in the former is not as wide as in the latter. The real difficulty is where the processing is undertaken to protect the vital interests of another person where the data subject's consent has been unreasonably withheld. In such a case, there does not appear to be a condition in Schedule 2 that could apply (bearing in mind the requirement for a condition in that Schedule in addition to one under Schedule 3 where the processing relates to sensitive personal data). Presumably the condition in Schedule 3 is intended to cover life-threatening situations where the data subject is incapable of giving consent (for example, where he or she is unconscious) or where a person other than the data subject is in such a situation but information needed to help the other person relates to the data subject. It is not an easy matter to think of possible scenarios where this would be the case. However, the wording in the Directive is narrower and allows processing only to protect the vital interests of the data subject or another person where the data subject is physically or legally incapable of giving consent. There seems to be no good reason for not extending the vital interests condition in Schedule 2 to persons other than the data subject.

The fourth condition allows processing of sensitive data by certain non-profit-making bodies and associations. It does not apply to all and there is a requirement that the body or association exists for political, philosophical, religious or trade union purposes. This will not extend to all charitable organisations, particularly if a narrow view is taken of the first three purposes. Political views, religious beliefs or beliefs of a similar nature and trade union membership all fall within the meaning of sensitive data by virtue of section 2. Beliefs of a nature similar to religious beliefs should mean philosophical beliefs which is the term used in Article 8(1) of the Directive. However, it is a moot point whether philosophical beliefs are similar to religious beliefs. Philosophical beliefs could include the application of reason and logic to observed phenomena to determine a scientific explanation of the creation of the universe which might be the very antithesis of religious explanations.

Recitals 33, 35 and 36 to the Directive suggest that it is the public interest that is key to this condition for processing sensitive personal data. Recital 34 mentions legitimate activities of certain associations or foundations the purpose of which is to permit the exercise of fundamental freedoms. Recital 35 on religious purposes is somewhat confusing and may contain a typographical error. Processing by political parties of data on people's political opinion is permitted as being in the public interest, subject to appropriate safeguards (recital 36).

Schedule 3 of the Data Protection Act 1998 requires that processing by a relevant non-profit-making organisation must concern only individuals who are members of the body or association or have regular contact with it in connection with its purposes (for example a person making regular contributions to the body) and is subject to appropriate safeguards for the rights and freedoms of others. A further requirement is that the processing must not involve disclosure of the personal data to a third party without the consent of the data subject. Of course, it must be remembered that this condition only applies to sensitive data. The body or association concerned may process other, non-sensitive data on the basis of Schedule 2. Not for profit organisations that do not exist for the purposes listed in paragraph 4(a)(ii) of Schedule 3 wishing to process sensitive personal data must seek the explicit consent of data subjects. The same should apply to a body that does exist for such purposes but wants to process sensitive personal data for any other, unrelated, purpose but the wording of paragraph 4 does not state this expressly, nor does the wording in the Directive.

The fifth condition is self explanatory (data made public by deliberate steps taken by the data subject) and the sixth and seventh conditions have been discussed in the previous section on the conditions in Schedule 2.

The eighth condition covers processing by health professionals and others having an equivalent duty of confidence. The processing must be necessary for medical purposes. The definition of "health professional" is very wide (see section 69) and includes appropriately registered medical practitioners, dentists, opticians, pharmacists, nurses, midwifes and health visitors amongst others. Medical purposes are not restricted to the provision of health care services but also extend to medical research and processing for the management of healthcare services.

Personal data containing information as to an individual's health are among the definition of sensitive personal data. Here, the impact of the law of breach of confidence may be felt. For example, in R v *Department of Health ex parte Source Informatics Ltd*[7] a data company, Source Informatics Ltd, tried to persuade general practitioners and pharmacists to hand over data relating to prescribing trends and habits. It was intended to make the data anonymous

---

[7] [1999] 4 All ER 185.

before being disclosed to the data company. The company considered such data and statistics would be commercially valuable to pharmaceutical companies. It was hoped that general practitioners and pharmacists would, for payment, copy onto magnetic disks details of the quantity and identity of drugs prescribed which would be passed on to the data company.

These proposed activities aroused concern at the Department of Health which issued a policy document warning of the complex legal and policy issues. The document advised against such disclosures and contained a recommendation that anyone contemplating disclosing such information should first take legal advice. In the view of the Department of Health, even if the data were rendered anonymous, disclosure might still involve a breach of confidence. Furthermore, in some cases, for example, where an individual was prescribed a rare combination of drugs, there might be a risk of identifying that person.

The data company sought a declaration in respect of the policy document on the grounds that disclosure of the data in anonymous form would not constitute a breach of confidence. It was argued that detriment was an essential requirement for a breach of confidence and the individual patients would suffer no detriment providing anonymity was secured.

At first instance, in the Queen's Bench Division, it was noted that the question of whether detriment was an essential feature of breach of confidence had never previously been the subject-matter of litigation. Latham J cited Megarry J's well-known description of the essentials for a breach of confidence action in *Coco* v *A N Clark (Engineers) Ltd*[8] (at 47) the third limb of which is "... *an unauthorised use of that information to the detriment of the party communicating it*". However, later in his judgment, Megarry J, *obiter*, doubted whether detriment was essential and suggested that there might be cases where a person might seek the aid of equity to prevent disclosure which may show him in a favourable light but might injure some friend or relative.

Differing views as to the requirement for detriment were expressed by Lord Keith of Kinkel and Lord Griffiths in *Attorney-General* v *Guardian Newspapers (No 2)*.[9] Lord Keith suggested that the public interest in respecting confidences was a sufficient reason to enforce an obligation even in the absence of detriment. However, Lord Griffiths suggested that detriment was essential. He said that the purpose of the remedy was to protect the person to whom the information belonged and not to punish the person making unauthorised use of the information. If that was the case, there was little point in extending the remedy to someone who is not in need of protection. In the present case, the

---

[8] [1969] RPC 41.
[9] [1990] 1 AC 109.

judge came to the conclusion that the situation was one in which there is a public interest in ensuring confidences are kept. He considered that patients should have the opportunity to make a decision as to whether data relating to their prescriptions should be disclosed even in anonymous form. Although most patients would not object if they felt confident that anonymity could be assured, a small number of patients would feel strongly that this information should not be disclosed without their consent, and certainly not for the financial gain of their general practitioner or pharmacist.

The proposed use of the disclosed information was accepted as being unauthorised use in the absence of the patients' express or implied consent. In addition to being a breach of confidence, such use was said to be an offence under section 5(2) of the Data Protection Act 1984 such as disclosing personal data to any person not described in the register entry or holding personal data for a purpose or purposes not described in the register entry (there are no direct equivalents to these offences under the 1998 Act). However, the correctness of this part of the judgment is questionable as, if personal identifiers were to be removed from the data, they could no longer be said to be personal data and would be outside the scope of both the 1984 and the 1998 Acts. Indeed, the subsequent appeal by Source Informatics to the Court of Appeal[10] was allowed.

The Court of Appeal did not consider that the planned action would involve a breach of confidence providing the identity of the patients was protected. The sole issue was the patients' right of privacy. Patients had no proprietary interest in the information and no right to control what happened to it subsequently providing their privacy was not put at stake. Thus, participation in the scheme by doctors and pharmacists would not expose them to a serious risk of successful breach of confidence actions. The Court considered that if the Department of Health was of the view that such a scheme operated against the public interest, then it could investigate taking appropriate legislative action.

If the data were disclosed without making them anonymous, then condition 8 of Schedule 3 could apply if appropriately notified to the Commissioner. However, that condition is limited to processing undertaken by health professionals or others with an equivalent duty of confidentiality. Two points can be made of that requirement in the context of the facts of the above case. First, would a private commercial enterprise be under such an equivalent duty of confidentiality? There would seem no reason why it should not. Personal data relating to health certainly have the necessary quality of confidence and, even in the absence of any express imposition of duty, it is almost certain that a duty of confidence would be implied. The law of confidence imposes a duty

---

[10] [2001] QB 424.

not to make an unauthorised use of the information and a duty not to disclose it further without consent. Those duties are absolute and broken by any unauthorised use or disclosure. The status or identity of the person responsible for the breach should not come into the calculation of whether what has occurred is a breach of confidence. The second point is that the processing must be *undertaken* by the health professional or other person having an equivalent duty of confidence. This suggests that it must be processed by such a person in fact and not processed on that person's behalf by a data processor. If a data processor is used, it would seem sensible, therefore, to impose an equivalent duty of confidence by contractual means which may go beyond the security provisions relating to data processors.

The ninth condition was the result of a late amendment to the Bill when it was realised that the Bill did not make specific provision for processing for ethnic monitoring. This allows processing for the purposes associated with equality of opportunity or treatment between persons of different racial or ethnic origins but is subject to appropriate safeguards for the rights and freedoms of data subjects. One might imagine that such safeguards would include high levels of security for such data and restricting access to it to only those persons within the data controller's organisation who carry out ethnic monitoring.

Data protection law is complex and it is difficult to predict all the situations and circumstances that might occur. Because of this the Secretary of State is given the power to modify the provisions of the Act. He is given the power to expand the conditions for processing sensitive personal data. Soon after Royal Assent it was realised that the late amendment allowing processing racial and ethnic data for the purposes of equal opportunity monitoring did not go far enough and other forms of equal opportunity monitoring should be permitted in terms of disability and religious beliefs. Other gaps were also spotted and the list of conditions in Schedule 3 were extended as described below.

FURTHER CONDITIONS FOR PROCESSING SENSITIVE PERSONAL DATA

Under paragraph 10 of Schedule 3 to the Date Protection Act 1998 the Secretary of State may to add the list of conditions in Schedule 3. The Data Protection (Processing of Sensitive Personal Data) Order 2000 sets out some further conditions. These include processing which is in the substantial public interest, which is necessary for the purposes of prevention or detection of any unlawful act, and which must necessarily be carried out without the explicit consent of the data subject so as not to prejudice those purposes. Further "substantial public interest" processing of sensitive personal data without the explicit consent of the data subject is permitted in relation to dishonesty, malpractice, seriously improper conduct or unfitness or incompetence in the context of mismanagement in the administration of, or failure in services provided by, any body or association. This extends to disclosure in the public interest for publication where the special purposes under section 3 of the Act apply (processing for the purposes of journalism, artistic purposes or literary purposes).

Some of these further conditions cover specific exemptions in the Act, such as the prevention or detection of crime under section 29. However, although specific exemption from some of the provisions of the Act were granted, without the addition of the further conditions, the exemptions could have been compromised or even rendered meaningless. It is no good being exempted from some provisions in the Act if the processing cannot proceed in the first place. As noted above, the conditions for processing are ousted by exemptions in only three cases (section 28 national security, section 32 journalism, literature and art and section 36 domestic purposes). The prevention and detection of crime exemption might typically involve disclosure of data relating to criminal convictions. Such data are sensitive personal data and could not otherwise be disclosed or otherwise processed under any of the conditions in Schedule 3 as originally enacted. Similar considerations apply to the regulatory activity exemption under section 33 in respect of, for example, investigations against managers for charities for suspected dishonestly. (An allegation of the commission of an offence is also sensitive personal data.)

Other conditions include processing for insurance and pension purposes of data relating to the physical or mental health or condition of parents, grandparents, great grandparents or siblings of the insured person or member of the pension scheme providing the information is not used to support measures or decisions with respect to the data subject and the processing is necessary where the data controller cannot reasonably be expected to obtain explicit consent of those relatives and is unaware of any withholding of consent. For example, an individual may apply for life assurance and be asked whether his parents are still alive and, if so, further information about their general health.

A further condition is in the context of confidential counselling, advice, support or any other service. Processing data relating to religious beliefs or beliefs of a similar nature or relating to physical or mental health or condition is permitted for equal opportunity purposes, something of an omission from the Act in its original form. The processing must not be used to support measures or decisions with respect to any data subject without that data subject's explicit consent and must not be so as to cause or be likely to cause substantial damage or substantial distress to any person. Furthermore, data subjects may give notice to data controllers to cease such processing. Of course, in many cases, equal opportunity monitoring is carried out anomalously and will be outside the scope of data protection law, provided equal opportunity forms are stored in a way such that the identity of the person completing a particular form cannot be subsequently retrieved.

Processing data about political opinions by registered political parties is allowed providing the data subject is not caused substantial damage or substantial distress and has not given notice of objection to such processing. Similarly, processing in the course of maintaining archives is permitted. A further condition which allows the processing of sensitive personal data is by a constable in the exercise of any functions conferred on him by law.

The Data Protection (Processing of Sensitive Personal Data) (Elected Representatives) Order 2002 provides for processing of sensitive personal data by, *inter alia*, members of the House of Commons, Scottish Parliament, Welsh and Northern Ireland Assemblies Parliament, UK members of the European Parliament, elected local authority members and elected mayors. They can process sensitive personal data in relation to their functions at the request of a data subject or on his or her behalf where the processing is necessary for the purposes of, and in connection with, action reasonably taken in response. Where the processing is as a result of a request made on behalf of the data subject, it is required that the data subject cannot give explicit consent, where the elected representative cannot reasonably be expected to obtain such consent and the processing must necessarily be carried out without explicit consent so as not to prejudice the action of the elected representative or is necessary in the interests of another individual where the data subject has unreasonably withheld explicit consent. Note, that it is the interests of another individual not the vital interests as in paragraph 3 of Schedule 3.

There are further provisions allowing disclosures by data controllers to elected representatives in relation to requests as above. Where Parliament or an Assembly is dissolved, the representative is treated as an elected representative until four days after an election. This does not apply to local authority councillors and the like.

TRANSFERS TO THIRD COUNTRIES

One of the main purposes of the Data Protection Directive was the removal of potential barriers to the freedom of movement of personal data throughout the European Community and, subsequently, throughout the European Economic Area ("EEA"). There had been some concerns that Member States with high levels of data protection would erect barriers to prevent the movement of personal data to other Member States which had weaker data protection laws or an absence of effective data protection laws. Although freedom of movement of personal data throughout the EEA was facilitated by the Directive, there was a danger that barriers would be erected around

Europe, with severe restrictions on the movement of personal data to countries outside the EEA, described as "third countries" in the language of the Directive. Many such third countries have no data protection law as such and some countries, such as the United States prefer a system based on self-regulation.

The ability to transfer personal data to any other country is vital to global commerce. Many organisations based in the United Kingdom transfer data to other countries for processing activities to be carried out. The growth of global telecommunications makes it relatively easy to transfer data to anywhere else in the world or to make massive databases located on computers in one country available to persons from any other country. One issue first of all is the difference between disclosures of and transfers of personal data. Neither "disclosure" nor "transfer" is defined in the Data Protection Act 1998 and the Directive offers no clue and, therefore, it would seem reasonable to look at dictionary definitions. The difference could be important because a mere disclosure to a person in a third country may not be deemed to be a transfer and outside the provisions on transfers to third countries. (Of course, a description of recipients to whom the data controller intends or may wish to disclose personal data is part of the registrable particulars and must be notified unless exempt from notification.)

The Oxford Concise English Dictionary defines "disclose" in terms of "make known, reveal, expose to view" whilst the relevant meaning of transfer includes "convey, remove, hand over, make over possession of". That being so, it would appear reasonable to assume that revealing personal data orally over the telephone is a disclosure but not a transfer. On the other hand transmitting a database containing personal data to another person who records that database on magnetic media is a transfer. But what about the situation where a database is located in the United Kingdom and persons from other countries, including third countries, access that database and retrieve and view some of the contents? If no permanent copy is made, for example, where the recipient simply views the data, the only copy being transient in the recipient's volatile computer memory, it would seem reasonable to describe this as disclosure and not transfer. Would it be both disclosure and transfer if the recipient saved a copy of all or part of the database on his computer's hard disk? The problem is that the word "transfer" connotes the idea that there is only one copy of the thing concerned which has moved from the first data controller to the second. This plainly cannot be right in the context of electronic transmission of data – the original copy is usually retained and it is a copy which is sent. It must be intended that this is within the meaning of transfer. Of course, transfers in the dictionary sense could be made in respect of manual data (unless it is a facsimile copy or photocopy which is sent).

It is submitted that accessing personal data where no permanent (or semi-permanent) copy is made is a disclosure only and not a transfer of those data. This is in line with the House of Lords decision in *R v Gold*[11] in which the House decided that a customer identification number and password held transiently in a computer's volatile memory (RAM) was not "recorded or stored" for the purposes of the Forgery and Counterfeiting Act 1980 and were not, consequently, false instruments under that Act. However, section 17(6) of the Copyright, Designs and Patents Act 1988 recognises that an infringing copy of a work may be transient.

It must also be noted that the wide definition of processing includes retrieval and disclosure by transmission and even storage. The provisions in the Directive on transfers to third countries refer to transfers of personal data which are undergoing processing or are intended for processing after transfer (Article 25(1)). As processing also includes storage ("holding" in the Act) there is no need for the transferee to perform any active processing for the transfer to be relevant for the purposes of the Act. A relevant transfer will have taken place where, for example, a copy of the data has been transmitted to the recipient who has saved the data file to his hard disk without opening the file.

One important point about distinguishing between disclosures and transfers is in the context of the internet. Say a data controller puts details of his key employees on his webpages. Those details will be personal data for the meaning of the Act and may be accessible by anyone, anywhere in the world. Many of the countries from which the data can be accessed will have no data protection law at all. If such access is deemed to be a transfer, then the provisions of the Act apply. Thus, the names and descriptions of all the countries or territories outside the European Economic Area must be given in any notification to the Commissioner. Fortunately, it is possible to notify "Worldwide" if more than 10 countries outside the EEA are involved.

The status of information made available on websites was not altogether clear. The Directive was made at a time when the significance of the internet was not fully appreciated by all, perhaps even including the European Commission. It took an application for a preliminary ruling from a Swedish court to the European Court of Justice to resolve the doubts.

In Case C-101/01 *Bodil Lindqvist*, 6 November 2003, Mrs Lindqvist was prosecuted for breaches of Swedish data protection law on the basis that she had processed personal data without notification, sensitive personal data without authorisation and that she had transferred personal data to third countries without authorisation. Mrs Lindqvist worked for a parish church in Sweden

---

[11] [1988] 2 WLR 984.

and set up webpages on her computer at home. At her request, the church set up a link to her website. It contained information about her colleagues. She had not asked their consent and the information also included the fact that one of them had injured her foot and was only working on a part-time basis as a result. Mrs Lindqvist had not notified her processing but removed the webpages once she realised that some of her colleagues did not appreciate them.

The Court of Justice noted that persons in third countries consulting the website had to take actions to connect to that website and then take the necessary actions to consult the pages. Mrs Lindqvist's computer did not contain the technical apparatus to send information automatically to persons who had not intentionally sought access to the pages (though the transfer provisions are certainly not limited to data transmitted automatically to a person who had not requested their transmission). The data were not, therefore, directly transferred from Mrs Lindqvist and the person seeking access. They were made available to such a person by virtue of the computer infrastructure of the company hosting the webpages.

The Directive contained no provisions in relation to transfers to third countries via the internet. Given the absence of express provision and the state of the internet at the time the Directive was drawn up, it was not possible to presume that the legislature intended to cover a situation where a person loads data onto a computer linked to the internet even though the data may be accessible to persons in third countries who have the technical means to access those data. A further problem would that, if it were otherwise, placing data on the internet would be transferring it all over the world and, even if just one country did not have adequate protection, Member States could be required to prohibit any personal data being placed on the internet. Of course, this would be subject to the derogations mentioned later.

The Court of Justice stressed that it was not considering the position of persons hosting webpages on behalf of others. It did note, however, that the Directive contained no provisions to determine whether operations performed by hosting providers occurred at their place of business or at the place where their computer infrastructure was located.

At first sight, this decision seems to run counter to the spirit of the Directive and provides an unfortunate loophole which could massively compromise individuals' right of privacy in relation to their personal data. It also suggests that a transfer of personal data requires a positive act by the data controller in transmitting data, rather than simply placing data where it can be accessed by others. It is regrettable that the Court eschewed the opportunity of interpreting the transfer provisions in the Directive in the context of the internet. The practical difficulties pointed to by the Court of Justice could have been easily overcome in such cases by ensuring that the explicit consent of data subjects was obtained prior to placing personal data on a website, something which Mrs Lindqvist unwisely failed to do. Before this case, the Information Commissioner's view was that placing data on a website involved a potential transfer all over the world and suggested that, where this was the case, notification of transfers to third countries should specify "Worldwide".

The *Lindqvist* case also fails to address the issue of whether placing personal data on the internet results in disclosure. If it does, the notification must give a description of recipients – everyone potentially in the world. Such a universal description would seem to defeat the fundamental principle of transparency. The same criticism applies to the description "Worldwide" for third countries to which data may be transferred. Hopefully, the European Commission will further investigate the issues raised by placing personal data on websites.

It is now to the specific provisions relating to transfers to third countries not having an adequate level of protection that we turn and the manner in which transfers of personal data may be made to such countries nonetheless.

The eighth data protection principle states that transfers of personal data shall not be made to countries or territories outside the European Economic Area not having an adequate level of protection for the rights and freedoms of data subjects in relation to the processing of personal data.

The major problem with this provision is that adequacy of protection is not a simple yes or no situation – it is a qualitative issue and some third countries will be adequate in some cases though not in others. This is because adequacy is determined by reference to a number of factors, in particular being: the nature of the data; the country or territory of origin and of final destination of the data; the purposes of and period for which the data are intended to be processed; the law in force in the country or territory in question; the international obligations and relevant codes of conduct in the country or territory in question (whether generally or by arrangement in particular cases); and any security measures taken in respect of the data in that country or territory. Thus, whilst it is possible to identify some countries as having adequate protection in all cases and in respect of which all transfers of personal data may be made without constraint, in most cases it will be a matter of determining adequacy in a particular case. However, in taking a somewhat pragmatic approach, there are some exceptions where the eighth principle will not apply. Schedule 4 to the Act contains a number of cases in which data transfers may take place notwithstanding that the third country does not, in a particular case, have an adequate level of protection. Schedule 4 is the United Kingdom's response to the derogations provided for in Article 26 of the Directive and follows those provisions closely. In other words, the United

Kingdom has chosen to take maximum advantage of the possible derogations from the restrictive prohibition in Article 25 of the Directive.

Under paragraph 15 of Part II of Schedule 1, where there are any proceedings where the question of adequacy arises and a Community finding has been made in relation to transfers of the kind in question, the question must be determined in accordance with that finding. A Community finding is a finding of the Commission under Article 31(2) of the Data Protection Directive to the effect that a country or territory outside the European Economic Area does, or does not, ensure an adequate level of protection for the purposes of Article 25(2) of the Directive. In determining such issues, the Commission will be assisted by a committee composed of representatives of Member States. The Working Party set up under Article 29 of the Directive shall, under Article 30(1), *inter alia*, give the Commission an opinion on the level of protection in the Community and in third countries. Thus far, a number of countries have been identified as having adequate protection, being Canada, Switzerland, Hungary, Argentina, Isle of Man, Guernsey and Jersey.

The difficulty with these provisions is that it may be difficult to accurately define "transfers of a particular kind" in the light of the various factors to be taken into account in determining adequacy where the country or territory in question does not have a model of data protection law equivalent to that under the Directive. Transfers of a particular kind could be specified in relation to the nature of the data, the purposes of processing, the duration of processing, security measures and relevant sectoral laws or codes of practice or a combination of these. In practice, it may prove easier to state what is acceptable rather than what is not.

Importantly, Schedule 4 to the Act disapplies the eighth principle (unless an order made by the Secretary of State rules otherwise), where:

1.   The data subject has given his consent to the transfer.

2.   The transfer is necessary -
     (a) for the performance of a contract between the data subject and the data controller, or
     (b) for the taking of steps at the request of the data subject with a view to his entering into a contract with the data controller.

3.   The transfer is necessary -
     (a) for the conclusion of a contract between the data controller and a person other than the data subject which -
          (i)   is entered into at the request of the data subject, or
          (ii) is in the interests of the data subject, or
     (b) for the performance of such a contract.

4.   (1) The transfer is necessary for reasons of substantial public interest.

(2) The Secretary of State may by order specify -
  (a) circumstances in which a transfer is to be taken for the purposes of sub-paragraph (1) to be necessary for reasons of substantial public interest, and
  (b) circumstances in which a transfer is not required by or under an enactment is not to be taken for the purpose of sub-paragraph (1) to be necessary for reasons of substantial public interest.

5. The transfer -
  (a) is necessary for the purpose of, or in connection with, any legal proceedings (including prospective legal proceedings),
  (b) is necessary for the purpose of obtaining legal advice, or
  (c) is otherwise necessary for the purposes of establishing, exercising or defending legal rights.

6. The transfer is necessary in order to protect the vital interests of the data subject.

7. The transfer is of part of the personal data on a public register and any conditions subject to which the register is open for inspection are complied with by any person to whom the data are or may be disclosed after the transfer.

8. The transfer is made on terms which are of a kind approved by the Commissioner as ensuring adequate safeguards for the rights and freedoms of data subjects.

9. The transfer has been authorised by the Commissioner as being made in such a manner as to ensure adequate safeguards for the rights and freedoms of data subjects.

Where the data subject's consent is obtained there is no problem. However, it should be noted that, although the Act is silent on this point, the Directive requires that the consent is unambiguous. This would seem to require that the consent is express and failing to tick a box on a form will not be sufficient. Ideally, there should be an appropriate statement on a form which the data subject signs, signifying his assent to the transfer. In the context of the internet, it has been suggested that only express consent will do, such as by requiring the data subject to click on a box to signify assent to the collection and further processing of personal data relating to him or her.

Paragraphs 2 and 3 above provide for transfers, notwithstanding problems over adequacy of protection, in the context of a contract involving the data subject. It is wider than situations where the data subject is a party to the contract and may apply where the contract has been entered into at the request of the data subject or is in the interests of the data subject. This latter possibility has been made much more likely under English law with the Contracts (Rights of Third Parties) Act 1999 which came into force on 11 November 1999 and which, under certain conditions, allows a third party to enforce a term in a contract. The Act does not apply to Scotland but there it is possible for third parties to have rights under contract on the basis of the principle *jus tertium*, derived from Roman law. Third party rights are relevant to the standard contractual clauses discussed below. It should be noted that the word "necessary" appears again but, in line with other provisions where the word appears, it is unlikely to be taken in a strong sense.

A contract entered into with someone other than the data subject but at the request of the data subject could cover a situation where the data subject is acting on behalf of the principal as agent or where the data subject is acting for another under a power of attorney.

The public interest is a nebulous concept in terms of transfers of personal data to countries or territories outside the EEA not having an adequate level of protection. It is not an easy matter to think of an example. Presumably this is why the Secretary of State is given the power to specify circumstance in which the transfer is necessary in the public interest. The Directive talks of transfers legally required in the public interest. Apart from such legally required transfers, the Secretary of State may also specify transfers which are not necessary in the public interest.

Transfers in relation to legal proceedings, legal advice or in connection with legal rights are permitted, as might be expected. This might be relevant where the data subject is party to legal proceedings in a third country, for example, where extradition proceedings are underway.

The vital interests of the data subject are included. The obvious example is the transfer of health data relating to a data subject who is taken ill whilst in a third country. Transfers of parts of public registers are permitted if the conditions for open inspection are complied with by any person to whom the data may be disclosed after the transfer. In other words it must be the recipient or recipients of the data after the data are transferred who must comply with any relevant condition. This could be the transferee or the person to whom the transferee discloses the data. There would not be a problem where the data are generally available to the public free of charge and without restriction. In other cases, where a copy of the data is supplied in return for payment a condition may be that it is not to be further copied without permission. Or it may be that information on a public register is available for inspection by persons showing an interest, such as entries on the Land Register. Of course, apart from other conditions, the law of copyright may be relevant. Material open for public inspection may be copied freely under certain conditions; see section 47 of the Copyright, Designs and Patents Act 1988. For example, information open to public inspection pursuant to a statutory requirement and which relates to matters of general scientific, technical, commercial or economic interest may be copied for the purposes of disseminating that information and is done with the authority of the appropriate person.

In relation to the eighth form of transfer (on terms of a kind approved by the Commissioner) the Commissioner may approve kinds of terms which ensure adequate safeguards or authorise the transfer as being made so as to ensure adequate safeguards. In any legal proceedings, as noted above, questions as to whether the eighth principle has been met are to be determined in accordance with any finding made by the European Commission under Article 31(2) of the Directive as to transfers of the kind in question.

Soon after the adoption of the Directive there was much work done on developing appropriate contractual terms and judging adequacy of protection.[12] The International Chamber of Commerce submitted proposals for contractual terms to the Commission. An important principle is that contracts should ensure that the data controller from the "home country" (that is, the transferor) retains decision-making control in respect of the processing carried out in a third country. Recommended contractual terms impose, on the transferee in the third country, similar obligations to those set out in the Data Protection Directive, whilst the transferor retains ultimate control of processing activity carried out in the third country.

Commission Decision 2001/497/EC of 15 June 2001 on standard contractual clauses for the transfer of personal data to third countries, under Directive 95/46/EC,[13] contains in the annex, standard clauses for transfers between a data controller in the EEA to a data controller outside. The clauses allow data subjects to enforce certain clauses including those covering rights to be informed, rights of access and rights to compensation. The Information Commissioner has issued guidance on the practical application of the clauses, for example, either as a word by word stand alone contract or by incorporation into a contract including other business terms. All such information, including links to the Commission's standard clauses and other materials can be found on the Information Commissioner's website at: www.information-commissioner.gov.uk.

The above decision cover transfers to data controllers outside the EEA. In terms of processors, Commission Decision 2002/16/EC of 27 December 2001 on standard contractual clauses for the transfer of personal data to processors established in third countries, under Directive 95/46/EC,[14] sets out in an annex standard contractual clauses offering adequate safeguards in the context of transfers from data controllers to processors established outside the EU. Again, data subjects can enforce certain clauses against the exporting data controller, and where the data controller has factually disappeared or has

---

[12] See particularly Appendix 10 to the Fourteenth Annual Report of the Data Protection Registrar, 1998.
[13] OJ L 181, 04.07.2001, p.19
[14] OJ L 6, 10.01.2002 p. 52.

ceased to exist at law, the data subject can enforce some clauses against the importing processor.

The United States approach is to offer "safe harbours", companies in the United States that agree to adhere to privacy principles but the problem remains about organisations that do not adopt effective internal privacy controls and another issue is in respect of the possibility of transfers from organisations in third countries to other organisations, either within that third country or another third country. Details of the safe harbour principles and lists of organisations subscribing to them may be found via the Information Commissioner's website.

Figure 7.2 shows, schematically, the basic mechanism for transfers outside the European Economic Area.

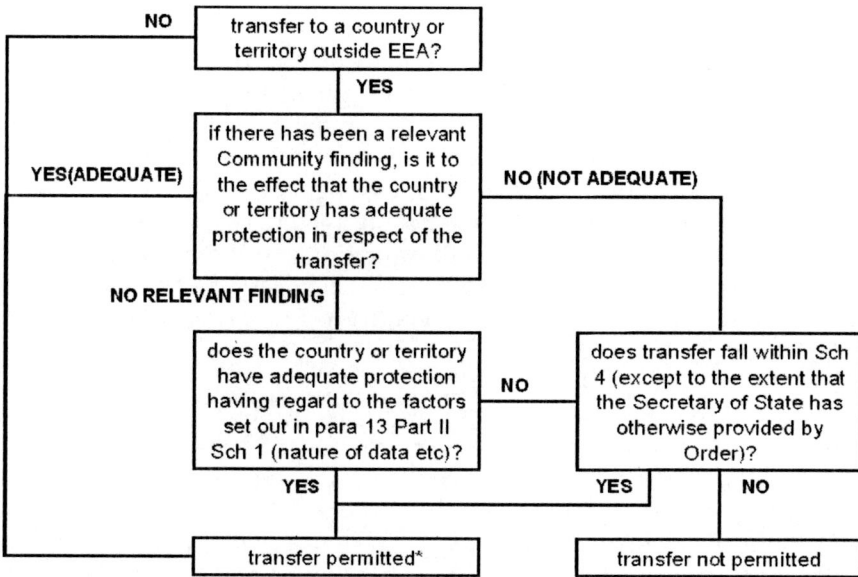

Providing otherwise within the data protection principles and scope of notification.

Figure 7.2 Transfers outside the EEA

CHAPTER 8
RIGHTS OF DATA SUBJECTS

INTRODUCTION

Until the Human Rights Act 1998 which gave force to the Council of Europe Convention for the Protection of Human Rights and Fundamental Freedoms ("the Human Rights Convention"), there was no general law of privacy in England. Before, legal protection of an individual's right to privacy, where it existed at all, came from a diverse variety of sources, such as the law of breach of confidence, the torts of defamation and malicious falsehood. To some extent also it derived, indirectly, from copyright through the enforcement of the economic rights by the owner of the copyright or, more recently, through the author's moral rights. A difficulty for legislators has been balancing the rights of individuals with freedom of expression and Parliament has seldom been prepared to legislate specifically in this area, leaving it to the courts to develop principles in a piecemeal fashion. The courts proceeded with extreme caution.

The advent of computer technology was perceived as a potential threat to privacy and individual freedoms and the Council of Europe Convention of 28 January 1981 for the Protection of Individuals with regard to the Automatic Processing of Personal Data attempted to impose a regulatory regime on the processing of computer data relating to individuals in such a way that risks to privacy and freedom would not be unduly compromised. The Data Protection Act 1984 was the United Kingdom's first response to the Convention but only took a minimalist approach. Providing data users (equivalent to data controllers under the 1998 Act) completed the necessary formalities for registration and complied with the data protection principles, data protection law had relatively little impact. Most individuals took very little notice of data protection law, had little awareness of it and relatively few individuals exercised their rights under the 1984 Act (unless they had a particular problem such as an inability to obtain credit due to inaccurate data). The 1998 Act significantly enhances pre-existing rights and provides for some important new rights including a right to prevent processing in some cases. Importantly, a right to compensation is provided for damage resulting from any contravention of the Act. Compensation for associated distress is also available and, where processing is for the special purposes, compensation for distress is available in the absence of damage. These data subject rights have now taken on some real importance but, in spite of the efforts of the Information Commissioner to raise awareness of them, for the year 2003/4, whilst 89% of data controllers were aware of data subjects' rights only 74% of individuals were aware of their rights under data protection law.[1]

In many situations where a data subject makes a claim for compensation under the Data Protection Act 1998, there will also be issues in relation to breach of confidence or the right of privacy under the Human Rights Convention, as in cases such as *Michael Douglas v Hello! Limited*[2] and *Naomi Campbell v MGN Ltd*.[3] Such cases show how the law of confidence has developed to give effect to Convention rights; see for example, Lord Nicholls of Birkenhead in *Naomi Campbell* at para 17 where he said:

> *"The time has come to recognise that the values enshrined in articles 8 and 10 are now part of the cause of action for breach of confidence. As Lord Woolf CJ has said, the courts have been able to achieve this result by absorbing the rights protected by articles 8 and 10 into this cause of action: A v B plc [2003] QB 195, 202, para 4. Further, it should now be recognised that for this purpose these values are of general application. The values embodied in articles 8 and 10 are as much applicable in disputes between individuals or between an individual and a non-governmental body such as a newspaper as they are in disputes between individuals and a public authority."*

Such cases also indicate that, to some extent, the rights provided under the Data Protection Act 1998 have their parallels to those protected by the law of confidence as it has developed.

Specific dangers are posed to individuals through the processing of genetic data, lifestyle data, impaired life databases, through the activities of private investigators and the growing use of surveillance, including CCTV. Techniques such as data matching (comparing data about an individual from several sources to detect inconsistencies that may point to a potential fraudster) and data warehousing (compiling massive databases from a number of individual databases) have become well used and have significant potential to adversely affect individuals' rights and freedoms, for example, as a result of inaccurate or incomplete data. Moreover, far more data of a sensitive nature is being processed by automatic means than was the case some time ago. Nor do

---

[1] Information Commissioner, *Annual Report and Accounts July 2004*: London, Stationery Office, 2004, HC669, p.88.
[2] [2003] EMLR 585.
[3] [2004] 2 All ER 995.

all the dangers which result from automated processing as structured manual files, (where information about a particular individual can be accessed readily), also present threats to privacy in the same way as certain forms of unstructured manual files, for example, relating to health data.

The Data Protection Directive, as well as extending data protection law to certain forms of manual processing, had two primary thrusts which consolidate and enhance individuals' rights and freedoms. These are the principles of *transparency* and *control*. Transparency is achieved by ensuring that individuals have rights to be informed of processing activities, in respect of the identity of the data controller and the purposes of processing, disclosures to third parties and by requiring more information to be supplied in response to subject access requests. Individuals' control over processing is improved by giving individuals rights to object to processing and, in some cases, requiring their consent to processing (possibly, express and unambiguous consent). That individuals have growing concerns about the processing of personal data is indicated by the number of requests for assessments submitted to the Information Commissioner, which are running at around twice as many as complaints made to the Registrar under the 1984 Act.[4] In the year 2003/4, 9,994 requests for assessment were received by the Information Commissioner's office (not including equivalent requests made under privacy in telecommunications and electronic communications legislation, standing at 1,670 for the same year).

TRANSPARENCY

An underlying theme of the Data Protection Directive was that processing activity should be as transparent as possible and that data subjects should be in a position to know who is processing personal data relating to them and for what purposes that processing is being carried out. For example, recital 38 to the Directive states that

> "... the data subject must be in a position to learn of the existence of a processing operation and, where data are collected from him, must be given accurate and full information, bearing in mind the circumstances of the collection".

Obligations are imposed on data controllers to provide individuals with information on collection of personal data from them and, in other cases, such as when those data are disclosed to a third party. Where the data have not been collected directly from the data subject (this includes the position where the

---

[4] Information Commissioner, *op cit* at p.89.

data were originally collected directly from the data subject but are now to be disclosed to a third party), the data subject must be informed when the data are recorded or at the latest when they are disclosed to a third party; see recital 39. Transparency is also ensured by giving individuals a right of access to their personal data. This is a right to be informed as to whether the data controller is processing data concerning the individual and, if so, a right of access to those data as well as the provision of other information concerning the processing activities.

In terms of transparency, the Directive went considerably further than was the case under the 1984 Act. Under that Act, transparency was achieved by virtue of the data protection register, a publicly available register of data users and computer bureaux together with a right of subject access. However, much of the information contained in the register was of a general nature and not particularly helpful as far as individuals were concerned (although, in practice, this is little better under the 1998 Act). To make matters worse, many organisations had several register entries and other cumbersome rules existed such as the requirement for every partner in a partnership to register separately as was the case with school heads and the board of governors of schools. Perhaps the worst feature was that, apart from obvious data controllers such as the individual's employer, bank and central and local government bodies, general practitioners and the Health Service, it was well-nigh impossible to discover the identity of all the other data controllers who held data relating to a particular individual. The individual might be alerted only when he received marketing material from a new source. A key aim of the Directive was to increase transparency. After all, the exercise of data subjects' rights under data protection law can only be really effective if individuals are better informed as to processing activities affecting them, whether by providing information directly to them or by establishing systems by which individuals can seek relevant information.

PROVIDING INFORMATION TO DATA SUBJECTS

Individuals have a fundamental right to be informed of processing activity which involves personal data relating to them. A data subject must be provided with certain information when data are collected from him or in other cases, for example, where the data, having originated from the data subject, are transferred to or disclosed to another data controller or where new data have been generated by a data controller. The only exceptions in the Directive were

> "... in particular for processing for statistical purposes or for the purposes of historical or scientific research ..."

where the provision of such information proves impossible or would involve a disproportionate effort or if recording or disclosure is expressly laid down by law. In such cases, Member States must provide appropriate safeguards; Article 11(2). Unless within the specific exceptions in the Act, this should enable data subjects to know the identity of data controllers processing personal data relating to them and the purposes for which they are processing those data. However, the exceptions in the Act, together with further exceptions from the requirement to notify contained within the Data Protection (Notification and Notification Fees) Regulations 2000, appear to intrude into the right to respect for private and family life in Article 8 of the Human Rights Convention. It is reasonable to assume there should be some synergy between the Data Protection Act 1998 and the Convention Rights (as data protection law is a child of the latter) but if the exceptions impede the ability for individuals to discover the identity of data controllers processing their personal data, this prejudices their ability to find out whether rights of privacy have been compromised. It is clear that the right of privacy under the Human Rights Convention is a proactive one and may give a right to an individual to obtain information to enable him or her to determine whether the right to privacy has been compromised; see for example, *Johnston* v *Ireland*[5] where the European Court of Human Rights stated (at para 55):

> "*Although the essential object of Article 8 ... is to protect the individual against arbitrary interference by the public authorities, there may in addition be positive obligations inherent in an effective 'respect' for family life.*"

Gaskin v *United Kingdom*[6] and *M G* v *United Kingdom*[7] both confirm that the right to privacy may impose a positive obligation to provide information.

An express statutory requirement to provide information to data subjects had no equivalent under the 1984 Act except to the extent that processing must be carried out fairly and lawfully under the first data protection principle. However, to some extent, case law before the Data Protection Tribunal (now the Information Tribunal) cured this omission. In cases such as *Innovations (Mail Order) Ltd* v *Data Protection Registrar*[8], *Linguaphone Institute Ltd* v *Data Protection Registrar*[9] and *British Gas Trading Ltd* v *Data Protection Registrar*[10] the Tribunal accepted that data subjects should be informed of "non-obvious" uses of personal data relating to them at the time of collection and that data

---

[5] [1986] ECHR 17.
[6] [1989] ECHR 13.
[7] [2002] ECHR 627.
[8] (Case DA/92 31/49/1) 29 September 1993.
[9] (Case DA/94 34/49/1) 14 July 1995.
[10] 24 March 1998.

subjects should not be required to expressly object to such at some time later, after the time the data were collected from the data subject. A data subject should be informed of non-obvious uses (such as list-trading for marketing purposes) at the time he volunteers his personal data and given an opportunity to object there and then, for example, by ticking a box on an order form or application form.

The basic provisions in the Data Protection Act 1998 require, in paragraph 2(1), Part II, Schedule 1, for processing to be treated as being fair:

(a) *in the case of data obtained from the data subject, the data controller ensures so far as practicable that the data subject has, is provided with, or has made readily available to him, the information specified in sub-paragraph (3) and,*

(b) *in any other case, the data controller ensures so far as practicable that, before the relevant time or as soon as practicable after that time, the data subject has, is provided with, or has made readily available to him, the information specified in sub-paragraph (3).*

Sub-paragraph (3) describes the information required to be given to the data subject as:

(a) *the identity of the data controller,*

(b) *if the data controller has nominated a representative for the purposes of this Act, the identity of that representative,*

(c) *the purpose or purposes for which the data are intended to be processed, and*

(d) *any further information which is necessary, having regard to the specific circumstances in which the data are or are to be processed, to enable the processing in respect of the data subject to be fair.*

This seems to favour the data subject by ensuring he or she is provided with information on collection of data and subsequently, for example where the data are disclosed to a third party. However, there are a number of "let-outs" for the data controller, apart from specific exemptions from the "subject information" provisions discussed in the following chapter. First, the amount of information provided may be relatively minimal. The identity of the data controller is essential (as is the identity of a nominated representative, if one has been notified). The purpose or purposes of the processing need not be given where the register entry itself has this information – paragraph 5 of Part II of Schedule 1 provides that the purposes of processing may be specified in a notice given to the data subject in compliance with the information provisions *or* by virtue of a notification under the Act. Further information to ensure fairness of processing will depend on the circumstances. It seems likely that this will apply to subsequent processing or disclosures that are not obvious or apparent at the time of collection, such as in the *Innovations* and other cases mentioned above. Furthermore, the data controller is excused from providing information if the data subject already has that information. This could be the case where a data controller, X, intends to transfer the data to data controller, Y, and X has already informed Y that this will happen beforehand and has identified Y and the purposes of the processing to be carried out by Y. In such a situation Y does not need to inform the data subject when he receives the data as the data subject already knows.

In cases other than where the data are collected from the data subject, another release from the obligation to provide information to the data subject is in cases prescribed by the Secretary of State. Article 11(2) of the Data Protection Directive excused the data controller from providing information in such cases,

> *"... in particular for processing for statistical purposes or for the purposes of historical or scientific research, the provision of such information proves impossible or would involve a disproportionate effort or if recording or disclosure is expressly laid down by law".*

The Data Protection (Conditions under Paragraph 3 of Part II of Schedule 1) Order 2000 excuses data controllers from providing information in cases other than where the data have been collected from the data subject where it would prove impossible or would involve a disproportionate effort or where the recording or disclosure is necessary to comply with a legal obligation to which the data controller is subject (other than a contractual obligation). Further conditions are laid down in the Order, in relation to cases other than where a legal obligation exists and this requires that the data controller makes a contemporary record of why he or she considers that provision of the information would require a disproportionate effort. The Order goes further than the Directive in that it is not limited to any forms of processing – apart from legal obligations, the Directive stresses statistics, historical or scientific research.

There may also be issues with the timing of giving information where data are not collected from the data subject. In such cases, the information must be provided before the relevant time or as soon as practicable after that time. Paragraph 2(2) of Part II of Schedule 1 defines the relevant time as follows:

> (a) the time when the data controller first processes the data, or

(b) in case where at that time disclosure to a third party within a reasonable period is envisaged-

    (i)   if the data are in fact disclosed to such a person within that period, the time when the data are first disclosed;

    (ii) if within that period the data controller becomes, or ought to become, aware that the data are unlikely to be disclosed, to such a person within that period, the time when the data controller does become, or ought to become, so aware; or

    (iii) in any other case, the end of that period.

There are a number of problems with this provision. The Act does not make it clear by whom the disclosure is envisaged. Is it the data controller, the data subject or both? The wording in the Directive in Article 11(1) seems to favour the disclosure being envisaged by the data controller. Recital 39 is the operative recital and this states that

"... data can be legitimately disclosed to a third party, even if the disclosure was not anticipated at the time the data were collected from the data subject; whereas, in all these cases, the data subject should be informed when the data are recorded or at the latest when the data are first disclosed to a third party".

This seems clearer than Article 11(1) and the equivalent provision in the Act.

If the disclosure in question is envisaged only by the data controller, this could result, under cases (ii) and (iii), in a data subject who has no idea that his data were intended to be disclosed to a third party, being informed that his data are not after all going to be so disclosed. This seems completely unnecessary. A more reasonable interpretation is that the disclosure is envisaged by both the data subject and the data controller, for example, if the data subject has filled out an order form and failed to tick the box preventing disclosure of his data to other organisations for marketing purposes. However, as at the time of completing the form, the data subject is unlikely to know the specific identity of the third parties to whom his data are intended to be disclosed, there seems little point in telling him his data are not going to be disclosed after all. A further problem is what constitutes a reasonable time? This may vary according to the circumstances. It might be different in a commercial context than in the case of data disclosed by a public body. But, in either case, it must also be a question of how long it is likely to be before the data become unreliable or inaccurate as a result of changes in the data subject's personal circumstances, unless details of such changes are incorporated in the collection of data in question. There is no equivalent to paragraph 2(2)(b)(ii) and (iii) in the Directive and these provisions seem completely pointless.

The principle of transparency is compromised by the amount of information that must be provided, under paragraph 2(3) Part II Schedule 1 as set out above. As regards the "further information" that should be given to the data subject to ensure that the processing is fair, the White Paper which preceded the 1998 Act suggested that it would be, in the first instance, the controller who would decide whether any further information was required to be given.[11] The Act is silent on this point. It is unlikely that many data controllers will volunteer any further information other than their own identity for, if the data controller has notified his processing (as he must do for automated processing and may do for manual processing), the notification itself may satisfy the requirement to give information as to the purposes of processing. Under paragraph 5 of Part II of Schedule 1, the purpose or purposes for which personal data are obtained may in particular be specified in a notice informing the data subject as required by paragraph 2 *or* in a notification given to the Commissioner under Part III of the Act. This seems to defeat the spirit of the Directive as data subjects would have to consult the register to discover the purpose or purposes of processing unless the data controller makes that information available to the data subject. Even though the register is available on the Information Commissioner's website, most data subjects will not consult it and, even if they do, may find it hard to discover the purpose or purposes relevant to their particular situation.

In cases where personal data are not collected from the data subject, for example, where data originally collected from the data subject are subsequently disclosed to a third party, the Directive goes further than the Act and suggests that the further information may be the categories of data, recipients or categories of recipients and the existence of access rights and the right to have inaccurate data corrected. Failure to provide information other than the identity of the data controller may result in the processing deemed to be unfair. Fairness should be assessed in the light of the data subject's rights under the Act. Particularly important is the need to know sufficient information to enable the data subject to exercise his or her rights, for example, rights to object to processing, rights of access and rights in respect of inaccurate data.

DISPROPORTIONATE EFFORT

The Data Protection Directive excuses the data controller from providing information to a data subject, where the data have not been obtained from the data subject, in cases where to provide the information, particularly in respect of

---

[11] Home Office (1997) *Data Protection: The Government's Proposals*, Cm 3725 at para.3.11.

"... processing for statistical purposes or the purposes or the purpose of historical or scientific research"

would prove impossible or would involve a disproportionate effort or if the recording or disclosure is expressly laid down by law; Article 11(2).

The approach of the Data Protection Act 1998 seems wider in that there is no reference to particular cases. The Act excuses the provision of information in cases where the data are not obtained from the data subject if, under paragraph 3(2) of Part II of Schedule 1:

(a) *the provision of that information would involve a disproportionate effort, or*

(b) *the recording of the information to be contained in the data by, or the disclosure of the data by, the data controller is necessary for compliance with any legal obligation to which the data controller is subject, other than an obligation imposed by contract.*

This applies in circumstances where, for example, the data have been generated by the data controller or, having been originally obtained from the data subject by one data controller, are now being disclosed to another data controller. The Act has no restrictions on the type of processing to which the provision applies. However, the Directive may not be as restrictive as it first appears as recital 40 simply gives research purposes as an example of when the provision of information could prove impossible or involve a disproportionate effort, presumably because of the sheer volume of data subjects or because the processing occurs long after collection of the data.

The Directive required appropriate safeguards to be provided where a data controller is permitted to rely on a disproportionate effort to excuse the provision of information to the data subject. Paragraph 3(1) of Part II of Schedule 1 to the Act empowers the Secretary of State to impose further conditions. Thus, the Data Protection (Conditions under Paragraph 3 of Part II of Schedule 1) Order 2000 imposes further conditions before the data controller can be excused from providing information to the data subject where the data have not been obtained from that data subject.

The Order contains two separate conditions. Article 4 applies both to disproportionate effort and recording or disclosures in compliance with a legal obligation. Article 5 of the Order only applies to disproportionate effort.

Article 4 of the Order excuses the provision of information only if the data subject has not notified the data controller in writing that he requires to be provided with the information in paragraph 2(3) of Part II of Schedule 1 to the

Act (identity of data controller and representative, if any; purposes of processing and any further information for processing to be fair). If the data subject's notice does not provide sufficient information to enable the data controller readily to determine whether he is processing personal data relating to that individual, the data controller must send an appropriate written notice[12] stating that he is unable to provide the information and stating his reason for that inability. The requirement that a notice be in writing is satisfied by transmission of the text of the notice by electronic means, which is received in legible form and which is capable of being used for subsequent reference. Thus, a notice by email should suffice.

Article 5 of the Order applies only where the data controller relies on disproportionate effort so as to excuse the provision of information. The requirement is that the data controller simply record his reasons for his view that the provision of information would involve a disproportionate effort. Article 5 is described as a "further condition" and this means that, in a case where disproportionate effort is relied on, both Article 4 and Article 5 apply; that is, that no notice has been received from the data subject *and* the data controller must record his reasons for his view why the provision of information would require a disproportionate effort.

There is no real guidance as to what constitutes a disproportionate effort although a factor must be the impact on fairness of processing. Although cost is likely to be the most common reason recorded, there should be a balance between the cost (whether financial or in terms of resources) and the potential risks to the data subjects' rights under data protection law. A broadly analogous situation applies in respect of informing third parties, to whom data have been disclosed, of inaccuracies. Third parties should be informed where reasonably practicable and this is determined, in particular having regard to the number of persons who would have to be notified. Where a copy of a customer database containing many thousands of entries is given to another data controller, perhaps in the context of list trading, having to notify every single individual of the disclosure could be seen as requiring a disproportionate effort. But, even here, if the risks to data subjects' rights are significant, this should override withholding information. Disproportionate effort should be seen in the context of the well-established concept of proportionality in European jurisprudence.

Bearing in mind that the provisions on informing data subjects relate to the first Data Protection Principle (fair and lawful processing), there may be many cases where reliance on disproportionate effort will not be appropriate. An example might be where the data subject has not consented to a particular

---

[12] *Linguaphone Institute Ltd* v *Data Protection Registrar* (Case DA/94 34/49/1) 14 July 1995.

disclosure or where a data controller generates new personal data relating to an individual which could compromise that individual or perhaps prejudice his rights of privacy, particularly if subsequent disclosures are likely to be made. Of course, simply falling within one of the conditions for processing should not, *per se*, excuse a data controller from providing information to data subjects.

Finally, it must be stressed that a data controller cannot rely on disproportionate effort where the data are obtained from the data subject, whether directly or through a processor engaged by the data controller to obtain the data or where the data subject has notified the data controller in writing that the information must be provided to the data subject. In such cases, the data controller is excused this obligation only if the data subject already has the information or it is readily available to him.

Subject access

The right of subject access has been significantly improved. Under the 1984 Act, data subjects had a right to be informed by the data controller whether he held personal data relating to them and, if so, to be given access to such data. Sections 7 to 9 of the 1998 Act deal with data subjects' right of access. Under section 7(1), subject to sections 8 and 9, a data subject is entitled:

(a) *to be informed by any data controller whether personal data of which that individual is the data subject are being processed by or on behalf of that data controller;*

(b) *if that is the case, to be given by the data controller a description of –*
   (i) *the personal data of which that individual is the data subject,*
   (ii) *the purposes for which they are being or are to be processed, and*
   (iii) *the recipients or classes of recipients to whom they are or may be disclosed;*

(c) *to have communicated to him in an intelligible form –*
   (i) *the information constituting any personal data of which that individual is the data subject, and*
   (ii) *any information available as to the source of those data, and*

(d) *where the processing by automatic means of personal data of which that individual is the data subject for the purpose of evaluating matters relating to him such as, for example, his performance at work, his creditworthiness, his reliability or his conduct, has constituted or is likely to constitute the sole basis for any decision significantly affecting him, to be informed by the data controller of the logic involved in that decision-taking.*

This is more extensive than was the case under the 1984 Act which, in effect, applied to only (a) and (c) above. Because the information provided is more extensive than before and individuals making subject access requests may not realise the scope of the provisions, the Data Protection (Subject Access) (Fees and Miscellaneous Provisions) Regulations 2000 treats a request for any information required to be given as extending to other information required to be given with the exception of the logic involved in any automatic decision-taking unless the individual makes it clear that he or she wants such information. Although a data subject could previously obtain information as to the description of the data, the purposes of processing and the recipients by consulting the register entry, under the 1998 Act this information must be provided in response to a subject access request, together with a description of the source of the data and of any logic employed in certain types of automated decision-taking, if requested.

Subject to the exemptions to granting subject access and other information to data subjects (set out and discussed in the following chapter), this is a significant enhancement in terms of transparency over the 1984 Act. Whilst in respect of information within (b) above, data controllers are likely only to provide the relevant extracts from their register entries, it must be remembered that this information must also be given in respect of automatically processed data exempt from notification and manual files caught by the Act for which notification may not have been sought by the data controller.

Under section 8(2) the obligation to communicate the information constituting personal data in intelligible form requires that a copy must be provided in permanent form unless it is not possible to supply such a copy or if it would involve a disproportionate effort or where the data subject agrees otherwise. It is no easy matter, given modern technology, to think of an example where it would prove impossible to provide a copy in permanent form. The Directive simply requires communication of the data in an intelligible form with no proviso. This simply follows the European Convention for the Protection of Individuals with regards to Automatic Processing of Personal Data 1981, Article 8 of which states, *inter alia*, that any data subject shall be entitled to obtain communication to him of personal data relating to him in an intelligible form.

Obviously, from the data subject's perspective, the ideal response is to be supplied with a copy in permanent form which can be retained by the data subject. Simply being shown the data without an opportunity to take a copy away will make it more difficult for the data subject to verify the accuracy of the data who also may want to double-check some of the information later. Often, it will only be later that the data subject realises the significance of some fact of which he or she may only have an imperfect recollection. If the data subject wants to carry out a second subject access request soon after the first, this may be refused on the basis that the second request, being identical or similar, has been made before the expiry of a reasonable period under section 8(3).

If software used to retrieve and present data is properly designed with a view to complying with subject access requests, supplying a copy in permanent form should not be onerous in relation to data processed by automatic means, subject to the problem of the copy disclosing data relating to other individuals, discussed later. A disproportionate effort may be involved in relation to manual files, apart from the cost of making copies, in that many other individuals may be identified in the copies which may require a mammoth exercise in concealing or erasing part of the information, a process known as redaction. Data controllers may charge, up to a maximum fee, for subject access. Even so, it is questionable whether cost is a relevant factor in determining whether the effort in providing permanent copies is disproportionate. However, and bearing in mind personal data includes image data, whether in a photograph, on video tape, CD, DVD or even on an X-Ray, complying with a subject access request can be quite costly. Factors which may be relevant in determining whether a disproportionate effort is involved include the technical, administrative and organisational measures required to produce a permanent copy. Again, the principle of proportionality is important and any potential compromise of the individual's rights under data protection should be taken into account. The greater the risk to individual's rights by not supplying a copy in permanent form, the greater the effort before it becomes disproportionate. In considering whether a disproportionate effort is involved Munby J said in *R (on application of Alan Lord)* v *Secretary of State for the Home Department* (at para 155).[13]

> *"Section 8(2)(a) exonerates a data controller from 'disproportionate' effort, but in determining what is proportionate one necessarily, as it seems to me, has to have regard to the intrinsic significance of the information whose disclosure is being sought and its importance for the data subject."*

In this case the matter was of some importance to the data subject as his liberty was at stake. The judge also noted that it was clear from the wording of section 8(2) that a copy of the information must be made available (unless impossible or where it would involve a disproportionate effort) and that it will not suffice to provide a summary of the information.

In some cases, the personal data will not be intelligible to the data subject without an accompanying explanation which may, in some cases, be better provided in oral form rather than as a supplementary statement. For example,

---

[13] [2003] EWHC 2073 (Admin).

a person who has undergone medical treatment who wishes to see his X-rays might prefer to have them explained to him by an appropriate health professional such as a radiologist. Providing permanent copies of X-Rays is expensive but data subjects generally want permanent copies, perhaps to take legal advice concerning an allegation of negligence. Unfortunately, some individuals see the subject access rights as a way to short-circuit the legal process of discovery, though this has been frowned on, for example, in *Durant* v *Financial Services Authority*[14] where Auld LJ said (at para 27) that the purpose of section 7 was not to obtain discovery of documents that might assist the individual in litigation.

The data controller can refuse to comply with a subsequent identical or similar request by a particular individual unless a reasonable interval has elapsed; section 8(3). In determining what a reasonable interval is, regard shall be had to the nature of the data, the purposes of the processing and the frequency with which the data are altered. The information to be given must be as it was when the request was received apart from deletions or amendments that would have been made notwithstanding the request.

The maximum fee that can be charged by a data controller in respect of a subject access request is £10 in most cases. For applications to credit reference agencies restricted to data relating to financial standing under section 9, in line with the Consumer Credit Act 1974 which governed such requests, the maximum is £2. There is a sliding scale as regards subject access to educational records where a permanent copy is handed over, rising to a maximum of £50.[15]

Where the request for subject access relates wholly or partly to personal data forming part of a health record and the request is not restricted to data processed or intended to be processed automatically only, the maximum fee is £50 where the data subject is provided with a permanent copy of the data. Originally, this was a transitional provision, reflecting the high cost of making copies of some health data such as X-Rays, scans and tissue samples and it was intended that the maximum fee would be reduced to £10 from 24 October 2001. However, as a result of increasing numbers of subject access requests in respect of health data, it has been decided to keep the £50 maximum until a final resolution of the problem of high costs incurred by data controllers complying with such requests has been resolved.[16] Issues identified as increasing the numbers of requests for access to health data, are:

---

14 [2003] EWCA Civ 1746.
15 Data Protection (Subject Access) (Fees and Miscellaneous Provisions) Regulations 2000.
16 The Data Protection (Subject Access) (Fees and Miscellaneous Provisions) (Amendment) Regulations 2001.

- the consolidation of the provisions of the Access to Health Records Act 1990 relating to living individuals into the Data Protection Act 1998;

- the setting of the maximum fee that may be charged for giving access to medical records at £50 regardless of actual costs incurred by the data controller;

- the development of conditional fee arrangements in litigation ("No Win, No Fee") and an associated increase in personal injuries claims;

- an increased awareness of data subject rights across society.[17]

Data controllers whose business activities make them susceptible to fraud were concerned about the provision of information concerning the logic of their automated decision-taking processes. For example, details relating to an individual applying for credit, such as postcode, employment and housing status, may be submitted to computer software which accepts or rejects the application for credit based upon a weighted assessment of a number of parameters. On the one hand, providing details of the logic could facilitate the activities of fraudsters who would simply be able to discover what the "right" answers are likely to be. On the other hand, it is possible for unfair or prejudicial factors or weightings to be used. The use of factors such as postcodes or the credit rating of a previous occupant of the dwelling now occupied by the data subject in question are inherently unfair even if they are reliable predictors. The dangers were highlighted in *CCN Systems Ltd* v *Data Protection Registrar, Equifax Europe Ltd* v *Data Protection Registrar* and *Infolink Ltd* v *Data Protection Registrar*[18] before the Data Protection Tribunal. The appellants, credit reference agencies, were extracting personal data relating to the financial status of individuals by reference to the current or previous address of the data subject together with financial information relating to any other individual who had been recorded as residing at any time at the same or a similar address as the data subject. The Data Protection Registrar issued an enforcement notice prohibiting the use of such third party data. However, the notice was amended by the Tribunal to allow the use of such data where there was a link between the data subject and the third party, such as a close family tie or financial relationship.

The requirement to be informed of the underlying logic does not apply to all forms of automated decision-taking. It applies where the purpose is to evaluate matters relating to the data subject such as performance at work, creditworthiness, reliability or conduct and has or is likely to constitute the sole basis for any decision significantly affecting him. The 1998 Act closely follows the language in Article 15(1) of the Directive although this states that

---

[17] Information Commissioner, Subject Access and Medical Records: Fees for Access, Guidance Note, 7 November 2001.
[18] All unreported, 1991.

the provisions apply also in relation to decisions having "legal effects" in addition to those significantly affecting the data subject. As the list of circumstances is non-exhaustive, it is not possible, apart from an application of the *ejusdem generis* rule, to predict other forms of purposes that will be caught. Certainly, in the first instance, the data controller is likely to take his own view on this matter, at least until such time as relevant codes of practice are available or guidance is offered by the Commissioner. Of course, any such guidance may be helpful but will not necessarily provide an accurate reflection of the true scope of the legislation on this point any more than it can on any other interpretation of the Act and statutory instruments promulgated under it.

It could be argued that, by addressing the concerns of data controllers about having to provide data subjects with information as to the logic in automated decision-taking, the 1998 Act has unduly compromised this right to information. This is especially so as section 8(5) of the Act excuses the data controller from providing such information if, and to the extent that, the information constitutes a trade secret. This appears to allow the data controller to refuse to provide any information as to the logic if he claims it is, in its entirety, a trade secret. This goes further than the Directive, recital 41 of which states that the right to information as to the logic in any automated decision-taking concerning the data subject must

> *"... not adversely affect trade secrets or intellectual property and in particular the copyright protecting the software; whereas these considerations must not, however, result in the data subject being refused all information" (emphasis added).*

Bearing in mind that the term "trade secret" is incapable of precise definition, data controllers may refuse to supply information relating to the logic of the automated decision-taking claiming it is, in its entirety, together with any information relating to it, a trade secret. Alternatively, data controllers may prepare some bland and generalised description of the logic that is little better than meaningless. The only way this can be tested is if a data subject asks the Commissioner for an assessment, since automated decision-taking, in common with other forms of processing, must comply with the data protection principles.

The maximum length of time to comply under the 1998 Act is the same as before, that is 40 days. One exception is in relation to requests made to credit reference agencies limited to personal data relating to an individual's financial standing, in which case the maximum period is only seven working days.[19] In respect of requests for access to accessible records which are educational

---

[19] Regulation 4 of the Data Protection (Subject Access) (Fees and Miscellaneous Provisions) Regulations 2000.

records within the meaning of Schedule 11 to the Act, the period is 15 school days as defined in section 579(1) of the Education Act 1996.

It could be argued that the 40-day period is unduly long, especially where the data are stored on computer. However, the data controller is not obliged to comply unless the request has been made in writing and the fee paid, (unless exempt), and he has been supplied with information such as he reasonably requires to satisfy himself as to the identity of the person making the request under section 7(3). Any failure to comply with a subject access request may result in a court order for compliance under section 7(9) of the Act.

Data controllers must exercise great care in verifying the identity of the individual making the request. In one case, a private investigator obtained personal information relating to famous people from British Telecom plc by deception and sold some of the information to the tabloid newspapers. She was prosecuted for six offences under section 5(6) of the 1984 Act for procuring the information and six offences under section 5(7) of the 1984 Act for selling the information to her clients. She was fined a total of £1,200.[20] Considering the gravity of the offences, this seems a relatively small fine and may reflect the failure of magistrates to take data protection offences seriously. The maximum fine for a single offence has been relatively low with many fines not exceeding £100. Absolute and conditional discharges account for a significant proportion of outcomes. In one case, a Clerk to the Justices was prosecuted under section 5(1) of the 1984 Act for failing to register. He was, perhaps not surprisingly, given an absolute discharge.[21]

Subject access where another individual would be identified

There are specific provisions which apply when compliance with a subject access request would disclose information relating to another identifiable individual. These are significantly different in comparison with the equivalent provisions under the 1984 Act. This is largely a result of the decision of the European Court of Human Rights in *Gaskin v United Kingdom*[22] discussed below. In some cases, supplying a copy of the personal data to a data subject following a subject access request will disclose data relating to another identifiable individual. In such cases, under section 7(4) the data controller is not obliged to comply with the request unless:

> (a) *the other individual has consented to the disclosure of the information to the person making the request, or*
> (b) *it is reasonable in all the circumstances to comply with the request without the consent of that other individual.*

---

[20] Data Protection Registrar, *Fourteenth Annual Report*, London: Stationery Office, 1998 at 21 & 54.
[21] Data Protection Registrar, *Fourteenth Annual Report*, *op cit* at 54.
[22] [1989] ECHR 13.

Information relating to another individual includes the situation where that other individual is the source of the information sought in the request, for example, where a social worker or person in charge of a home for children in care has written a report on the person now making the subject access request. The above provision does not excuse the supply of as much information as can be supplied without disclosing the identity of the other individual; section 7(5). For example, this may be done by omitting the name or other identifying particulars of that other individual.

In determining whether it is reasonable in all the circumstances to comply without the consent of the other, factors that may be taken into account include, under section 7(6):

(a) *any duty of confidentiality owed to the other individual,*
(b) *any steps taken by the data controller with a view to seeking the consent of the other individual,*
(c) *whether the other individual is capable of giving consent, and*
(d) *any express refusal of consent by the other individual.*

In part, these provisions on subject access where supplying information containing data relating to another identifiable person are intended to comply with the judgment of the European Court of Human Rights in *Gaskin* v *United Kingdom*.[23] In that case, Gaskin claimed he had been ill-treated whilst he was in care. Liverpool City Council kept a confidential file on him and he sought access to records concerning him. The City Council resolved to give Gaskin access provided the persons who were the source of the documents in the file consented. Only 19 out of 46 of these gave their consent and the relevant documents were made available to Gaskin. However, the remainder of the documents, where the contributors refused consent or could not be traced, were not disclosed to him. It was held by the European Court of Human Rights, in a split decision, that this was a breach of his right to respect for his private and family life under Article 8 of the European Convention on Human Rights. Although the United Kingdom could not be said to have inter-fered with his private life, there may be certain circumstances where a positive obligation arose inherent in respect for private life. Whether such an obli-gation arose in a particular case was a matter of balance and, on the basis of the principle of proportionality, required that an independent authority decided whether access should be granted or denied if a contributor to such records withheld consent or did not answer. That had not happened in Gaskin, hence the breach of Article 8.

---

[23] [1989] ECHR 13.

In another case, *M G* v *United Kingdom*,[24] the applicant was denied access to full social records on the basis that the local authority would be in breach of confidence to others, including the applicant's siblings. As the events occurred before the Data Protection Act 1998 came into force, there was no right of appeal to an independent authority and therefore, following Gaskin, there was a breach of the applicant's right of respect for his private and family life under Article 8 of the Human Rights Convention. However, the Court did accept that it might be compatible with that right to withhold documents where consent was lacking.

Where data relating to another identifiable person would be disclosed, the data controller may feel the easiest way to comply with a subject access request would be to omit or conceal information revealing the identity of that other person, that is, to redact that information. However, the data controller may be faced with a dilemma. Does he:

(a) *supply the information after redaction, or*
(b) *seek the consent of the other persons and then, applying the factors in section 7(6) (and other factors that might be relevant to the circumstances – the list of factors in section 7(6) is not exhaustive),*
     (i) *supply the information without redacting it, or*
     (ii) *supply the information after redaction?*

Of course, where the other individuals can be contacted relatively easily and consent, there is no problem and the information may be supplied in unredacted form (although the data controller may still want to redact information which is not within the meaning of personal data).

In *Durant* v *Financial Services Authority*,[25] it was alleged that the defendant had taken a blanket decision to redact the names of all other individuals and this was not reasonable in all the circumstances under section 7(4)(b). Auld LJ said (at para 54):

"... *the protection given by section 7 of the 1998 Act to other individuals when a data subject seeks access under that provision to his personal data, for example where such data may identify another individual as the source of the information. In such a case both the data subject and the source of the information about him may have their own and contradictory interests to protect. The data subject may have a legitimate interest in learning what has been said about him and by whom in order to enable him to correct any inaccurate information given or opinions expressed. The other may have a*

---

[24] [2002] ECHR 627.
[25] [2003] EWCA Civ 1746.

justifiable interest in preserving the confidential basis upon which he supplied the information or expressed the opinion. ... The protection that the 1998 Act gives to other individuals is similarly qualified [as in the Directive], reflecting, in this respect, the principle of proportionality in play between the interest of the data subject to access to his personal data and that of the other individual to protection of his privacy."

As with so much of data protection law, the principle of proportionality is important and it is a matter of balancing the interests of the data subject and those of the other person. Where the other person refuses consent, or is incapable of giving consent or cannot be found, the data controller should go through this balancing exercise. Auld LJ considered that the scheme in the Act raised a presumption that information identifying the other person should not be disclosed without consent. That presumption can be rebutted if the data controller nevertheless considers it reasonable to release that information in all the circumstances including those in section 7(6). Another point is that the question is whether it is reasonable to comply, not whether it is reasonable to refuse to comply. Auld LJ also thought that the data controller was not bound to seek consent although, of course, failure to seek consent may affect the issue of whether it was reasonable in all the circumstances to comply.

In *Durant*, the defendant reviewed its decision to redact all references to other individuals and decided that it could disclose some of the information after balancing the interests involved. However, it maintained that some of the information should still be redacted. In one of those cases, the individual concerned had expressly refused consent because of the claimant's abusive behaviour. The right to privacy of the other individual would be a highly relevant though not determinate factor. However, consideration should also be given to what, if any, legitimate interest the data subject had in having information identifying another individual made available to him or her. Auld LJ said that data controllers should go through a two stage process. First, was the information about another individual necessarily part of the personal data that the data subject had requested? If so, then the second stage leads to the section 7(4) balance. In the end, the court accepted that the remaining redactions were appropriate as they were of little legitimate value to the claimant.

In *R (on application of Alan Lord) v Secretary of State for the Home Department*,[26] the claimant had been convicted of murder and was sentenced to life imprisonment. He was a Category A prisoner. Category A prisoners are considered dangerous and every effort is made to prevent their escape. Three categories of risk of escape exist for such prisoners, standard, high and exceptional. Although he had been in the higher categories, the claimant at the relevant

[26] [2003] EWHC 2073 (Admin).

time was in the standard category. Annual reviews are made of such prisoners which result in the writing of a report called a Category A Report by prison officers and others, such as psychiatrists. Normally, prisoners are not shown these reports but instead are shown a summary, known as the "gist" in which the identities of the report writers are kept anonymous. There was, therefore, an expectation of confidentiality by those writing the reports. The claimant sought full disclosure of the Category A Reports concerning him and he applied for subject access under the Data Protection Act 1998. A substantial amount of information was provided but not the Category A Reports. He then complained to the Information Commissioner but this was still under investigation when he applied to the court under section 7(9) of the Act seeking an order for compliance with his request for access to the reports in full or subject to such redaction as was necessary for the purposes of section 29(1) of the Act (the exemption for the purposes of the prevention or detection of crime, discussed in the following chapter).

Munby J said that section 7(4) requires a balancing exercise, in this case, balancing the interests of the prisoner against the rights of the prison officers and others who compiled the Category A Reports. He also noted that section 8(2)(a) (refusal to supply a copy of the information sought on the basis of disproportionate effort) involves a similar type of balancing exercise, albeit that the balance that has here to be struck is between the interests of the prisoner and what might be called the administrative interests of the prison service. The authors of the Category A Reports had not consented to their disclosure to the claimant. Munby J said (at para 148):

> "I accept [counsel's] argument that the proper balance called for by section 7(4)(b) between the legitimate interests of the prisoner and of the authors of the reports can be held by a system of targeted non–disclosure. The blanket policy of non–disclosure of anything which is not contained in the gist is not, in my judgment, a proportionate response to the undoubted problems and concerns identified by [two witnesses]. The Secretary of State's present blanket policy is not, in my judgment, a 'necessary measure' to safeguard – in my judgment, and for all the reasons given by [counsel], it goes significantly further than is necessary to safeguard – the interests of the authors of the reports."

However, Munby J went on to accept that there may be cases where the Home Secretary could rely on section 7(4) to refuse access to reports, for example, where there is a danger of revenge attacks. The problem was that there was a blanket policy and consideration to disclosure was not made on a case by case basis. Munby J ordered disclosure of the reports in full and in unredacted form.

The fact that there must be a balance between the interests of the data subject and the interests of other individuals is reinforced by recital 42 of the Directive to the effect that Member States may, in the interests of the data subject or so as to protect the rights and freedoms of others, restrict rights of access and information.

Section 7(9) provides that a court may order compliance with a request under the subject access provisions in section 7 where a data controller has failed to comply with the request. In *Durant*, it was confirmed that the court does indeed have discretion to order compliance. Auld LJ noted that it could even be possible for a court to hold that it was reasonable to comply with a subject access request on the basis of section 7(4) and yet refuse to order compliance with the request without the other individual's consent.[27] The court also has a discretion under section 14 in relation to ordering rectification, etc.[28] In particular, the court will not exercise its discretion where to do so would amount to an abuse of process by a litigant, for example, "... *in order to ventilate challenges which were clearly apt to be ventilated in earlier proceedings in which the claimant was a party*".[29]

Credit reference

Under section 9 an application to a credit reference agency is taken to be limited to financial information relating to the data subject unless a contrary intention is expressed. The data controller must include a statement of the data subject's rights under section 159 of the Consumer Credit Act 1974, to the extent required as prescribed. Section 62 of the Data Protection Act 1998 modifies section 158 of the Consumer Credit Act 1974 and the right under that section to obtain a copy of a file applies only in relation to partnerships. For other individuals the right to a copy of the file is under section 9 of the 1998 Act although the right of correction of wrong information remains under section 159 of the Consumer Credit Act. Basically, the regime seems much as before but credit reference agencies present particular problems in terms of personal data.[30] Particular concerns relate to the use and disclosure by credit reference agencies of "white data" and "grey data", the former being data indicating that a data subject has a good credit record and the latter being where the data indicate that the data subject has been in default but not for a period sufficient for the data to be regarded as "black data".

Another concern relates to the use by credit reference agencies of personal data of other persons with the same last name at the same address of a person

[27] See also *R (on application of Alan Lord)* v *Secretary of State for the Home Department* [2003] EWHC 2073 (Admin).
[28] *R v Wozencroft* [2002] EWHC 1724 (Fam).
[29] Per Wilson J in *Wozencroft*.
[30] See for example, *Equifax Europe Ltd* v *Data Protection Registrar* (Case DA/90 25/49/7) 28 June 1991.

seeking financial credit. Before *Equifax* and other cases in the early 1990s, processing of information about other persons previously at the address who had different names was deemed to be unfair. One problem for credit reference agencies was that information about such third parties was useful in predicting whether the person applying for credit was likely to default on a loan. There was also a problem because individuals applying for subject access would be given a copy of their personal data that might also identify other persons in the household. Under the present regime, use of data of others with the same last name in the same household still applies, though under new proposals, lenders will be given only data about the person applying for credit and financial partners. Credit reference agencies will give individuals an opportunity to opt out and be assessed in their own right, subject to conditions.[31]

The law of breach of confidence has long since regulated the disclosure of personal data by financial institutions. In *Tournier* v *National Provincial and Union Bank of England*[32] it was held that a bank could disclose information about its customers where the disclosure was required by law, where there is a public duty to disclose, where the interests of the bank require disclosure, or where the customer has consented, expressly or impliedly. Apart from the duty of confidence and the data protection principles, particularly that processing must be fair and lawful, there are further restrictions on disclosures of white data and grey data. The *Tournier* principles are limited in that disclosure may be permitted if it is in the institution's interests, which it may be if it intends to disclose white data, for example to a credit reference agency in return for subsequent disclosures from the credit reference in respect of other data subjects. Of course, white data are valuable in relation to activities other than the decision to grant credit, such as in targeted marketing. Except where the data subject concerned has submitted an application for credit, any other disclosure of white data could be perceived as an infringement of the basic right to privacy under Article 8 of the Human Rights Convention. At one time, the Data Protection Registrar considered that disclosure of white data and grey data without the consent of the data subject did not fall within the third *Tournier* exception.[33]

As noted above, credit reference agencies must comply with a subject access request within seven working days where the request is restricted to data relating to the financial standing of the individual making the request.

---

[31] Information Commissioner, *Annual Report and Accounts July 2004*: London, Stationery Office, 2004, HC669, pp.38–40).
[32] [1924] 1 KB 461.
[33] Data Protection Registrar, *Tenth Annual Report*, London: HMSO, 1994 at 66.

Enforced subject access

Enforced subject access occurs, typically, where a prospective employee is required to carry out a subject access request with the police to confirm to the employer that the individual does not have any previous criminal convictions or police cautions before a job offer is confirmed. This practice has been deprecated by the Data Protection Registrar under the 1984 Act. The Information Commissioner also disapproves of this practice. An example, of the views of the then Data Protection Registrar can be found in the Data Protection Registrar's *Tenth Annual Report*, London: HMSO, 1994 at p.24. In the year to March 1994, there were some 11,500 subject access requests made in respect of the Police National Computer System, the majority of which were believed to be enforced subject access requests.

This practice can result in serious injustice. For example, in *R v Chief Constable of 'B' ex parte R*,[34] R, who was 29 years old at the time, wanted to travel to a foreign country to teach English to adults and had to apply for a visa. He was required by the Consulate General of that country to provide a certificate of prosecution and conviction history. Unfortunately, R had a spent conviction for a minor offence of theft committed when he was 19 years old for which he received a conditional discharge and was ordered to pay compensation. Although the Chief Constable supplied a statement to the effect that R had "no citeable convictions", it was not on the standard form issued under the Data Protection Act 1984 as required by the Consulate General. This form would show R's spent conviction (the Code of Practice for Data Protection used by the Association of Chief Police Officers generally requires "reportable" offences to be retained for 20 years, even though some will be spent convictions). However, the Data Protection Act 1984 contained no discretion to exclude some information from being provided under a subject access request and, according to Laws LJ in the Divisional Court of the Queen's Bench Division, section 21 of that Act clearly required all the information constituting the personal data to be supplied. Any conflict with the Rehabilitation of Offenders Act 1974 was removed by section 26(4) of the 1984 Act which stated that the subject access provisions apply notwithstanding any enactment or rule of law prohibiting or restricting disclosure or withholding information. The judge expressed his sympathy for *R* whom he described as having lived down his conviction, gaining a series of academic and professional qualifications and subsequently leading an exemplary and productive life.

In the above case, Laws LJ said it was no comfort to the applicant for the enforced subject access that legislation is in place which is intended to obviate the problems he had encountered. This was not strictly true as the Bill was yet to be introduced into Parliament and, in its original form it had no restrictions

---

[34] (Unreported) 24 November 1997.

on enforced subject access (the Bill had its first reading in the House of Lords on 14 January 1998). Nor did the Data Protection Directive mention enforced subject access except, perhaps, obliquely by requiring subject access to be "without constraint"; Article 12(a). Provisions dealing with enforced subject access were included in the Bill in an amendment in the House of Lords.

Although giving employers access to criminal records can be justified in some cases, such as where a potential employee will work with children or vulnerable persons, widespread and uncontrolled use of it undermines the principle of rehabilitation of offenders. It was generally welcomed therefore that the Data Protection Act 1998, as enacted, made enforced subject access a criminal offence. However, section 56 has not been brought into force and it seems increasingly unlikely that it will be brought into force in the near future. In practical terms, section 56 cannot be brought into force until certain provisions of the Police Act 1997 dealing with certificates of criminal records and the like are brought into force.[35] There are difficulties in that the Criminal Records Bureau is in place in England and Wales and there is similar provision in Scotland but there are no plans to bring in its equivalent in Northern Ireland. Bearing in mind the unhappy outcome of the above case, it is regrettable that there will be any further delay to bringing section 56 into force.

When brought into force, section 56, will apply in relation to the recruitment of another as an employee, the continued employment of another person, any contract for the provision of services *by another person*, or the provision of goods, facilities or services *to any person* (this extends also to the supply of a relevant record by a third party). It covers "relevant records", being those showing convictions and cautions where the data controller is a specified chief officer of police or the Secretary of State. Also included are specified functions of the Secretary of State such as under section 92 of the Powers of Criminal Courts (Sentencing) Act 2000, the Prison Act 1952, the Social Security Contributions and Benefits Act 1992, the Social Security Administration Act 1992, the Jobseekers Act 1995 or in relation to certificates of criminal records under Part V of the Police Act 1997 (with necessary amendments for Scotland and Northern Ireland).

The offence will be one of strict liability. However, the provisions will not apply where the requirement is authorised or required by law or court order or justified as being in the public interest but this does not include the ground that it would assist in the prevention or detection of crime. Specific provision will be made to allow enforced subject access in specific cases.

---

[35] Section 75(4) of the Data Protection Act 1998. See also the explanatory note to the Data Protection Act 1998 (Commencement Order) 2000.

Requiring someone to provide a health record is controlled under section 57, which is in force. Any term or condition in a contract is void in as much as it purports to require the supply of, or producing to another person, a record, copy or part of a record consisting of information contained in any health record as defined in section 68(2). A health record is one containing information relating to the physical or mental health or condition of an individual which was made by or on behalf of a health professional. "Health professional" is widely defined in section 69. There is no criminal sanction for what is effectively enforced subject access to health records.

Subject access fees

The subject access fees are set out in the Data Protection (Subject Access) (Fees and Miscellaneous Provisions) Regulations 2000. The general rule is that the maximum fee which can be charged is £10 under regulation 3. However, where the request relates only to the financial standing of the data subject and is made to a credit reference agency, the maximum fee is £2. These fees mirror the position immediately prior to the coming into force of the 1998 Act.

Where access is requested to educational records under regulation 5, no fee may be charged unless a copy of the information constituting the personal data in permanent form is supplied to the data subject as a means of complying with the requirement in section 7(1)(c)(i) of the Act. Where this is so the fee structure in the Schedule to the regulations applies. Where the copy includes material in any form other than a record in writing on paper (for example, on magnetic disk in digital form), the maximum fee is £50. However, where the copy consists solely of a record in writing on paper, a sliding scale applies and the maximum fee varies from £1 if the copy comprises fewer than 20 pages to £50 where the copy comprises 500 or more pages.

There were some transitional provisions in relation to requests in connection with health records. Where the request related wholly or partly to personal data forming part of an accessible record, being a health record for the purposes of section 68(2) of the Act and did not relate exclusively to data within section 1(1)(a) and (b) (automatically processed data) and the request was made before 24 October 2001, the maximum fee was £50 where compliance with giving access to the data requires a copy in permanent form to be supplied to the data subject. However, because of the growing number of subject access requests in respect of health data and the high costs in complying with such requests, the Data Protection (Subject Access) (Fees and Miscellaneous Provisions) (Amendment) Regulations 2001 retained the £50 maximum.

In other cases where access is requested to accessible health records, the data controller can make no charge if at least part of the record was made after the beginning of the period of 40 days immediately preceding the date of the request. In making the request, an individual may specify that the request relates only to data made within that 40 day period. Of course, accessible records are unstructured manual data, not being within (a), (b) or (c) of section 1(1) of the Act (the definition of "data").

CONTROL OVER PROCESSING ACTIVITY

Prior to the implementation of the Data Protection Act 1998, individuals had relatively little control over processing of personal data. Areas of law other than data protection law may have been appropriate in a few cases, such as the laws of breach of confidence, copyright and defamation but, generally, the 1984 Act failed to empower individuals in this respect. Providing a data user kept his processing within the principles and his registered particulars, the data subject had little effective control. The 1998 Act, in line with the Data Protection Directive, has significantly changed this.

A data subject now has the right to object to processing likely to cause substantial damage or substantial distress (to him or her or to any other person), an absolute right to prevent processing for the purposes of direct marketing and can prevent certain forms of automatic decision-taking. Furthermore, as noted in previous chapters, the data subject's consent may be required in some cases, for example, as being one of the conditions for processing. Another aspect is that the meaning of "personal data" and "processing" are very much wider than was the case under the previous law.

In the lead-up to the 1998 Act, many data controllers expressed concern at the inclusion of provisions giving data subjects rights to object to or prevent processing of their personal data or to withhold consent to the processing of their personal data. The spectre of individuals interfering with or preventing the processing of personal data was raised. However, it is probably true to say that the substance of the new law and the experience under it is less fearsome for data controllers than was feared during proposals for the Data Protection Directive.

RIGHT TO PREVENT PROCESSING LIKELY TO CAUSE SUBSTANTIAL DAMAGE OR SUBSTANTIAL DISTRESS

Under section 10(1) of the Data Protection Act 1998, a data subject can require the data controller to cease or not to begin processing for a specified purpose or in a specified manner on the ground that, for specified reasons, it is unwarranted as causing or being likely to cause substantial damage or substantial distress to him or another. However, this right does not apply to processing under conditions 1 to 4 in Schedule 2, being processing:

- where the data subject has given consent;

- where necessary in relation to a contract;

- where necessary for compliance with a legal obligation; or

- where necessary to protect the vital interests of the data subject.

The Secretary of State may order other exceptions, though none have yet been ordered. It is no easy task to think of examples where this right would apply bearing in mind that the first data protection principle requires processing to be fair and lawful. It is self-evident that processing that is fair is unlikely to cause damage or distress. The government Consultation Paper on the Data Protection Directive gave an example, being where personal data might be disclosed in such a way that in practice it might come into the hands of a person known to the data subject but did not elucidate further.[36] Presumably an example could be where the data subject in question has an embarrassing illness, is terminally ill or has a criminal record.

Where the right was most likely to have proved important is where processing is for journalistic purposes but it is severely curtailed in this respect. There are numerous exemptions from the new law for processing which is for the "special purposes" being, under section 3, the purposes of journalism and artistic and literary expression. By virtue of section 32(2), exemption is from all the principles (except the seventh dealing with security measures): subject access; the right to prevent processing likely to cause substantial damage or substantial distress; rights in relation to automated decision-taking and some of the rights of rectification, blocking, erasure or destruction of personal data. These exemptions apply only if compliance is incompatible with the special purposes and the processing is undertaken with a view to publication and the data controller reasonably believes that publication is in the public interest, having regard to the special importance of the public interest in freedom of expression. Otherwise, the exemptions do not apply and, importantly, individuals may still have a right to compensation for damage and/or distress as discussed later in this chapter. Although an individual may not be able to prevent processing for the special purposes, he may be entitled to compensation if he can show that the data controller wrongly relied on the exemption.

To give effect to the right, the data subject has to give notice in writing to the data controller, specifying the purpose or manner of processing objected to

---

[36] Home Office (1996) *Consultation Paper on the EC Data Protection Directive*, at p.30.

and the reasons why he or another is likely to be caused substantial damage or substantial distress. Within 21 days, the data controller must give written notice stating that he has complied with the data subject's notice or intends to do so or stating why he considers the notice unjustified to any extent and the extent, if any, to which he has complied or intends to comply. As with other provisions involving data subjects' rights, the right is backed by the power of the court to order compliance. If the data subject does not exercise his or her right to prevent processing under section 10(1), this does not prejudice his or her other rights.

Impact on the laws of defamation and passing off

The law of defamation gives a person a cause of action in respect of published information or words concerning him, directly or by innuendo, which "*tend to lower the plaintiff in the estimation of right thinking members of society generally*".[37] Although there is no satisfactory single definition of defamation, it is tested through the eyes of the ordinary, reasonable person and there will be no remedy where some people see or read the information carelessly or incompletely. In *Charleston* v *News Group Newspapers*,[38] a Sunday newspaper carried a photograph of a man and a woman who appeared to be engaged in sexual intercourse. Superimposed on the photographs were images of the faces of the claimants, actors who played Harold and Madge Bishop in the television soap *Neighbours*. The captions ran "*Strewth! What's Harold up to with our Madge?*" and "*Porn Shocker for Neighbours Stars*". The text underneath made it clear that the image had been produced as part of a pornographic computer game which had used the images of the claimants without their permission.

The House of Lords held that the article as a whole was not defamatory, rejecting the argument that the headlines and photographs could found a claim in libel in isolation from the related text even though Lord Bridge accepted that some readers would not read the text. Those readers, who might not take the trouble to read the text to discover what the article was about, according to Lord Bridge, could hardly be described as "*ordinary, reasonable, fair minded readers*". This case shows a serious failing in the law of defamation as, although held not to be defamatory, the publication would almost certainly have caused the claimants substantial distress.

The law of passing off is unlikely to be much help in such situations either because of the requirement for a common field of activity or because no account is taken of whether "*a moron in a hurry*" might be fooled by the defendant's misrepresentation.[39] However, in *Alan Kenneth McKenzie Clark* v

---

[37] Per Lord Atkin in *Sim* v *Stretch* [1936] 2 All ER 1237.
[38] [1995] 2 AC 65.
[39] Per Foster J in *Morning Star Cooperative Society Ltd* v *Express Newspapers Ltd* [1979] FSR 113.

Associated Newspapers Ltd,[40] the late Alan Clark MP was successful in a passing off action (and also in respect of false attribution of authorship under copyright law) after complaining about a spoof diary which appeared in the London Evening Standard based on what a journalist imagined Alan Clark might record in his Diary. The newspaper column was headed *"Alan Clark's Secret Political Diaries"* and included a photograph of Alan Clark. Below was a statement identifying the journalist as the author and the basis for the articles. Nevertheless, the court held that, to be actionable as passing off, the deception had to be more than momentary and inconsequential and the article had to be looked at as a whole to decide whether a substantial number of readers would think that Alan Clark had written the articles. Nor was it a defence to claim that readers of the column would not be misled had they been more careful. In the event, the defendant was permitted to continue to publish the "diaries" providing the identity of the true author was made sufficiently clear. Of course, as Alan Clark had written his own diaries, there was a common field of activity.

With the advent of information technology it is very easy to manipulate text and images. Situations such as the *Neighbours* and *Alan Clark* cases will become more and more common. Such material may be placed on a webpage on the internet, making it available on an unprecedented scale. Data protection law may provide some control over such activities, particularly where the material is placed on a computer situated within the European Economic Area. The definition of personal data under the Data Protection Act 1998 extends to data comprising information which relates to a living individual who can be identified from those data, or from those data and any other information which is in the possession of, or is likely to come into the possession of, the data controller. This includes any expression of opinion about the individual and any indication of the intentions of the data controller or any other person in respect of the individual; section 1(1). "Information" is not a precise term, but Article 2(a) of the Directive states that personal data is defined by reference to identifiers such as an identification number or one or more factors specific to the individual's physical, physiological, mental, economic, cultural or social identity and recital 14 confirms that processing sound and image data are within the scope of the Directive. However, recital 16 limits the scope of this by excluding processing such as video surveillance carried out for the purposes of public security, defence, national security or State activities relating to criminal law or other activities outside the scope of Community law.

If sound and image data identifying living individuals are processed automatically, that is, by computer, or are intended to be so processed, or are or are intended to form part of a relevant filing system, they will fall within the

---

[40] [1998] RPC 261.

scope of data protection law and will be subject to the rights given to individuals. These rights include a right to prevent processing causing or likely to cause substantial damage or substantial distress to the individual concerned. That would certainly be applicable to the *Neighbours* case. Although the right to prevent processing is suppressed where the processing is for the special purposes, which include journalism, it is still available unless the data controller reasonably believes that publication is in the public interest.

Another concern is the use of images and, perhaps, voices of famous deceased persons. The technology already exists to create new films, photographs and advertisements using images and voice patterns belonging to personalities who have died such as Elvis Presley, Marilyn Monroe and Sidney James. Relatives and friends may find these activities particularly distressing. The Data Protection Act 1998 is unhelpful in that "personal data" are defined as data which relate to a living individual by section 1(1). There is a precedent for giving "rights" to deceased persons as, under copyright law, there is a right not to have a work falsely attributed to a person as author or film director – section 84 of the Copyright, Designs and Patents Act 1988. This right endures for 20 years after the death of the person falsely attributed and is exercisable by his personal representatives. It might apply in some cases where there is an underlying copyright work and the personality could be taken to be the author of the work. It is perhaps a pity that limited data protection rights should have been secured for a reasonable period of time for recently deceased persons, enforceable by their personal representatives or administrators. Such rights would not be onerous to respect. The Directive defines data subjects as being identifiable natural persons. "Natural" can mean having a physical existence as opposed to a spiritual one. It seems unlikely that this extends to recently deceased persons though there appears to be nothing in the Directive to prevent Member States extending at least some of the safeguards to protect the dignity of the recently deceased.

RIGHT TO PREVENT PROCESSING FOR DIRECT MARKETING

To some people, being inundated with junk mail is a real nuisance. Until the 1998 Act came into force there was little one could do about it apart from joining the Mailing Preference Service, operated by the Direct Marketing Association, but even that was not foolproof. As careful as one might be in ticking boxes on forms, objecting to one's personal data being used for marketing purposes, some marketing material still seems to get through. On the other hand, direct marketing is an effective way for commercial organisations to inform persons of their products or services. As the content and use of marketing databases becomes more sophisticated, more effective targeted marketing is possible, delivering marketing material which is far more likely to be of direct interest to the recipient.

On the whole the availability of opt-out registers such as that under the Mailing Preference Service (and the equivalent for electronic communications, discussed in Chapter 14) has been reasonably effective to prevent unwanted marketing materials and information in the United Kingdom. Organisations involved in marketing are required to consult these registers from time to time so they can avoid sending marketing material to persons and organisations choosing to opt-out. The right in the Data Protection Act to prevent processing for direct marketing (and equivalent rights in respect of electronic communications) is a useful supplement to the Mailing Preference Service which does not cover all marketing mailing lists (it is estimated that the Service has around 90 per cent coverage). The Directive contained two ways of controlling direct marketing from the data subject's point of view; Article 14(b). One possibility was the right to object, on request and free of charge. The other was to be informed before personal data are disclosed for the first time to third parties or used on their behalf for the purposes of direct marketing, and to be expressly offered the right to object free of charge to such disclosures or uses. The Directive also required that Member States take necessary measures to ensure that data subjects were aware of the existence of their rights in respect of direct marketing. The Data Protection Act 1998 elects the former approach, giving the data subject a right, by giving written notice, to require a data controller to cease within a reasonable time in the circumstances or not to begin processing his personal data for the purposes of direct marketing – section 11. "Direct marketing" is defined as the communication by any means of any advertising or marketing material which is directed at particular individuals. The right to object is an absolute one, notwithstanding the existence of the Mailing Preference Service. The data controller must give the data subject a written notice within 21 days of receipt of the data subject's notice stating what steps he has taken or will take to comply with the notice. There are no exceptions to this right and, under section 11(2), the court may order compliance if the data controller fails to comply with the data subject's notice.

Unaddressed unsolicited mail is not caught by these provisions as the material is not directed at particular individuals. However, this can be prevented by informing the Post Office which holds an opt-out register for this purpose. The government has no plans to prohibit direct marketing by mail, pointing out that it generates additional work for the Post Office, thereby keeping postage rates lower that they would otherwise be.

Copies of the electoral register are sold to direct marketing companies. In *R (Robinson)* v *Wakefield Metropolitan District Council*,[41] the claimant asked the local authority not to place his name and address on the electoral register as he

---

[41] [2002] QB 1052.

was opposed to it being made available to marketing organisations. This request was refused and the claimant sought judicial review of that decision as failure to complete the registration form was a criminal offence. It was held that section 11 of the Data Protection Act 1998 complied with Article 14(b) of the Directive, which had direct effect, and gave the claimant the right to object to processing for marketing purposes. It was therefore incumbent on the local authority's electoral registration officer to give effect to that right and the Regulations concerning the electoral register had to be construed in the light of the right to prevent processing for the purposes of direct marketing. As a result, the Representation of the People (England and Wales) (Amendment) Regulations 2002 (with equivalent Regulations for Scotland and Northern Ireland) provide for two copies of the register to be kept. A full copy and an edited copy with the names of those persons indicating that they did not want to receive marketing material.

RIGHTS IN RELATION TO AUTOMATED DECISION-TAKING

Decisions taken by computer with no direct human intervention pose real threats in terms of fairness and prejudice to individuals. For example, a person may be denied credit or some other advantage simply because of his post code or because the previous occupant of his dwelling or some other person living at the same address had a bad record as in *Equifax Europe Ltd* v *Data Protection Registrar, supra*. Statistically predictive measures which may find their way into automated decision systems may operate unfairly in individual cases. Unless controlled, automated decision-taking could easily breach the first data protection principle.

In its initial form, the Data Protection Bill, following the Directive, only allowed decisions taken solely by automated means in the context of a contract with the data subject or where authorised by a law which also lays down measures to safeguard the data subject's legitimate interests. In terms of contracts, if the request of the data subject was not satisfied, there had to be suitable measures to safeguard his interests, such as arrangements allowing him to put forward his point of view. Controlled decisions were those producing legal effects concerning the data subject or significantly affecting him and were based solely on the automated processing of data intended to evaluate certain personal aspects relating to him, such as his performance at work, creditworthiness, reliability, etc.; Article 15. The list is not exhaustive. Data subjects were given the right to object to such processing. The mechanism in the Directive was, therefore, to:

1. allow automatic decision-taking (subject, of course, to the general scheme of data protection law);
2. give a data subject a right to object to processing where it produces legal effects concerning him or which significantly affects him where

the processing evaluates personal aspects of the type listed (including ejusdem generis rights);

3. deny a data subject a right to object to processing where the processing is in the context of a contract providing that:
    (a) the data subject's request is satisfied, or if not
    (b) suitable measures exist to safeguard his interests, for example, allowing him to put his point of view;

4. deny a data subject a right to prevent processing authorised by law which also safeguards the data subject's legitimate interests.

The Data Protection Act 1998 has implemented this by having two sets of provisions in section 12. One deals with automated decisions in 2. above, the other with decisions in 3. and 4. above, which are described as "exempt decisions", the reason being that they are excluded from the more generous data subject's rights that apply to decisions in 2. above.

Exempt decisions are covered by section 12(5) to (7). They are decisions which are:

- taken in the course of steps taken:
    — for the purpose of considering whether to enter into a contract with the data subject;

    — with a view to entering into such a contract; or

    — in the course of performing such a contract; or

- authorised or required by or under any enactment.

An exempt decision is also one which is made in such circumstances as the Secretary of State may prescribe by order. No such order has been made.

To qualify as an exempt decision, the condition in section 12(7) must apply. That is that either the effect of the decision is to grant that the data subject's request or steps have been taken to safeguard his legitimate interests, for example, by allowing him to make representations. The Act does not specifically require the data controller to do anything further although, if a data subject's legitimate interests are to be safeguarded, this implies that the representations the data subject makes are taken seriously and action is taken if, for example, the processing would otherwise be unfair. Of course, if the data subject suspects that the processing is unfair, he could apply to the Information Commissioner for an assessment under section 42.

In relation to other forms of automated decisions, that is decisions that are not exempt decisions but are within 2. above (subject to an omission, see later), data subjects are given a right to object to such processing. Section 12(1) states that:

"An individual is entitled, at any time, by notice in writing to any data controller, to require the data controller to ensure that no decision taken by or on behalf of the data controller which significantly affects that individual is based solely on the processing by automatic means of personal data of which that individual is the data subject for the purpose of evaluating matters relating to him such as, for example, his performance at work, his creditworthiness, his reliability or his conduct."

The omission is the reference to decisions producing legal effects on the data subject. To that extent the Act does not fully implement the Directive. Of course, in many cases decisions producing legal effects on the data subject will be set in the context of contracts and will be exempt decisions subject to section 12(5) to (7). However, there may be other decisions producing legal effects which are not in relation to contracts with the data subject. Examples are decisions which affect the data subject's status, (other than in the context of a contract), and which are entitlement to benefits, exemptions or penalties. In an Orwellian world, an example of the latter could be where a convicted offender is sentenced by a computer system which calculates the level of fine or even term of imprisonment.

To give effect to the right to object, under section 12(3), the data subject must serve a written notice on the data controller who must respond in 21 days of receiving it by stating in a written notice what steps he intends to take to comply with the notice. There is no express requirement that the data controller must comply within those 21 days or any other period but the court may order compliance. An appropriate form of words for the notice is to use the language of section 12(1) itself unless the individual is concerned about a type of decision which is not amongst those specifically mentioned. The notice cannot affect the provisions relating to exempt decisions.

Even if an individual has not served a notice, he or she still has other rights in relation to an automated decision, not being an exempt decision. The individual can require that the decision is reviewed. In such cases, under section 12(2)(a), the data controller must notify the individual that the decision was taken on the basis of processing as set out in section 12(1). Under section 12(2)(b), the data subject then has 21 days from receipt of that notification from the data controller, by written notice, to require that the data controller reconsiders the decision or takes a new decision by other means. Again, a court can order compliance with that notice. The only problem is where a data controller fails to inform the data subject that the decision was taken by automatic means. The data controller may believe notwithstanding that the processing in question falls outside the matters described in section 12(1), that the decision is based solely on processing by automatic means. This could be so where the decision concerns something not expressly mentioned in the section. Another problem is where the data controller simply does not inform the data subject of the automated decision-taking. This may be deliberate even though the decision is caught by section 12(1) or it may be inadvertent because the data controller was unaware of the duty to notify the data subject under section 12(2)(a). In such cases, one might wonder how the data subject is to know or even suspect that his or her right to have the decision reviewed are available unless it is apparent to the data subject that this is the case. Furthermore, in practice, few data subjects are likely to exercise their right to object to automated decision-taking.

REQUIREMENTS FOR INDIVIDUALS' CONSENT

For processing to be within the first Data Protection Principle, one of the conditions in Schedule 2 to the Act must be met and, in the case of sensitive personal data, as defined in section 2, one of the conditions in Schedule 3 must also be met. In both Schedules, one of the conditions is the data subject's consent. Therefore, if the data controller has that consent, in either case, this requirement is satisfied. For non-sensitive data, the wording is simply that the data subject has given his consent to the processing, whilst for sensitive data, the expression used is that the data subject has given his explicit consent to the processing of the personal data. From this it would seem that consent may be implied for non-sensitive processing, for example, by the data subject failing to tick the ubiquitous objection to the marketing box on a form he completes, but for sensitive personal data express and informed consent appears to be required. This is reinforced by the language in the Directive which also requires consent to be explicit where sensitive data are concerned and Article 2(h) refers to consent as any freely given specific and informed indication of the data subject's wishes. However, even in terms of sensitive personal data, it may be processed without the data subject's explicit consent if one of the other conditions in Schedule 2 and one of the other conditions in Schedule 3, applies. This will be so in many cases.

In relation to processing non-sensitive data, many data controllers will be able to rely on the condition that processing is necessary for the purposes of the legitimate interests of the data controller or a third party to whom the data are to be disclosed (although this must not be unwarranted in any particular case by reason of prejudice to the rights and freedoms or legitimate interests of the data subject).

Processing with appropriate safeguards by a non-profit making body which exists for political, philosophical, religious or trade-union purposes is one of the conditions for processing sensitive data, which is defined as including personal data relating to political opinions, religious beliefs or other beliefs of a similar nature and trade union membership. However, the data may not be disclosed to a third party without the consent of the data subject. Considering that explicit consent is one of the conditions for processing sensitive data, it seems reasonable to assume that consent here also ought to be explicit, that is, express and informed consent.

Another situation where the data subject's consent may be required is in the context of transfers of personal data to third countries not having an adequate level of protection. A "third country" is one outside the European Economic Area. The term is not used in the Act but derives from the Directive: see Articles 25 and 26. The basic rule is that personal data must not be transferred to such countries, but it was possible for Member States to derogate from this in certain circumstances under Article 26(1). Again, there is a set of conditions and the data controller has to satisfy only one. These are set out in Schedule 4 to the Act. The data subject's consent is one possibility. However, again the ability of the data subject to prevent transfers of data outside the European Economic Area is seriously prejudiced because one of several other conditions may be relied on by the data controller instead of seeking consent. An important one is where the transfer is necessary for the performance of a contract between the data subject and the data controller, or for taking steps at the request of the data subject with a view to his entering into a contract with the data controller or where the transfer is necessary for the conclusion of a contract between the data controller and a person other than the data subject, entered into at the request of the data subject, or is in the interests of the data subject, or for the performance of such a contract; paragraphs 2 and 3 of Schedule 4.

Other conditions include where the transfer is necessary for reasons of substantial public interest or for the purpose of, or in connection with, any legal proceedings (including prospective legal proceedings) or obtaining legal advice or is in order to protect the vital interests of the data subject or the data is on a public register or is authorised by the Commissioner. A further condition is where the transfer is made on terms which are of a kind approved by the Commissioner as ensuring adequate safeguards for the rights and freedoms of data subjects; paragraph 8 of Schedule 4.

Although various forms of processing will be subject to the data subject's consent, this will be so only in a minority of cases as consent is generally only one of a number of alternative conditions. In many cases, except in the case of disclosures by non-profit–making bodies where there is no alternative to consent, an alternative ground for processing can be relied upon by the data controller. That being so, the data subject's right to prevent processing by withholding his consent will apply in some circumstances only, such as where consent to the disclosure of personal data for the purposes of marketing is required.

COMPENSATION

By virtue of section 13, data subjects are entitled to compensation from the data controller for damage resulting from a contravention of any of the requirements in the Act. Although similar in operation, this is much wider than under the 1984 Act as the entitlement to compensation now extends to *any* contravention of the 1998 Act. Compensation for distress is also available where there is also damage or where the contravention concerns processing for the special purposes (journalism, literary or artistic purposes). The right to compensation is tempered by the existence of a defence similar to that under the 1984 Act, being where the data controller can prove that he took such care as was in all the circumstances reasonably required to comply with the requirement which has been contravened.

In some circumstances, claims for compensation under the Data Protection Act 1998 will go arm in arm with claims for breach of confidence. This is understandable as the law of confidence has developed, and is likely to continue to develop, to give effect to the right of privacy under Article 8 of the Human Rights Convention. However, a claim to compensation need not be the result of a breach of confidence. It may result because of the loss of a contract or some other opportunity or benefit because personal data relating to an individual has been lost or is inaccurate. It could be argued in such cases, that the right to privacy is also engaged as the Convention right is widely construed.

A claim to compensation under data protection law may give rise to an award of damages where they are awarded on the basis of some other head, such as a breach of confidence. It would be usual to determine the total award and then to distribute it between the heads of damage, in which case, the award under data protection law is likely to be the smaller. In *Douglas* v *Hello! Ltd*[42] photographs were taken surreptitiously at the wedding of Michael Douglas and Catherine Zeta-Jones. This was held to be a breach of confidence and a breach of the first data protection principle (unfair processing). The couple had sold the sole rights to take photographs to OK! Magazine and strict controls to prevent any unauthorised photography. Nevertheless, someone unknown managed to take some unauthorised photographs. In the award of costs[43] Lindsay J awarded the couple £15,000 for the breach of confidence and only £50 each compensation under section 13 of the Data Protection Act.

If there are two distinct claims concerning the same events, it will not usually be possible to run one after a settlement has been awarded in respect of circumstances such that the settlement really addresses both claims. There

---

[42] [2003] 3 All ER 996.
[43] [2004] EMLR 13.

would have to be a distinct head of damage for the other claim to stand any chance of success. In *Ogle* v *Chief Constable of Thames Valley Police*[44] a claim was brought for compensation under the Data Protection Act in respect of an inaccurate entry on the Police National Computer. An attempt by Thames Valley Police to have the entry corrected to reflect the claimant's successful appeal against the length of his disqualification failed. The claimant had been arrested by Surrey police on the basis that he was driving whilst disqualified and he was held for two and a half hours. However, his disqualification from driving had expired. He settled out of court for £950 with Surrey police in respect of his wrongful arrest. Soon after, he made a claim for compensation under the Data Protection Act 1984 against the defendant on the basis that the data were inaccurate. Although the Court of Appeal recognised that a claim for the common law tort of false imprisonment and a claim for compensation under the Data Protection Act were distinct causes of action, the claim against the defendant under the Act failed. The damage suffered had been met by the settlement and to allow the action to proceed would be an abuse of process.

Compensation may be available where a data controller relies on one of the exemptions under the Act if it is shown that the exemption does not apply, in whole or in part. *Naomi Campbell* v *MGN Ltd*[45] involved newspaper reports of the claimant's treatment for drug addiction which included photographs of her leaving a meeting of Narcotics Anonymous and details of her treatment. At first instance, Morland J found that this was a breach of confidence and a breach of the first data protection principle. He awarded her £2,500 damages and £1,000 aggravated damages in total without distinguishing between the two heads of claim. The Court of Appeal overturned this decision, accepting that the "publishers" defence under section 32 of the Act applied,[46] but the House of Lords reinstated the first instance decision.[47]

Like any claim, it is important to comply with the Civil Procedure Rules, in particular to ensure that the particulars of the claim are concise and set out the facts on which the claimant relies. It is not sufficient to simply claim compensation on the basis that the defendant is in breach of the Act. Concise reference should be made to the facts giving rise to the breach and the provisions of the Act claimed to be breached. In *X* v *Chief Constable of Greater Manchester*[48] a large number of claims were made against the defendant in respect to a murder investigation involving the claimant, who had undergone a gender re-assignment. One of the claims was headed "Actual Malice" and was a claim to compensation under the Data Protection Act 1984 (it should

---

[44] [2001] EWCA Civ 598.
[45] [2002] EWHC 499 (QB).
[46] [2003] QB 633.
[47] [2004] 2 All ER 995.
[48] [2004] EWHC 262 (QB).

have been the 1998 Act) for damage to character and reputation and hurt feelings for a breach of the Act by the defendant. As with most of the other claims, this was vague in the extreme and it was hard to know the nature of the cause of action. The statement of case was struck out as disclosing no cause of action and as being an abuse of process.

Compensation for distress is not available in the absence of damage save where processing for the special purposes is concerned. However, an application under Article 8 of the Human Rights Convention might overcome this problem. In *M G* v *United Kingdom*[49] the European Court of Human Rights awarded 4,000 euros to the claimant who had been given only limited access to social records.

RIGHTS IN RELATION TO INACCURATE DATA, ETC.

Section 14 of the Act gives data subjects a right to rectification, blocking, erasure or destruction of personal data. The 1984 Act was in terms of rectification or erasure only. "Blocking", although not defined in either the Directive or the 1998 Act, would appear to cover automatic processing where the data in question are not deleted but are marked or flagged as not to be processed. Thus a number of entries in a database of individuals may be so marked such that report-generating software ignores those entries when producing a specific report. The use of the word blocking may reflect the practicalities of computer software whereby, in some systems, an entry may appear to be deleted but in reality still exists but is suppressed from further processing. The inclusion of the word "destruction" is to cover the destruction of manual files, whether relevant filing systems or accessible records.

There are two forms of the right. The first applies in respect of data that are inaccurate. The second form applies where the data subject has suffered damage resulting from any contravention of the Act such that the data subject would be entitled to compensation under section 13. This second right to have data rectified, etc. could apply where the data subject has suffered damage as a result of the data being excessive for the purposes of the processing or where the data are accurate but processed unfairly in breach of the first data protection principle. Both forms of the right require the data subject to apply to a court for the remedy.

The first form of the right is examined first. Under section 70(2), data are inaccurate if they are incorrect or misleading as to any matter of fact (this is the same definition as under the 1984 Act). Inaccurate data may be ordered by a court, on application by the data subject, to be rectified, blocked, erased or

---

49 [2002] ECHR 627.

destroyed if the court is satisfied that they are inaccurate. This extends to other data which contain an expression of opinion about the data subject which is based upon such inaccurate data; section 14(1). It would seem that a statement of intention based on inaccurate data is not within the right. That seems reasonable because the "accuracy" of an intention can only be determined with the benefit of hindsight.

Paragraph 7 of Part II of Schedule 1 (interpretation of the principles) states that it is not a contravention of the fourth principle (data shall be accurate and, where necessary, kept up to date) if the data accurately record information given by the data subject or a third party where, having regard to the purpose or purposes for which the data were obtained and further processed, the data controller has taken reasonable steps in the circumstances to ensure the accuracy of the data and, if notified by the data subject of his view that the data are inaccurate, the data indicate that fact. Where this is the case, the court may instead of ordering rectification, etc., require a supplementary statement of the true facts. If data accurately record information received or obtained from the data subject or a third party but paragraph 7 of Part II of Schedule 1 does not apply (for example, where the data controller has failed to take reasonable steps to ensure accuracy), the court may, instead of ordering rectification etc., make an order to secure compliance with or without a further order for a supplementary statement of the true facts; section 14(2).

Under section 14(3), where a court has made an order for rectification, blocking, erasure, or destruction, if satisfied that the data are inaccurate, it may, where it considers it reasonably practicable, require that third parties to whom the data have been disclosed are notified accordingly by the data controller. In determining whether it is reasonably practicable to inform third parties of the inaccuracy, regard is to be had, in particular, to the number of persons who would have to be notified. (In the Directive third parties are required to be notified unless it proves impossible or involves a disproportionate effort.)

The second form of the right of rectification etc. provides a court with a general power to order rectification, blocking, erasure or destruction where the data subject has suffered damage (such that there is a right of compensation under section 13) and where there is a substantial risk of further contravention in respect of those data in such circumstances. This could apply, for example, where data are excessive or have been kept longer than is necessary for the notified purposes of processing or where the processing activity itself does not conform because it is unfair, unlawful or where none of the conditions allowing processing exist.

In addition to a court order in the second form of the right, the court may, where it considers it to be reasonably practicable, order the data controller to notify third parties to whom the data have been disclosed of the rectification, blocking, erasure or disclosure. In the context of the second form of the right, the court could order that third parties be notified even though the data are accurate but otherwise objectionable, such as being excessive. As with the first form of the right, in determining whether third parties should be notified, regard is to be had in particular to the number of persons who would have to be informed.

There is a transitional right of rectification, etc. in respect of exempt manual data under section 12A. This curious section is inserted by paragraph 1 of Schedule 13 to the Act. It is intended to give equivalent rights in respect of manual data that were in existence before 24 October 1998, the latest date for implementation of the Directive. There is also a right under section 12A to require a data controller to cease processing exempt manual data in a way that is incompatible with the data controller's legitimate interests. The effect of these transitional rights, which expire on 23 October 2007, to be replaced by full rights, is described in the following chapter in the section on the transitional provisions.

JURISDICTION AND PROCEDURE

In England and Wales, data subjects seeking to enforce their rights under the Act must proceed in the High Court or a county court; section 15. Where there is an issue as to whether a data subject is entitled to subject access under section 7 (including information as to the logic in any automated decision-taking), the data subject or his representative will not have access to the information unless and until the court determines the matter of right of access in favour of the data subject. However, the court may require that the information constituting the data and, where relevant, the information as to the logic involved in any automated decision-taking, must be made available to the court for inspection; section 15(2). An example of this happening can be seen in *R (on application of Alan Lord)* v *Secretary of State for the Home Department*[50] involving an application for subject access by a prisoner who wanted sight of reports relating to him made by prison officers and others. He had been given summaries (gists) of the reports only. Munby J ordered that the reports be made available to the prisoner in full and unredacted form.

In *Johnson* v *Medical Defence Union Ltd*,[51] Laddie J noted that section 15(2) was not determinative of the question of whether documents should be disclosed according to the discovery rules under the Civil Procedure Rules where they were required for some other purpose, such as a claim to compensation or

---

[50] [2003] EWHC 2073.
[51] [2004] EWHC 2509 (Ch).

rectification under the Data Protection Act 1998. The claimant's application to renew his membership of the defendant union, which provided professional indemnity insurance, had been rejected. He applied for subject access under section 7 but was not convinced he had been given everything to which he was entitled. He applied to the court under section 7(9) for access to further information but also submitted claims under section 10 (to prevent processing likely to cause distress) and section 14 for rectification. He also claimed compensation under section 13 of the Act. When his application for access to further documents was rejected under the Act (on the basis that they were not within the Act, being held in unstructured manual files and, in any case, not being personal data), he applied for discovery under the Civil Procedure Rules to support his other claims.

Laddie J held that, although not determinative, and even though section 15(2) has no direct bearing on whether there should be disclosure under CPR, it does have some indirect impact. As with section 7(4) to (6), section 15(2) reflects the concerns of the legislature that confidential information relating to third parties should not be disclosed to the data subject in some cases. A court should bear these concerns in mind when deciding whether or not to grant an order for specific disclosure and may take a view that disclosure should be refused in whole or in part or the documents ordered to be disclosed should be redacted.

CHAPTER 9
EXEMPTIONS AND TRANSITIONAL PROVISIONS

EXEMPTIONS

There were a great many exemptions from some of the provisions under the 1984 Act. Some were very wide and effectively exempted many from the regime of data protection afforded by the Act. The national security exemption extended to Part II (the notification requirements) and the rights of data subjects under the Act. Other exemptions related to the subject access provisions and others related to the non-disclosure provisions. The crime and taxation exemptions contained examples of both exemptions whilst the exemption in respect of judicial appointments, granted exemption from the subject access provisions only. Urgent disclosures for the purpose of preventing injury or damage to health were exempt from the non-disclosure provisions.

The Data Protection Act 1998, as supplemented by a number of statutory instruments, contains a number of these previous exemptions with necessary changes to take account of the changes in the model of data protection posited under the new Act. However, there are some significant changes and some new exemptions, not previously available. Like before, there are two defined types of exemptions. The subject access provisions become the subject information provisions. Whilst some exemptions are tailor made and relate to one or more of the principles and one or more sections or Parts of the Act, as appropriate, the cross-cutting exemptions are set out in section 27 as follows:

> *'subject information provisions' meaning the first principle in as much as it requires compliance with paragraph 2 Part II of Schedule 1 (providing information to the data subject on collection or in other cases) and section 7 (subject access);*

> *'non-disclosure provisions' means the first data protection principle (but not with respect to the requirement that one of the conditions in Schedule 2 is met and, for sensitive data, one of the conditions in Schedule 3 is also met),*

the second to the fifth data protection principles, section 10 (the right to prevent processing likely to cause damage or distress) and section 14(1) to (3) (right of rectification, etc. in relation to inaccurate data) to the extent that they are inconsistent with the disclosure in question.

If nothing more, these two sets of provisions can simply be seen as a word-saving device. One point of note is that the exemptions are available in most cases only to the extent that the purpose of the exemption would be prejudiced by the full application of the Act and rights under it. So, for example, the data controller is exempt from the subject information provisions in the context of negotiations with the data subject but only to the extent that those provisions would be likely to prejudice those negotiations; paragraph 7, Schedule 7.

Except as provided for in the exemptions, the subject access provisions are unaffected by any enactment or rule of law prohibiting or restricting the disclosure, or authorising the withholding of information; section 27(5).

The exemptions are, for no apparent reason, set out in two distinct places in the Act. Some appear in Part IV whilst the remainder are set out in Schedule 7. The only distinction that can be made is that the exemptions in the Schedule only relate to either the subject information provisions or the subject access provisions. Others, some of which are very important, are set out in statutory instruments. In the context of health, education and social work, section 30 provides that the Secretary of State may make exemptions from the subject information provisions and there are three statutory instruments giving effect to these exemptions. In other cases, the Secretary of State may make further exemptions from the subject information provisions personal data, the disclosure of which is prohibited or restricted by or under any enactment, if and to the extent that he considers it necessary for the safeguarding of the interests of the data subject or the rights and freedoms of any other individual that the prohibition or exemption ought to prevail over those provisions; section 38(1). Under section 38(2), the Secretary of State may by order exempt from the non-disclosure provisions disclosures made in circumstances specified in the order, if he considers it necessary for the safeguarding of the interests of the data subject or the rights and freedoms of any other individual. The Secretary of State is also empowered to make orders in relation to Crown employment and Crown and Ministerial appointments under paragraph 4 of Schedule 7. Some orders have been made and are discussed below.

Two of the exemptions are outside the scope of the Directive (see Article 3(2)) including public security and defence and processing by an individual for a purely personal or household activity. Nevertheless, specific exemptions are included in the Act for national security and domestic purposes. Although such processing is outside the scope of the Directive, there is nothing to prevent Member States making provision for controls or exemptions in relation to such processing, providing other EC legislation is not thereby prejudiced. Indeed, Article 13(1) of the Directive mentions national security, defence and public security as areas where restrictions on many of the rights provided for in the Directive may be permissible. Transitional exemptions are contained in Schedule 8 and are described later in this chapter. Some of these are of only historical interest as the first transitional period expired on 23 October 2001.

Before looking at the exemptions in more depth, it will be useful to set them out very briefly so as to obtain an overall perspective on them and their range and scope (of course, in this form it is not possible to set out the precise scope of the exemption). Unfortunately, it is not an easy matter to categorise them as to the nature of the exemption, as will be seen. Therefore, they are set out in the order they appear in the Act, followed by the further exemptions contained in Orders made under the Act. Although, where appropriate, they will be combined in the narrative that follows Table 9.1, for example, when an order has been made under a provision in the Act. It should be noted that specific exemptions from the need to notify only are set out in Chapter 6 on notification. It should also be noted that some of the exemptions are conditional or subject to other qualifications which are described in more detail later.

A final point of interest is that the power to grant exemptions derives from Article 13 of the Directive which is considerably shorter than the equivalent provisions of the new domestic law. Perhaps the key provision in the Directive, which enables many of the exemptions in the United Kingdom version of data protection law, is Article 13(1)(g) which allows restrictions on certain rights and provisions in some cases, including, where necessary, to safeguard "the protection of the data subject or the rights and freedoms of others".

Table 9.1 *Overview of Exemptions under the Data Protection Act*

Statutory provision	Description	Exemption
section 28	national security	– all the Data Protection Principles – Parts II, III and V of the Act (rights of data subjects, notification, enforcement) – section 55 (unlawful obtaining etc. of personal data)
section 29	crime and taxation	– 1st Data Protection Principle (but not the conditions for processing) – section 7 (subject access) – further limited exemption from the non-disclosure provisions
section 30	health, education and social work	– exemptions from subject information provisions by order (see later)

Table 9.1 *Overview of Exemptions under the Data Protection Act (continued)*

Statutory provision	Description	Exemption
section 31	regulatory activity	– subject information provisions
section 32	journalism, literature and art	– all the Data Protection Principles except for the 7th Principle (security measures) – section 7 (subject access) – section 10 (right to prevent processing likely to cause substantial damage or substantial distress) – section 12 (rights in respect of automated decision-taking) – section 14(1) to (3) (rights to rectification, etc.)
section 33	research, history, statistics	– further processing not incompatible with the 2nd Data Protection Principle (processing only for the purpose for which the data were obtained) – data used for such purposes may be kept indefinitely notwithstanding the 5th Data Protection Principle (data not to be kept longer than necessary for the purposes of processing) – section 7 (subject access) – subject to conditions
section 33A	manual data held by public authorities (from 1 January 2005)	– 1st, 2nd 3rd, 5th, 7th and 8th Data Protection Principles – 6th Data Protection Principle except in so far as it relates to data subjects rights under sections 7 and 14 – sections 10 to 12 – section 13 except as far as it relates to damage caused by a contravention of section 7 or the 4th Data Protection Principle or distress also suffered as a result – Part III (notification) – section 55 (criminal offences)
section 34	information available to the public by or under any enactment	– subject information provisions – 4th Principle (data to be accurate and up to date) – section 14(1) to (3) (rights to rectification, etc.) – non-disclosure provisions
section 35	disclosures required by law or in connection with legal proceedings, etc.	– non-disclosure provisions

Table 9.1 *Overview of Exemptions under the Data Protection Act (continued)*

Statutory provision	Description	Exemption
section 36	domestic purposes	– all the Data Protection Principles – Part II (data subjects' rights) – Part III (notification)

Exemptions contained in Schedule 7 to the Act

para 1	Confidential references by data controller	– section 7 (subject access)
para 2	armed forces	– subject information provisions
para 3	Judicial appointments, honours	– subject information provisions
para 4	Crown employment, etc.	– subject access provisions (by order, see later)
para 5	Management forecasts	– subject information provisions
para 6	corporate finance	– subject information provisions (order adding conditions, see later)
para 7	negotiations	– subject information provisions
para 8	examination marks	– section 7 (subject access) – temporary
para 9	examination scripts	– section 7 (subject access)
para 10	legal professional privilege	– subject information provisions
para 11	self-incrimination	– section 7 (subject access)

Exemptions contained in orders

SI 2000/413	health	– subject information provisions (for specified types of data) – section 7 (subject access)
SI 2000/414	education	– subject information provisions (for specified types of data) – section 7 (subject access)
SI 2000/415	social work	– subject information provisions (for specified types of data) – section 7 (subject access)
SI 2000/416	Crown appointments	– subject information provisions
SI 2000/184	corporate finance	– simply sets further conditions for the exemption under para 6 of Schedule 7
SI 2000/419 and SI 2000/1865	human fertilisation and embryology and adoption records and reports	– section 7 (subject access)

The exemptions will now be considered in more detail.

NATIONAL SECURITY

This exemption is provided under section 28 of the Data Protection Act 1998 and is the most wide-ranging of all and exempts from all the data protection principles, Parts II, III and V of the Act (rights of data subjects, notification and enforcement) and the offences under section 55. Indeed, there is little left of the Act. Even the basic duty of data controllers to comply with the principles under section 4(4) is disapplied. Under section 56, the offence whereby a person is required to supply or for example, produce a record, indicating criminal convictions, still applies though this has not yet been brought into force. Even then, this offence does not apply if required by law or by or under any enactment or if it is in the public interest. A further exemption, with effect from 26 April 2004 is in relation to the Information Commissioner's powers to inspect personal data recorded in the Schengen information system, the Europol information system and the Customs information system.

The exemption applies if it is required for the purpose of safeguarding national security. Note the use of the word "required" when so many provisions of the Act, in line with the Directive, use the word "necessary". Could this mark a shift from an objective test to a subjective one?

For the exemption to apply, a Minister of the Crown must sign a certificate certifying that the exemption is required for the purpose of safeguarding national security. Subject to an appeal to the Information Tribunal, such a certificate is conclusive evidence of that fact. A certificate may even be retrospective as section 28(2) also covers the past. The exemption need not take complete advantage of all the provisions exempted but may be restricted. A certificate may identify personal data to which it relates by means of a general description and may take effect prospectively.

Appeals to the Information Tribunal may be brought in two ways. First, any person directly affected may appeal and, applying the principles of judicial review, if the Tribunal finds that the Minister did not have reasonable grounds for issuing the certificate, the Tribunal may quash it. The second way is an appeal brought by a party to proceedings under the Act in which a data controller claims that a certificate, identifying personal data to which it applies by a general description, applies to *any* personal data. Such an appeal is based on the ground that the certificate does not apply to the personal data in question, that is, these data are outside the scope of the certificate. In such a case, the Tribunal may decide that the certificate does not apply in that particular case otherwise the certificate must be conclusively presumed to apply.

There are evidential presumptions that apply to certificates. A document purporting to be a certificate shall be received in evidence and deemed to be such unless the contrary is proved. A document certified as a true copy shall be evidence of the certificate if it purports to be signed by a Minister of the Crown.

The power to make certificates may only be exercised by a Minister of the Crown who is a member of the Cabinet or the Attorney General or the Attorney General of Scotland. No powers exercisable by virtue of Part V of the

Act (enforcement) may be exercised in relation to personal data exempted under section 28 from the relevant provision. There are special rules of procedure before the Tribunal in respect of appeals arising under section 28. These are discussed in Chapter 11.

The Tribunal, when dealing with appeals under section 28 is a court within section 42 of the Supreme Court Act 1981.[1]

CRIME AND TAXATION

The crime and taxation exemption covers a number of purposes and, in some cases, exemption is from section 7 (subject access), in other cases, exemption is from the subject information provisions or the non-disclosure provisions. In one case partial exemption from the first data protection principle is allowed. The exemption is set out in section 29.

Where personal data are processed for the purposes of the prevention or detection of crime, the apprehension or prosecution of offenders or the assessment or collection of any tax or duty (including impositions of a similar nature), exemption is granted from the first data protection principle (but the conditions for processing in Schedules 2 and 3 still apply) and from the subject access provisions; section 29(1). The exemption is allowed to the extent that compliance with those provisions would be likely to prejudice any of the above purposes. As is usually the case with exemptions under the Act, the exemption is not absolute and some value judgement is required. Thus, if a data controller relying on the exemption is challenged, he must be able to show that it would be likely to prejudice any of the relevant purposes.

As the conditions for processing to be fair in Schedules 2 and 3 still apply, this exemption does not, *per se,* allow processing for the prevention and detection of crime, etc. It simply excuses the data processor from some of the provisions of the Act, in particular, the requirements set out in Part II of Schedule 1 (interpretation of the principles) which relate to the first principle. Thus, the manner in which the data are obtained is not an issue (most of the remainder of the interpretation covers the provision of information to data subjects which may be excused under the subject information provisions in any case). Therefore, it may be perfectly acceptable to deceive a person to provide information about himself in the pursuit of the prevention or detection of crime, etc.

The scope of the equivalent exemption under the 1984 Act came under scrutiny in *Agreement in the Enforcement Action against the Halifax Building*

---

[1] *Re Ewing*, 20 December 2002, Queen's Bench Division.

Society, 6 January 1992 before the Data Protection Tribunal. An individual complained that he had not received all the information he was entitled to following a subject access request. The building society withheld data it considered to be "system security data", claiming the crime prevention exemption applied. The Data Protection Registrar (now Information Commissioner) issued an enforcement notice and the Building Society appealed against it to the Tribunal. It claimed to have been concerned about maintaining the secrecy of its customers' accounts and the desirability of restricting information about these accounts. Eventually an agreement was reached to the effect that the building society would not normally give details of transactions on the data subject's account, card number, computer terminal and location of the automated teller machine in response to a subject access request. Other information would be supplied, however. It was agreed that persons making subject access requests would be informed of this and that the Building Society would consider requests for this other information if there was a genuine need for the data subject to see it. The Building Society also agreed to inform data subjects that they could complain to the Data Protection Registrar if not satisfied with this response.

Under section 29(2), this exemption applies also to anyone discharging a statutory function who has obtained the data from a person who held the data for any of the above purposes. However, the exemption in this case is limited to the subject information provisions only. This might apply where personal data processed by an auditor assessing tax liabilities is later disclosed to and processed by the Inland Revenue. This is reinforced by section 29(3) which provides that personal data processed for any of the purposes under section 29(1) are also exempt from the non-disclosure provisions if the application of those provisions would be likely to prejudice any of the purposes set out in section 29(1). In *James Martin's Application for Judicial Review*, 20 December 2002, discussed in Chapter 7, the disclosure to the partner of previous allegations of physical and sexual abuse of children by the applicant for judicial review was exempt from the non-disclosure provisions under section 29(3) as being for the prevention of crime. To fall within the provisions of section 29, concerning the prevention or detection of crime, the data controller does not have to be a police authority or directly concerned with the investigation of criminal offences, apprehending and prosecuting suspected offenders. In that case, it was a social worker who made the disclosure.

A straightforward example of the application of section 29 can be seen in the case of *R v Chief Constables of C and D ex parte A*.[2] A local authority asked the police force in its area to obtain information from another police force in pursuance of a child access vetting enquiry in respect of an applicant for a job that involved working with children. The information related to previous

---

[2] *The Times*, 7 November 2000.

police investigations into allegations of inappropriate behaviour with children. The job offer was subsequently withdrawn. In an application for judicial review, it was contended that the disclosure was in breach of the Data Protection Act 1998. It was held that, as the personal data were processed for the purposes of the prevention or detection of crime, this clearly fell within the framework of the 1998 Act and the Data Protection (Processing of Sensitive Personal Data) Order 2000. Therefore the disclosures were exempt from the non-disclosure provisions.

Some local authorities, under section 163 of the Criminal Justice and Public Order Act 1994 and section 111 of the Local Government Act 1972 use video surveillance in order to promote the prevention of crime and may disclose copies of video recordings to the media in connection with this purpose. In *R v Brentwood Borough Council, ex parte Peck*[3] a man was filmed walking down Brentwood High Street with a knife in his hand. He later slashed his wrists in a suicide attempt but this was not recorded and he was not charged with any offence. However, the video recording was later shown on television and in a publication and some people who knew the man recognised him. He applied for judicial review but his application was dismissed. It was held that the statutory provisions permitted the local authority to take the actions it had. In any case, the local authority had not known of the objection until after the broadcast. The Directive makes it clear that personal data can include image data and, in such a case, apart from relying on the statutory provisions allowing video surveillance, a local authority acting in the same way should be able to rely on the exemption in section 29 which could include covertly recording the data, not informing the individual that it has been recorded and denying subject access to the data. It should also permit the disclosure to the media if the purpose still subsists. However, the European Court of Human Rights disagreed and held that there was a violation of Article 8.[4] Peck had not been charged with a criminal offence and the Council had taken insufficient care to ensure that his identity was not revealed by the television company or the publisher nor had it sought Peck's consent to the disclosure of the footage. The disclosure was disproportionate and, furthermore, there was a breach under Article 13 of the Human Rights Convention because Peck had no effective domestic remedy (the facts happened before the Data Protection Act 1998 and the Human Rights Act 1998 came into force).

As Peck had not committed a criminal offence, there was no overriding requirement in the public interest justifying the interference with his right to privacy by broadcasting and publishing the images in such a way that he could be identified. Had the commission of a criminal offence been involved, then such publication could be justified, for example, as an attempt to identify the culprit as in the *Crime Watch* television programme.

---

[3] [1998] EMLR 697.
[4] *Peck v United Kingdom* [2003] EHCR 44.

Bearing in mind that data protection law flows from the Council of Europe Convention for the Protection of Human Rights and Fundamental Freedoms ("the Human Rights Convention"), it is not surprising that there are parallels between provisions in the Data Protection Directive and the Convention. In particular, the right to respect for private and family life in Article 8(1) is subject to possible derogation in Article 8(2) which covers, *inter alia*, the prevention of public disorder and crime. In part, section 29 is the expression of that derogation. In *R (on application of Ellis) v Chief Constable of Essex Police*[5] it was accepted that the position under the Data Protection Act 1998 was the same as under Article 8 of the Convention. In that case, the issue was whether an offender naming scheme was within the exemption. Whether it was necessary to include a particular person in the scheme would depend on the circumstances and depended on whether it was proportionate. Lord Woolf CJ said (at para 33):

> "... this is a genuine initiative on the part of the police and that their objective is in the public's interest since it is to reduce crime and increase the confidence of the public in the effectiveness of the police and the criminal justice system generally. We attach considerable significance to this last point. We have very much in mind that we have not only to take into account the rights of the offender who is to be the subject of the Scheme but those of the public as well. It is necessary to remember that the sort of crimes targeted by the Scheme are ones that cause very deep concern to the victims of those crimes as well as the general public. As against this, it is also necessary to take into account the dangers to which Mr Cavadino refers of the Scheme interfering with the rehabilitation of offenders. This is also in the public interest since it reduces crime."

However, the scheme required monitoring, bearing in mind the risks to the offender's family and an informed structured assessment of the risks involved.

Section 64(1A) of the Police and Criminal Evidence Act 1984, inserted by the Police and Criminal Justice Act 2001, allows the retention of fingerprints and DNA samples taken from persons under investigation for committing criminal offences, even though they had been subsequently acquitted or where no charges were brought. Even then, the samples could only be used for the prevention and detection of crime. In *R (on application of S and another) v Chief Constable of South Yorkshire*[6] this was held to be compatible with Article 8 of the Human Rights Convention. Even though the retention of the samples was contrary to Article 8(1), it was justified under Article 8(2). Again, the principle of proportionality was important. The risks to the individual were outweighed by the benefit to the public, bearing in mind that the samples had, in the first

---

[5] [2003] EWHC 1321 (Admin).
[6] [2003] 1 All ER 148.

place, been taken legally. The value of the database of such samples would be significantly reduced otherwise.

The final exemption in section 29 is in subsection (4) in relation to personal data processed by means of a classification system for risk assessment for one of the following purposes:

- the assessment or collection of any tax or duty or imposition of a similar nature; or

- the prevention or detection of crime, or the apprehension or prosecution of offenders in cases;

- where the offence concerned involves an unlawful claim for payment out of public funds or an unlawful application of public funds.

This only applies where the data controller is a "relevant authority", being a government department, local authority or any other authority administering housing benefit or council tax benefit; section 29(5). "Public funds" include funds provided by any Community institution.

HEALTH, EDUCATION AND SOCIAL WORK

Section 30 of the Data Protection Act 1998 gives the Secretary of State the power to make orders granting exemptions from the subject information provisions in the context of health, education and social work. In particular, exemption is allowed from the subject access provisions where compliance would be likely to cause serious harm to the physical or mental health of the data subject or another. Three Orders have been made under section 30, one each for health, education and social work. Although there are some common themes, each is considered separately below.

Health

The Data Protection (Subject Access Modification) (Health) Order 2000 grants exemption from the subject information provisions in one case and the narrower subject access provisions in another case. First, it is important to note what data is covered by the exemption and it is personal data consisting of information as to the physical or mental health or condition of the data subject. The Order does not apply to data exempted from subject access under section 7 of the Act by virtue of an Order made under section 38(1) which empowers the Secretary of State to make further exemptions. One example is personal data concerning human fertilisation and embryology which is covered by its own exemption (see later).

There are two forms of exemption. The first is from the subject information provisions, under Article 4 of the Order. Personal data are exempt if processed by a court and consisting of information supplied in a report or other evidence supplied by a local authority, Health and Social Services Board, Health and Social Services Trust, probation officer or other person in the course of proceedings under a number of rules (for example, the Family Proceedings Courts (Children Act 1989) Rules 1991) if the information could be withheld from the data subject in whole or in part by the court in accordance with those rules. This simply extends the court's power to withhold personal data in such circumstances to relevant data controllers.

The second form of exemption is more complex and applies to the subject access provisions. The basic reason for exemption is that granting subject access would be likely to cause serious harm to the physical or mental health or condition of the data subject or any other person. Where the data controller is a health professional, widely defined in section 69 of the Act, exemption on such grounds is granted to the extent it is required to prevent the likelihood of such harm. However, where the data controller is not a health professional, there is a basic duty to consult such an appropriate health professional. This might be the case where the data controller is an employer in the health sector who employs health professionals or engages health professionals as consultants.

An "appropriate health professional" is the one currently or most recently responsible for the clinical care of the data subject as regards the information subject to the request. Where there is more than one such health professional it is the one most suitable to advise on matters to which the information relates. Where there is no such health professional or the data controller is the Secretary of State and the personal data are processed in the exercise of his functions under the Child Support Acts 1991 or 1995, the health professional is one with the necessary experience and qualifications to advise on matters to which the information relates.

Figure 9.1 shows the working of the exemption where the data controller is not a health professional. The provisions apply in two ways, first that there is a principle that applies – the data controller *shall not withhold* the personal data unless he has first consulted an appropriate health professional regarding the exemption; Article 5(2). If the health professional is of the opinion that the exemption does apply, the data controller may withhold the personal data and rely on the exemption. The second approach is to require that such a data controller *shall not communicate* the personal data unless he has first consulted an appropriate health professional; Article 6(1). However, under Article 6(2), this does not apply if the data controller is satisfied that the data subject has previously seen the information subject to the request or already has knowledge of it. This only applies *to the extent* that the data subject has seen or

is data controller
satisfied data
YES subject has
previously seen
to the extent data information or
subject has seen/has has knowledge
knowledge of it?

NO

has there been a has 6 months
prior elapsed from
YES consultation with **YES** date of prior
opinion exemption an appropriate opinion consultation and
does not apply in health exemption subject access
respect of all professional? applies request & fee?
information

NO   **YES   NO**

first consult is it reasonable
appropriate **YES** in the
health circumstances to
professional re-consult?

NO

'opinion' **NO**
exemption
applies?

YES

COMMUNICATE	WITHHOLD
PERSONAL	PERSONAL
DATA*	DATA

* But see other exemptions described in text

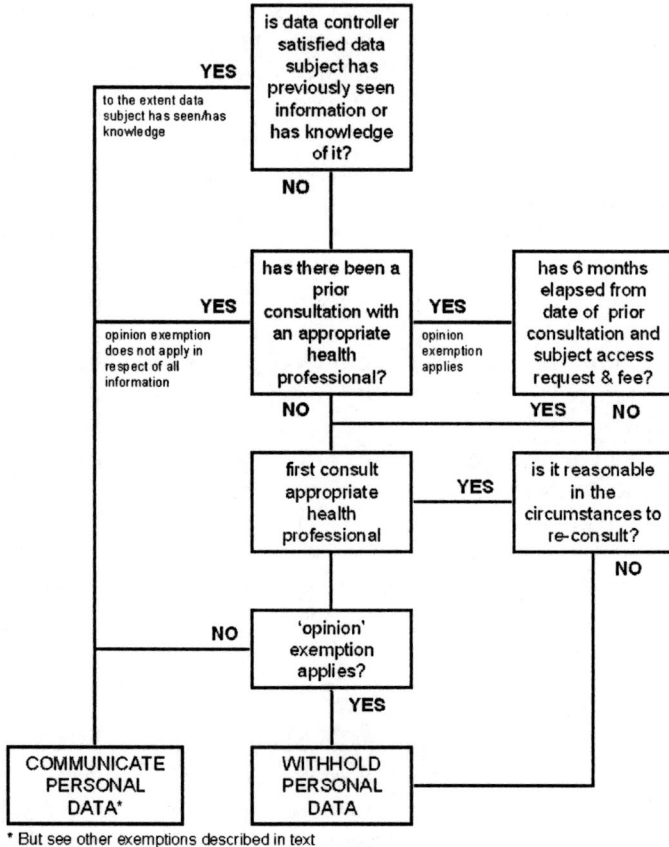

Figure 9.1 Exemption from subject access in relation to a data controller who is not a health professional

has knowledge of it and in some cases, the exemption will apply partially, that is, to those parts of the data comprising information of which the data subject has no knowledge and has not seen.

There are further provisions to allow a data controller who is not a health professional to engage in prior consultations with appropriate health professionals and these are set out in Article 7 of the Order.

The health professional's opinion must be given in writing. Where the health professional is of the opinion that the exemption applies, any prior consultation has an effective life of six months up to the date that the data controller received the subject access request. An exception is where the prior consultation took place not more than six months before but it is reasonable in the circumstances for the data controller to re-consult the appropriate health professional.

To take an example, say that there are three individuals, Amanda, Boris and Christine and the data controller is a health authority. All three have been receiving treatment for schizophrenia. On 29 March 2004, the authority consulted the psychiatrist who has been treating them about whether disclosing their personal data to each of them would be likely to cause each of them or any other person serious harm to their physical or mental health or condition. In other words, did the exemption in Article 5(1) of the Order apply in all three cases? The psychiatrist gives his opinion, in writing, that the exemption applies and, in each case, if a subject access request is made by any of them, the information constituting the personal data should be withheld.

On 18 May 2004, the health authority receives a subject access request from Amanda. Relying on the prior consultation, it withholds the personal data from Amanda. On 22 June 2004, the health authority receives a similar request from Boris. However, because Boris has responded well to treatment and his condition has improved since March, the health authority decides it ought to re-consult the psychiatrist which it does. Even though there has been some improvement to Boris's condition, the psychiatrist still considers access to the personal data would be likely to cause serious harm to Boris's mental health or condition and the request is refused. On 4 October 2004 the health authority receives a subject access request from Christine. As more than six months has elapsed from the last consultation, the health authority must re-consult. It does so and the psychiatrist confirms in writing that the exemption still applies.

Where the prior consultation results in the appropriate health professional being of the opinion that the exemption does not apply, there is no time limit if a data controller wishes to rely on that as confirmation that the exemption *does not apply* and subject access can be granted. Of course, in such a case, the data controller would be wise to re-consult if the circumstances suggest that the exemption might now apply.

A person may be entitled by law to make a subject access request on behalf of another, such as where a person has parental responsibility or where the data subject is incapable of managing his own affairs and that other person has been appointed by a court to manage those affairs, such as by the Court of Protection or where a person has been granted an enduring power of attorney. In such a case, the data controller is exempt from complying with the subject access request if, and to the extent that, to do so would disclose information provided by the data subject in the expectation that it would not be disclosed to the person making the request on his behalf or where the information has been obtained as a result of any examination or investigation consented to by the data subject in the expectation it would not be so disclosed. Exemption is also available to the data controller if the data subject has expressly indicated that the data should not be so disclosed.

As the exemption only applies in respect of personal data consisting of information as to the physical or mental health or condition of the data subject, other personal data held by the data controller, for example relating to name and address, appointment dates and the like, may be caught by the subject access provisions, if within the scope of the Act. The Department of Health made it clear that this exemption should be relied on only in exceptional circumstances.

The underlying basis of the health exemption was confirmed by the House of Lords in *Sidaway* v *Board of Governors of the Bethlem Royal Hospital*[7]. It was accepted that a doctor's duty (and that of a health authority) was to act at all times in the best interests of the patient. In some circumstances, this could require that information be withheld. In *R* v *Mid-Glamorgan Family Health Services, ex parte Martin*[8] a patient was refused access to his health records going back to before 1990 on the basis that it would be detrimental for him, personally, to see those records. The patient argued that there was a common law right of access. However, the Court of Appeal, in refusing the grant access on the "best interests" principle, denied that there was a common law right of access. However, Nourse LJ said that a health authority does not have an absolute right, no more than a private doctor, to deal with medical records any way that it chooses and it must always act in the best interests of the patient.

A data controller may be excused from complying with a subject access request where the personal data would necessarily disclose information about another identifiable individual. However, under section 7(4) of the Act, this does not apply if the other individual has consented or it is reasonable in the circumstances to comply without such consent. Article 8 of the Order adds a further limb to this and for the purposes of health records adds a new paragraph (c) to section 7(4) to the effect that the data controller must still comply if the other individual is a health professional who compiled or contributed to the health record or has otherwise been involved in the care of the data subject as a health professional. Therefore, a data controller must comply with a data subject request in respect of a health record even though it discloses information about the health professional, such as his name and, possibly, his opinion about the patient's physical or mental health or condition.

For the purposes of the Data Protection (Subject Access Modification) (Health) Order 2000, section 7(9) of the Act is substituted. This allows applications to be made to the court in respect of a data controller about to comply or who has failed to comply with a subject access request in contravention of the Order. The application may be made by the person making the subject access request or by any other person to whom serious harm to his physical or

---

[7] [1985] AC 871.
[8] [1995] 1 All ER 356.

mental health or condition would be likely to be caused by compliance with a subject access request in contravention of the subject access provisions, including those provisions and modifications in the Order.

Education

The education exemptions are provided for by the Data Protection (Subject Access Modification) (Education) Order 2000. In some respects this exemption is similar to that applying in the case of the health exemption above. The Order applies to educational records as defined in Schedule 11 to the Act. Typically, it is information relating to past or present pupils at a local authority maintained school or special school as defined in section 6(2) of the Education Act 1996. The information must have originated from or been supplied by or on behalf of an employee at that school, teachers or employees of certain other schools, the pupil himself or the parent of the pupil (or a person having parental responsibility or a person who has care of the pupil; section 576(1) Education Act 1996). The Schedule contains modifications to the definition for Scotland and for Northern Ireland.

There are some exceptions to the above information such as information processed by a teacher for his own use. Furthermore the Order does not apply to data within the scope of the Data Protection (Subject Access Modification) (Health) Order 2000. Also, data exempt under section 38(1) (the power of the Secretary of State to make further exemptions) are outside the scope of the education order. One example is data relating to adoption records.

There is an equivalent exemption from the subject information provisions where information may be withheld by a court in accordance with a provision of one of a number of rules such as the Magistrates' Courts (Children and Young Persons) Rules 1992. The list of rules is less extensive than those under the health exemption.

The exemption from subject access is granted on the same basis as that for the equivalent health exemption, that is that disclosure of the information would be likely to cause serious harm to the physical or mental health or condition of the data subject or any other person; Article 5(1) of the Order. However, there is alternative ground on which the data controller can refuse to comply with a subject access request. This is where the request is made by a person with parental responsibility and the data subject is a child or where the person making the request is entitled to do so on behalf of the data subject because that person has been appointed by the court to manage the data subject's affairs. In such cases, the exemption from subject access applies if information would be disclosed as to whether the data subject is, has been or may be at risk of child abuse. Exemption is granted to the extent that compliance would not be in the best interests of the data subject.

There are modifications for Scotland where the data controller is an education authority and the request relates to information believed to have originated from or have been supplied by the Principal Reporter. In certain cases, the Principal Reporter must be informed that the request has been made and the data controller must not communicate the information to the data subject unless the Principal Reporter is of the opinion that the subject access exemption does not apply.

As noted in the previous section, a data controller may be excused from complying with a subject access request where information about another identifiable individual would be disclosed. Under section 7(4) of the Act, this does not apply if the other individual has consented or it is reasonable in the circumstances to comply without such consent. Article 7 of the Data Protection (Subject Access Modification) (Education) Order 2000 adds a further limb for the purposes of educational records. The data controller must still comply if the other individual is a "relevant person", being as defined in paragraph 4(a) or (b) of Schedule 11 (for example, an employee of a local education authority or teacher or employee at various other types of school, with appropriate modifications for Scotland and Northern Ireland as set out in the Schedule), or the person making the request. The definition of 'relevant person" is inserted into the Act by a new section 7(12). The inclusion of the person making the request is puzzling. It means that a data controller cannot refuse a request if that person would be identified unless to comply would be likely to cause serious harm to the physical or mental health or condition of that person or any other person.

For the purposes of the Data Protection (Subject Access Modification) (Education) Order 2000, section 7(9) of the Act is substituted. This allows applications to be made to the court in respect of a data controller about to comply or who has failed to comply with a subject access request in contravention of the Order. The application may be made by the person making the subject access request or by any other person to whom serious harm to his physical or mental health or conditions would be likely to be caused by compliance with a subject access request, in contravention of the subject access provisions, including those provisions and modifications in the Order.

Social work

Like the two previous exemptions, this one, under the Data Protection (Subject Access Modification) (Social Work) Order 2000, has two forms of exemption. The first is in relation to information which may be withheld by a court pursuant to certain reports or evidence or the provisions of a number of rules. The relevant reports, evidence and rules are set out in paragraph 2 to the Schedule to the Order and the exemption is from the subject information provisions. The second exemption applies in relation to subject access but is not complete and covers the information to be provided under section 7(1)(b) to (d). That is, under this Order, the duty to inform a data subject whether the data controller is processing personal data relating to the data subject still applies.

The type of information within the subject access exemption is set out in paragraph 1 of the Schedule. It is information concerned primarily with social work or obtained in connection with it. For example, it covers personal data processed by a local authority for social services functions and other bodies such as a Health Authority, NHS Trust, the National Society for the Prevention of Cruelty to Children and probation committees. It also applies to data processed by a guardian ad litem appointed under section 41 of the Children Act 1989 or equivalent legislation having effect in Scotland or Northern Ireland as appropriate. The apparent complexity of paragraph 1 to the Schedule is compounded by the differences in legislation and terminology in Scotland and Northern Ireland but the overall effect should be similar. The purpose of the exemption is that full compliance with the subject access provisions would be likely to prejudice the carrying out of social work because of serious harm to the physical or mental health or condition of the data subject or any other person likely to be caused by compliance; Article 5(1). Social work is construed in accordance with the provisions of paragraph 1 of the Schedule.

The Order does not apply to data consisting of information as to the physical or mental health or condition of data subjects where either the Data Protection (Subject Access Modification) (Health) Order 2000 or the Data Protection (Subject Access Modification) (Education) Order 2000 applies.

There are similar provisions to the "health" Order where another person, such as a person with parental responsibility or appointed by the court to manage the data subject's affairs, is legally entitled to request access on behalf of the data subject. In this case expectations or express indications by the data subject that the information would not be disclosed to the person acting on his behalf mean that the exemption applies, even though the test above might not (access would be prejudicial to the carrying out of social work by reason of serious harm to the physical or mental health or condition of the data subject being likely to be caused).

Again, as with the "education" Order there are provisions in Scotland for the Principal Reporter to be consulted in certain circumstances and modification of section 7(4) of the Data Protection Act 1998 where personal data relating to another identifiable individual would be revealed. Here, the data controller cannot refuse access, *inter alia*, if that other individual is a relevant person. For the purposes of the "social work" Order, a relevant person is:

- a guardian ad litem appointed under section 41 of the Children Act 1989 (or the equivalent outside England and Wales) or the Principal Reporter in Scotland;

- a person employed by a body referred to in paragraph 1 in connection with the functions relating to the data in question;

- a person who has provided for reward, a service specified in paragraph 1(a)(i), (b), (c) or (d) of the Schedule (social services functions) and the information relates to that person or he supplied it in his official capacity or in connection with the provision of the service.

REGULATORY ACTIVITY

This exemption is provided for under section 31 and is from the subject information provisions to the extent that the application of those provisions would be likely to prejudice the proper discharge of any of a number of specified functions ("relevant functions") which are designed to protect the public against dishonesty, mismanagement and other malpractice in certain cases, to protect charities and the property of charities and to protect persons in respect of health and safety. The exemption applies like the others within the section in the context of processing personal data in the discharge of the function concerned.

Relevant functions are those conferred on any person by or under any enactment, any function of the Crown, a Minister of the Crown or government department or any other function of a public nature exercised in the public interest.

Section 31(2) sets out the purposes of the functions within this exemption and is fairly self-explanatory. For example, one of the purposes is to protect the public against financial loss resulting from dishonesty, malpractice or seriously improper conduct by, or the unfitness or incompetence of, persons concerned in the provision of banking, insurance, investment or other financial services. In such cases, for example, the exemption would apply to the appropriate regulatory body. The exemption also applies in respect of financial loss due to the conduct of bankrupts and dishonesty, etc. of persons authorised to carry on a profession or other activity. Thus, in many cases, professional bodies will be able to rely on the exemption. This could be useful if such a body is investigating allegations of misconduct by one of its members and would prevent that member finding out, for example, that he is under preliminary investigation.

The exemption in the context of charities is designed to protect charities against misconduct or mismanagement in their administration, whether by trustees or others or for protecting the property of charities from loss or misapplication or for the recovery of the property of charities.

The exemption in relation to health and safety extends to the health, safety and welfare of persons at work or the health and safety of others against risks arising from or in connection with the actions of persons at work.

Section 31(4) covers functions conferred by or under any enactment on certain Commissions or Commissioner such as the Parliamentary Commissioner for Administration and the Commission for Local Administration in England (and equivalent and other bodies in Wales, Scotland and Northern Ireland). The functions are those designed to protect the public against maladministration by public bodies, failures in services provided by public bodies or a failure of a public body to provide a service which it was its function to provide. As above, the exemption is from the subject information provisions, to the extent that compliance would be likely to prejudice the discharge of that function.

Section 31(4A), inserted by section 233 of the Financial Services and Markets Act 2000, covers processing for the purpose of discharging any function conferred by or under Part XVI of that Act on the body established by the Financial Services Authority for the purposes of that Part. Such processing is exempt from the subject information provisions in any case to the extent to which the application of those provisions would be likely to prejudice the proper discharge of the function.

A further exception from the subject information provisions is contained in section 31(5). This applies to the discharge of any function conferred on the Office of Fair Trading which is designed:

- to protect members of the public against conduct which may adversely affect their interests by persons carrying on a business;

- for regulating agreements or conduct having, as their object or effect, the prevention, restriction or distortion of competition in connection with any commercial activity; or

- for regulating abuses of dominant positions in the market.

The latter two, in particular, reflect the controls over anti-competitive practices contained in the Competition Act 1998.

New sub-section (6) was inserted by the Health and Social Care (Community Health and Standards) Act 2003, with effect from 1 June 2004. It applies to personal data processed for the purpose of the function of considering a complaint under section 113(1) or (2) or section 114(1) or (3) of that Act or section 24D or section 26, 26ZA or 26ZB of the Children Act 1989. Such processing is exempt from the subject information provisions in any case to the extent to which the application of those provisions to the data would be likely to prejudice the proper discharge of that function.

Finally, it should be noted, in common with many other exemptions, that the regulatory activity exemption applies only to the extent that the relevant function would be prejudiced by the application of the subject information provisions. It is not necessarily an absolute exemption and, in some cases, the provisions may be complied with in whole or in part without a likelihood of the discharge of the function being prejudiced.

SPECIAL PURPOSES – JOURNALISM, LITERATURE AND ART

Article 9 of the Data Protection Directive required Member States to provide exemptions and derogations where the processing of personal data is carried out solely for journalistic purposes or the purposes of artistic or literary expression. However, the exemptions and derogations must be such as to be necessary to reconcile the rights to privacy with the rules governing freedom of expression. The United Kingdom has tried to reach this difficult balancing act by providing wide-ranging exemptions for the processing of data for the special purposes bearing in mind the special importance of the public interest and the reasonable belief of the data controller that publication is in the public interest and that the provision to which the exemption relates would be incompatible with the publication. Of course, as many judges have said, what is of interest to the public is not necessarily *in* the public interest.

It should be noted when looking at the exemptions provided for under section 32 that the Information Commissioner's powers of enforcement are severely constrained where a data controller claims to be processing data only for the special purposes. Thus, in a court action in relation to the exercise of data subjects' rights or in respect of compensation brought under sections 7(9), 10(4), 12(8), 12A(3) or 14, if the data controller claims that he is processing data only for the special purposes with a view to the publication of material not previously published by him at a time 24 hours before he makes that claim, the proceedings must be stayed until the Information Commissioner makes a determination under section 45 as to whether the special purposes do apply or the claim is withdrawn. Proceedings must also be stayed if it appears to the court that the special purposes apply; section 32(4) and (5).

The exemption itself is very wide-ranging and, under section 32(2), exemption is from all the data protection principles (except the seventh principle relating to security measures) and many of the rights of data subjects, being the right of subject access, the right to prevent processing likely to cause substantial damage or substantial distress, rights in relation to automated decision-taking and most of the rights of rectification, etc. The exemption applies if the processing is undertaken with a view to publication of any journalistic, literary or artistic material and the data controller reasonably believes that publication is in the public interest having regard, in particular, to the special importance of the public interest in freedom of expression. A further requirement is that the data controller reasonably believes that compliance with the exemption in question is incompatible with the special purposes.

In determining whether the data controller's belief that publication is in the public interest is reasonable, regard may be had to his compliance with any relevant code of practice designated by the Secretary of State for this purpose; section 32(3). As noted previously, the Secretary of State can order the Information Commissioner to prepare and disseminate codes of practice after consultation with trade associations and data subjects or persons representing data subjects. The Data Protection (Designated Codes of Practice) (No 2) Order 2000 lists in its Schedule those codes of practice designated for the purposes of section 32(3). These are specified codes of practice issued or published by the Broadcasting Standards Commission, the Independent Television Commission, the Press Complaints Commission, the British Broadcasting Corporation and the Radio Authority. They are obviously important in determining whether the data controller's belief in the publication concerned being in the public interest is reasonable.

The Press Complaints Commission issued a revised Code of Practice which came into force on 1 June 2004. Clause 3 deals with privacy and states:

(i) *Everyone is entitled to respect for his or her private and family life, home, health and correspondence, including digital communications. Editors will be expected to justify intrusions into any individual's private life without consent.*

(ii) *It is unacceptable to photograph individuals in private places without their consent.*

Private places are public or private property where there is a reasonable expectation of privacy. This is highly relevant in the context of the *Naomi Campbell* case, discussed below in that, in some circumstances, it may be a breach of the right to privacy to be photographed in a public place, even if the person photographed is a famous person who normally seeks publicity.

Under section 32(6), "publication" in this context means making available to the public or any section of the public.

The availability of the section 32 defence, sometimes referred to as the publishers' defence (though it is of wider ambit than just the media) came up for consideration in the litigation between Naomi Campbell and the Mirror Group Newspapers. The newspaper ran a story about the model undergoing treatment for drug addiction at Narcotics Anonymous after she had repeatedly and publicly denied any such addiction. She sued for damages for breach of confidence and also sought compensation under section 13 of the Data Protection Act 1998. The newspaper relied on the section 32 defence in relation to the data protection claim. If effective, it gives exemption from a large number of provisions in the Act including the right to compensation. At first instance, *Campbell* v *Mirror Group Newspapers*[9] Morland J held that the defence (better described as an exemption) applied only up to the time of publication and its purpose was to prevent someone obtaining a "gagging order" but grants no protection after publication has taken place.

The Court of Appeal disagreed.[10] Section 32(4) and (5) concerns stays in proceedings in circumstances such as where the data controller claims that the processing is only for the special purposes and the processing is with a view to publishing previously unpublished material. The stay remains until the Commissioner makes a determination under section 45 or where the stay was based on such a claim it is withdrawn. It can be inferred from these purely procedural provisions that, where a stay is ordered, and it has to be ordered where the data controller makes such a claim, the data controller may publish the material before the Commissioner makes a determination. As it is clear that the purposes of these provisions is to prevent gagging orders interfering with publication, there would be no need for section 32(1) to (3). Lord Philips MR said (at para 118):

> "Sub-sections (1) to (3), on their face, provide widespread exemption from the duty to comply with the provisions that impose substantive obligations upon the data controller, subject only to the simple conditions that the data controller reasonably believes (i) that publication would be in the public interest and (ii) that compliance with each of the provisions is incompatible with the special purpose – in this case journalism. If these provisions apply only up to the moment of publication it is impossible to see what purpose they serve, for the data controller will be able to obtain a stay of any proceedings under the provisions of sub-sections (4) and (5) without the need to demonstrate compliance with the conditions to which the exemption in subsections (1) to (3) is subject."

The Court of Appeal also accepted that it would be illogical to grant exemption before publication but to leave the data controller exposed to the full rigours of the Act thereafter. Interpreting section 32 to apply also to post-publication was in line with the overall scheme of things in the Directive and

---

9   [2002] EWHC 499 (QB).
10 *Campbell* v *MGN Ltd* [2003] QB 633.

agreed with the views expressed by Lord Williams of Mostyn in Hansard[11]. The procedural provisions prevented individuals interfering with pre-publication activities (without such provisions, the right of freedom of expression could be seriously prejudiced). After publication, it was a question of whether the data controller had reasonable belief that publication was in the public interest and compliance with the relevant provision would have been incompatible with the public interest.

The House of Lords, by a 3:2 majority, allowed Naomi Campbell's appeal against the Court of Appeal decision.[12] However, it did not rule on the section 32 aspect as it was generally accepted that, whatever the outcome on the breach of confidence point, the decision would be the same under data protection law. The only conclusion that one can draw is that their tacit acceptance, at least by the majority judges, that the defendant's belief that publication was in the public interest was not a reasonable belief in the circumstances.

Whether the data controller's belief that publication is in the public interest is reasonable, apart from relevant codes of practice, is a matter to be determined from the circumstances. Relevant factors are likely to include the manner in which the personal data were collected, the motivation underlying the publication and whether it provided enlightenment for the public or relevant part of the public or disabused the public of some mistaken belief or informed the public of some matter of importance. If data are obtained surreptitiously and published merely for financial gain, it is unlikely that the data controller's belief in public interest will be held to be reasonable. A good example is provided by *Douglas* v *Hello! Ltd*[13] in which photographs were taken surreptitiously of the couple's wedding and reception and published in Hello! Magazine. The couple had sold the exclusive right to publish photographs to a rival magazine, OK! for a large sum of money. As to the possibility of the section 32 exemption applying, Lindsay J said he had no credible evidence of such reasonable belief, nor any room for any conclusion that the data controller reasonably held a belief that publication was in the public interest. He said (at para 232):

"That the public would be interested is not to be confused with there being a public interest."

Section 32 is most likely to be relevant in relation to processing by the media but it is not limited to this. Processing for the special purposes also covers artistic or literary expression so it can extend, *inter alia*, to images made by

[11] HL Deb, 2 February 1998, c 442.
[12] *Campbell* v *MGN Ltd* [2004] 2 All ER 995.
[13] [2003] 3 All ER 996.

painters or works of literature providing these involve personal data within the meaning of data protection law. Examples, may be where a photographer places a portrait of someone on his webpage or a writer publishes an electronic version of a biography. The stress on electronic publication reflects the fact that such works may not be, or are not part of, a relevant filing system and are unlikely to fall within the meaning of accessible records or recorded information held by a public authority. Automatic processing of personal data, or holding personal data with a view to such processing, is within (a) or (b) of the definition of data and there is no requirement for any form of structure or ease of accessibility. One worrying factor is that, in relation to the work of artists, particularly avant-garde artists, the notion of public interest might be strained. The Data Protection Directive does not use reasonable belief that publication is in the public interest as a requirement for the exemptions.

RESEARCH, HISTORY AND STATISTICS

A great deal of data kept or processed for research purposes are in anonymous form, where personal identifiers have been stripped out. Providing the individuals and their associated data cannot be subsequently matched together, then the data are not personal data and are outside the scope of the Act. Nor would it appear in such cases that a duty of confidence can arise in respect of such anonymous data. In *R v Department of Health ex parte Source Informatics Ltd*[14], the Court of Appeal held that data relating to patients' prescriptions transferred by doctors and pharmacists to a company wishing to analyse those data was not a breach of confidence as all the personal identifiers had been stripped from the data before transfer. The Court did not consider the disclosure would be a breach of confidence providing the identity of the patients was protected; the sole issue being the right of privacy of the patients.

In some cases research data will contain identifiers or the data controller may have other information which when combined with the data permits the identification of the individuals to whom the data relate. Bearing in mind the importance of research in many disciplines and the value of statistical research, special provision is made to allow appropriate research data to be kept indefinitely. Furthermore, data processed for research purposes (defined as including statistical or historical purposes) may be so processed even if those were not the purposes for which the data were first obtained. In some cases, exemption is also available from the subject access provisions. There is a specific safeguard in that the exemption applies only if the "relevant conditions" apply being, under section 33(1), that the data are not processed to support measures or decisions with respect to particular individuals and the data are not processed in such a way to cause or be likely to cause substantial

---

[14] [2001] QB 424.

damage or substantial distress to any data subject.

The use of the term "particular individuals" in the first limb of the relevant conditions indicates that the measures or decisions are not limited to those taken in respect of the data subjects to whom the research data relate. However, the second limb (substantial damage or distress) does appear to be so limited.

Where the relevant conditions are complied with, under section 33(2), there is partial exemption from the second data protection principle in that further processing only for research purposes is not to be regarded as incompatible with the purposes for which the data were obtained. Again, where the relevant conditions are complied with, section 33(3) allows personal data processed only for research purposes to be kept indefinitely notwithstanding the fifth data protection principle.

Section 33(4) grants exemption from the subject access provisions under section 7 if the data are processed in compliance with the relevant conditions and the results of any research or resulting statistics are not made available in any form which identifies any of the data subjects.

The exemptions require that the data are processed only for research purposes but section 33(5) confirms that certain mere disclosures are not treated as processed other than for the research purposes. The disclosures are:

• to any person for research purposes;

• to the data subject or a person acting on his behalf;

• at the request or with the consent of the data subject or person acting on his behalf (this covers disclosures to persons other than the data subject or person acting on his behalf); or

• where the circumstances are such that the person making the disclosure has reasonable grounds for believing any of the above apply.

In the latter case, if the data controller has reasonable grounds, in the circumstances, for believing that a person to whom he discloses the data is going to process the data for research purposes and, in fact, that person goes beyond those purposes, the data controller will be able to rely on the exemption in any case but, of course, that other person will not.

MANUAL DATA HELD BY PUBLIC AUTHORITIES

Section 33A was inserted by the Freedom of Information Act 2000 and came into force on 1 January 2005 (the same date as access rights commenced under that Act). Sweeping exemption is granted to public authorities in relation to data falling within (e) of the definition of data, that is recorded information held by a public authority that does not fall within (a) to (d) of the definition. That is, it is not automatically processed (or intended to be so processed), it is not part of a relevant filing system and it is not an accessible record.

The exemption is in relation to all the data protection principles except the fourth (data shall be kept accurate and up to date) and, except in as much as it applies to the right of access under section 7 and the right of rectification etc. under section 14, the sixth data protection principle. Further exemption is granted in respect of sections 10 to 12 (rights to prevent processing and in respect of automatic decision-taking) and section 13 except in so far as it relates to damage caused by a contravention of section 7 or of the fourth data protection principle and to any distress which is also suffered by reason of that contravention. The exemption also extends to notification (though being manual data, they would otherwise be exempt from notification anyway) and the criminal offences under section 55.

INFORMATION AVAILABLE TO THE PUBLIC

This exemption, under section 34, applies in cases where the data consist of information which the data controller is required to make available to the public whether by publication or making it available for inspection or otherwise and whether or not a fee is charged. The exemption is from the subject information provisions, the fourth data protection principle (that data are accurate and, where necessary, kept up to date), the right of rectification, blocking, erasure and destruction under section 14(1) to (3) and the non-disclosure provisions. Where information is available to the public, it would be completely unnecessary to apply the subject information provisions and the non-disclosure provisions. The exemption from the fourth data protection principle and the rights of rectification, etc. may seem more controversial. However, in most cases, the enactment under which information is required to be made publicly available will include its own mechanism for the correction of errors.

We saw in Chapter 8 that disclosing the electoral register to marketing companies caused issues in relation to the right to object to processing for the purposes of direct marketing and that, as a result, two versions of the register are now kept. From the second version, which is made available, *inter alia*, to companies wishing to engage in direct marketing, the names of those exercising their right to prevent such processing are excluded.

DISCLOSURES REQUIRED BY LAW ETC.

Section 35 contains exemptions from the non-disclosure provisions where the disclosure in question is required by law or made in connection with legal proceedings or for the purpose of obtaining legal advice or otherwise necessary for the purposes of establishing, exercising or defending legal rights.

The equivalent exemption under the Data Protection Act 1984 was considered in *Rowley* v *Liverpool City Council*.[15] The claimant brought a personal injury action against her former employer and made an application for discovery to obtain information about payments, subsequent to her injury, made to three "comparative earners". This information was required so that the loss of earnings up to the trial included in the special damages could be calculated. The defendant refused to disclose such data, claiming that it was prohibited by the 1984 Act. The defendant relied on the exemption from registration on the basis of the payroll and accounts exemption. (This particular exemption was available until 24 October 2001 under the transitional provisions – under the 1998 Act, exemptions from notification are provided for by the Data Protection (Notification and Notification Fees) Regulations 2000.)

Although section 32(2) of the Data Protection Act 1984 made the exemption conditional upon the data not being disclosed except in limited circumstances relating to payroll and accounts, section 34(5) of that Act (broadly similar to the equivalent exemption in the 1998 Act) allowed disclosure if required by law or in the course of legal proceedings. Therefore, the disclosure requested did not contravene the Act and was allowed because it was in the course of legal proceedings in which the defendant was a party and, furthermore, it was in compliance with an order of the court.

The application of section 35 appears to be simple enough though there may be other issues involved such as breach of confidence or even a breach of the right to privacy.

There may be a slight distinction between circumstances where the disclosure is required by or under any enactment compared with disclosures required by any rule of law or by court order. The former may result in an express challenge to the statutory provision based on the law of confidence or the right to privacy. In *Guyer* v *Walton (Inspector of Taxes)*[16], Guyer, a solicitor who carried on mainly conveyancing work, submitted a self-assessment tax return. The Inland Revenue sought more information from Guyer in the form of invoices and details of bank accounts. Even then, the Revenue was unable to trace all

[15] (unreported) 26 October 1989.
[16] [2001] STC (SCD) 75.

the cash flows and asked for sight of additional material including his client cash-book and ledger under section 19A of the Taxes Management Act 1970. Guyer refused on the basis that, in respect of the further information sought, he was under a duty of confidentiality to his clients and disclosure would also be a breach of his clients' right of privacy under the Human Rights Convention and, furthermore, he was precluded from disclosing information about his clients under data protection law.

Section 35(1) of the Data Protection Act 1998 provided for disclosure required, *inter alia*, by or under any enactment. This was clearly the case here as the Revenue's request was based on the Taxes Management Act. The confidence point also fell away as this duty was overridden by a general duty to obey the law. Of the right of privacy under Article 8(1) of the Convention, there was ample justification for interfering with the right under Article 8(2) as the Revenue's notices had been issued in accordance with law in the pursuit of a legitimate aim necessary in a democratic society for protecting the tax and revenue system.

Where disclosure is required by order of the court, the data controller is likely to refuse to disclose the information to which access is sought in the absence of such order on the ground that, otherwise, it would be in breach of data protection law. In *Andersen* v *Halifax plc*[17] (a case under the equivalent provision in the 1984 Act) a bank refused to disclose details of the recipient of a large amount of money withdrawn from the account of a recently deceased man to his wife. The bank adopted a neutral stance though and said a court order would be needed. Such an order was granted by the High Court of Northern Ireland which confirmed that the order was required to overcome the statutory prohibition on disclosure under the Act.

The power to require a copy of the register of company members to be furnished to any person under section 356(6) of the Companies Act 1985 is a discretionary one but, if the discretion is exercised to require a copy to be supplied, the exemption under data protection law cannot prevent the supply of that copy as it is by way of court order. In *Pelling* v *Families Need Fathers Ltd*,[18] the applicant sought a copy of the register of members of the defendant company but was refused and therefore, eventually, applied to the court for an order. He had originally been a member of the company. The company argued that supplying a copy of the register would, *inter alia*, be a breach of data protection law. The Court of Appeal decided that it could either grant the order subject to safeguards such as maintaining confidentiality or decline if the company agreed to act as a postbox for communications made by the applicant for the order.

---

[17] [2000] NI 1.
[18] [2002] 2 All ER 440.

In cases where the disclosure required by or under any enactment is challenged, the court may be called upon to determine whether the statutory provision complies with the right of privacy under Article 8 of the Human Rights Convention. If there is some ambiguity, the court will have to interpret the relevant provision in line with the Convention or, where there is a clear conflict, make a declaration of incompatibility. In cases where disclosure is ordered by the court, it can be assumed that the court will take due account of confidentiality and privacy issues.

DOMESTIC PURPOSES

The Directive does not extend to processing of personal data by a natural person in the course of a purely personal or household activity; Article 3(2). Express exemption is required in the Data Protection Act 1998 otherwise such processing would otherwise be caught by the Act. An alternative approach might have been to exclude such processing from the definition of processing to take it right outside the Act. The exemption under section 36 of the Act is very broad, being exemption from the data protection principles, the rights of data subjects and the requirements as to notification, but it is not a complete exemption from the Act altogether. Some of the enforcement powers of the Information Commissioner remain (although it is unlikely that they will be of any relevance, except for Information Notices) and the offences under section 55 may apply, not in respect of the private individual, but where another person may deceive the individual into disclosing personal data to another person. It will, of course be extremely rare that this could apply in circumstances where the exemption under section 36 applies. However, the private individual remains a data controller under the Act.

The scope of the exemption as specified in section 36 is in relation to the processing of personal data by an individual for that individual's personal, family or household affairs (including recreational purposes). Of course, if the individual processes personal data for other purposes, he may lose the benefit of the exemption. In particular, an individual who carries out work for clients at home will be a data controller under the Act. One example under the 1984 Act was a self-employed accountant who worked on client accounts. Initially, he worked for a company at the company's premises and also put some of his other clients' accounts on that computer. He then bought his own computer and transferred his clients' accounts to that computer and worked from home. It was held by the Divisional Court of the Queen's Bench Division that the accountant was a data user (equivalent to data controller under the 1998 Act) and, consequently should have been registered under the Act.[19]

---

[19] *Data Protection Registrar* v *Griffin* (unreported) 22 February 1993.

An interesting aspect of the case is that it was held that the self-employed accountant was not a computer bureau even though he only processed data solely for purposes required by his clients. Under the 1998 Act it would seem reasonable to accept that such a self-employed person working at home, using his own computer but manipulating data relating to clients is a data controller and not a data processor. He should therefore, unless otherwise exempt, notify under the Act even though the processing is on behalf of his clients. In the *Griffin* case, it was accepted that the accountant had, at least, joint control of the data on his computer.

SCHEDULE 7 EXEMPTIONS

Section 37 refers to further miscellaneous exemptions in Schedule 7 of the Act.

Confidential References

Paragraph 1 of the Schedule grants exemption from the subject access provisions where a reference is given or is to be given by the data controller for the purposes of the education, training or employment (actual or prospective) of the data subject or the appointment or prospective appointment of the data subject to any office or the provision or prospective provision by the data subject of any service. The reference must be in confidence. In some cases, a written or typed reference will not constitute or be part of a relevant filing system, accessible record or recorded information held by a public authority within the Freedom of Information Act 2000 and, therefore, will be outside the scope of the Act and there can be no right of access under the Act (though there may be on the basis of the right of privacy under the Human Rights Convention). It will be different if the reference is stored electronically, is on a *pro forma* or if it is included in a structured file, in which case, the data controller may rely on the exemption.

Following *Spring* v *Guardian Assurance plc*[20] it should be noted that a person writing a reference about an employee or former employee owes a duty of care to that employee and could be liable in negligence if the reference turned out to be inaccurate and the employee suffered damage as a result. This case emphasises the need to ensure that references are confidential though this should not excuse the need for persons writing references to do so carefully.

Of course, the existence of the exemption does not prevent the data controller giving access to a confidential reference that he has written. The recipient of the reference, for example a prospective employer, cannot give access to it, however, without running the risk of an action for breach of confidence.

---

[20] [1995] 2 AC 296.

Even if a reference is marked confidential, if it has an adverse effect on the individual about whom it relates, the Information Commissioner has been prepared to serve a preliminary enforcement notice requiring access to the reference to be given to that individual. In one case, a job offer made by a local authority was withdrawn after it received a confidential reference from a previous employer. The individual had by then already resigned from her previous job and was obviously concerned that if she continued to give her previous employer as a reference, as she would probably have to do, this could prevent her obtaining suitable work. Although the local authority had a policy of showing references to interviewees, it declined to do so in this case as the reference was marked confidential. The former employer was unable to provide a compelling reason why the reference should not be shown to the individual but after serving the preliminary enforcement notice, the reference was shown to the individual.[21] Although no further facts were given in the report, the reference may not even have been within the scope of the Act as far as the local authority was concerned. For example, if the reference was typed on a computer, the previous employer would be a data controller within the Act and the data would also fall within the definition of data, being processed automatically. If the reference was sent to the local authority printed on paper, it would not be personal data within the Act from the perspective of the local authority, unless it intended to process the data by automatic means, for example, by scanning it into a computer file. Of course, it would be quite different if the reference had been sent by email.

It is worth noting that it is the data controller who writes the confidential reference who can take advantage of the exemption from subject access. The recipient remains under a duty of confidence. That being so, there seems no justification for serving a preliminary enforcement notice on the local authority (though such notices are not provided for by the Act and are informal) as compliance would force the authority to be in breach of its obligation of confidence owed to the previous employer. The individual would not be completely without a remedy as the right of privacy under Article 8 of the Human Rights Convention would be likely to give her a right of access in respect of the previous employer.

Armed forces

This exemption is from the subject information provisions and applies to the extent that the application of those provisions would be likely to prejudice the combat effectiveness of any of the armed forces of the Crown; paragraph 2.

Depending on the circumstances, this exemption could fall foul of the Human Rights Act 1998. Although not concerning this particular exemption, a case

---

[21] Information Commissioner, *Annual Report 2004*, HC699, pp.48–49.

which is not too removed is *McGinley & Egan* v *United Kingdom*[22] in the European Court of Human Rights. The two applicants, when they were soldiers, witnessed nuclear testing carried out by the United Kingdom in 1957 and 1958 at Christmas Island. They both subsequently suffered health problems which they thought might be caused by their exposure to radiation. They submitted claims for war pensions but these were turned down and the government refused to disclose documents containing details of radiation levels. The Court held that access to the documents would have either allayed their fears or allowed them to assess the danger to which they had been exposed and this raised an issue under Article 8 of the European Convention on Human Rights (right of respect for private and family life, home and correspondence).

Article 8 can give rise to positive obligations which require a balance between the interests of individuals and the general interest of the community. In cases where a government engaged in hazardous activities which could have adverse consequences on the health of those involved, Article 8 requires that an accessible and effective procedure was in place to enable such persons to seek all relevant and appropriate information. This could cause a conflict between the Convention and the armed forces exemption where there is a subsisting conflict. However in the *McGinley* case there was no breach of Article 8 because the applicants failed to appeal under rule 6 of the Pensions Appeals Tribunals (Scotland) Rules 1981. This could have given them an opportunity to apply for an order for disclosure of the relevant documents and this procedure meant that the United Kingdom had fulfilled its obligations under Article 8 in such a case.

A request for revision of that judgment was refused by a majority of the European Court of Human Rights.[23] It was argued that the submission of the United Kingdom government about the efficacy of the rule was misleading.

Judicial appointments and honours

Paragraph 3 of Schedule 7 gives exemption from the subject information provisions in respect of personal data processed for the purposes of assessing a person's suitability for judicial office or the office of Queen's Counsel or the conferring of any honour by the Crown. The exemption is absolute and it is not expressed in terms of prejudice to those purposes.

Crown employment etc.

Exemption from the subject information provisions may be granted by Order of the Secretary of State in respect of processing of personal data for the

---

[22] [1998] ECHR 51.
[23] [2000] ECHR 44.

purposes of assessing any person's suitability for employment by or under the Crown or any office to which appointments are made by Her Majesty, by a Minister of the Crown or by a Northern Ireland Department. Again the exemption is absolute and there is no requirement for a likelihood of prejudice, for example, to the process of making appointments. The Data Protection (Crown Appointments) Order 2000 lists those appointments already covered by the exemption, being appointments made by Her Majesty as follows:

- Archbishops, diocesan and suffragan bishops in the Church of England;

- Deans of cathedrals of the Church of England;

- Deans and Canons of the two Royal Peculiars;

- The First and Second Church Estates Commissioners;

- Lord-Lieutenants;

- Masters of Trinity College and Churchill College, Cambridge;

- The Provost of Eton;

- The Poet Laureate;

- The Astronomer Royal.

Management forecasts

This exemption is contained in paragraph 5 of Schedule 7 and is from the subject information provisions. It applies to personal data processed for the purposes of management forecasting or management planning to assist the data controller in the conduct of any business or other activity; paragraph 5. The exemption only applies if and to the extent that compliance would be likely to prejudice the conduct of that business or other activity. The exemption may be useful where a company is considering a take-over bid, restructuring, downsizing or merging with another company. It could be relevant in the context of personal data relating to present or potential employees or actual or potential investors or intentions to replace members of the board of directors.

Corporate finance

The main purpose of paragraph 6 of Schedule 7 is to provide exemption from the subject information provisions where, for example, it is required to safeguard important economic or financial interests of the United Kingdom. The exemption is intended to promote the orderly functioning of financial markets or the efficient allocation of capital and guards against the inevitable prejudicial effect of the application of the subject information provisions. In particular, these provisions could affect decisions in respect of subscriptions to or the issue of shares which may affect business activity. The exemption applies where personal data are processed for the purposes of, or in connection with, a corporate finance service provided by a relevant person.

Important definitions are "corporate finance service", being a service consisting in underwriting in respect of the placing of issues of any instrument (or a service relating to such undertaking) or advice to undertakings on capital structure, industrial strategy and related matters and advice and service relating to mergers and the purchase of undertakings. An "instrument" is one as set out in Schedule 1 to the Investment Services Regulations 1995.

A 'relevant person' is:

- any person authorised under Chapter III of Part I of the Financial Services Act 1986 or an exempt person under Chapter IV of Part I of that Act;

- any person who, but for Part III or IV of Schedule 1 to that Act would require authorisation under that Act;

- any European investment firm within the meaning in regulation 3 of the Investment Services Regulations 1995;

- any person who, in the course of employment, provides his employer with a service relating to mergers and the purchase of undertakings or a service related to underwriting in respect of issues of, or the placing of issues of, any instrument (this extends also to any partner who provides to the other partners in the partnership such a service).

Exemption from the subject information provisions is given:

- to the extent to which the application of those provisions (or the data controller reasonably believes the application of those provisions) could affect the price of any instrument already in existence or likely to be or may be created (price includes value); and

- to the extent that the data are not exempt from the subject information provisions by virtue of the above, they are exempt from those provisions if the exemption is required for the purpose of safeguarding an important economic or financial interest of the United Kingdom.

In terms of the latter, matters to be taken into account and circumstances in which the exemption is, or is not, to be taken to be required may be specified by order of the Secretary of State. This is the purpose of the Data Protection (Corporate Finance Exemption) Order 2000.

Under the Order, a matter to be taken into account is the inevitable prejudicial effect on the orderly functioning of financial markets or the efficient allocation of capital within the economy which will result from the application, whether on an occasional or regular basis, of the subject information provisions to particular data. The data referred to are those personal data to which the application of the subject information provisions could, in the reasonable belief of the relevant person, affect:

- any decision of any person whether or not to deal in, subscribe for or issue any instrument which is in existence or is to be or may be created; or

- any decision of any person to act or not to act in a way that is likely to have an effect on business activity including, in particular, an effect on the industrial strategy of any person (whether it is or is to be pursued independently or in association with others), the capital structure of an undertaking or the legal or beneficial ownership of a business or asset.

Negotiations

Personal data consisting of records of the intentions of the data controller in relation to any negotiations with the data subject are exempt from the subject information provisions; paragraph 7 of Schedule 7. The exemption is only to the extent that compliance would be likely to prejudice the negotiations. This exemption has no equivalent under previous data protection law though it should be noted that indications of intentions in respect of individuals did not fall within the definition of personal data under the Data Protection Act 1984, hence the need for the exemption. It might be relevant in the context of forthcoming negotiations with an employee concerning that employee's future prospects or pay but is clearly much wider. It may relate to intentions in respect of forthcoming negotiations with third parties such as consultants, suppliers or trade union negotiators, for example.

Examination Marks

This exemption is similar to the equivalent one under the 1984 Act. It gives a temporary exemption from the subject access provisions. By virtue of paragraph 8 of Schedule 7 of the Data Protection Act 1998, the exemption applies to personal data consisting of marks or other information processed by the data controller:

- for the purpose of determining the results of an academic, professional or other examination or enabling such determination; or

- in consequence of the determination of any such results.

"Examination" includes a process for determining the knowledge, intelligence, skill or ability of a candidate by reference to his performance in any test, work or other activity.

The normal period for responding to a subject access request is 40 days though this does not apply in all cases. For example, the maximum period in respect of educational records which are accessible records, is 15 school days. Where the period of 40 days is used below, it is to be taken to be 40 days or such other period as may be prescribed. In some cases, where the examination takes place in a primary or secondary school, the provisions relating to educational records may also apply.

Normally, a data controller must comply with a data subject request within the prescribed period. However, if the day that the request is received (the "relevant day") falls before the day the results are announced, the period during which the data controller must respond is either the end of five months beginning with the relevant day or 40 days after the day the results are announced (published or made available or communicated to candidates) whichever is the earlier. This 40 day period is not the "prescribed period" and applies even if the examination results are contained in an educational record. However, and to compensate for this, if the request is complied with later than the prescribed period, the response by the data controller must include all the information held at the time of the request *and* subsequently.

Examination scripts

This exemption is granted in respect of the subject access provisions. The meaning of "examination" is as above and the exemption relates to personal data consisting of information recorded by candidates during an academic, professional or other examination. The exemption is absolute and there is no qualitative test to determine whether or not it applies. In practice, the exemption is likely to be very narrow as, in many cases, an examination script will not fall with the meaning of data in the Act and, even if it does, it may not be personal data. However, although many examination scripts are anonymous (as far as the markers are concerned) a University or other educational body will hold other information recording the candidate's name with the associated number used on the examination script. Where an examination takes place on computer, for example, in the case of a computer-based multiple choice test, the resulting "script" will fall within these provisions. A student taking such an examination may want access to this, for example, to challenge the mark awarded to him or her. This provision allows access to be denied. However, Article 8 of the Human Rights Convention may be a different route open to a student requiring access in such a case or even an application for disclosure under the Civil Procedure Rules.

Unlike some of the exemptions, there is no particular purpose that may be prejudiced by granting access. It appears to be an absolute exemption against subject access. There is no equivalent provision in the Data Protection Directive although Article 13 allows Member States to grant exemptions, *inter alia*, to protect the data subject or the rights and freedoms of others. It is very questionable that this justifies the exemption which does not really serve any significant purpose apart from, perhaps, the embarrassment of an educational body which has poor or defective assessment methods.

Legal professional privilege

Paragraph 10 of Schedule 7 grants this exemption from the subject information provisions if the data consist of information in respect of which a claim to legal professional privilege could be maintained in legal proceedings. In Scotland it applies where a claim to confidentiality between client and professional legal adviser could be so claimed.

Self-incrimination

A request under the subject access provisions in section 7 (or an order under that section) need not be complied with to the extent that to do so would expose the person to whom the request has been made, or who has been ordered to comply, to proceedings for an offence where compliance would reveal evidence of the commission of that offence. This does not apply, of course, to an offence under the Data Protection Act 1998. However, information disclosed by any person in compliance with a request or order under section 7 shall not be admissible against him in proceedings for an offence under the Data Protection Act 1998. Of course, the Information Commissioner may be able to use his powers of enforcement under the Act in appropriate cases, and any data subjects affected may be able to bring civil action for compensation and rectification, etc.

Miscellaneous subject access exemptions

Pursuant to his powers under sections 38(1) and 67(2) of the Data Protection Act 1998, the Secretary of State may, after consultation with the Information Commissioner, make further exemptions from the subject information provisions. Such exemptions must be in respect of personal data, the disclosure of which is prohibited or restricted by or under any enactment, if and to the extent that he considers it necessary for safeguarding the interests of the data subject or the rights and freedoms of any other individual. A further requirement is that the prohibition or restriction ought to prevail over the subject information provisions.

Further exemptions have thus been provided for by the Data Protection (Miscellaneous Subject Access Exemptions) Order 2000. It states that personal data, consisting of information the disclosure of which is prohibited or restricted by the enactments or instruments listed in the Schedule to the Order, are exempt from the subject access provisions under section 7 of the Data Protection Act 1998. These are various provisions under the Human

Fertilisation and Embryology Act 1990, the Adoption Act 1976 (as amended by the Parental Orders (Human Fertilisation and Embryology) Regulations 1994), the Education (Special Educational Needs) Regulations 1994, the Family Proceedings Rules 1991 and the Family Proceedings Courts (Children Act 1989) Rules 1991. The Schedule also contains a list of equivalent and supplementary legislation relating to Scotland and Northern Ireland in respect of the above legislation which does not extend to those countries. In particular, in Scotland, there are provisions concerning information provided by the Reporter for the purposes of children's hearings.

THE TRANSITIONAL PROVISIONS

INTRODUCTION

The Data Protection Act 1998 contains some important and complex transitional provisions, some of which endure until 24 October 2007 and beyond. These provisions are an attempt to take full advantage of the derogations permitted in the Data Protection Directive and are primarily aimed at processing which was already underway before 24 October 1998, the latest date for implementing the Directive.

One provision of immediate relevance to all data controllers at the time was that applications to register processing activity were, until commencement of the new provisions on notification on 1 March 2000, dealt with under the Data Protection Act 1984 and such registrations continued to be valid until 24 October 2001 by virtue of paragraph 2 of Schedule 14 to the 1998 Act. Furthermore, those applications were to be determined in accordance with the 1984 Act (paragraph 2(3) of Schedule 14 of the 1998 Act).

Schedule 8 to the Data Protection Act 1998 contains the main transitional provisions. There are two transitional periods defined in paragraph 1, Part I of the Schedule defines these as follows:

> 'he first transitional period' means the period beginning with the commencement of this Schedule and ending with 23rd October 2001; and

> 'the second transitional period' means the period beginning with 24th October 2001 and ending with 23rd October 2007.

The first period applies to automated processing already underway and has also to deal with the exemptions under the 1984 Act which were no longer available under the 1998 Act (although some continued in modified form as a result of Orders made under the Act). The second period relates only to manual files. Processing for historical research, whether automated or manual, is separately provided for and the transitional provisions that apply here have no time limit.

A major issue for the application of the transitional provisions is what is meant by processing already underway. For example, could a database consisting of or including personal data subject to processing on 23 October 1998 lose the advantage of the exemptions in the transitional provisions if new personal data were subsequently added to the database after that date? There were three possibilities:

- the database as a whole could continue to take advantage of the transitional provisions;

- the database as a whole was caught by the new law;

- only the new personal data had to comply with the law under the 1998 Act in all respects but the pre-existing data did not have to.

The Data Protection Directive is somewhat ambiguous on this point and is couched in terms of processing already underway but the Data Protection Act 1998 seems clearer but less helpful to data controllers. The exemptions in the transitional provisions are expressed mainly in respect of "eligible data" which are defined in paragraph 1, Part I of Schedule 8 in the following terms

> "...personal data are "eligible data" at any time **if, and to the extent that**, *they are at any time subject to processing which was already under way immediately before 24th October 1998" (emphasis added).*

Eligible automated data are eligible data processed or to be processed by automatic means and eligible manual data are simply eligible data which are not eligible automated data. Because of the very wide definition of processing in section 1(1) of the Act, there is no need for the data to have been actively processed on 23 October 1998. Simply being in possession of them is sufficient.

Two points can be made about the definition of eligible data. First, there is no express requirement that the data are being processed by or on behalf of the data controller. Simply the fact that they are subject to processing by any data controller should suffice; that is, data that existed before 24 October 1998 are eligible data. The second point is that the phrase "if, and to the extent that," implies that data created on or after 24 October 1998 are not eligible data and subject immediately to the full rigours of the Data Protection Act 1998. This suggests the third alternative interpretation above is the correct one. A further question is what the effect is of commencing some new processing activity in relation to personal data that existed before 24 October 1998. The definition suggests, to that extent, the data will no longer be eligible data.

THE FIRST TRANSITIONAL PERIOD

This first transitional period has now passed. This applied to automated processing and manual processing (full derogation) until 24 October 2001. In relation to manual data, the provisions appear at first sight to be unduly complex but the provisions were intended to fully comply with the Directive.

Manual data

The basic rule was that eligible manual data, other than data forming part of an accessible record, were exempt from the data protection principles and Parts II and III of the Act (data subjects' rights and notification) during the first transitional period. However, if the manual data consisted of information relevant to the financial standing of the data subject and the data controller was a credit reference agency, the exemption was limited and did not extend to the right of access of data subjects (under section 7 as modified by section 9 in relation to credit reference agencies) and a right to rectification, erasure, blocking or destruction of inaccurate or incomplete data and a right to require the data controller to cease holding exempt manual data in a manner incompatible with the data controller's legitimate interests.[24] These latter rights are provided by section 12A of the Act which is inserted until 24 October 2007 by paragraph 1 of Schedule 13 to the Act.

Where the data were part of an accessible record, whether eligible data or not, the exemptions were largely subject to the same rights of data subjects as apply to credit reference agencies. Thus, pre-existing and new data contained in accessible records such as health records, educational and certain local authority records enjoyed exemption from the principles (except in so far as the sixth principle in as much as it relates to subject access under section 7 and section 12A), other rights of data subjects (such as the rights to prevent processing) and the notification requirements. The complexity of these provisions can be explained by the fact that the 1998 Act incorporated some other legislative provisions, allowing access to personal data such as the Consumer Credit Act 1974 (access to credit reference agencies data – the right to have incorrect data rectified still remains under section 159 of the Consumer Credit Act 1974) and the Access to Personal Files Act 1987, which was repealed by the Data Protection Act 1998.

Eligible automated data – general exemption

The model for data protection law under the 1998 Act is significantly different to that under the Act it replaced and, apart from anything else, the transi-

---

[24] In line with the Directive, it is the data controller's legitimate interests that are relevant, not those of the data subject.

tional provisions had to cope with a number of differences between the two Acts, particularly in respect to a number of exemptions under the 1984 Act that were not provided for in the Directive. However, in modified form and to a limited extent, some of these exemptions were perpetuated by the Data Protection (Notification and Notification Fees) Regulations 2000 which provides further exemptions from notification unless the processing is assessable processing.

Paragraph 13 of Schedule 8 to the Act gave general exemption to all eligible automated data and was intended to place such data generally (apart from the "lost" exemptions described below) in the same position as applied under the 1984 Act. The exemptions, which provided an excellent guide to some of the major differences between the old law and the new law, are set out below:

- The data controller was excused from the requirement to provide data subjects with information when data are obtained from him and in other cases (such as disclosures to third parties).

- There was no need for any of the conditions for processing in Schedule 2 to exist nor, in the case of sensitive data, any of the conditions in Schedule 3.

- There was no obligation to impose security obligations on processors in writing or evidenced in writing (of course, computer bureaux had a duty in respect of security under the 1984 Act).

- The provisions controlling transfers to personal data to third countries not having an adequate level of protection did not apply.

- The requirement to give additional information in response to a data subject request compared to that required under the 1984 Act (for example, a description of the data, the purposes of processing, and the recipients) did not apply.

- The data controller was exempt from the right of data subjects to prevent processing causing or likely to cause substantial damage or substantial distress, and the right to prevent processing for the purposes of direct marketing and the rights of data subjects in respect of automated decision-taking.

- The enhanced rights of data subjects to compensation did not apply and were restricted to those under the 1984 Act.

Notwithstanding these exemptions, the data controller was still subject to a general duty under the first data protection principle to ensure that the processing is fair.

Eligible automated data – particular exemptions

Other exemptions for automated processing concerned the fact that a number of exemptions provided for under the 1984 Act disappeared, though in some cases, exemption from notification might now be available. Under the Data Protection Act 1984, processing was required to be by reference to the data subject. This did not include operations performed only for the purpose of preparing the text of documents (the "word processing" exception). Paragraph 5 of Schedule 8 extended the benefit of this exemption for a further three years for eligible automated data.

An important exemption which was relied on by many organisations under the 1984 Act related to processing for payroll and accounts (the exemption was from registration and data subjects' rights). Paragraph 6 of Schedule 8 to the 1998 Act attempted to continue this for a further three years. It provided that eligible automated data processed for one or more of the purposes concerned were exempt from the data protection principles and Parts II and III (data subjects' rights and notification) during the first transitional period. The purposes were

> *"... calculating amounts payable by way of remuneration or pensions in respect of service in any employment or office or making payments of, or of sums deducted from, such remuneration or pensions, or for keeping accounts relating to any business or other activity carried on by the data controller or keeping records of purchases, sales or other transactions for the purpose of ensuring that the requisite payments are made by or to him in respect of those transactions or for the purpose of making financial or management forecasts to assist him in the conduct of any such business or activity ...".*

However, the data could not be processed for any other purpose, although the exemption was not lost by any processing for any other purpose if the data controller could show that he had taken such care to prevent it as in all the circumstances was reasonably required. The burden of proof to show this was so was imposed on the data controller.

Under the Data Protection (Notification and Notification Fees) Regulations 2000, except where the processing is assessable processing, processing for purposes associated with staff administration and accounts and records are exempt from the notification requirements. Thus, in most cases, the previous exemption will continue indefinitely but in a much more limited form, being restricted to notification only.

Under the transitional provisions in relation to payroll and accounts, some disclosures were also permitted such as to any person by whom the remuneration or pensions was payable, for the purpose of obtaining actuarial advice, for the purpose of giving information as to the person in any employment or office for use in medical research into the health of, or injuries suffered by, persons engaged in particular occupations or working in particular places or areas. The data subject (or a person acting on his behalf) could also request or consent to the disclosure either generally or in the circumstances in which the disclosure in question was made. The exemption still applied if the person making the disclosure has reasonable grounds for believing that the data subject requested or consented to the disclosure. Further disclosures were permitted which included the purpose of audit or for the purpose only of giving information about the data controller's financial affairs.

Unincorporated members' clubs and mailing lists had wide-ranging exemption under the 1984 Act and the transitional provisions again attempted to perpetuate this for a further three years. The exemption was again from the data protection principles and Parts II and III of the Act. The conditions which applied to unincorporated members' clubs and mailing lists, such as the requirement to ask data subjects whether they object to the processing of personal data relating to them still apply now (these provisions are equivalent to those in section 33(2) to (5) of the Data Protection Act 1984 and the language used is very similar). In spite of these transitional provisions, the Data Protection (Notification and Notification Fees) Regulations 2000 provides exemption from notification in respect of certain processing by non-profit-making organisations.

A further exemption under the 1984 Act was from the subject access provisions where the data were solely for back-up purposes, for example to replace data on a computer in the event that they were accidentally erased or corrupted in some way. This was continued until 24 October 2001.[25]

THE SECOND TRANSITIONAL PERIOD

The second period applies only to manual processing and is a partial derogation for 12 years, that is, until 24 October 2007, and applies to eligible manual data and accessible records, whether eligible or not. It does not apply to eligible manual data processed only for the purposes of historical research for which there is separate provision. The exemption is from the first data protection principle (except to the extent to which it requires compliance with the requirements to inform data subjects when the data are obtained from the data subject or in other cases), the second, third, fourth and fifth data protection principles, and section 14(1) to (3) which contains the basic rights to rectification, blocking, erasure and destruction. Of course, there is no requirement generally to notify manual processing (except where the processing is assessable, though processing already underway immediately

[25] The effect was identical to the exemption in section 34(4) of the 1984 Act.

before 24 October 1998 is not subject to any of the requirements in respect of assessable processing). Data subjects still have a right of access to such data and a right to be informed in accordance with the first data protection principle. Although exemption is granted in respect of some of the rights of rectification under section 14(1) to (3), this is of little consequence as the processing is subject to section 12A instead.

Before the Data Protection Directive was adopted, concern was expressed about the fact that, in some cases, data controllers might find it very difficult and expensive to comply fully even by 24 October 2007 in relation to manual data. This is particularly the case where an organisation has substantial amounts of archived data which it may want to retain, for example for future research purposes or for defending legal claims. In order to assuage such concerns, the Council and Commission made a joint statement to the effect that, in certain circumstances:

> "... at the end of the 12 year transitional period, controllers must take all reasonable steps relating to the requirements of Articles 6, 7 and 8, which do not prove impossible or involve a disproportionate effort in terms of cost."[26]

The exemption does not prevent individuals exercising their right of subject access, their right to prevent processing and their rights to compensation. The security obligations also apply and data controllers need to review this aspect in relation to manual files. For example, whether manual files are kept in secure locked cabinets and rooms and only made available to employees and agents on a "need to know" basis.

PROCESSING FOR HISTORICAL RESEARCH (PARTIAL DEROGATION)

Section 33 of the Act provides exemption from some of the provisions of the Act where processing is only for research purposes. "Research purposes" are defined as including statistical or historical purposes. The particular exemption in Schedule 8, the transitional provisions, is more limited in its scope in that it applies to processing only for the purposes of historical research, notwithstanding the difficulty in trying to define historical research or other forms of research covered by section 33.

The exemption in respect of historical research in Schedule 8 is indefinite and there is no time limit to it. After 23 October 2001, eligible manual data processed only for the purpose of historical research in compliance with the

---

[26] Home Office, *Consultation Paper on the EC Data Protection Directive*, March 1996, at 48. The statement drew attention to the need for controllers to bear in mind the need to ensure the protection of the rights and freedoms of individuals.

"relevant conditions" (as set out in section 33(1) of the Act) and relevant auto-mated data which are processed only for the purpose of historical research, in compliance with the relevant conditions, and otherwise than by reference to the data subject, are exempt from the first data protection principle (but not as regards informing data subjects), the second, third, fourth and fifth data protection principles, and the rights of rectification, blocking, erasure and destruction under section 14(1) to (3).

To reiterate the relevant conditions, they are that the data are not processed to support measures or decisions with respect to particular individuals and that they are not processed in such a way that substantial damage or substantial distress is, or is likely to be, caused to any data subject.

Other eligible automated data processed only for the purpose of historical research in compliance with the relevant conditions are exempt from the first data protection principle to the extent to which it requires compliance with the conditions in Schedules 2 and 3 (the conditions for processing). This more limited exemption applies where, in spite of the other conditions being present, the data are processed by reference to the data subject.

In respect of these exemptions, and in line with section 33(5) in respect of the general exemption for processing only for research purposes, personal data are not to be treated as processed otherwise than for the purpose of historical research merely because the data are disclosed:

(a) to any person, for the purpose of historical research only;

(b) to the data subject or a person acting on his behalf;

(c) at the request, or with the consent, of the data subject or a person acting on his behalf; or

(d) in circumstances in which the person making the disclosure has reasonable grounds for believing that the disclosure falls within para-graph (a), (b) or (c).

Section 12A does not apply to eligible manual data processed for historical research.

If the relevant conditions are not met, the exemption for eligible automated data is of the more restricted variety and applies only in respect of the first data protection principle but subject to the conditions for processing.

ASSESSABLE PROCESSING

Where, by its nature, processing activity is likely to cause substantial damage or substantial distress to data subjects or is likely otherwise to significantly prejudice the rights and freedoms of data subjects, section 22 of the 1998 Act provides that the processing will be subject to a preliminary assessment by the Information Commissioner before processing can proceed. The types of processing affected will be specified by order of the Secretary of State and are likely to be relatively limited covering processing of genetic data, data matching and processing by private investigators. However, by virtue of paragraph 19 of Schedule 8, processing which was already underway immediately before 24 October 1998 is not assessable processing for these purposes. This applies both to manual and automated data. At the time of writing, no Orders have been made under section 22.

CHAPTER 10

ENFORCEMENT AND CRIMINAL OFFENCES

INTRODUCTION

Simply granting individuals rights in relation to personal data is not necessarily an effective way of policing and enforcing data protection law and ensuring data controllers and others comply with the requirements of the legislation. The author is not aware of any great rush by individuals to exercise their rights of rectification, etc. nor to apply to the court for compensation, apart from a few high profile cases. It may be that most cases where individuals have applied to a court to enforce their rights go unnoticed and are not given publicity. It would appear that, rather than exercise their rights of rectification and prevention of processing directly, many individuals instead complain to the Information Commissioner. This would be in line with experiences under the 1984 Act and, indeed the number of complaints made is growing under the 1998 Act and now stands at around 10,000 per year.[1] The provisions are different under the 1998 Act and, strictly speaking, "complaints" are "requests for assessment" under section 42 of the Act. The Information Commissioner is not obliged to make an assessment and might decline, for example, on the basis that the individual should first make a subject access request or if there has been an undue delay in submitting the request.

The Data Protection Act 1998 gives the Information Commissioner powers of enforcement by way of notices and also provides for a number of criminal offences, for example, failing to notify non-exempt processing and procuring the disclosure of personal data without the data controller's consent. The most draconian notice is the enforcement notice which may order a data controller to cease a particular processing activity that is contrary to the Act. Other forms of notice are aimed at obtaining information about processing activity so that the Information Commissioner can take a view on the legality of the

---

[1] 9,994 in the year 2003/4 – Information Commissioner, *Annual Report 2004*, HC699 p.89.

processing or whether it falls within the special purposes (journalism or artistic or literary purposes). Where processing is claimed to be within the special purposes, the Information Commissioner is also given the power to make a determination as to whether this is so.

One point that can be made is that the numbers of notices served and the number of prosecutions under the Act are fairly low. In the year 2002/3 (the latest for which full figures are available for the number of notices served) a total of 12 notices, including preliminary notices were served. In the year 2003/4, there were 8 prosecutions, all under section 55(1) in respect of obtaining or disclosing personal data without the data controller's consent. One man was found guilty of 10 offences and asked for 165 other offences to be taken into consideration. He was fined a total of £10,000.

SYSTEM OF NOTICES

The Information Commissioner has at his disposal three forms of notice provided for by the Data Protection Act 1998, namely:

* the enforcement notice;

* the information notice; and

* the special information notice.

As was the case under the 1984 Act, the Information Commissioner has also adopted a system for preliminary notices. In some cases, the preliminary notice (although not provided for in the Act) will be sufficient to resolve any issue about the processing activity or the provision of information by the data controller. In some cases, a preliminary notice may lead to the formal notice. However, a preliminary notice is not an essential precursor to the formal notice and an enforcement notice or one of the two forms of information notice may be served on a data controller with no prior warning. This is unlikely to come as a complete surprise as the data controller has most likely already been involved in correspondence with or investigation by the Information Commissioner. Under section 47, failing to comply with an enforcement notice, information notice or special information notice is a criminal offence. An offence is also committed if a person makes a statement in purported compliance which he knows to be false in a material respect or recklessly makes such a statement. There is a due diligence defence in relation to failing to comply with a notice.

ENFORCEMENT NOTICE

Under section 40, if the Commissioner is satisfied that the data controller has contravened or is contravening any of the data protection principles, he may serve a notice requiring the data controller to take or refrain from taking specified steps within a specified time and/or refrain from processing after a specified time:

- any personal data;

- personal data of a specified description; or

- for a specified purpose or purposes or in a specified manner.

Where an enforcement notice relates to a breach of the fourth data protection principle (inaccurate data), the Commissioner may, if reasonably practicable, require the data controller to notify third parties to whom the data have been disclosed. In determining what is reasonably practicable, regard is to be had to the number of third parties who would have to be notified. There are also similar powers to those of the court in respect of inaccurate data that accurately record information provided by the data subject or a third party.

In deciding whether to serve the notice, any personal damage or distress caused or likely to be caused has to be taken into account. The provisions as to the service of enforcement notices are subject to restrictions as regards processing for the special purposes (journalism, literary and artistic purposes).

Enforcement notices cannot take effect until the period for appeal has expired or pending an appeal unless the case is a matter of urgency in which case the time for compliance is seven days. This happened in *Midlands Electricity Board v Data Protection Registrar*, 7 May 1999. However, the appeal to the Tribunal was successful on that point and, although the Tribunal held that it had been right to serve an enforcement notice, the part of the notice requiring compliance as a matter of urgency was struck out at a preliminary hearing. The Tribunal did not find any evidence of any likelihood to cause any person damage or distress. This is a factor in whether to serve an enforcement notice. In the end the Tribunal extended the time for compliance for 18 months. It would take the data controller a significant amount of time to modify its software to overcome the problem as there was no ability to record persons who had opted out. The original complaint arose from an innocuous booklet, enclosed with power supply bills and statements, which contained information about power and energy and related products but which also contained information about products unconnected with power supply.

An enforcement notice may be cancelled or varied by the Commissioner. This may be done on the Commissioner's own initiative or following a written application by the data controller after the period for appeal has expired where he can show that by reason of a change in circumstances some or all of the provisions of the notice need not be complied with to ensure compliance with the data protection principles; section 41.

Under the 1984 Act, in *British Gas Trading Ltd* v *Data Protection Registrar,* 24 March 1998, the Tribunal held that the Registrar was right to serve an enforcement notice rather than accept an undertaking from British Gas Trading Ltd.

INFORMATION NOTICE

Under section 43, an information notice may be served by the Information Commissioner as a result of a request for assessment (see later) by or on behalf of an individual who believes that he is directly affected by processing, as to whether it is likely or unlikely to comply with the Act. Alternatively, the Information Commissioner may serve an information notice if he reasonably requires the information to determine whether the data controller has complied with or is complying with the data protection principles.

The notice will require the data controller to furnish information within a time and in a form specified in the notice. Where the notice results from a request for assessment, the notice must state this and the processing to which the request relates. In other cases, there must be a statement to the effect that the Information Commissioner regards the specified information as relevant for the purpose of determining whether the data controller has complied with or is complying with the data protection principles and the reasons why it is relevant for that purpose. The notice must also give particulars of the right of appeal to the Information Tribunal under section 48. Furthermore, the time stated for providing the information sought must not expire before the time allowed for an appeal, being 28 days. If an appeal is brought, then the data controller need not furnish the information until the appeal has been determined or withdrawn.

The notice may contain a statement that compliance is required as a matter of urgency, giving reasons, within seven days from the day on which the notice is served. Legal professional privilege is preserved so the data controller does not have to furnish information so protected and it applies in respect of any person representing the data controller. The rule against self-incrimination also applies, other than in respect of an offence under the Data Protection Act 1998.

Under section 46(3) an information notice may not be served on a data controller in respect of processing for the special purposes unless a determination under section 45 has taken effect.

SPECIAL INFORMATION NOTICE

These notices relate to processing for the special purposes (the purposes of journalism, artistic purposes or literary purposes). These provisions are, in many respects, similar to those for information notices and must contain particulars of the right of appeal and, unless compliance is required within seven days as a matter of urgency, must not take effect until the time for bringing an appeal to the Information Tribunal has expired or, if an appeal is brought, until determination of the appeal or withdrawal. There are also parallel provisions on legal professional privilege and the right against self-incrimination.

Under section 44, the notice may be served if the Commissioner has received a request for assessment under section 42 (the Act is silent on whether there is, on its face, an issue in the request relating to the special purposes but this seems a reasonable assumption to make) or if the Commissioner has reasonable grounds for suspecting that, in a case where proceedings have been stayed under section 32, the data are not being processed only for the special purposes or with a view to publication for the first time by the data controller.

A stay under section 32(4) may be ordered by the court where the data controller claims that the processing is only for the special purposes and with a view to publication by any person of any journalistic, literary or artistic material which, at the time 24 hours immediately before the time of the claim, had not previously been published by the data controller. In this context, "publish" means making available to the public or any section of the public.

The proceedings referred to in section 32(4) are in relation to subject access, processing likely to cause damage or distress, automated decision-taking or rights in relation to inaccurate data. The stay applies until a determination under section 45 takes effect or the data controller withdraws the claim. The purpose of the provisions relating to stays is to prevent interference with the right of freedom of expression, for example, by the imposition of a "gagging order".

Unless the notice is sent after a request for assessment is made, the notice may only be sent where a data controller has used the exemption under section 32 (special purposes) as a shield in any proceedings to obtain a stay.

The purpose of the notice is to obtain information so that the Information Commissioner can determine whether the exemption for the special purposes does indeed apply or whether the data are being processed with a view to publication by any person of journalistic, literary or artistic material not previously published by the data controller. This envisages a situation where the data controller, who has not previously published the material, intends to disclose the data to another person who will publish it, hence the reference to publication by any person. This must also include the data controller himself.

PROCESSING FOR THE SPECIAL PURPOSES – RESTRICTIONS ON NOTICES AND DETERMINATIONS

Under section 46, an enforcement notice may not be served on a data controller with respect to processing for special purposes unless a determination by the Information Commissioner under section 45(1) has taken effect *and* the court has given leave to serve the notice. A court will not grant leave unless satisfied that the Information Commissioner has reason to suspect a contravention of the principles of substantial public importance and, except where the case is one of urgency, the data controller has been given notice, in accordance with the rules of court, of the application for leave to serve the notice.

The Commissioner may not serve an information notice with respect to processing for special purposes unless a determination by the Commissioner as to the special purposes has taken effect.

A determination under section 45 may be that the personal data are not being processed only for the special purposes or are not being processed with a view to publication by any person of journalistic, literary or artistic material not previously published by the data controller. The determination must be in writing and notice of it must be given to the data controller and contain details of rights of appeal under section 48. It cannot take effect until the end of the period during which an appeal can be brought or pending the determination or withdrawal of an appeal where there is one.

The Commissioner's powers of entry and inspection are described later in this chapter but a warrant must be obtained from a judge before those powers may be exercised. However, no warrant shall be issued in respect of processing for special purposes of journalism, literary or artistic purposes unless the Information Commissioner has first made a determination under section 45.

APPEALS

Appeals go to the Information Tribunal (formerly known as the Data Protection Tribunal) and may, under section 48, be made in respect of:

- enforcement, information or special information notices;
- a refusal by the Commissioner to cancel or vary an enforcement notice;

- where a notice contains a statement that the notice must be complied with as a matter of urgency within seven days, the Commissioner's decision to include the statement or the effect of the inclusion of the statement as regards any part of the notice; or

- a determination under section 45.

The Tribunal may allow the appeal, substitute another notice if it considers that the notice is not in accordance with the law or, where it involved an exercise of discretion by the Information Commissioner, and that discretion ought to have been exercised differently, cancel or vary a notice, rule ineffective statements made by the Commissioner requiring compliance as a matter of urgency (in respect of the whole or part of a notice) or cancel a determination of the Commissioner, as appropriate.

The rules of procedure have been made under powers in Schedule 6 to the Act which also deals with the constitution of the Tribunal, *ex parte* proceedings in cases involving certificates in relation to national security and the power to remit to the High Court for contempt. The Tribunal may review any determination of fact on which the notice in question was based. Appeals from the Tribunal on a point of law go to the High Court in England or Wales, the Court of Session in Scotland or the High Court of Justice in Northern Ireland, depending on the address of the appellant.

REQUESTS FOR ASSESSMENT

If a person believes processing is being carried on which directly affects him, he or a person on his behalf may apply for an assessment as to whether the processing is likely to or unlikely to comply with the provisions of the Act (section 42). The Information Commissioner shall upon receipt of such a request make such assessment, providing he has been furnished with sufficient information to identify the person making the request and the processing in question.

The matters to which the Information Commissioner may take into account to determine the manner in which it is appropriate to make an assessment include:

- the extent to which the request appears to the Commissioner to raise a matter of substance;

- any undue delay in making the request; and

- whether the person making the request is entitled to make a subject access request.

The Commissioner shall notify the person whether an assessment has been made as a result of the request and any view formed or action to be taken, having regard in particular to any exemption from subject access, of any view formed or action taken as a result.

In the year 2003/4, the Information Commissioner received a total of 11,664 requests for assessment (including 1,670 under the telecommunications and electronic communications regulations). Of the recorded outcomes, advice was given in 57% of cases and the request was declined in 12% of cases (or insufficient information was provided by the person making the request). It was thought that compliance with the principles was likely in 15% of cases and unlikely in 16% of cases.[2]

OFFENCES

Data controllers must ensure that their employees and agents who process personal data on their behalf are reliable and trustworthy. Under paragraph 10 of Part II of Schedule 1 (interpretation of the seventh data protection principle), data controllers are under an obligation to ensure the reliability of employees having access to personal data and, under paragraph 11, data processors processing data on behalf of the data controller are required to process under a contract made or evidenced in writing which imposes the equivalent security obligations as the data controller is under by virtue of the seventh principle.

The dangers of employees disclosing personal data in an unauthorised manner was highlighted in a prosecution concluded in July 1998 where a father and son were found guilty of a number of offences under the 1984 Act.[3] The son worked for the National Westminster Bank and had passed on information concerning some of the bank's customers to his father who was a private investigator. Total fines of £6,000 in respect of nine offences were imposed, the son being fined £1,000 only. The activities of private investigators continue to cause concern under the 1998 Act. The Information Commissioner refers to the organised and systematic obtaining of personal data by deception (known as "blagging"). In many cases, employees disclose personal data to private investigators and the like, usually in return for payment. Such disclosures have been made by persons working for DVLA, the police and the Inland Revenue. A number of persons have been charged with the offence of misconduct in public office which carries a maximum penalty of five years' imprisonment. Persons such as private investigators who paid

[2] Information Commissioner, *Annual Report 2004*, HC699, p.91.
[3] Press release, Office of the Data Protection Registrar, 15 July 1998.

these persons to disclose the personal data to them have been charged with the offence of aiding, abetting, counselling or procuring the offence. This also carries a maximum of five years' imprisonment. The offence of misconduct in public office has more teeth than offences under the Data Protection Act 1998, none of which carry custodial sentences.

Proceedings for offences under the Act may be brought, in England and Wales, only by the Commissioner or by or with the consent of the Director of Public Prosecutions (in Northern Ireland, the Director of Public Prosecutions for Northern Ireland); section 60(1). There is potential for the Commissioner, including past Commissioners, to be prosecuted under the Act in respect of disclosures of confidential information (under section 59). If this unlikely event should occur, presumably the prosecution would be by or with the consent of the Director of Public Prosecutions. The Commissioner can hardly prosecute himself!

Senior officers of corporate bodies (director, manager, secretary or similar officer) may also be charged with an offence under the Act if the offence was committed by the body corporate with the consent or connivance of or through the neglect of the senior officer; section 61. The same applies to any person purporting to act in any such capacity.

OFFENCES RELATED TO NOTIFICATION

Where notification is required under the Act, failure to notify is an offence of strict liability; section 21(1). Under section 21(2), it is also an offence to fail to notify changes but this is subject to a due diligence defence. A data controller who can show that he exercised all due diligence to comply with the duty to notify changes has a defence under section 21(3). As data controllers may have to make changes to their processing activities very quickly in response to market or other pressures, a period of 28 days is allowed within which the Information Commissioner must be notified by virtue of regulation 12(2) of the Data Protection (Notification and Notification Fees) Regulations 2000. Even so, it is incumbent on data controllers to continually review their processing activities and to have procedures in place to flag changes to their processing activities which will impact upon their registered particulars. If such "good practice" systems are in place, it is likely that the due diligence defence will succeed. The burden of proving due diligence is, of course, on the data controller but the standard of proof will be that commonly applicable to defences for criminal offences, being proof on a balance of probabilities. It is not thought that this is a case of adducing sufficient evidence to raise the defence, leaving it to the prosecution to disprove it. That would be to introduce unnecessary technicality in what is, after all, a relatively minor offence.

Section 22(6) makes it an offence to commence processing before a notification has been given to the Information Commissioner in respect of assessable processing requiring a preliminary assessment by the Commissioner and before the period during which the Commissioner can serve a notice on the data controller has expired (within 28 days or the period as extended up to a maximum of 42 days). This is an offence of strict liability and could be very easy to commit. No orders have yet been made by the Secretary of State specifying processing of a type coming within these provisions. However, when such orders are made (and it seems likely that orders may be made in respect of processing genetic data, data matching and processing by private investigators) the wide definition of processing may catch out data controllers. Simply collecting and having personal data fall within the definition of processing. It is likely that a data controller may be tempted to obtain personal data in advance of notifying the Commissioner on the assumption that what is controlled is active processing. Indeed, it may be difficult for the Commissioner to carry out an effective preliminary assessment if the data controller has no examples of the type of data he wishes to process for the Commissioner to examine.

Where a data controller has elected not to notify processing which is exempt, for example manual processing, the data controller is under a duty to provide the relevant particulars to any person on request in writing and within 21 days of receipt of that request. The relevant particulars are those referred to in paragraphs (a) to (f) of section 16(1), that is, the registrable particulars except, of course, a statement that notification does not extend to exempt data which are being processed. However, the duty to provide the relevant particulars does not apply to processing exempt from the notification provisions in Part III of the Act.

Where the duty arises, the relevant particulars must be made available in writing and free of charge. Failure to comply is an offence under section 24(4). This is, however, subject to a defence that the person charged exercised all due diligence to comply with the duty; section 24(5).

The imposition of this duty and the possibility of criminal proceedings may be one reason why data controllers choose to notify processing activity exempt from the notification requirements in respect of which the duty arises. Another factor is that notification of processing that would otherwise be exempt may relieve the data controller of the obligation to inform data subjects as to the purposes of processing, when data are collected from the data subject or in other cases subject, of course, to the overriding proviso that such information must be given to ensure that the processing is fair under the first data protection principle.

OFFENCES RELATED TO NOTICES SERVED BY THE COMMISSIONER

There are two offences associated with notices. Under section 47(1), a person who fails to comply with an enforcement notice, information notice or special information notice commits an offence. Section 47(3) provides a defence if the person charged can prove that he exercised all due diligence to comply with the notice. Data controllers who have taken effective action to comply with notices should have a defence, especially if they keep a careful record of the steps they take to comply and can show that those steps are reasonable and appropriate in the context of the notice.

A person who makes a statement knowing it to be false in a material respect, or recklessly makes a statement which is false in a material respect in purported compliance with an information notice or special information notice, commits an offence; section 47(2). Of course, there is no due diligence defence for this. Until recently, it appeared that recklessness was an objective concept based on the ordinary prudent adult and whether such a person would think there was an obvious risk of the prohibited consequence using the test set out by Lord Diplock in *R v Caldwell*.[4] However, the House of Lords overruled *Caldwell* in *R v G*[5] reinstating the subjective test that applied before *Caldwell*.

The term "recklessness" was also used in respect of the 1984 Act and it came up for consideration in *Data Protection Registrar v Amnesty International (British Section)*, 8 November 1994, in which Amnesty International was charged with offences under sections 5(2)(b) and (d) of the 1984 Act (there are no equivalent offences under the 1998 Act). Amnesty International had disclosed its mailing list to another charitable organisation. At first instance, the stipendiary found that Amnesty International had not been reckless because the disclosure of the list did not cause a serious harmful consequence. He relied on Lord Diplock's judgment in *R v Lawrence*[6] where he spoke of an "obvious and serious" risk, rather than simply an "obvious risk". The Data Protection Registrar appealed to the Queen's Bench Divisional Court by way of case stated. The appeal was allowed and it was confirmed that, for the purposes of the Data Protection Act 1984, there is no requirement that the risk of harm should be serious, it must simply be an obvious risk. But now *Caldwell* has been consigned to the history books (and most lawyers are only too happy to see that happen as it resulted in some very unreasonable findings of guilt) and where recklessness is the relevant form of *mens rea* (the mental element), the prosecution will have to show that the accused knew that there was a risk of the forbidden consequence occurring as a result of his acts or omissions.

---

[4] [1982] AC 341.
[5] [2003] UKHL 50.
[6] [1982] AC 510.

OBTAINING, DISCLOSING, PROCURING AND SELLING OFFENCES

Offences of procuring the disclosure of personal data and selling such data were inserted into the 1984 Act by section 161 of the Criminal Justice and Public Order Act 1994. Activities leading to such offences represent serious threats to the rights of privacy in relation to processing personal data. Section 55 of the Data Protection Act 1998 restates and expands these sorts of offences. There were a number of successful prosecutions under the 1984 Act. In one case, a private investigator obtained personal information relating to famous people from British Telecom by deception, some of which she sold to tabloid newspapers.[7] She was prosecuted for six offences under section 5(6) of the 1984 Act for procuring the information and six offences under section 5(7) of the 1984 Act for selling the information to her clients. She was fined a total of £1,200. The offences under the 1998 Act of obtaining, disclosing, procuring the disclosure of personal data without the data controller's consent and selling such data are probably the most important ones under the Act and, in the year to 31 March 2004, all offences charged involved either obtaining or disclosing personal data without the data controller's consent.

Under section 55(1), the *mens rea* for the offences of obtaining or disclosing personal data or the information contained in the data or procuring the disclosure of information contained in personal data without the consent of the data controller is knowledge or recklessness (which now must be judged subjectively). There are some specific defences in section 55(2) including the prevention of crime, public interest, reasonable belief in a right in law to obtain or disclose the data and reasonable belief that the data controller would have consented. It is also an offence for a person who has obtained personal data in contravention of section 55(1) to sell those data; section 55(4). This offence does not require *mens rea* although, of course, the original obtaining does. However, under section 55(5), it is also an offence to offer to sell personal data obtained or subsequently obtained in contravention of section 55(1). There is no requirement for the person offering to sell the data to be the same person responsible for the obtaining, disclosure or procuring the disclosure of the data. This offence, therefore, appears to be of strict liability and could be committed by an "innocent" third party to whom the data have been disclosed by the person originally responsible for acquiring them in contravention of section 55(1). Furthermore, an advertisement indicating that the data are or may be for sale is within the meaning of an offer to sell. Although not defined in the Act, it seems appropriate to take a dictionary meaning of "advertisement", being a public notice or announcement. A conversation in a public house between two persons, a potential seller and buyer of the data, is unlikely to be considered an advertisement. The same should apply where a

---

[7] Data Protection Registrar, *Fourteenth Annual Report*, London: Stationery Office, 1998 at 21 & 54.

person simply makes it known to a small number of persons, such as journalists, that he or she has personal data to sell. It is questionable what the purpose of this provision is as anyone wishing to sell personal data of doubtful pedigree is hardly likely to place an advertisement in Exchange & Mart.

OBSTRUCTING OR FAILING TO GIVE ASSISTANCE IN RESPECT OF OVERSEAS INFORMATION SYSTEMS

A new offence under section 54A was inserted into the Data Protection Act 1998 by the section 81 of the Crime (International Co-operation) Act 2003, and took effect on 26 April 2004. Sub-section (1) gives the Information Commissioner the power to inspect the Schengen information system, the Europol information system and the Customs information system for the purpose of assessing whether or not any processing has been or is being carried out in compliance with this Act. Section 54A(6) makes it an offence to intentionally obstruct a person exercising that power or, without reasonable excuse, to fail to give any person exercising the power any assistance he may reasonably require.

ENFORCED SUBJECT ACCESS

Forcing a person to carry out a subject access request to confirm to a prospective employer that the person has no record of criminal convictions or police cautions has long been seen as an abuse of data protection law. Section 56 would make this an offence in some cases but, because of difficulties with the Police Act 1977 and the position in Northern Ireland, this provision has not yet been brought into force and it does not appear that it will be brought into force for some time, if ever.

Requiring an individual to supply certain types of records concerning him– or herself will be made a criminal offence where it is done so in connection with recruitment of that person as an employee or the continued employment of that person or in respect to any contract for the provision of services by that person to the person requiring the supply of the record; section 56(1). Under section 56(2), a person who is concerned with the provision of goods, facilities or services to the public, whether or not for payment, must not, as a condition of such provision or offer of such provision to another person, require that other person to supply him with a relevant record or produce it to him. The types of records caught are described as "relevant records" and relate to convictions and cautions, imprisonment or detention and certain functions concerning social security contributions and benefits. A table in section 56, which may be amended by the Secretary of State, sets out the data controllers and subject-matter within the enforced subject access provisions and should be referred to for further detail. Therefore, an employer who requires that a prospective employee provide a certificate of his criminal convictions and cautions would commit an offence unless one of the defences in section 56(3) applies.

Contravention of either section 56(1) or (2) will be an offence but, under section 56(3) it will be a defence to show that the imposition of the requirement was required or authorised by or under any enactment, by any rule of law or by order of a court or, in the particular circumstances, the imposition of the requirement was justified in the public interest. However, in terms of certificates of criminal records and the like under Part V of the Police Act 1997, the imposition of the requirement is not justified in the public interest on the ground that it would assist in the prevention or detection of crime.

MISCELLANEOUS OFFENCES

The Information Commissioner and the staff of the Commissioner's Office have access to all manner of information which is obtained or supplied under the Data Protection Act 1998 or under the Freedom of Information Act 2000. Much of this information will be publicly available, such as the registrable particulars and there are no issues of confidentiality in respect of such information. However, other information is confidential. An example is details of a data controller's security arrangements (although very bland descriptions are acceptable, such as confirmation that appropriate standards are adhered to). Another example may be responses by data controllers to information and special information notices, in as much as there has not been any public hearing before the Tribunal. Much other confidential information may be in the hands of the Commissioner and agents and staff. Some will relate to enforcement and pending criminal prosecutions. Other information may involve private and unpublished information relating to data subjects or information which is commercially sensitive. Issues of privacy may occur in relation to individuals and organisations. Because of this the Commissioner, and previous Commissioners, members of the Commissioner's staff and agents of the Commissioner who knowingly or recklessly disclose unpublished information obtained by or furnished to the Commissioner under or for the purposes of the Data Protection Act 1998 or the Freedom of Information Act 2000 (this was inserted with effect from 30 November 2000) will commit an offence; section 59. The information must relate to an identified or identifiable individual or business and must not have been made available to the public from other sources before or at the time of the disclosure complained of.

There is a defence of lawful authority under section 59(2). This applies in a number of cases, the first is where the disclosure is made with the consent of the individual or person carrying on the business. It also applies where the information was provided for the purpose of being made available to the public under the Data Protection Act 1998 or the Freedom of Information Act 2000, for example, this would apply where the information disclosed was part of the registrable particulars but which had not at, the time of the disclosure, been entered on the register. Another case of lawful authority is where the disclosure is for the purposes of, and is necessary for, the discharge of any function under either Act or any Community obligation. Disclosure for the purposes of any civil or criminal proceedings (whether arising under either Act or otherwise) is a further form of lawful authority. The final form of lawful authority is where the disclosure is necessary in the public interest, having regard to the rights and freedoms or legitimate interests of any person.

It is noteworthy that information relating to businesses is within these provisions. An example is where the information concerns the security measures taken by a limited company in respect of its processing of personal data. "Business" is defined in section 70(1) as including any trade or profession. It would not seem to cover public bodies or authorities.

The Commissioner's powers of entry and inspection are contained in Schedule 9 to the Act and are described towards the end of this chapter. Under paragraph 12 of the Schedule, any person who intentionally obstructs a person in the execution of a warrant issued under the Schedule or who fails without reasonable excuse to give any person executing such a warrant such assistance as he may reasonably require for the execution of a warrant, commits an offence. This is the only offence in the Act which is not triable either way and the maximum penalty is a fine not exceeding level 5 on the standard scale; section 60(3).

Finally, it should be noted that the Information Tribunal can commit a person to the High Court (or, in Scotland, the Court of Session) where a person is guilty of any act or omission in respect of proceedings before the Tribunal if it would be such as to amount to contempt of court if the proceedings were proceedings before a court. The Tribunal cannot punish the person itself but must certify the matter for the court. The court can then deal with the matter as if it were contempt of court. The maximum penalty is two years imprisonment; section 14(1) Contempt of Court Act 1981.

Under section 77 of the Freedom of Information Act 2000, where a request for information has been made to a public authority, and under section 1 of that Act or section 7 of the Data Protection Act 1998, the applicant would have been entitled (subject to payment of any fee) to communication of any information in accordance with that section, any person (a public authority and any person in it employ, or who is an officer of, or is subject to the direction of the pubic authority) is guilty of an offence if he alters, defaces, blocks, erases, destroys or conceals any record held by the public authority, with the intention of preventing the disclosure by that authority of all, or any part, of the information the communication of which the applicant would have been entitled. The maximum penalty is a fine not exceeding level 5 on the standard scale. The offence is triable summarily only.

LIABILITY OF EMPLOYEES, SENIOR OFFICERS ETC.

Some of the offences in the Act may be committed by employees or agents of the data controller, for example, knowingly or recklessly disclosing personal data without the consent of the data controller under section 55. In other cases, an employee of the data controller as well as the data controller may commit an offence. One possible example is the offence of requiring a person to supply a record indicating criminal convictions and cautions under section 56. For example, if the managing director of a company required the supply of such a record, both he and the company could be prosecuted. Other offences, such as failing to notify processing activity, may be committed only by the data controller and not by an employee of the data controller.

The usual provisions apply with respect to offences committed by a body corporate where it is proved that the offence was committed with the consent or connivance or was attributable to any neglect on the part of any director, manager, secretary or similar officer or person purporting to act in such a capacity; section 61. That person, as well as the body corporate, is liable to prosecution. This also applies where the affairs of the body corporate are managed by its members. They are treated as directors for the purposes of this provision. In Scotland, where an offence has been committed by a Scottish partnership, if the offence is proved to have occurred with the consent or connivance of, or is attributable to any neglect on the part of a partner, that partner may also be prosecuted. Where directors, managers, etc. are prosecuted under these provisions, the same maximum penalties apply.

MODE OF TRIAL AND PENALTIES

None of the offences carry custodial sentences (apart from the equivalent of contempt before the Tribunal) and it is unlikely that punishments meted out by magistrates' courts will increase by any significant amount if at all. That being so and bearing in mind the number of prosecutions each year is only a few dozen, the teeth of data protection law in terms of criminal liability are not particularly sharp and do little to encourage full compliance with the result that, in many cases, individuals' rights under data protection law may be seriously compromised. As the vast majority of prosecutions in the past have been for failing to register, the danger is that a culture of "register and ignore" the data protection principles will be tacitly encouraged.

Apart from the offences relating to warrants, under section 60(2) the maximum penalties are:

> *"on summary conviction, a fine not exceeding the statutory maximum, or on conviction on indictment, a fine."*

The warrant offences carry a maximum of a fine not exceeding level 5 on the standard scale. Of course, the court may impose other sentences such as an absolute discharge or conditional discharge. In Scotland, an admonishment is possible.

POWERS OF ENTRY AND INSPECTION

The Information Commissioner has powers of entry and inspection which are set out in Schedule 9 to the Act. The basic mechanism is that the Commissioner first gives the occupier of the premises in which evidence of a contravention of the principles or the commission of an offence under the Act may be found, seven days' notice demanding access at a reasonable hour. If that access is refused or granted but the occupier unreasonably refuses to comply with a request from the Commissioner or officers or staff of the Commissioner to search, inspect, examine etc., the Commissioner may then apply to a circuit judge or district judge (or the magistrates' court) for a warrant.

The occupier must then be notified that an application for a warrant is to be made so that the occupier can have an opportunity to be heard on the question of whether the warrant should be issued. The circuit judge or district judge will grant a warrant if satisfied, after considering information given on oath and supplied by the Commissioner, that there are reasonable grounds for suspecting that a data controller has contravened or is contravening any of the data protection principles or that an offence under the Act has been or is being committed. Furthermore, the judge must be satisfied that there is evidence of the contravention or the commission of the offence to be found on premises specified in the information. However, the judge will not issue the warrant where the relevant data are being processed for the special purposes unless the Commissioner has made a determination under section 45 of the Act.

A warrant may be granted without a prior demand for access where the judge is satisfied that the case is one of urgency and the object of entry would be defeated if the normal procedure is complied with. In such cases, the occupier will have no prior knowledge of the warrant until it is executed.

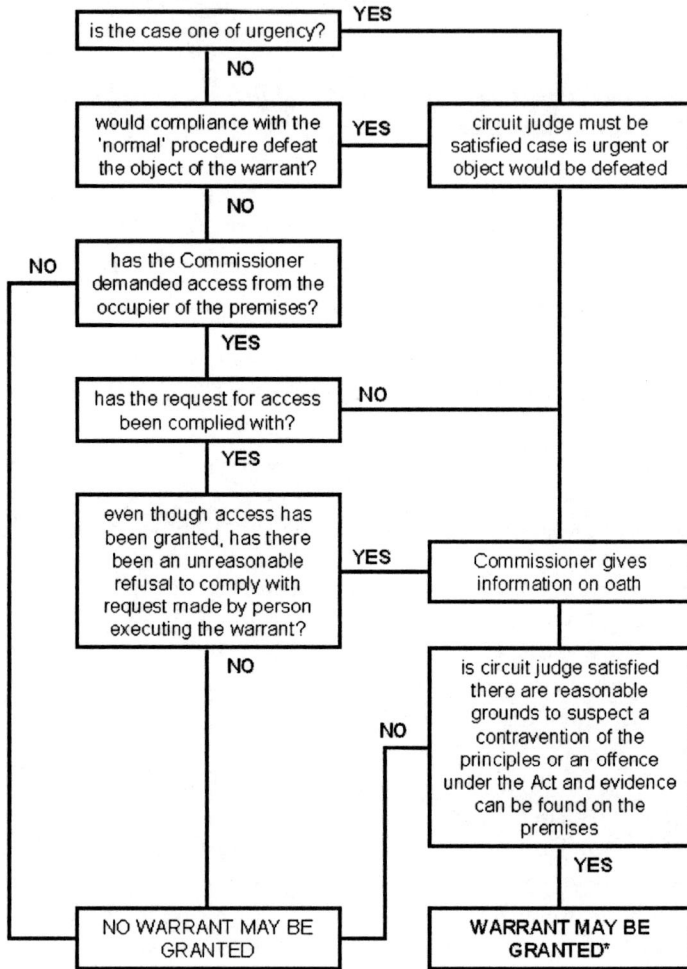

* If the data controller claims processing is for the special purposes, the Commissioner must make a determination under section 45.

Figure 10.1 Grant of warrant

"Premises" includes any vessel, vehicle, aircraft or hovercraft and the person in charge of such things is deemed to be the occupier of premises. Figure 10.1 shows the possible routes to the grant of a warrant.

A circuit judge or district judge granting a warrant will also issue two copies, certified as copies. The grant of a warrant gives the Commissioner, officers or staff, within seven days of the date of the warrant, the power to enter the premises, to search them, to inspect, examine, operate and test any equipment found therein which is used or intended to be used for processing personal data. Documents or other material may be inspected and seized as evidence of a contravention of the principles or the commission of an offence.

"Document" is not defined in the Act. If a restrictive view is taken, being that it means written or printed material, the inclusion of "other material" should be sufficient to cover computer storage media such as magnetic disks. Of course, the operation of any equipment may result in a printed record of, say, the contents of a database comprising information about individuals.

Reasonable force as may be necessary may be used in the execution of a warrant. It must be executed at a reasonable hour unless there are grounds for suspecting the evidence would not be found if executed at a reasonable hour. For example, it may be that it is suspected that unlawful processing only takes place late at night and, immediately after, all evidence of such processing is erased. When the warrant is executed, if the occupier is present, he shall be shown the warrant and given a copy of it. Otherwise, a copy must be left at a prominent place on the premises.

A receipt must be given for anything seized and things seized may be retained for as long as necessary in the circumstances. The occupier may ask for a copy of anything seized and this request should be complied with by the person executing the warrant if he considers he can do so within a reasonable time.

There are a number of restrictions on the powers of inspection and seizure. The powers cannot be exercised in respect of personal data which is exempt under section 28 (national security). Certain communications, documents, copies or other records in relation to certain legal advice given by a professional legal adviser and his client are also exempt. This applies where the advice relates to the client's obligations, liabilities or rights under the Act or in respect of communications in connection with or in contemplation of proceedings arising out of or under the Act, including proceedings before the Tribunal. Where the person in occupation of the premises objects to inspection or seizure of any material on the basis that part of it is exempt from the powers of inspection or seizure, he must still provide that much of the material to which the exemption does not apply.

Warrants must be returned to the issuing court after execution or, if not executed, within seven days of its date. Where it has been executed, the person executing it must endorse the warrant stating what powers have been exercised by him under the warrant.

Schedule 9 contains appropriate modifications in respect of terminology for Scotland and Northern Ireland.

Equivalent powers of search and seizure are given to the Information Commissioner in respect of evidence likely to be found on premises indicating failures to comply with Part I of the Freedom of Information Act 2000 (access to information held by public authorities), decision notices, enforcement or information notices under the Act or offences under section 77 of that Act (altering, etc records held by a public authority with the intention of preventing disclosure) by virtue of Schedule 3 to that Act.

FORFEITURE, ETC.

Where a person has been convicted of one of a number of specific offences under the Act, the court may order the forfeiture, destruction or erasure of any document or other material used in connection with the processing of personal data and appearing to be connected with the commission of the offence; section 60(4). However, the court must give any person, other than the offender, claiming to be the owner of or otherwise having an interest in the document or other material an opportunity to be heard as to why the order should not be made.

The offences to which these provisions apply are as follows:

- processing personal data without having an entry on the register where this is required – section 21(1);

- carrying on assessable processing before receipt of a notice from the Commissioner (or expiry of the time for the Commissioner to respond – section 22(6));

- unlawful obtaining, disclosing or procuring offences under section 55;

- requiring a person to supply or produce a relevant record (for example, a record indicating criminal convictions) – section 56;

- failing to notify changes in the registrable particulars and security measures in relation to assessable processing – section 21(2) but only in respect of processing within section 22;

- failure to comply with an enforcement notice – section 47(1).

In many cases, the order will include an order for erasure where the relevant material is in digital form stored on computer media. The use of the word "erasure" indicates that "other material" must extend to computer data.

CHAPTER 11

THE INFORMATION COMMISSIONER AND THE INFORMATION TRIBUNAL

INTRODUCTION

The present Information Commissioner is Richard Thomas. Previously the post was held by Elizabeth France who was appointed, originally, as the second Data Protection Registrar (the title under the 1984 Act) in 1994 following the retirement of Eric Howe, the first Data Protection Registrar. Under section 6(2) of the Data Protection Act 1998, the Information Commissioner is appointed by Her Majesty by Letters Patent. The role of the Commissioner is somewhat widened, reflecting the changes to data protection law brought about by the Data Protection Directive, however, a number of the general duties are largely as before and powers of entry and inspection are basically the same as under the previous Act. Elizabeth France probably oversaw the greatest changes to the role of Information Commissioner with the inclusion of responsibilities under privacy in telecommunications (now electronic communications) and the Freedom of Information Act 2000. She also had three consecutive titles, Data Protection Registrar, Data Protection Commissioner and, finally, Information Commissioner. The Tribunal's name also changed from Data Protection Tribunal to Information Tribunal.

The Information Tribunal under the 1998 Act is very much like that under the previous law but its jurisdiction is modified to take account of the differences in notices served by the Commissioner and the power of the Commissioner to make determinations. The jurisdiction has also subsequently been extended to hear appeals brought under the Privacy and Electronic Communications (EC Directive) Regulations 2003 (formerly under the Telecommunications (Data Protection and Privacy) Regulations 1999) and appeals under the Freedom of Information Act 2000. As before, a different procedure is implemented in respect of appeals relating to certificates signed by a Minister of the Crown making exemptions on the ground of national security.

First, the office of the Information Commissioner and his role is described, followed by the constitution and jurisdiction of, and the procedure before, the Information Tribunal.

THE INFORMATION COMMISSIONER

Part I of Schedule 5 to the Data Protection Act 1998 sets out the status, capacity and tenure of the Commissioner and other provisions relating to salary, officers and staff, accounts, etc. The functions of the Commissioner are set out in sections 51 to 54 in Part VI of the Act.

THE OFFICE OF INFORMATION COMMISSIONER

Paragraph 1(2) confirms that the Commissioner, officers and staff of the Commissioner are not to be regarded as servants or agents of the Crown. Under paragraph 2, tenure of office is for a period not exceeding five years but the Commissioner may be re-appointed for a maximum term of office not exceeding 15 years. However, there is the possibility of further re-appointment if there are special circumstances and such re-appointment is in the public interest. The Commissioner must retire in any case at the age of 65 years. The Commissioner may be relieved of his office by Her Majesty at the Commissioner's own request or may be removed by Her Majesty following an Address from both Houses of Parliament.

The Commissioner's salary and pension are specified by a resolution in the House of Commons which is charged on and issued out of the Consolidated Fund; paragraph 3.

Up to two deputy Commissioners (presently Frances Aldhouse and Graham Smith) are appointed by the Commissioner under paragraph 4 of Schedule 5 which also allows the Commissioner to appoint a number of other officers and staff as he may determine at a remuneration, pensions, etc. and conditions of service determined by the Commissioner. Apart from the appointment of the deputy Commissioners (the power to appoint two was introduced by the Freedom of Information Act 2000), the establishment of the office of Commissioner and remuneration, pensions, etc. and conditions of service are subject to the approval of the Secretary of State. The deputy Commissioners perform functions conferred on the Commissioner during any vacancy in that office or during any time during which the Commissioner is, for any reason, unable to act. Without prejudice to these provisions, the Commissioner may delegate the performance of functions under the Data Protection Act 1998 and the Freedom of Information Act 2000 to any of the Commissioner's officers and staff. The Commissioner is not required to take out insurance under the Employer's Liability (Compulsory Insurance) Act 1969.

Paragraphs 6 and 7 of Schedule 5 to the Act deal with matters of authentication. The application of the seal of the Information Commissioner is authenticated by his signature or that of some other person authorised for the purpose. Any document purporting to be an instrument issued by the Commissioner and duly executed under the Commissioner's seal or to be signed by or on behalf of the Commissioner is receivable in evidence and deemed to be such an instrument unless the contrary is shown. Thus, there is a presumption that such documents are what they appear to be.

In terms of financial matters, under paragraph 8, the Secretary of State may make payments to the Commissioner out of money provided by Parliament. Unless the Secretary of State, with the consent of the Treasury, otherwise directs, money received by the Commissioner in the exercise of his functions under the Data Protection Act 1998, under section 159 of the Consumer Credit Act 1974 or under the Freedom of Information Act 2000, shall be paid to the Secretary of State, paragraph 9. Such sums received by the Secretary of State are paid into the Consolidated Fund. Money received under the Data Protection Act 1998 is primarily in respect of notification.

Other fees are charged by the Commissioner, for example, in respect of certified copies of register entries and, under section 51, with the approval of the Secretary of State, the Commissioner may charge in respect of services rendered under Part VI of the Act, for example, where the Commissioner assesses processing with the consent of the data controller under section 51(7). The function referred to under section 159 of the Consumer Credit Act 1974 refers to orders made following applications by either a consumer or credit reference agency in respect of notices to correct wrong information held by a credit reference agency. Section 62(2) to (4) of the Data Protection Act 1998 makes the necessary changes to section 159 of the 1974 Act, giving the Information Commissioner the power to hear applications and make orders under section 159.

Finally, under paragraph 10, the Commissioner has a duty to keep proper accounts and prepare an annual statement of account, sending copies to the Comptroller and Auditor General who shall examine and certify the statement and lay copies before each House of Parliament. The relevant financial year is the period of 12 months beginning with 1 April.

Some of the above provisions do not extend to Scotland, in particular those relating to authenticity.

FUNCTIONS OF THE INFORMATION COMMISSIONER

The powers and functions of the Information Commissioner in respect of notification, enforcement, prosecution of offenders and powers of entry and inspection are described in the relevant parts of this book. What we are concerned with here are the specific functions set out in Part VI of the Data Protection Act 1998. They can be classified as follows:

- duties to promote good practice and compliance;

- dissemination of information;

- involvement in respect of drawing up codes of practice;

- dissemination of Community findings in relation to transfers to third countries;

- assessing processing with the consent of data controllers;

- laying reports and codes of practice before each House of Parliament;

- assisting individuals where processing is for the special purposes;

- participating in international co-operation;

- power to inspect personal data in certain overseas information systems.

Good practice and compliance

"Good practice" is defined for the purposes of section 51 as practice in the processing of personal data as appears to the Commissioner to be desirable having regard to the interests of data subjects and others. This includes, but is not limited to, compliance with the requirements of the Act. The danger is that the formulation of good practice may be an attempt by the back door to introduce further forms of constraint than those provided for directly by the Act. That being so, however, good practice can never be determinative of the law but may help in interpreting what is reasonable and what constitutes due diligence where these are issues under the Act and subordinate legislation. With this in mind, data controllers would do well to take note of what constitutes good practice in the eyes of the Commissioner.

A basic duty is the promotion of the following of good practice by data controllers under section 51(1). This also extends to the performance of the Commissioner's functions under the Act to promote the observance of its requirements by data controllers. This latter duty does not necessarily mean that the Commissioner must take enforcement action or commence a prosecution where a contravention of the Act is discovered. The promotion of observance of the requirements of the Act may be achieved through explanation and guidance. Indeed, when the parts of the 1984 Act concerning registration came into force, initially, the Registrar adopted a helpful approach to those data users who did not realise they should have been registered under the Act. The basic provisions on enforcement and information notices clearly gives the Commissioner a discretion by the use of the word "may" such as in the phrase "the Commissioner may serve him with a notice …".

As was the case under the 1984 Act, the Information Commissioner continues to provide guidance for data controllers and data subjects alike about the requirements and operation of data protection law.

Dissemination of information

Section 51(2) requires the Information Commissioner to disseminate information to the public about the operation of the Act, good practice and other matters within the scope of the Commissioner's functions. Furthermore, the Commissioner may give advice to any person as to such matters. The Commissioner decides the form and manner of dissemination and will give such information as appears expedient.

There are also duties to disseminate codes of practice for guidance and to disseminate information concerning to transfers of personal data to outside the European Economic Area: see below.

Codes of Practice

The Information Commissioner may be involved in the preparation of codes of practice in two ways. The first is where the Secretary of State orders, (or the Commissioner considers it appropriate to do so), the preparation and dissemination of codes of practice for guidance as to good practice; section 51(3). Appropriate trade associations, defined as including any body of data controllers, data subjects or persons representing data subjects must be consulted before the codes are prepared. Dissemination is to such persons as the Commissioner considers appropriate. The preparation of codes of practice by the Commissioner is a new function and, previously, the Commissioner could only encourage the preparation and dissemination of codes of practice, as noted below.

The Commissioner, where he considers it appropriate to do so, may also encourage the preparation of codes of practice by trade associations and the dissemination of such codes to members of the association; section 51(4). If a trade association submits a code of practice to the Commissioner for consideration, the Commissioner shall notify the trade association whether, in the opinion of the Commissioner, the code promotes the following good practice. The Commissioner must consult data subjects or representatives of data subjects as appears appropriate before notifying the trade association.

Under the 1984 Act, the Data Protection Registrar was very active in the encouragement of codes of practice. Some examples included codes relating to employee data, data matching, disclosures of information in magistrates' courts, and in relation to the work of trading standards and environmental health officers.

Codes of practice designated under section 32(3) of the Act by the Secretary of State are those by the Broadcasting Standards Commission, the Independent Television Commission, the Press Complaints Commission, the British Broadcasting Corporation's Producers' Guidelines and the Radio Authority Code; Data Protection (Designated Codes of Practice) (No 2) Order 2000. The designation of such codes is in relation to processing for the special purposes and not within the provisions in Part VI. Although such codes of practice are designated by the Secretary of State, he has a duty to consult the Information Commissioner under section 67(3). This is a general duty to consult which applies in the case of all orders and regulations made under the Act except for commencement orders and the notification regulations.

Dissemination of Community findings in relation to transfers to third countries

Section 51(6) requires that the Commissioner disseminates in such form and in such manner as he considers appropriate, a Community finding in respect of countries outside the European Economic Area (EEA) regarding adequacy of protection for personal data, certain decisions of the European Commission and other information concerning processing of personal data outside the EEA.

In respect of third countries not having adequate protection, a "Community finding" is, under paragraph 15(2) of Schedule 1 to the Act, a finding of the European Commission that a country or territory outside the EEA does, or does not, ensure an adequate level of protection for personal data within the meaning in Article 25(2) of the Data Protection Directive. This requires adequacy to be assessed in the light of all the circumstances surrounding the transfer particularly having regard to the nature of the data, the purpose and duration of the proposed processing operation, the countries of origin and final destination, general and sectoral rules of law in the third country and professional rules and security measures complied with in that country. This is very similar to the interpretation of the eighth data protection principle set out in paragraph 13 of Schedule 1 to the Act. Thus, if the European Commission, under the procedure in Article 31(2) of the Data Protection Directive, decides that a particular third country has, or has not, an adequate level of protection, the Commission will inform Member States accordingly and, in the United Kingdom, the Information Commissioner will then disseminate that finding as appropriate. A useful place to disseminate such findings is by placing them on the Commissioner's internet website.

It is notable that a Community finding can be to the effect that a third country (that is, a country outside the EEA) does ensure adequacy of protection for personal data. It would appear, because the test for adequacy is a qualitative question depending on the circumstances, that the finding might be that a third country has adequacy of protection in respect of certain types of processing of certain descriptions of personal data. On the other hand, if the third country adopts a model of data protection equivalent to that in the Data Protection Directive, there seems no reason why the Community finding cannot be to the effect that the third country in question has adequate protection in all cases where processing is allowed under the Directive. Indeed, a number of countries have been designated as adequate, being Canada, Switzerland, Argentina, the Isle of Man, Guernsey and Jersey.

Decisions of the European Commission which the Information Commissioner has a duty to disseminate are those under Article 26(3) or (4) of the Data Protection Directive taken under Article 31(2), being decisions with respect to authorisations for transfers to third countries not having an adequate level of protection where the data controller adduces adequate safeguards, for example, by the use of contractual clauses or where the Commission decides that certain contractual clauses offer sufficient safeguards.

The information to be disseminated in connection with Community findings and relevant decisions of the Commission may be supplemented by other information to be disseminated by the Commissioner. Such other information must be such as appears to the Commissioner to be expedient to give to data controllers in relation to personal data about the protection of the rights and freedoms of data subjects in connection with processing personal data outside the EEA.

Assessing processing with the consent of data controllers

Under section 51(7), the Information Commissioner may, with the consent of the data controller, assess any processing of personal data as to whether it is in accordance with good practice and shall give the data controller the results of such assessment. A data controller who is unsure of whether his processing activity will comply with good practice (in reality, the data controller will only be concerned that the processing concerned complies with the requirements of the Act) may approach the Commissioner for such assessment or it may be that the first approach is made by the Commissioner. In practice, it is unlikely that many data controllers will seek the views of the Commissioner and most will be more likely to be influenced by guidance issued by the Commissioner, Community findings and the like disseminated by the Commissioner, relevant codes of practice, trade associations or the views of the data controller's legal advisers.

Section 51(8) permits the Commissioner to charge a fee for any services under this Part of the Act, including assessments, with consent of the data controller. However, the Secretary of State must give consent to this.

Laying reports and codes of practice before each House of Parliament

As under the previous legislation the Commissioner has a duty to lay annually before each House of Parliament a general report on the exercise of the Commissioner's functions under the Act; section 52(1). These annual reports (the 20th such report was published in 2004) are an invaluable source of information for those involved with data protection law. They are now published on the Commissioner's internet site. As well as looking at the Commissioner's experience in terms of enforcement and prosecutions, such reports look at caseload and developments and are usually very forward looking. The Commissioner may lay other reports before each House in respect of the Commissioner's functions as he thinks fit.

Any code of practice prepared under section 51(3) in compliance with a direction of the Secretary of State must also be laid before each House of Parliament unless such code of practice is included in the annual report or any other report laid before each House of Parliament; section 52(3).

Assisting individuals where processing is for the special purposes

Where processing is for the special purposes, an individual who is a party or prospective party to proceedings (including prospective proceedings) before a court to enforce rights of subject access, the right to prevent processing likely to cause substantial damage or substantial distress, rights in respect of automated decision-taking, rights of rectification or compensation, may apply to the Information Commissioner for assistance under section 53. Until 23 October 2007, also included are proceedings with respect to section 12A(3) – the right of rectification, etc. and a right to require the data controller to cease holding personal manual data (within the meaning of exempt manual data) in a way incompatible with the data controller's legitimate purposes.

As soon as practicable, the Commissioner must consider the application and decide whether and to what extent to provide assistance but will do so only if, in the Commissioner's opinion, the case involves a matter of substantial public importance. Whatever the Commissioner decides, he must inform the applicant as soon as is practicable and, where the decision is not to provide assistance, the Commissioner may, if he thinks fit, give reasons for that decision.

The fine detail is contained in Schedule 10 to the Act. It may include arrangements for the Commissioner to bear the costs of legal advice or representation and, where assistance is provided in respect of the conduct of proceedings, the Commissioner must indemnify the applicant in respect of costs or expenses and the Commissioner may also indemnify the applicant in respect of costs or expenses where a compromise or settlement is reached and may indemnify the applicant in respect of damages awarded pursuant to any interlocutory or interim relief.

In cases where the Commissioner gives assistance to an individual, the person against whom the proceedings have been or are commenced must be informed of that fact. There are also provisions for the Commissioner to have first charge for any expenses incurred on any award made to the applicant in the proceedings or any compromise or settlement.

Thus far, it does not appear that any such assistance has been given to individuals under section 53.

International co-operation

The European Convention for the Protection of Individuals with Regard to Automatic Processing of Personal Data ("the Data Protection Convention") requires co-operation between members of the Data Protection Convention in respect of data protection. The Data Protection Directive also contains provisions for co-operation between the supervisory authorities of Member States. Of course, in the United Kingdom, the Information Commissioner is the supervisory authority. Section 54 of the Data Protection Act 1998, supplemented by two statutory instruments, contains the provision to implement these requirements as regards the functions of the Commissioner. Under the Directive, there is also a Working Party established which is comprised of representatives from the supervisory authorities of Member States, representatives of the authority or authorities established for the Community institutions and a representative of the Commission.

Where the term "data protection functions" is used in section 54, which provides for international co-operation, it means functions relating to the protection of individuals with respect to the processing of personal information.

Co-operation under the Data Protection Convention

Under section 54(1), the Information Commissioner is the designated authority for the purposes of Article 13 of the Data Protection Convention and is the United Kingdom supervisory authority for the purposes of the Data Protection Directive. The functions under Article 13 of the Convention to be performed by the Commissioner are set out in the Data Protection (Functions of Designated Authority) Order 2000, made by the Secretary of State under section 54(2). The Order requires the Commissioner to provide information to other Data Protection Convention countries and, also in accordance with Article 13, allows the Commissioner to request information from other Convention countries.

Article 13 of the Data Protection Convention requires that the parties agree to render each other mutual assistance so as to implement the Convention and to designate one or more authorities. The information to be furnished relates to the law and administrative practice in the field of data protection and parties to the Convention must take, in conformity with their domestic law and for the sole purpose of protection of privacy, all appropriate measures for furnishing factual information relating to specific automatic processing carried out in its territory, with the exception, however, of the personal data being processed.

There are also requirements for the Commissioner to assist persons resident outside the United Kingdom in exercising their rights under Article 8 of the Data Protection Convention which are rights in respect of subject access and rectification or erasure of data processed contrary to the provisions of the relevant domestic law. In particular the Commissioner may notify the person concerned of the data controller's address for receipt of subject access requests. If it appears to the Commissioner that there has been a breach of one of the data protection principles, the Commissioner must either inform the person making the request of the rights and remedies available to him under Part II of the Act or, if the Commissioner considers that this would not help the person making the request or would be otherwise inappropriate, the Commissioner may treat the request as a request for assessment under section 42 of the Act.

If a person, resident in the United Kingdom, requests assistance in respect of the rights under Article 8 of the Data Protection Convention, where the relevant processing is taking place in a Convention country other than the United Kingdom, the Commissioner will forward the request to the supervisory authority of that other country, providing the Commissioner is satisfied that the request contains all the necessary particulars referred to in Article 14(3) of the Data Protection Convention. Those particulars are:

- the name, address and any other relevant particulars identifying the person making the request;
- the automated personal data file to which the request pertains, or its controller;
- the purpose of the request.

As the Data Protection Convention was only concerned with automated processing of personal data, it is reasonable to assume that, where the other Convention country is a member of the EEA, that these particulars should include details of manual filing systems within the meaning of "personal data filing system" in the Data Protection Directive, where appropriate.

Where the Commissioner receives information as a result of a request from a foreign designated authority or made by the Commissioner to such an authority, that information may only be used for the purposes specified in the request.

Co-operation with the European Commission and other supervisory authorities

The Secretary of State has made the Data Protection (International Co-operation) Order 2000 under section 54(3) of the Data Protection Act 1998. The Order sets out the provisions as to co-operation in respect of the exchange of data and the exercise of the Information Commissioner's powers, at the request of another supervisory authority.

Article 3 of the Order applies where the Commissioner is satisfied that a transfer or proposed transfer of personal data to a third country involved or would involve a contravention of the eighth data protection principle. The Commissioner must inform the European Commission and other supervisory authorities of his reasons for this view. If an enforcement notice has been served, the Commissioner must delay informing the European Commission and other supervisory authorities until such time as the notice has expired or, where an appeal is pending, until the outcome of the appeal. Of course, if an appeal against such an enforcement notice is successful completely or in all relevant respects (or an appeal by the Commissioner against such a decision of the Information Tribunal fails), then the Commissioner should not make his initial views known to the European Commission or other supervisory authorities. Although the Article does not specifically state that it applies to transfers from the United Kingdom to third countries, it would appear to so apply, as Article 4 is couched in terms of transfers authorised by other Member States.

If a transfer has been authorised by another Member State by virtue of the derogation from the general prohibition of transfers to third countries not having adequate protection for personal data under Article 26(2) and the Commissioner is satisfied that the authorisation does not comply with those provisions, he may inform the European Commission, giving particulars of the authorisation and his reasons for considering that the authorisation does not comply with Article 26(2). It would seem that the Commissioner has discretion in this case as Article 4(2) of the Order states that the Commissioner *may* inform the European Commission.

The Data Protection Act 1998 only applies to data controllers established in the United Kingdom or, if not so established nor in any other EEA State, data controllers who use equipment in the United Kingdom for processing personal data except only for the purposes of transit through the United Kingdom; section 5(1). For example, an American company which has a processing operation located in the United Kingdom will be subject to the United Kingdom Act. On the other hand, a company established in France will be subject to French data protection law (which is, of course, very similar to United Kingdom law, being based on the Data Protection Directive). If that same French company processes data also in the United Kingdom, as it is established in France, it remains subject to French law and, at first sight, the United Kingdom Act does not apply to it. However, Article 5 of the Data Protection (International Co-operation) Order 2000 allows the United Kingdom Commissioner to exercise his powers of enforcement under Part V of the Act against the French data controller in respect of processing in the United Kingdom if the French supervisory authority so requests. The same applies in respect of all the other EEA States. Article 5 requires that the processing concerned must be within the scope of the functions of the supervisory authority in the other EEA State.

In such cases, the United Kingdom Information Commissioner must send to that other supervisory authority, as soon as reasonably practicable, a statement of the extent of the action he has taken as he thinks fit. If the Commissioner decides not to exercise those functions under Part V of the Act, he must send to that other supervisory authority, as soon as reasonably practicable after making that decision, his reasons for that decision.

Where a data controller is subject to United Kingdom law under section 5(1) of the Act, but is processing data in another Member State, the United Kingdom Commissioner can request the supervisory authority to exercise its equivalent powers of enforcement, based on Article 28(3) of the Data Protection Directive. Such a request must specify the data controller's name and address in that other EEA State in so far as is known and such details of the circumstances of the case as the Commissioner thinks fit to enable that other supervisory authority to exercise those functions.

The Information Commissioner may, under Article 7 of the Order, supply the European Commission or any other supervisory authority, with such information which, in the opinion of the Commissioner, is necessary for the performance of the data protection functions of the European Commission or other supervisory authority. This is a general duty and is not limited to information relating to enforcement in other jurisdictions.

These provisions usefully extend the potential jurisdiction of supervisory authorities in terms of enforcement and prevent the possibility of a data controller setting up his establishment in one EEA State but carrying out most of his data processing operations in another EEA State so as to avoid the rigours of data protection law.

Co-operation in relation to transfers to third countries

The European Commission may make a decision as to whether a third country (that is, a country or territory outside the EEA) affords adequate protection for personal data in accordance with the procedure in Article 31(2) of the Data Protection Directive. Also in accordance with that provision the European Commission may decide that certain contractual clauses offer sufficient safeguards as required by Article 26(2) so as to allow a particular transfer or set of transfers of personal data to third countries.

In either case, under section 54(6), the Information Commissioner must comply with the decision in exercising his functions under paragraph 8 or 9 of Schedule 4 to the Act, being that the transfer is made on the basis of such approved contractual terms or is authorised by the Commissioner. In both cases, the key is that the use of the terms or the manner of transfer is so as to ensure adequate safeguards for the rights and freedoms of individuals.

Under section 54(7), the Commissioner must inform the European Commission and the supervisory authorities in the other EEA States of any approvals he makes under paragraph 8 of Schedule 4 or authorisations he grants under paragraph 9.

Other potential functions

The Secretary of State may by order direct the Information Commissioner to carry out data protection functions to enable Her Majesty's government in the United Kingdom to give effect to any international obligations of the United Kingdom; section 54(4).

If the Secretary of State so directs, the Commissioner must provide any authority exercising data protection functions under the law of any colony, with assistance in relation to the discharge of data protection functions, as directed by the Secretary of State; section 54(5). The terms of the assistance, and payment for the assistance are as directed or approved by the Secretary of State.

Power to inspect overseas information systems

Section 54A was inserted by the Crime (International Co-operation) Act 2003 with effect from 26 April 2004. It gives the Information Commissioner the power to inspect personal data recorded in certain overseas information systems being:

- Schengen information system established under Title IV of the Convention implementing the Schengen Agreement of 14th June 1985;

- Europol information system established under Title II of the Convention on the Establishment of a European Police Office; and

- Customs information system established under Chapter II of the Convention on the Use of Information Technology for Customs Purposes.

The power is exercisable only to ensure processing is in accordance with the Data Protection Act 1998 but includes a power to inspect, operate and test equipment used in such processing. Except in a case of urgency, the Information Commissioner must give prior written notice to the relevant data controller. Anyone obstructing a person exercising the above power or failing without reasonable excuse to give any person exercising the power any assistance he may reasonably require is guilty of an offence.

Information provided to the Commissioner or Tribunal

Section 58 prevents hindrances on persons providing information to the Commissioner or Tribunal necessary for the discharge of their functions under the Data Protection Act 1998 or the Freedom of Information Act 2000. No enactment or rule of law prohibiting or restricting the disclosure of information shall preclude any person providing such information. This could include, for example, information in respect of which the person furnishing the information would otherwise be under, or claim to be under, a duty of confidence.

THE INFORMATION TRIBUNAL

The purpose of the Information Tribunal ("the Tribunal") is primarily to hear appeals from data controllers in respect of notices served by the Commissioner or determinations made by the Commissioner as to whether processing is for the special purposes. A data subject does not have a right to appeal to the Tribunal against a decision of the Commissioner and may only become a party to a hearing before the Tribunal in rare cases involving the national security exemption, if he is a person directly affected by a certificate made under the exemption or where he is a party to proceedings and claims that a general description of personal data in such a certificate does not extend to the data in question. In practice, the Tribunal only handles a small number of appeals each year. It now also has jurisdiction to hear appeals by public authorities against enforcement or information notices served by the Commissioner under the Freedom of Information Act 2000 (this is with effect from 30 November 2002 as a result of the Information Tribunal (Enforcement Appeals) (Amendment) Rules 2002).

The status of the Information Tribunal came under consideration in *Re Ewing*, 20 December 2002. This involved an appeal under section 28(4) against a certificate issued in respect of the national security exemption. Section 42 of the Supreme Court Act 1981 contains provisions relating to vexatious litigants and an order under that provision was made preventing the applicant instituting civil proceedings in the High Court of any inferior court without the leave of the High Court. Ewing argued that leave was not required as the Tribunal was not a court for the purposes of the Act. This argument was rejected and it was held that the Tribunal was a court for the purposes of section 28(4) of the Data Protection Act 1998. By parity of reasoning, the same should apply to section 60(1) of the Freedom of Information Act 2000 which allows appeals against national security certificates issued under section 23(2) or (3) of that Act. In *Re Ewing*, Davis J said (at para 42):

> "... *s.42 extends to all bodies which (having regard to their functions, characteristics and procedures), are constituted as bodies having judicial characteristics and exercising judicial functions by means of judicial procedures, such that they can properly be categorised as courts.*"

He also said that whether a body is labelled as a court does not necessarily mean that it is one, nor does the name Tribunal mean that it is not a court.

CONSTITUTION

The constitution of the Information Tribunal is provided for under section 6(5) and (6) and Part II of Schedule 5 to the Data Protection Act 1998. There is a chairman, appointed by the Lord Chancellor after consulting the Secretary of State and such number of deputy chairmen as the Lord Chancellor so appoints. The Secretary of State is responsible for appointing other members of the Tribunal who shall be:

- persons representing the interests of data subjects;
- persons representing the interests of persons who make requests for information under the Freedom of Information Act 2000;
- persons representing the interests of data controllers; and
- persons representing the interests of public authorities.

The number of members to be appointed is a matter for the Secretary of State to determine.

The chairman and the deputy chairman or chairmen shall have a seven year general qualification within the meaning of section 71 of the Courts and Legal Services Act 1990 (or solicitors or advocates in Scotland of at least seven years' standing or members of the bar of Northern Ireland or solicitors of the Supreme Court of Northern Ireland of at least seven years' standing). There are no particular professional qualification requirements for other members of the Tribunal.

Members of the Tribunal hold and vacate office in accordance with their terms of appointment and are eligible for re-appointment. A member wishing to resign must do so in writing to the Lord Chancellor. The chairman and deputy chairmen must vacate office on attaining the age of 70 years but this is subject to the Judicial Pensions and Retirement Act 1993 and, consequently, it is possible for a such a person to be authorised to continue in office up to the age of 75 years.

The Secretary of State determines remuneration and allowances to be paid out of money provided by Parliament and also may appoint such officers and staff as he thinks necessary for the proper discharge of the Tribunal's functions. Expenses of the Tribunal are determined by the Secretary of State, to be paid out of money provided by Parliament.

Schedule 6 gives some basic detail concerning appeal proceedings, leaving the fine detail to be dealt with by rules, described later. The Tribunal normally sits with a chairman or deputy chairman and an equal number of representatives of data subjects and representatives of data controllers (in the case of an appeal under the Data Protection Act 1998) and the determination of the Tribunal shall be by a simple majority. As under the 1984 Act, it is usual for the Tribunal to sit with the chairman or a deputy chairman and two members.

The appeal procedures are different in national security cases, that is, where the appeal is brought in respect of the national security exemption under section 28. In such cases, the appeal will usually be held *ex parte* before three persons (from amongst the chairman and deputy chairmen of the Tribunal) except where the appeal is disposed of summarily in which case, the appeal is heard *ex parte* by one or more of such persons. An appeal brought under section 48(3) in respect of a statement in a notice served by a Commissioner requiring compliance or the provision of information as a matter of urgency, is heard *ex parte* before the chairman or a deputy chairman sitting alone, unless the Commissioner is asked to give evidence or be heard on any matter relating to the appeal.

JURISDICTION

Except in the case of appeals brought under section 28 (the national security exemption) the rights of appeal are set out in section 48 of the Act. Appeals may be brought under that section against:

- an enforcement, information or special information notice;

- a refusal by the Commissioner to cancel or vary an enforcement notice, following an application by the person on whom the notice has been served;

- the Commissioner's decision to include a statement in a notice to the effect that compliance (in the case of an enforcement notice) or the provision of information (in the case of either an information notice or a special information notice) is required as a matter of urgency within seven days or the effect of the inclusion of such a statement as respects any part of the notice; or

- a determination under section 45.

The first three of the above rights are exercisable by the person on whom the notice has been served whereas the last right to appeal belongs to the data controller in respect of whom the determination has been made. There seems no reason for this subtle change in terminology as the provisions on the service of notices are clear that such notices may only be served on data controllers.

An appeal may be brought under section 28(4) by any person directly affected by the issue of a certificate made for the purposes of the national security exemption. Under section 28(6), where a data controller claims that a certificate made under section 28(2), which identifies the personal data to which it applies by means of a general description, applies to any personal data, in any proceedings in which such a claim is made, any other party may appeal to the Tribunal on the ground that the certificate does not apply to the personal data in question.

PROCEDURE

In proceedings before the Tribunal, in the case of appeals other than in respect of the national security exemption, the procedure is not unlike that before the courts. The Data Protection Tribunal (Enforcement Appeals) Rules 2000 set out the fine detail of the procedure and Figure 11.1 indicates that procedure in simplified form.

Notice of appeal and reply by Commissioner

Appeals must usually be brought within 28 days of the date on which the relevant notice was served on or given to the appellant (rule 4 of the Data Protection Tribunal (Enforcement Appeals) Rules 2000) but the Tribunal may extend that time if, because of special circumstances, it considers it just and right to do so. An appeal must be brought by written notice of appeal served

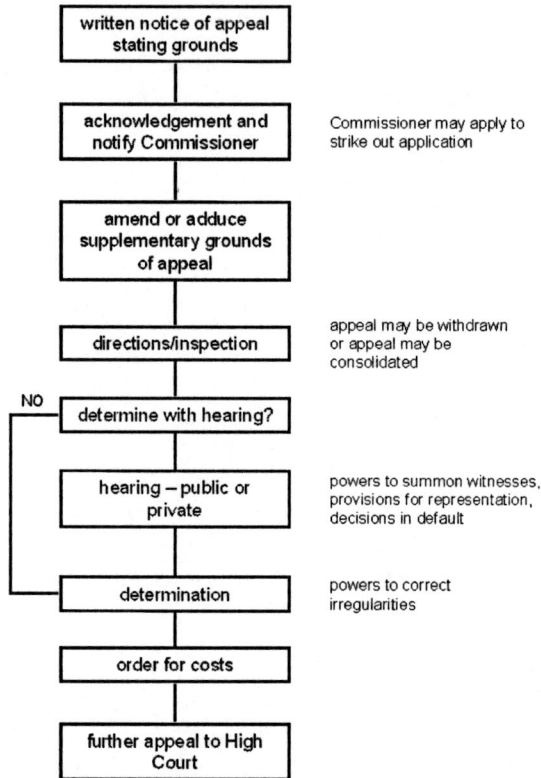

Figure 11.1 Basic procedure before the Tribunal

on the Tribunal and must identify the disputed decision and the date on which that decision was served on or given to the appellant. It must also state the name and address of the appellant, the grounds of appeal, whether the appellant considers that he is likely to wish a hearing to be held or not, and an address for service. If the appeal is brought out of time (that is, exceeding the 28-day limit), the appellant, in his notice of appeal, must also state the special circumstances which he considers justify the Tribunal in accepting juris-diction. Where a notice of appeal is served by post and sent to the proper officer of the Tribunal (either by recorded delivery or registered letter), it is treated as being served on the date on which it is received for dispatch by the Post Office. The "proper officer" is the person appointed by the chairman of the Tribunal to perform the duties of the proper officer under the relevant rule.

When the notice of appeal is received by the proper officer he then will send an acknowledgement to the appellant and a copy of the notice of appeal to the Commissioner. The acknowledgement of service must include a statement of the Tribunal's power to award costs against the appellant. If the notice of appeal relates to appeal under section 48(3) (an appeal in relation to a statement that compliance or the provision of information is required as a matter of urgency within seven days), the proper officer must instead send to the Commissioner a copy of the notice of appeal if the Tribunal considers that the interests of justice require the Commissioner to assist the Tribunal by giving evidence or being heard and, if this is done, the jurisdiction of the Tribunal must not be heard *ex parte*.

There is no specified time limit for acknowledgement of notice of appeal and notification to the Commissioner but it would seem that it should be by return of post. The Commissioner should reply, sending to the Tribunal a copy of the notice relating to the disputed decision and to both the Tribunal and the appellant, a written reply acknowledging service of the notice of appeal and stating whether or not the Commissioner intends to oppose the appeal and, if so, what grounds will be relied upon in opposing the appeal. The reply should be within 21 days except in relation to an appeal under section 48(3) where notice of appeal has been sent to the Commissioner, in which case the time limit is such period as the Tribunal allows, not exceeding 28 days. In such cases, it might be expected that the period allowed should be quite short, preferably before the seven day period for compliance of the provision of information has expired, if that is possible. The Commissioner may ask for an extension to the time to reply, stating the special circumstances which the Commissioner considers makes it just and right to have longer to reply.

Where the appellant has indicated that he is not likely to wish a hearing to be held, the Commissioner, in his reply, must inform the Tribunal and the appellant whether he considers that a hearing is likely to be desirable.

The normal procedure is for an appeal in respect of an information notice brought under section 48(1) to be heard by the chairman sitting alone. However, in such a case, the Commissioner may include in the reply a statement of representation as to why it might be necessary in the interests of justice for the appeal to be heard otherwise than by the chairman sitting alone.

The reply may include a request for an early hearing of the appeal and, if it does, the reasons for that request must be included in the reply.

Amendment, application for striking out, withdrawal and consolidation

The appellant, with the leave of the Tribunal, may amend his notice of appeal or add supplementary grounds of appeal. The usual provisions apply relating to acknowledgement and the sending of a copy to the Commissioner. The Commissioner may amend his reply and, if so, a copy of the amended reply must be sent to the Tribunal and appellant. The normal time periods, including the provisions for extension, apply as in the case of the first reply.

Except where the appeal is brought under section 48(3) (an appeal in relation to a statement that compliance or the provision of information is required as a matter of urgency within seven days), the Commissioner may include a notice requesting that the appeal should be struck out. Possible grounds are that the Commissioner is of the opinion that an appeal does not lie to, or cannot be entertained by, the Tribunal or that the notice of appeal discloses no reasonable grounds of appeal. The strike out notice must state the grounds for the Commissioner's opinion. Where an application for strike out is made, that may be heard as a preliminary issue or at the beginning of the hearing of the appeal.

An appeal may be withdrawn at any time by the appellant. To do this, a notice signed by or on behalf of the appellant must be sent to the Tribunal. The proper officer will then send a copy to the Commissioner. If the notice is sent by either registered letter or recorded delivery, it takes effect when received for dispatch by the Post Office. Although there is no specific requirement for the notice of appeal or Commissioner's reply to be signed there is such a requirement in the case of notice of withdrawal.

There is no mention in the Rules about sending notices in ways other than by post, although rule 27 states that notices may be sent by post in a registered letter or by recorded delivery. It would seem reasonable to suggest that they may be validly served by facsimile transmission or electronic mail. The only downside is that the presumptions as to when the notice takes effect do not apply in such cases.

Where an appeal has been withdrawn, a new appeal cannot be brought by the appellant in respect of the same disputed decision except with the leave of the Tribunal.

Where there are two or more appeals which, in the view of the Tribunal, concern some common question of law or fact or, for some other reason, it is desirable so to proceed, the Tribunal may order that the appeals are consolidated or heard together. Before making such an order, the parties must be given an opportunity to show cause why such an order should not be made.

Directions and inspection

The Tribunal may, on its own motion or on the application of any party, give such directions at any time as it thinks proper to enable the parties to prepare for the hearing of the appeal or to assist the Tribunal to determine issues. Typically, directions may provide that a particular matter is dealt with as a preliminary issue at a pre-hearing review and for a process of discovery, subject to privilege in respect of documents or other material as applies in a court. The recipient of any information or document supplied may only use it for the purposes of the appeal. The Tribunal may also request that any party sends to the Tribunal and the other party:

- statements of facts and evidence to be adduced;

- a skeleton argument;

- a chronology of events;

- other particulars or supplementary statements reasonably required for the determination of the appeal;

- any document or other material required by the Tribunal which the party has the power to deliver;

- an estimate of time needed for the hearing; and

- a list of witnesses to be called to give evidence.

The Tribunal may limit the length of oral submissions and the time for the examination and cross-examination of witnesses and limit the number of expert witnesses to be heard on either side.

Notice of directions must be served on the parties. The Tribunal may, on the application of any party, set aside or vary the directions given.

The Tribunal has a power to require entry to premises for the purposes of inspecting, examining, operating or testing any equipment therein which is used or intended to be used in connection with the processing of personal data. Documents or other material connected with the processing of personal data also may be inspected, examined or tested. The order requiring entry shall also require the occupier to permit the Tribunal to be accompanied by the parties and such number of officers or members of staff of the Tribunal as it considers necessary. Copies of the order are served on the occupier (who may himself be a party) and the parties. The order must specify a time when the Tribunal can enter the premises but this must be at least seven days following the service of the copy.

There is immunity from inspection, etc. in relation to documents or other materials which are privileged, that is, that their production by the appellant on the trial of an action in the relevant part of the United Kingdom could not be compelled. Note that this rule is stated to apply only in respect of the appellant (the equivalent rule relating to the process of discovery applies to either party) and does not appear to benefit an occupier who is not also the appellant but basic principles ought to apply here.

Power to determine without a hearing

The Tribunal may determine an appeal, or any particular issue, without a hearing where the parties so agree in writing or where it appears to the Tribunal that the issues raised have been determined in a previous appeal brought by the appellant on the basis of facts not materially different from those in the present appeal. In this case, the parties must be given an opportunity to make representations to the effect that there should be a hearing. Before the Tribunal determines any matter without a hearing, it may, if it thinks fit, direct any party to provide in writing further information about any relevant matter within a time set by the Tribunal. The Tribunal will then make its determination (see the section later on determination and costs).

The hearing

Where there is to be a hearing, the Tribunal sets the time and place for the hearing. The Tribunal has to give due regard to the convenience of the parties and any request for an early hearing. The proper officer will then send a notice to the parties informing them accordingly. However, a notice will not be sent to the Commissioner where the appeal is brought under section 48(3) (appeal in relation to a statement that compliance with an enforcement notice or the provision of information is required as a matter of urgency within seven days) and the Commissioner is not a party.

The notice must contain information as to the provisions relating to default of appearance which allow the Tribunal to dismiss the case or determine the appeal or any particular issue in the party's absence unless that party has furnished sufficient reason for his absence. The Tribunal may also make an order for costs as it thinks fit in the party's absence.

The time of the hearing must not be less than 14 days from the date the notice of the hearing is sent unless the parties agree or, where the appellant agrees and the appeal is one under section 48(3). The Tribunal has the power to postpone or adjourn a hearing or change the venue. Each party must be notified as must any witnesses be summoned.

The attendance of witnesses may be ordered by summons (citation in Scotland). At least seven days notice must be given unless the witness accepts shorter notice. Where a witness attends in obedience to a summons, he shall be entitled to such sum as the Tribunal considers reasonable in respect of his attendance and travel to and from the place of the hearing. Where the summons is issued at the request of a party, that sum will be paid by that party.

Each party may conduct the case himself or be represented by any person whom he appoints. There is no requirement for the representative to be legally qualified. The Commissioner may or may not be a party in respect of an appeal brought under section 48(3).

Where the appeal is brought under section 48(1) and relates to an information notice, the normal procedure is for the hearing to take place before the chairman sitting alone, and any determination is made by the chairman sitting alone. However, this does not apply if it appears to the chairman necessary in the interests of justice that a hearing or determination should be by the Tribunal constituted as normal, that is, a chairman or deputy chairman (who presides) and equal numbers of persons representing the interests of data subjects and persons representing the interests of data controllers. In making that decision, the chairman must take into account any representations made by the appellant or Commissioner as to why the hearing should not, in the interests of justice, be heard and determined by the chairman sitting alone.

As regards matters preliminary to or incidental to the appeal, the chairman may act for the Tribunal in certain cases, such as in respect to notices served out of time, amendment, withdrawal of appeal, directions, setting the time and place for a hearing and summoning witnesses.

All hearings, including preliminary hearings must be in public. However, having regards to the desirability of safeguarding the privacy of data subjects or commercially sensitive information, the Tribunal may direct that a hearing or any part of it will take part in private. Where a hearing, or part of it, is in private (in addition to the parties) the chairman, any deputy chairman or member of the Tribunal, who are not part of the Tribunal for the purposes of the hearing, may also attend. Furthermore, whether or not the hearing is in public, a member of the Council on Tribunals or the Scottish Committee of the Council on Tribunals may attend in that capacity and may remain present during deliberations but must not, of course, participate in such deliberations.

Each party must be given an opportunity to address the Tribunal, amplify orally written statements previously furnished, give evidence, call witnesses and put questions to any person giving evidence before the Tribunal, make representations on the evidence (if any) and on the subject matter of the appeal generally. Where evidence is taken, the opportunity to make representations on the evidence and on the subject matter of the appeal must come after the completion of the taking of evidence. Where the appeal is under section 48(3), the Commissioner is not a party but, if the Commissioner is asked to assist the Tribunal, he may do so by giving evidence or being heard on any matter relating to the appeal.

The Tribunal may receive in evidence documents or information which would be inadmissible in a court of law but no person may be compelled to give evidence or produce any document which he could not be compelled to give or produce on the trial of the action in a court of law in the relevant part of the United Kingdom, where an appeal from the Tribunal lies to be determined. The Tribunal may require witnesses giving oral evidence to do so on oath or affirmation and the chairman or the proper officer shall have the power to administer oaths or take affirmations.

Except as provided by the Data Protection Tribunal (Enforcement Appeals) Rules 2000 the Tribunal has a duty to conduct the proceedings in such manner as it considers appropriate in the circumstances for discharging its functions and shall, as appears to the Tribunal appropriate, seek to avoid formality in the proceedings.

The burden of proof lies on the Commissioner and it is for the Commissioner to satisfy the Tribunal that the disputed decision should stand. The only exception is in respect of an appeal under section 48(3) in which case it is the appellant who bears the burden of proof. The usual civil standard of proof applies.

Determination and costs

The Tribunal may allow the appeal, substitute another notice if it considers that the notice is not in accordance with the law or, where it involves an exercise of discretion by the Commissioner, that the discretion ought to have been exercised differently, cancel or vary a notice, rule ineffective statements made by the Commissioner requiring compliance as a matter of urgency (in respect of the whole or part of a notice) or cancel a determination of the Commissioner, as appropriate. Appeals from the Tribunal on a point of law go to the High Court in England or Wales.

The chairman must certify in writing the determination as soon as practicable and must sign and date the certificate which must include any material finding of fact and the reasons for the decision. The proper officer will then send a copy to all the parties. Arrangements must be made for the Tribunal to publish the determination but shall, in doing so, have regard for the desirability of safeguarding the privacy of data subjects and commercially sensitive information. Amendments may be made to the text for this purpose. For example, this could involve not disclosing a data subject's identity.

The Rules contain provisions in respect of irregularities and the correction of clerical mistakes. An irregularity does not, of itself make the proceedings void but the Tribunal may give such directions or take such steps before reaching its decision to cure or waive the irregularity if it considers any person may have been prejudiced by the irregularity. Clerical mistakes in a document recording or certifying a direction, decision or determination of the Tribunal or chairman or errors in such documents arising from accidental slips or omissions may be corrected at any time by the chairman by a certificate signed by him.

The Tribunal may make an order awarding costs, including in a case where the appeal has been withdrawn. The award may be made against the appellant and in favour of the Commissioner where the Tribunal considers that the appeal was manifestly unreasonable. If it considers the disputed decision was manifestly unreasonable, the Tribunal may make an order awarding costs against the Commissioner in favour of the appellant. In cases where a party has been responsible for frivolous, vexatious, improper or unreasonable action or has failed to comply with a direction or has been responsible for any delay which with diligence could have been avoided, an award of costs may be made against that party in favour of the other party. It is common for there to be no order for costs.

PROCEDURE – NATIONAL SECURITY

In cases where an appeal is brought under section 28 of the Act, the exemption relating to national security, a different appeal procedure applies and is contained in the Data Protection Tribunal (National Security Appeals) Rules 2000. There are some similarities with the procedure in enforcement appeals and some of the provisions that apply there apply in a similar fashion to national security appeals, *mutatis mutandis*. However, there are some significant differences which flow from two main factors. The first is that the appeal should not be such as to disclose information contrary to national security and this constrains some of the procedural aspects such as the hearing itself, which will normally be in private, the issue and content of notices and the content of the published determination. The second factor is that, in one of the two cases in which an appeal may be brought, a Minister of the Crown may attend and be heard even though the Minister is not, strictly speaking, the respondent in the appeal.

To remind ourselves of the two forms of appeal under section 28, the first is under section 28(4) and is an appeal brought by any person directly affected by the issue of a certificate signed by a Minister of the Crown to the effect that exemption, from all or any of the provisions for which exemption is possible under this exemption,[1] is required for the purpose of safeguarding national security. The second form of appeal lies under section 28(6) and is where a data controller claims that such a certificate which identifies the personal data to which it applies by means of a general description, applies to any personal data. The other party to the proceedings may bring an appeal on the basis that the certificate does not apply to the personal data in question and the Tribunal may rule that the certificate does not so apply.

---

[1] the data protection principles, Parts II, III and V of the Act and section 55.

In the following description of the rules relating to national security appeals, the emphasis is on those rules which are significantly different to those applying in the case of enforcement appeals. Of course, in national security appeals, it is a certificate which is in dispute not a notice served by the Commissioner. Where the appeal is brought under section 28(4), the other party is the relevant Minister (the one responsible for signing the certificate) and, where an appeal is brought under section 28(6), it is the respondent data controller who is the other party, notwithstanding that the relevant Minister will, nevertheless be involved.

In *Re Ewing*,[2] it was argued that the Crown Minister did not have *locus standi* in an application to seek leave by a vexatious litigant to institute proceedings under section 28(4). Davis J in the Queen's Bench Division of the High Court rejected this argument.

Constitution and general duty of the Tribunal

Under paragraph 3 of Schedule 6 to the Act, unless the Tribunal sits *ex parte*, it will consist of three persons designated by the Lord Chancellor from among the chairman and deputy chairman, being persons capable of hearing national security appeals, one of whom will preside. *Ex parte* hearings are only in respect of summary disposal of an appeal where jurisdiction is exercised by one of more of the persons so designated by the Lord Chancellor.

When exercising its functions under the Rules, the Tribunal has a basic duty to secure that information is not disclosed contrary to national security. This includes information indicating the existence or otherwise of any such material. The jurisdiction to hear an appeal under section 28(4) or 28(6) shall be exercised *ex parte* only in the case of summary disposals of appeals but if the Tribunal proposes to dismiss an appeal forthwith, it must notify the appellant and the relevant Minister and the appellant must be given an opportunity to make written representations and request a hearing.

Bringing appeal, acknowledgement and reply

This procedure will be described first in relation to an appeal brought under section 28(4) by a person affected by the certificate. Following this, the main differences with respect to appeals brought under section 28(6) will be highlighted.

The appellant must serve a written notice of appeal on the Tribunal which identifies the disputed certificate and states the name and address of the appellant, the grounds of appeal and an address for the service of notices and other documents on the appellant. An appeal may be brought any time during

---

[2] (unreported) 20 December 2002.

the currency of the certificate and the usual rules apply as regards service by registered letter or recorded delivery, that is, it is treated as being served when received for dispatch by the Post Office.

When the Tribunal receives the notice of appeal, the proper officer will then send an acknowledgement of service to the appellant and a copy of the notice of appeal to the relevant Minister and the Commissioner. The acknowledgement of notice will be accompanied by a statement of the Tribunal's powers to award costs against the appellant.

The relevant Minister must then reply within 42 days of receiving the copy of the notice of appeal and is required to send a copy of the disputed certificate and a written notice stating whether or not he intends to oppose the appeal and, if so, a summary of the circumstances relating to the issue of the certificate and the reasons for its issue, the grounds upon which he relies in opposing the appeal and a statement of the evidence upon which he relies in support of those grounds. There is no provision for the relevant Minister to ask for an extension of the 42-day period.

The proper officer of the Tribunal will then send a copy of the Minister's notice to the appellant and the Commissioner unless the Tribunal proposes to deal with the appeal by summary disposal or where the Minister objects to disclosure of his notice on the basis of national security. Such an objection must be sent with the notice in reply and must state reasons. If possible, without disclosing information contrary to the interests of national security, a "sanitised" version of the notice which can be shown to the appellant can be submitted along with the full notice in reply. Where the Minister has objected to disclosure, the Tribunal must not disclose the relevant information unless the Tribunal decides to overrule the objection.

Where the appeal is brought under section 28(6), the notice of appeal must also include a statement of the date the respondent data controller made the relevant claim, an address for service of notices and other documents on the respondent data controller and, where applicable, a statement of the special circumstances which the appellant considers justify the Tribunal accepting notice of an appeal served out of time. Unlike an appeal under section 28(4) where an appeal may be brought at any time during the currency of the certificate, in this case there is a time limit of 28 days from the date upon which the relevant claim was made by the respondent data controller.

When the Tribunal receives the notice of appeal, the proper officer will also send a copy of the notice of appeal to the respondent data controller who has 42 days to reply. The reply must acknowledge service of the copy of the notice of appeal and must state whether or not the data controller intends to oppose the appeal and, if so, the grounds on which he relies. The respondent data controller may ask for an extension to the 42 day period if he applies before the expiry of that period and can show cause why, by reason of special circumstances, it is just and right to do so.

Except where the Tribunal proposes to deal with the appeal by summary disposal, the proper officer will then send a copy of the data controller's reply to the relevant Minister. A copy may only be sent to the appellant and Commissioner after a period of 42 days following receipt by the Minister of the respondent data controller's reply, unless the Minister has indicated that he does not object to the copy of the reply being sent earlier. The Minister may object to the disclosure of the respondent data controller's reply to the appellant and to the Commissioner and again, a sanitised version may be sent. In this case, notice of objection must be sent within 42 days of the date on which the Minister receives the data controller's reply.

Pre-hearing

There are provisions for amendment and the adding of supplementary grounds which are similar though slightly more complicated because of the presence of a respondent data controller in some cases. There are also provisions for withdrawal of appeal, consolidation and directions which are broadly similar to those which apply to enforcement appeals. However, where the Tribunal proposes to give or vary any direction, to summon witnesses, to determine the appeal without a hearing (not being a summary disposal) on the basis that the issues have been determined on a previous appeal brought by the appellant on the basis of facts not materially different, or to certify or publish a determination, it must first notify the Minister of the proposal. The Minister may then ask the Tribunal to reconsider the decision if he considers it would cause information to be disclosed contrary to the interests of national security.

The Tribunal then has to determine the relevant Minister's objections to the proposal in the absence of the parties but the Minister or a person acting on his behalf may attend, whether or not a party to the appeal. This procedure also applies in the case of an objection by the Minister to disclosures of notices or replies to notices. In this case, the Tribunal must invite the Minister to make oral representations. No material subject to an unsuccessful objection may be disclosed by the Tribunal if the relevant Minister decides not to rely on it in opposing the appeal.

Objections against Tribunal proposals as mentioned above may be considered either as a preliminary issue or at the hearing of the substantive appeal. An objection against disclosure of a notice or reply must be considered as a preliminary issue.

The hearing

The provisions on determination of an appeal without a hearing are similar to those in respect of enforcement appeals except that the relevant Minister may ask the Tribunal to reconsider unless the decision to do so was based on written agreement by the parties. Similar provisions apply in respect of the setting of the time and place of the hearing, summoning witnesses and representation (but subject to exclusion of parties or where the hearing is a determination of the Minister's objections). Any party may be excluded, other than the relevant Minister, from the hearing or any part of it, on the basis of securing that information is not disclosed contrary to the interests of national security. The provisions in respect of non-appearance of a party are as before.

The normal position is for hearings, including preliminary hearings, to be in private. However, with the consent of the parties and the relevant Minister, the Tribunal may direct that the hearing or any part of it shall be held in public. Where the Tribunal sits in private it may, with the consent of the parties and the relevant Minister, admit such persons on such terms and conditions as it considers appropriate.

Other provisions as to the conduct of proceedings, preliminary and incidental matters, evidential matters and dealing with costs and irregularities are similar as for enforcement appeals, *mutatis mutandis*. Also, determinations are similar in practice with the exception that amendments may be made to the text of any certificate on the basis of national security in addition to the desirability of safeguarding the privacy of data subjects and commercially sensitive information.

CHAPTER 12

THE FIRST REPORT OF THE COMMISSION ON THE IMPLEMENTATION OF THE DATA PROTECTION DIRECTIVE

INTRODUCTION

Under Article 33 of the Directive, the Commission is required to report to the Council and the European Parliament at regular intervals, not exceeding three years from the 24 October 1998 (three years from the date of adoption of the Directive, being the latest date for compliance), on the implementation of the Directive. Appropriate proposals for amendment are to be attached if considered necessary. In particular, the Commission should examine the application of the Directive towards the processing of sound and image data relating to individuals and submit appropriate proposals as necessary, taking account of developments in information technology and in the light of the state of progress in the information society. The report must be made public.

The report was delayed by approximately 18 months and was published in 2004.[1] The reason given was that a number of Member States had been late implementing the Directive. In December 1999, the Commission decided to take France, Germany, Ireland, Luxembourg and the Netherlands to the European Court of Justice for failing to notify all the measures necessary to implement the Directive. Notifications were later submitted for those States. The main features of the report are discussed in this chapter.

NO AMENDMENT OF THE DIRECTIVE

The Commission considered that no modifications were needed to the Directive by the time of its report. Few of those partaking in consultations

---

[1] (COM/2003/0265 final).

desired modifications. However, detailed proposals for amendments were submitted jointly by Austria, Sweden, Finland and the United Kingdom. These concerned only a few provisions, being Article 4 on applicable law, Article 8 on the processing of sensitive personal data, Article 12 on the right of access, Article 18 on notification and Articles 25 and 26 on transfers to third countries. The Netherlands later also adhered to these proposals. However, the Commission thought it unwise to make any changes yet, in particular, because experience with the Directive was limited in view of the problems of implementation in some Member States.

Some of the issues raised could be dealt with by better implementation of the Directive or by closer cooperation between supervisory authorities to achieve convergence. These approaches should be given an opportunity as, apart from anything else, they are likely to be effective more quickly than by modifying the Directive, within which there is at least some scope to deal with some of the difficulties encountered. A number of amendments that had been proposed were aimed at reducing the burdens on data controllers. Although the Commission recognises this as a legitimate goal, there would have to be careful consideration of the impact of such changes to ensure that they did not prejudice the protection afforded by the Directive.

The Commission noted that there was considerable scope for improving implementation of the Directive as it stands and addressing this issue was, in itself, likely to resolve at least some of the issues raised. The Commission is also committed to concentrating on clear breaches of data protection law and on divergent implementations which may cause problems in relation to the internal market. A particular issue is the transfer of personal data to third countries and harmonisation is needed as a priority so as to facilitate legitimate transfers whilst avoiding unnecessary barriers to transfers to countries outside the European Economic Area.

ON-LINE SURVEY

The Commission carried out an on-line survey inviting data subjects and data controllers to give their views as to various aspects of data protection law. Some 9,156 individuals and 982 data controllers submitted responses. The results are summarised below:

- Level of protection. Nearly half of individuals considered the protection afforded to be a minimum even though the Commission claims that the Directive provides a high level of protection

- Awareness. Over three-quarters of individuals thought that the level of awareness of data protection was insufficient, bad or very bad and less than 15 per cent thought it sufficient, good or very good. Data controllers also were negative on awareness.

- Acceptance by business. More than two-thirds of data controllers accepted that data protection was necessary with less than three per cent only considering that it was completely unnecessary.

- Subject access. Nearly two-thirds of data controllers did not think responding to requests for subject access involved an important effort for their organisations. Most data controller either had no available figures or received less than 10 requests for subject access.

The Commission recognised that the survey cannot be regarded as representative but carried out another survey during 2003. This still found a lack of awareness amongst individuals but more data controllers accepted the need for privacy laws.[2] In relation to awareness, it should be noted that the United Kingdom Information Commissioner found a level of awareness of data protection law of 74 per cent.[3] The Commission is working towards increasing awareness of data protection law amongst individuals, noting that this varied considerably throughout the Community.

MAIN FINDINGS IN THE REPORT

The Commission noted that the Directive fulfilled one of its main objectives, being the removal of barriers to the free movement of data throughout the Community. At the time the Directive was published only Italy and Greece did not have specific data protection laws, yet these were some of the first Member States to transpose the Directive into domestic law. No instance of any problems concerning the free movement of data was notified to the Commission. Although there seems to be little evidence that barriers to the free movement of data was much of an issue before the Directive, the Commission clearly thought that this could become a major problem if it was not addressed as Italy and Greece had no data protection laws at all.

GENERAL DISPARITIES IN IMPLEMENTATION

The Directive provides for a high level of protection for personal data but allowed some divergence, as it did not seek to attain full convergence. Rather, in line with the principle of subsidiarity, the Directive sought approximation of data protection law in Member States. One problem is that not having complete harmony makes it difficult for multi-national organisations to

---

[2] Single Market News, Nr 33, May 2004.
[3] Annual Report 2004, HC669, p.88.

develop pan-European data protection policies. This may lead to greater calls for convergence in domestic laws and their application and in terms of greater cooperation between supervisory authorities.

Even where a provision in the Directive offers little or no scope for divergence, there are disparities between Member States' implementations which will have to be addressed. Examples include the definitions and "closed lists" such as the conditions for processing, providing information to data subjects, exemptions and exceptions regarding transfers to third countries. Nevertheless, the Commission considers it better to proceed other than by modifying the Directive, at least initially. It pointed out that data protection law applies to a large number of sectors and in relation to many contexts and this goes against adding more detail. Disparities between Member States' implementation of the Directive can be dealt with by the Commission invoking the procedure under Article 226 of the EC Treaty where such disparities reflect imperfect implementation of the Directive. Under Article 226, the Commission, after giving the Member State an opportunity to submit observations, delivers a reasoned opinion on the state's failure to fulfil its obligation. If the state does not comply within the stated time with the opinion, the Commission may bring the matter to the European Court of Justice.

Although partly based on anecdotal evidence, the Commission is of the view that national supervisory authorities gave enforcement of data protection a low priority, compliance by data controllers was patchy and data subjects had a relatively low level of knowledge of their rights. Some data controllers probably are reluctant to change their practices to comply with the regulatory framework under the Directive which they perceived as burdensome and they probably thought the chances of enforcement action taken against them as being low.

Full implementation of the Directive required primary legislation and a secondary stage requiring a review of other legislation that may possibly conflict with the Directive and implementation of safeguards in relation to exceptions provided for in the Directive. The Commission noted that this second phase had not even commenced in some Member States. One issue in a number of states was the need to clarify the application of Article 7(f) (the "legitimate interests" condition for processing) but nothing had yet been done about this. Clarification of the meaning of sensitive personal data had also been called for by a number of Member States. A reasonable and flexible interpretation of this and of anonymous data was suggested by some representative organisations and by Member States including the United Kingdom.

APPLICABLE LAW

Article 4 of the Directive deals with applicable law and this is the law of the country or countries in which the data controller has its establishment(s) and the processing is carried out in relation to that or those establishments. It also applies the law of the country in which a data controller, who is not established within the territory of any of the Member States, uses equipment for processing personal data where the equipment is situated in that country.

This is an important provision and its correct implementation is vital to the functioning of the internal market. However, there are differences in how this has been implemented in the Member States. One problem for data controllers established in a number of Member States is that compliance with disparate data protection rules is required. Another problem identified by Member sScontrollers not established within the Community. Further clarification of this was sought. However, the Commission thought more experience with this aspect of data protection law was needed before any proposals to change Article 4 could be contemplated. The Commission did note, however, that some Member States' implementation of Article 4 as it stands was deficient and they would have to make changes to their laws to comply.

TRANSFERS TO THIRD COUNTRIES

There were very wide disparities between Member States as to the implementation of the provisions on transfers to third countries. The approach of some Member States to determining adequacy of protection was to leave this to the data controller to decide and the Commission thought this did not comply with Article 25(1) which places the requirement on Member States. Some Member States require authorisation to transfers but this may conflict with the aim of providing adequate protection without making it difficult to transfer personal data to third countries. However, mere notification of proposed transfers to third countries under Article 19 should not result in de facto authorisations. One problem with disparities of approach is that data controllers may choose as point of export the Member State with the least burdensome implementation of the provisions on transfers to third countries.

The Commission noted that, in the reality of global telecommunications networks, an over-strict approach would not meet the legitimate needs of international trade. This would create a gap between law and practice but such a gap could result from a lack of enforcement which was apparent from the low numbers of notifications of authorised transfers submitted to the Commission. More use should be made of "block authorisations" under Articles 25(6) and 26(4) (Commission findings that third countries afford adequate protection and standard contractual clauses approved by the Commission).

Although coming after the Commission's report, Case C-101/01 *Bodil Lindqvist*, 6 November 2003, discussed in Chapter 7 in this context, shows that more consideration needs to be given to the situation where personal data is placed on a website. In that case, the European Court of Justice held that placing data passively on a website did not involve a transfer to third countries.

SOUND AND IMAGE DATA

During the drafting of the Directive, concern was expressed by some people about the effects of technological developments on the processing of sound and image data when the Directive seemed focused on processing text. Article 33 specifically required the Commission to consider the application of the Directive, in particular, to such data and to submit any necessary proposals. As recital 14 specifically states that the Directive applies to sound and image data, the possibility was that subsequent developments in information technology may prejudice the right of privacy in respect of such data, requiring modification to some of the Directive's provisions.

The laws of all the Member States apply also to sound and image data and this aspect of the Directive does not appear to have raised any specific problems. Some countries treat sound and image data the same as other data (in line with the technology-neutral approach in the Directive) whilst Germany and the Netherlands have specific provisions for sound and image data. Denmark, Sweden and Portugal have separate laws dealing with video surveillance. It is this latter form of processing that seems to require further public debate to determine the limits to be placed on this form of processing. One problem the Commission will face is trying to reconcile the use of video surveillance as a weapon in the fight against crime and anti-social behaviour with risks to individuals' right and freedoms.

Clarification is probably needed in some cases, for example, whether a single fingerprint or isolated image are within the scope of the Directive in cases where identification of the person is impossible or highly unlikely. The Commission accepts that it needs to provide more guidance in such cases.

SUMMARY AND CONCLUSIONS

A number of other disparities between Member States' implementation of the Directive were identified, in particular, in relation to processing for historical, statistical or research purposes, the data subject's consent (particularly important in the context of on-line transactions), providing information to data subjects and the notification requirements. In respect of the latter, the Commission noted that, despite calls to simplify notification, the Directive itself contains provisions for exemption from and simplification of notification and some Member States had not taken advantage of these. The report includes an action plan which involves more collaboration and discussion between the Working Party, Member States and supervisory authorities. Particular issues are bringing all Member States' legislation into full and uniform compliance (allowing for the fact that the Directive contains a number of options and derogations), enforcement, providing data subjects with information, simplifying the rules on transfers to third countries and promoting privacy enhancing technologies. During 2004, the Working Party held a first discussion on harmonising the data subject information requirements under Article 10 of the Directive and adopted the following conclusion:

> *The Art. 29 Working Party welcomes the efforts to develop a standard for comprehensible data protection information. Comprehensive, intelligible and easily accessible information about the data processing is an indispensable condition to guarantee the data protection rights to the persons concerned. We encourage the institutions and companies involved to continue their tasks.*

Given that the legislation in Member States is still bedding down, it is a little early to make firm concrete proposals to change the Directive. Further complications will ensue as an indirect result of the enlargement of the European Union, though representatives of some of the new Member States attended meetings of the Working Party since 2002. As experiences of applying data protection law grow, it is likely that changes will have to be made to keep a fair balance between free movement of personal data and basic rights and freedoms. Of course, that some Member States have transposed the Directive inadequately or badly must be addressed more urgently and it is likely that the Commission will use its powers under Article 226 of the EC Treaty sooner rather than later. During 2000, the Commission decided to take five Member States to the European Court of Justice under Article 226 for failing to notify the measures taken to implement the Directive. Further information about the activities of the Commission (and about data protection law generally) is available at the Commission's data protection website, the address of which is: *http: //europa.eu.int/comm/internal_market/privacy/index_en.htm.*

CHAPTER 13

PROCESSING PERSONAL DATA AND THE COMMUNITY INSTITUTIONS

INTRODUCTION

Community institutions, especially the Commission, as part of their normal operations, regularly process personal data relating to individuals in Member States. There may also have been doubts as to whether these institutions and like bodies would be governed by any Member State's data protection law as they are supra-national entities. Article 286 of the EC Treaty states that, as from 1 January 1999, Community acts on the protection of individuals with regard to the processing of personal data and the free movement of such data shall apply to the Community institutions and bodies established by or under the Treaty. Article 286 required that a supervisory authority should be established before 1 January 1999 but it was not until 17 January 2004 that the European Data Protection Supervisor and his deputy were appointed. The European Parliament and the Council subsequently adopted Regulation (EC) 45/2001 on the protection of individuals with regard to the processing of personal data by the Community institutions and bodies and on the free movement of such data.[1] The appointment of the European Data Protection Supervisor was made by Decision 2004/55/EC of the European Parliament and of the Council of 22 December 2003 appointing the independent supervisory body as provided under Article 286 of the EC Treaty (European Data Protection Supervisor).[2] Appointment is for a period of five years. Generally, data protection law applies to the Community institutions and bodies as it does under the Data Protection Directive. That being so, this chapter concentrates on the differences between the model of data protection as it applies under the Regulation and that set out in the Data Protection Directive ("the Directive").

---

[1] OJ L 8, 12.01.2001, p.1 ("the Regulation").
[2] OJ L 12, 17.01.2004, p.47.

DEFINITIONS AND SCOPE

The definitions are set out in Article 2 of the Regulation and closely follow those in the Directive. The definition of controller is different as one might expect and it is "... the Community institution or body, the Directorate-General, the unit or any other organisational entity which alone or jointly with others determines the purposes and means of the processing of personal data; where the purposes and means of processing are determined by a specific Community act, the controller or the specific criteria for its nomination may be designated by such Community act". Otherwise, to all intents and purposes, the definitions are the same.

Under Article 3, the Regulation applies to the processing of personal data by all Community institutions and bodies insofar as such processing is carried out in the exercise of activities all or part of which fall within the scope of Community law. Processing caught by the Regulation, as with the Directive, is automatic processing and processing other than by automatic means of personal data in a filing system or intended to form part of a filing system. A filing system is a structured personal data filing system accessible by specific criteria (equivalent to "relevant filing system" under the Data Protection Act 1998). The range of bodies caught by the Regulation is large and comprises the European Parliament, the Council of the Union, the European Commission, the Court of Justice and the Court of Auditors. The bodies set up by the EC, ECSC and EAEC Treaties are also included: the European Central Bank, the European Investment Bank, the Economic and Social Committee, the Committee of the Regions. The Regulation also applies to bodies set up under secondary Community legislation being the European Centre for the Development of Vocational Training, the European Foundation for the Improvement of Living and Working Conditions, the European Environment Agency, the European Training Foundation, the European Monitoring Centre for Drugs and Drug Addiction, the European Agency for the Evaluation of Medicinal Products, the Office for Harmonisation in the Internal Market (Trade Marks and Designs), the European Agency for Safety and Health at Work, the Community Plant Variety Office and the Translation Centre for the Bodies of the Union.

PRINCIPLES RELATING TO DATA QUALITY

These principles are set out in Article 4 of the Regulation and closely follow the equivalent principles in the Directive. However, in relation to the fifth principle ("kept in a form which permits identification of data subjects for no longer than is necessary ..."), in the Directive, Member States are required to lay down appropriate safeguards in relation to data kept longer for historical, statistical or scientific use. The Regulation goes further and states that the

"... Community institution or body shall lay down that personal data which are to be stored for longer periods for historical, statistical or scientific use should be kept either in anonymous form only or, if that is not possible, only with the identity of the data subjects encrypted. In any event, the data shall not be used for any purpose other than for historical, statistical or scientific purposes."

Thus, appropriate safeguards are translated as meaning that the data must be anonymised (as the preferred solution) or, if that is not possible, the data must be kept in encrypted form. No guidance is given as to who will be entitled to hold the encryption key or as to the standard to be used.

Under Article 6, a change to the purposes of processing is possible if the change of purpose is expressly permitted by the internal rules of the institution or body. Personal data collected exclusively for ensuring the security or the control of the processing systems or operations shall not be used for any other purpose, with the exception of the prevention, investigation, detection and prosecution of serious criminal offences. This is all without prejudice to Article 4 (data quality), Article 5 (lawfulness of processing) and Article 10 (processing special categories of data).

LAWFULNESS OF PROCESSING AND SPECIAL CATEGORIES OF DATA

These provisions are equivalent to the conditions for processing under the Data Protection Act 1998 which derive from the Directive. For "non-sensitive" personal data a condition in Article 5 of the Regulation must apply to allow processing to be lawful. For special categories of data ("sensitive" data), a condition in Article 10 must also be engaged.

Article 5 states that personal data may be processed only if:

(a) processing is necessary for the performance of a task carried out in the public interest on the basis of the Treaties establishing the European Communities or other legal instruments adopted on the basis thereof or in the legitimate exercise of official authority vested in the Community institution or body or in a third party to whom the data are disclosed, or

(b) processing is necessary for compliance with a legal obligation to which the controller is subject, or

(c) processing is necessary for the performance of a contract to which the data subject is party or in order to take steps at the request of the data subject prior to entering into a contract, or

(d) the data subject has unambiguously given his or her consent, or

(e) processing is necessary in order to protect the vital interests of the data subject.

Condition (a) replaces the "legitimate interests" and "public interests" processing under the Directive and is intended to be equivalent though there is no balance in respect of individuals' rights and freedoms. The other conditions are the same though differently ordered.

Article 10 applies to special categories of personal data defined the same as in the Directive. There is a blanket prohibition and then a list of exceptions. Member States may provide that data relating to administrative sanctions or judgments in civil cases may be processed under the control of official authority under the Directive but there is no mention of this in the Regulation. However, otherwise the Regulation conditions follow those in the Directive reasonably closely, *mutatis mutandis*.

INFORMING DATA SUBJECTS AND THEIR RIGHTS

The Regulation is more specific in what information should be provided to the data subject when data are obtained from him or her and is, under Article 11:

(a) the identity of the controller;
(b) the purposes of the processing operation for which the data are intended;
(c) the recipients or categories of recipients of the data;
(d) whether replies to the questions are obligatory or voluntary, as well as the possible consequences of failure to reply;
(e) the existence of the right of access to, and the right to rectify, the data concerning him or her;
(f) any further information such as:
    (i)   the legal basis of the processing operation for which the data are intended,
    (ii) the time limits for storing the data,
    (iii) the right to have recourse at any time to the European Data Protection Supervisor, insofar as such further information is necessary, having regard to the specific circumstances in which the data are collected, to guarantee fair processing in respect of the data subject.

However, with the exception of (a), (b) and (c), provision of information may be deferred as long as this is necessary for statistical purposes although it must be provided as soon as the reason for which the information was withheld no longer applies. The Directive is silent on legal basis and time limits and the right of recourse to the supervisory authority but, in both the Regulation and Directive, the provision of the further information is required only if necessary to guarantee fair processing.

Where the data have not been obtained directly from the data subject, under Article 12, the information to be provided is the same with the addition of information about the categories of data and the origin of the data (except where the controller cannot disclose this for reasons of professional secrecy). A disproportionate effort provision applies similar to that in the Directive. In both cases, where the data are obtained from the data subject and in other cases, the controller is absolved from providing the information where the data subject already has it.

A right of access is granted under Article 13 of the Regulation similar to that in the Directive. However, the Regulation is more specific in relation to rectification, blocking and erasure. In particular, Article 15 gives the data subject a right to have data blocked. The concept of "blocking" is not defined expressly but from the provisions in the Regulation it appears to mean disabling access to, or processing of, data in such a way that the data can later be retrieved if appropriate. The right to blocking applies where the data subject contests the accuracy of the data (this is temporary for a period to allow the controller to verify the accuracy or completeness of the data); where the controller no longer needs the data for its tasks but requires to keep them for the purposes of proof; or where the processing is unlawful but the data subject requires them to be blocked instead of erased. The latter could apply where the data subject may want to be able to obtain access to the data at a later stage, for example, for the purposes of legal proceedings. Defending potential legal proceedings may be the reason why a controller might want to block data it no longer requires for the purposes of processing for which they were originally acquired.

Data in automated filing systems shall be blocked by technical means in such a way that it is clear that the data may not be used. Blocked personal data may only be processed for the purposes of proof, with the data subject's consent or for the protection of the rights of a third party. Where data have been blocked at a data subject's request, he or she must be informed before the data are unblocked.

Data subjects also have rights to object to processing. These are similar to those under the Directive. However, there is no exception in relation to a contract with the data subject from automated individual decisions in the Regulation.

CONFIDENTIALITY AND SECURITY OF PROCESSING

These provisions are more detailed than in the Directive in respect of security of processing by automatic means. Basic requirements of confidentiality are placed on employees of Community institutions and bodies, whether as controllers or processors, only to act under the instructions of the controller unless required to do so by virtue of national or Community law. The basic statement of security measures is equivalent to that in the Directive. Having regard to the state of the art and the cost of their implementation, the controller shall implement appropriate technical and organisational measures to ensure a level of security appropriate to the risks represented by the processing and the nature of the personal data to be protected. The purpose of the measures is, in particular, to prevent any unauthorised disclosure or access, accidental or unlawful destruction or accidental loss, or alteration, and to prevent all other unlawful forms of processing. The Regulation then states, in Article 22(2), that where personal data are processed by automated means, measures shall be taken as appropriate in view of the risks in particular with the aim of:

(a)   preventing any unauthorised person from gaining access to computer systems processing personal data;
(b)   preventing any unauthorised reading, copying, alteration or removal of storage media;
(c)   preventing any unauthorised memory inputs as well as any unauthorised disclosure, alteration or erasure of stored personal data;
(d)   preventing unauthorised persons from using data-processing systems by means of data transmission facilities;
(e)   ensuring that authorised users of a data-processing system can access no personal data other than those to which their access right refers;
(f)   recording which personal data have been communicated, at what times and to whom;
(g)   ensuring that it will subsequently be possible to check which personal data have been processed, at what times and by whom;
(h)   ensuring that personal data being processed on behalf of third parties can be processed only in the manner prescribed by the contracting institution or body;
(i)   ensuring that, during communication of personal data and during transport of storage media, the data cannot be read, copied or erased without authorisation;
(j)   designing the organisational structure within an institution or body in such a way that it will meet the special requirements of data protection.

There is no equivalent to this in the Directive although it could be argued that these specific requirements are implicit in the general statement of security measures to be adopted. They do, at least, alert controllers to particular risks associated with processing personal data by automated means. Point (g) would seem to prevent the placing of personal data on a website. These requirements may also provide a useful touchstone by which data controllers generally under data protection law can assess whether their security measures are appropriate.

The position as regards processors is similar to that in the Directive and requires that the processing is carried out under a contract or other legal act.

DATA PROTECTION OFFICERS

Each Community institution and body is required to appoint at least one data protection official under Article 24 of the Regulation. The duties of the data protection official include making controllers and data subjects aware of their rights and obligations; responding to requests from, and cooperating with, the European Data Protection Supervisor; ensuring in an independent manner the internal application of the Regulation; keeping a register of the processing operations carried out by the controller, containing the items of information (see below); and notifying the European Data Protection Supervisor of any processing operations likely to present specific risks under the prior checking provisions set out in Article 27.

The information that must be kept in the register (not dissimilar to that in the register kept under the Data Protection Act 1998) is:

(a) the name and address of the controller and an indication of the organisational parts of an institution or body entrusted with the processing of personal data for a particular purpose;
(b) the purpose or purposes of the processing;
(c) a description of the category or categories of data subjects and of the data or categories of data relating to them;
(d) the legal basis of the processing operation for which the data are intended;
(e) the recipients or categories of recipient to whom the data might be disclosed;
(f) a general indication of the time limits for blocking and erasure of the different categories of data;
(g) proposed transfers of data to third countries or international organisations;
(h) a general description allowing a preliminary assessment to be made of the appropriateness of the measures taken pursuant to Article 22 to ensure security of processing.

Changes must also be notified to the Data Protection Official. Apart from item (h), the register must be available for inspection by any person directly or indirectly through the European Data Protection Supervisor.

Prior checking under Article 27 is to be carried out by the European Data Protection Supervisor after notification by the Data Protection Official. Processing subject to prior checking is likely to include:

(a) processing of data relating to health and to suspected offences, offences, criminal convictions or security measures;

(b)   processing operations intended to evaluate personal aspects relating to the data subject, including his or her ability, efficiency and conduct;

(c)   processing operations allowing linkages not provided for pursuant to national or Community legislation between data processed for different purposes;

(d)   processing operations for the purpose of excluding individuals from a right, benefit or contract.

Where there is any doubt, the Data Protection Official must consult the European Data Protection Supervisor. The opinion of the European Data Protection Supervisor must be delivered within two months. However, this period can be extended to allow time to obtain further information needed and there is provision for a further two-month extension. Failure to deliver an opinion in the time allowed results in a deemed favourable opinion. The European Data Protection Supervisor must keep a register of processing notified under this provision.

The Annex to the Regulation sets out the tasks, duties and powers of Data Protection Officials to be implemented by each Community institution or body, being as follows.

1.   *The Data Protection Officer may make recommendations for the practical improvement of data protection to the Community institution or body which appointed him or her and advise it and the controller concerned on matters concerning the application of data protection provisions. Furthermore he or she may, on his or her own initiative or at the request of the Community institution or body which appointed him or her, the controller, the Staff Committee concerned or any individual, investigate matters and occurrences directly relating to his or her tasks and which come to his or her notice, and report back to the person who commissioned the investigation or to the controller.*

2.   *The Data Protection Officer may be consulted by the Community institution or body which appointed him or her, by the controller concerned, by the Staff Committee concerned and by any individual, without going through the official channels, on any matter concerning the interpretation or application of this Regulation.*

3.   *No one shall suffer prejudice on account of a matter brought to the attention of the competent Data Protection Officer alleging that a breach of the provisions of this Regulation has taken place.*

4.   *Every controller concerned shall be required to assist the Data Protection Officer in performing his or her duties and to give information in reply to questions. In performing his or her duties, the Data Protection Officer shall have access at all times to the data forming the*

subject-matter of processing operations and to all offices, data-processing installations and data carriers.

5.   *To the extent required, the Data Protection Officer shall be relieved of other activities. The Data Protection Officer and his or her staff, to whom Article 287 of the Treaty shall apply, shall be required not to divulge information or documents which they obtain in the course of their duties.*

TRANSFERS OF PERSONAL DATA

The Regulations envisage three forms of transfers of personal data. The first is within or between Community institutions and bodies. The second form of transfer is to recipients other than Community institutions and bodies but who are subject to national laws implementing the Data Protection Directive. Both of these forms of transfer are stated to be without prejudice to Articles 4 (data quality principles), 5 (lawful processing), 6 (change of purposes) and 10 (special categories of data). The final form of transfer is to recipients in third countries and international organisations not subject to the Data Protection Directive. Transfers are permitted in more limited cases than is the case under the Directive.

TRANSFERS WITHIN OR BETWEEN COMMUNITY INSTITUTIONS OR BODIES

Article 7 covers these transfers. Transfers are possible if necessary for a legitimate task covered by the competence of the recipient. If the transfer is at the recipient's request, both the controller and the recipients are made responsible for the legitimacy of the transfer. In such cases, the controller must verify the competence of the recipient and make a provisional evaluation of the necessity of the transfer and, if the controller has any doubts about this, the controller must seek further information from the recipient. The recipient must ensure that the necessity of the transfer can be subsequently verified. Finally, the recipient must not process the data for any purpose other than that for which they were processed.

TRANSFERS TO RECIPIENTS SUBJECT TO THE DIRECTIVE

This applies where the recipient is not a Community institution or body but is subject to national laws implementing the Directive. This could apply, for example, where the recipient is a government department. Under Article 8, the transfer may take place if the recipient establishes that the data to be transferred are necessary for the performance of a task carried out in the public interest or subject to the exercise of public authority. Transfers are also possible if the recipient establishes the necessity of the transfer and there is no reason to assume that data subjects' legitimate interests might be prejudiced.

TRANSFERS TO RECIPIENTS NOT SUBJECT TO THE DIRECTIVE

This applies to controllers in third countries, or international organisations, not subject to the Directive. Transfers in such cases are governed by a set of rules not dissimilar to transfers to third countries under the Directive, providing similar safeguards.

Under Article 9 of the Regulation, transfers may proceed only if an adequate level of protection is ensured within the country of the recipient or within the recipient international organisation and the data are transferred solely to allow tasks covered by the competence of the controller (that is, the Community institution or body transferring the data) to be carried out.

Adequacy is determined in a similar manner as in the Directive. Adequacy is assessed in the light of all the circumstances surrounding the transfer operation or set of operations and particular consideration is given to the nature of the data, the purpose and duration of the processing operation or set of operations, the recipient third country or international organisation, the rules of law in force (both general and sectoral), professional rules and security measures complied with in that third country or international organisation. There are provisions for Community institutions and bodies to inform the Commission and the European Data Protection Commissioner of cases where they consider third countries or international organisations do not have an adequate level of protection and dissemination of this information to Member States. Community institutions and bodies must take the measures necessary to comply with Commission decisions to the effect that a third country of international organisation does not provide adequate protection.

As with transfers to third countries under the Directive, a pragmatic approach is taken by making provision for transfers where protection is inadequate. Article 9(6) still allows transfers if one of the following conditions is met:

(a) *the data subject has given his or her consent unambiguously to the proposed transfer; or*

(b) *the transfer is necessary for the performance of a contract between the data subject and the controller or the implementation of pre-contractual measures taken in response to the data subject's request; or*

(c) *the transfer is necessary for the conclusion or performance of a contract entered into in the interest of the data subject between the controller and a third party; or*

(d) the transfer is necessary or legally required on important public interest grounds, or for the establishment, exercise or defence of legal claims; or

(e) the transfer is necessary in order to protect the vital interests of the data subject; or

(f) the transfer is made from a register which, according to Community law, is intended to provide information to the public and which is open to consultation either by the public in general or by any person who can demonstrate a legitimate interest, to the extent that the conditions laid down in Community law for consultation are fulfilled in the particular case.

Furthermore, under Article 9(7), transfers may take place if authorised by the European Data Protection Supervisor where the controller adduces adequate safeguards with respect to the protection of the privacy and fundamental rights and freedoms of individuals and as regards the exercise of the corresponding rights; such safeguards may in particular result from appropriate contractual clauses. There is a duty placed on controllers to inform the European Data Protection Supervisor of transfers under Article 9(6) or (7).

REMAINING PROVISIONS

Exemptions and restrictions are similar to those in the Data Protection Directive. Chapter IV of the Regulation contains an equivalent set of provisions relating to privacy in telecommunications. This should now be read in the light of Directive 2002/58/EC of the European Parliament and of the Council of 12 July 2002 concerning the processing of personal data and the protection of privacy in the electronic communications sector,[3] (indeed, Article 19 of that Directive states that references to the privacy in telecommunications Directive are to be construed as references to Directive 2002/58/EC). These provisions in Directive 2002/58/EC are discussed in the following chapter, as implemented in the United Kingdom.

Controllers have duties to consult with, provide information, cooperate and react to allegations by the European Data Protection Supervisor under Articles 28 to 31. Chapter V of the Regulations deals with the establishment, appointment and duties of the European Data Protection Supervisor. The primary duties are, under Article 41:

---

[3] OJ L 201, 31.07.2002, p.37.

to ensure that the fundamental rights and freedoms of natural persons, and in particular their right to privacy, are respected by the Community institutions and bodies;

to monitor and ensure the application of the provisions of the Regulation and any other Community act relating to the protection of the fundamental rights and freedoms of natural persons with regard to the processing of personal data by a Community institution or body; and

to advise Community institutions and bodies and data subjects on all matters concerning the processing of personal data.

Articles 46 to 48 set out the duties and powers more completely. Recital 30 to the Regulation states that it may be necessary to monitor computer networks and provides that the European Data Protection Supervisor can determine under what conditions computer networks under the control of Community institutions or bodies should be monitored to prevent unauthorised use.

The European Data Protection Supervisor is appointed for a term of five years and a deputy is also appointed for the same term. A Secretariat is established to assist the European Data Protection Supervisor who shall be chosen from persons whose independence is beyond doubt and who are acknowledged as having the experience and skills required to perform the duties of European Data Protection Supervisor, for example because they belong or have belonged to the supervisory authorities under the Data Protection Directive. The first European Data Protection Supervisor is Mr Peter Johan Hustinx and his assistant is Mr Joaquin Bayo Delgado, both of whom where appointed on 17 January 2004 as a result of Decision 2004/55/EC of the European Parliament and of the Council of 22 December 2003 appointing the independent supervisory body as provided under Article 286 of the EC Treaty (European Data Protection Supervisor).[4] The European Data Protection Supervisor is to act in an independent manner but may be dismissed or deprived of his or her right to a pension or other benefits in its stead by the Court of Justice at the request of the European Parliament, the Council or the Commission, if he or she no longer fulfils the conditions required for the performance of his or her duties or if he or she is guilty of serious misconduct.

The European Court of Justice has jurisdiction to hear disputes under the Regulations and individuals have a right to complain to the European Data Protection Supervisor and a right to damages under Article 288 of the EC Treaty. Actions against decisions of the European Data Protection Supervisor go to European Court of Justice under Article 32 of the Regulation. Employees

---

[4] OJ L 12, 17.01.2004, p.47.

of Community institutions and bodies may also complain to the European Data Protection Supervisor under Article 33.

Community institutions and bodies are charged with ensuring that processing already underway at the date the Regulation came into force are brought into conformity with it within one year; Article 50. The Regulation came into force on the 20th day following the date of publication in the official journal which was 12 January 2001.

CHAPTER 14
PRIVACY IN ELECTRONIC COMMUNICATIONS

INTRODUCTION

New and sophisticated technical developments in public telecommunications such as Integrated Services Digital Networks (ISDN) and digital mobile networks and the other developments such as video on demand and inter-active television pose new threats to privacy which were not fully addressed by the Data Protection Directive. The same can be said of electronic mail and other means of communicating electronically. Now, it is possible to use a computer as a telephone with video and mobile telephones have the ability to transmit and store images. In many ways, conventional computer technology and mobile communications are converging. One problem was that the growing use of new means of communication might be hindered if users did not have confidence that their privacy would not be put at risk. Taking a lead from the Data Protection Directive and on the basis that confidentiality in communications is guaranteed, in particular, by the European Convention for the Protection of Human Rights and Fundamental Freedoms, the European Parliament and the Council adopted Directive 97/66/EC of 15 December 1997 concerning the processing of personal data and the protection of privacy in the telecommunications sector[1] This Directive was implemented in the United Kingdom by the Telecommunications (Data Protection and Privacy) Regulations 1999, amended by the Telecommunications (Data Protection and Privacy) (Amendment) Regulations 2000.

It was not long before it became apparent that the growing use of computer technology, particularly advanced digital technologies and electronic mail, caused the European Commission to re-visit this form of data protection in the light of further technological developments and the response was Directive 2002/58/EC of the European Parliament and the Council of 12 July 2002 concerning the processing of personal data and the protection of privacy

---

[1] OJ L 24, 30.01.1998, p.1.

in the electronic communications sector (Directive on privacy and electronic communications).[2] This Directive repealed and replaced Directive 97/66/EC and Article 19 of the Directive on privacy and electronic communications states that references to the repealed Directive are to be construed as references to this Directive. The Directive effectively translates the principles set out in the Data Protection Directive into the electronic communications sector.

The Directive on privacy and electronic communications was implemented in the United Kingdom by the Privacy and Electronic Communications (EC Directive) Regulations 2003, which came into force on 11 December 2003 and revoked the above-mentioned telecommunications Regulations. The new Regulations have already been amended to give corporate subscribers the right to be included on opt-out registers in relation to unsolicited telephone calls for marketing purposes. The amendment was made by the Privacy and Electronic Communications (EC Directive) (Amendment) Regulations 2004, with effect from 25 June 2004.

This chapter looks specifically at the provision of the Regulations with appropriate references to the Directive on privacy and electronic communications, as appropriate. Particular aspects of the Regulations relate to security of systems, confidentiality of communications, traffic and billing data, calling and connected line identification, location data, malicious, nuisance and emergency calls, automatic calling systems and automatic call forwarding, subscriber directories and unsolicited direct marketing communications.

RELATIONSHIP WITH THE DATA PROTECTION DIRECTIVE AND DATA PROTECTION ACT 1998

The Privacy and Electronic Communications (EC Directive) Regulations 2003 (hereinafter referred to as "the Regulations"), in line with the Directive, are an attempt to transpose the principles of data protection law as set out in the Data Protection Directive in the field of electronic communications. Consequently, where expressions used in the Regulations are not defined there, they are taken to mean the same as in the Data Protection Act 1998. Furthermore, if an expression is defined in neither the Regulations nor the Act, they are to be taken to mean the same as in the Data Protection Directive; regulation 2(2) and (3).

The Regulations should not prejudice the Data Protection Act 1998 and regulation 4 states that nothing in the Regulations is to relieve a person of his obligations under the Act in relation to processing personal data.

---

[2] OJ L 201, 31.07.2002, p.37.

SECURITY AND CONFIDENTIALITY

Providers of public electronic communications services are required to keep their systems secure by taking appropriate technical and organisational measures; regulation 5. A public electronic communications service is defined in section 151 of the Communications Act 2003 (from where a number of other definitions are derived) as an electronic communications service provided so as to be made available for use by members of the public. Where necessary measures may be taken in conjunction with the network provider who shall comply with any reasonable request by the service provider. If, in spite of the measures taken, there remains a significant risk, subscribers must be informed of the nature of that risk (free of charge except for the cost to the subscriber of obtaining or collecting that information), measures that may be taken by the subscriber against that risk and the likely costs of taking such measures. A measure is appropriate if, having regard to the state of technological development and the cost of implementation, it is proportionate to the risks to be safeguarded against.

It is not uncommon for cookies to be installed on a person's computers, for example to collect information about a previous visit to a website or to remember a user's password. Other information may be collected from computers such as addresses of websites visited and the like. In many circumstances, the person using the computer will not object to this as it may help to provide a better service when visiting websites. However, there is a risk to privacy if individuals are unaware that this is going on. Therefore, under regulation 6, an electronic communications network is not to be used to store information, or to gain access to information stored, in the terminal equipment of a subscriber or user unless the subscriber or user is provided with clear and comprehensive information about the purposes of the storage of, or access to, that information and is given the opportunity to refuse the storage of or access to that information. The condition to provide information and give the opportunity to refuse only applies to the first occasion where the same person stores or accesses information on more than one occasion. The requirement not to store or access information on the subscriber's or user's terminal equipment does not apply where the sole purpose is to carry out or facilitate the transmission of a communication over an electronic communications network or where strictly necessary for the provision of an information society service requested by the subscriber or user.

TRAFFIC DATA AND ITEMISED BILLING

Limitations are placed on the retention of traffic data. Traffic data are defined as any data processed for the purpose of the conveyance of a communication on an electronic communications network or for the billing in respect of that communication and includes data relating to the routing, duration or time of a communication. Under regulation 7, when no longer required for the purposes of transmission of communication, traffic data are to be erased or, in the case of an individual, modified so that they no longer constitute personal data of that subscriber or user or, in the case of a corporate subscriber, modified so that they do not constitute personal data of that subscriber if it was an individual. Thus, retention beyond transmission of the communication is only possible if personal identifiers are stripped out (or the equivalent of such identifiers in the case of a corporate subscriber).

There are some exceptions to this basic rule where the data are required for payment of charges or interconnection payments when they can be retained until the expiry of the period during which legal proceedings may be brought in respect of payments due, or alleged to be due. Where legal proceedings are brought within that period, the data may be processed until the proceedings are finally determined, including allowances for the time for any appeal or, if there is an appeal, the determination of the appeal proceedings. References to an appeal include an application for permission to appeal. In other words, those data may be retained until such time as the expiry of the appropriate limitation period (for example, for six years from the date of an alleged breach of contract or, if proceedings are brought before the end of the limitation period, until the conclusion of those proceedings).

Another exception to the obligation to erase or remove personal identifiers or the equivalent is in the case of traffic data relating to a subscriber or user where the data are processed and stored for the purpose of marketing electronic communications services, or for the provision of value added services to that subscriber or user in cases where the subscriber or user has consented to such processing or storage. If this is so, the processing and storage may be undertaken only for the duration necessary for the marketing purposes. The consent of the subscriber or user may be withdrawn at any time. The reference to storage in addition to processing is really redundant as the Data Protection Directive includes storage in the meaning of processing (though the Data Protection Act 1998 uses the term "holding" instead). The consent referred to must, under regulation 8, be informed consent.

A public communications provider or person acting under his authority may only process traffic data under regulation 7 for the following activities:

(a) the management of billing or traffic;
(b) customer enquiries;
(c) the prevention or detection of fraud;
(d) the marketing of any telecommunications services provided; or
(e) the provision of a value added service.

This does not prevent the furnishing of traffic data to a person who is a competent authority for the purposes of any provision relating to the settling of disputes (by way of legal proceedings or otherwise) which is contained in, or made by virtue of, any enactment.

Regulation 9 enables a subscriber to request from a provider of a public electronic communications service a bill that is not itemised. OFCOM[3] has a duty, when exercising its functions under Chapter 1 of Part 2 of the Communications Act 2003 (electronic communications and networks), to have regard to the need to reconcile the rights of subscribers receiving itemised bills with the rights to privacy of calling users and called subscribers, including the need for sufficient alternative privacy-enhancing methods of communications or payments to be available to such users and subscribers.

CALLING OR CONNECTED LINE IDENTIFICATION

Regulations 10 and 11 concern the identification of calling or connected lines. A number of issues arise such as the ability to suppress the number of a line from which a call is made and the ability to see that a number is being withheld and to elect not to take a call. Another issue is that of nuisance calls and the possibility of tracing such calls even though the calling number is withheld.

Regulation 10 applies to outgoing calls where the facility to enable the presentation of calling line identification is available. In such cases, providers of public electronic communications services must provide users originating a call with a simple means to prevent identification of the calling line on the connected line. This applies to a user not necessarily the subscriber. However, the regulation goes on to require that a subscriber shall have the right, in respect of their line and all calls originating from that line, with a simple means of preventing presentation of the identity of that subscriber's line on any connected line. Thus, a corporate subscriber may require that his number is withheld in respect of all calls made from his line. These rights to suppress the calling line number are subject to the provisions relating to malicious and nuisance calls and emergency calls, for which see later. The rights to suppress calling line identification must be provided free of charge.

The identity of incoming calls can be presented on the receiving equipment. Where this is so, regulation 11 requires that the provider of a public electronic communications service ensures that the called subscriber has a simple means

---

[3] The Office of Communications as established by section 1 of the Office of Communications Act 2002.

to prevent, without charge for reasonable use of the facility, presentation of the identity of a calling line on the connected line. Where presentation on the connected line of the identity of the calling line is available before the call is established, that is, before the call is answered, the relevant telecommunications service provider must ensure that the called subscriber has, as respects all or particular calls in the case of which such presentation has been withheld by the caller, a simple means of rejecting such calls.

Where a facility enabling the presentation of connected line identification is available, the provider of a public electronic communications service shall provide the called subscriber with a simple means to prevent, without charge, presentation of the identity of the connected line on any calling line. This enables a subscriber the ability to avoid the capture of his number or other communications gateway. A "called subscriber" is the subscriber receiving a call by means of the service in question whose line is the called line (whether or not it is also the connected line).

Providers of public electronic communications services must publicise the availability of facilities for calling or called line identification including options for preventing identification of a line under regulation 12. Communications providers are required to comply with any reasonable requests made by the provider of the public electronic communications service by means of which facilities for calling or connected line identification are provided; regulation 13.

LOCATION DATA

It is now possible to locate the geographic position of a mobile telephone to some degree of accuracy. Clearly there are implications for privacy here as the movements of a particular person could be logged and disclosed to others. Regulation 14 provides for restrictions on the processing of location data though this is without prejudice to the processing of traffic data.

Location data are data processed in an electronic communications network indicating the geographical position of the terminal equipment of a user of a public electronic communications service. This includes data relating to the latitude, longitude or altitude of the terminal equipment, the direction of travel of the user or the time the location information was recorded.

Location data relating to a user of a public electronic telecommunications network or service may only be processed where the user or subscriber cannot be identified from the data or where necessary for the provision of a value added service with the informed consent of the user or subscriber, which may be withdrawn at any time, even on a call by call basis, by simple means and free of charge. Processing may only be carried out by the relevant public communications provider or by relevant third party providing the value added service or persons acting under their authority. Where processing is carried out in relation to a value added service, it must be limited to that necessary for the purposes of providing that service.

MALICIOUS OR NUISANCE CALLS

Under regulation 15, a communications provider may override anything done to block calling line identification where a subscriber has requested the tracing of malicious or nuisance calls received on his line and the provider is satisfied that such action is necessary and expedient for the purposes of tracing such calls. Any term of a contract for the provision of public electronic communications services concerning the suppression of a calling line is subject to this. A communications provider is not prevented, for the purposes of any action relating to the tracing of malicious or nuisance calls, from storing and making available, to a person with a legitimate interest, data containing the identity of a calling subscriber which were obtained in this way. This could apply, for example, in providing OFCOM or the police with information about nuisance calls.

EMERGENCY CALLS

Preventing identification of a calling line or the processing of location data could have serious consequences in cases of emergency, for example, where a badly injured person calls the emergency services. Regulation 16 therefore removes the restrictions on the processing of location data and the right to block calling line identification. It also provides that no person is entitled to prevent the presentation on the connected line of the identity of the calling line. An emergency call is one using the national emergency number (999) or the single European emergency number (112).

AUTOMATIC CALL FORWARDING

Call forwarding is where a call is automatically redirected to another number when a line is engaged or not accepted within a set period of time or even unconditionally without connection to the called line being attempted. It can even be selective where certain calling lines only are forwarded. A subscriber's provider of an electronic communications service is required, free of charge and without avoidable delay, to prevent automatic call forwarding where the subscriber requests this. Every other communications provider shall comply with any reasonable requests made by the subscriber's provider to assist in the prevention of that call forwarding.

DIRECTORIES OF SUBSCRIBERS

Telephone and other directories contain information that may be very useful to persons wanting to find the telephone number or fax number of someone they want to contact for legitimate reasons, including marketing purposes. However, that information can also assist those with other purposes and could pose a threat, for example to females living alone or to persons involved in sensitive work which may attract the attention of pressure groups. The facility to "go ex-directory" is important as is the possibility of suppressing certain information such as a title which gives away the sex of the subscriber. Organisations too may have reasons for being ex-directory or having information relating to the organisation restricted or limited in some way. That could apply, for example, in relation to organisations involved in research involving live animals or to fur farmers.

The provisions relating to subscribers' directories are contained in regulation 18 and apply to directories of subscribers, whether in printed or electronic form, which are made available to members of the public or a section of the public, including by means of a directory enquiry service. The personal data of an individual subscriber shall not be included in a directory unless that subscriber has, free of charge, been informed by the collector of the personal data of the purposes of the directory in which his personal data are to be included, and given the opportunity to determine whether such of his or her personal data as are considered relevant by the producer of the directory should be included in the directory.

In a case where individual subscriber's personal data are to be included in a directory which can be accessed solely by means of a telephone number, the information to be provided must include that fact, and the express consent of the subscriber to the inclusion of his or her data must be obtained. Where data relating to an individual subscriber has been included in a directory, he or she has the right, without charge, to verify, correct or withdraw those data at any time. If a request to be withdrawn from the directory is made, it only takes effect as regards subsequent editions of the directory (this include revisions). Telephone number has the same meaning as in section 56(5) of the Communications Act 2003, which is a wide definition but for the purposes of regulation 18 does not include any number which is used as an internet domain name, an internet address or an address or identifier incorporating either an internet domain name or an internet address, including an email address.

AUTOMATED CALLING SYSTEMS

Automatic calling equipment is telecommunications apparatus capable of automatically initiating a sequence of calls to more than one number. This allows large numbers of calls to large number of recipients in a short period of time and at relatively little cost to the person initiating those calls. This is clearly open to abuse and must be controlled. The types of abuse of such systems include the delivery of recorded messages, initiating calls which, if answered, result in a recorded message or silence because there are not enough operators to service all calls answered or simply sending unsolicited facsimile messages.

Under regulation 19, a person must not transmit or instigate the transmission of communications of recorded matter for direct marketing by means of automated calling systems unless the subscriber has previously notified the caller that, for the time being, he consents to such communications. A subscriber must not allow his line to be used for automated calling systems without such consent. An automated calling system is defined as one capable of automatically initiating a sequence of calls to more than one destination in accordance with instructions stored in the system and transmitting sounds that are not live speech for reception by persons at some or all of the destinations so called.

DIRECT MARKETING PURPOSES

The ability to prevent unsolicited communications for the purposes of direct marketing is quite important. It is one thing receiving direct marketing material by post (this can be reduced by use of the "opt-out" scheme under the Mailing Preference Service or individuals can exercise their right to object under section 11 of the Data Protection Act 1998). Receiving unsolicited direct marking communications by telephone, facsimile transmission or electronic mail can be even more irritating. The introduction of a Telephone Preference Service and Fax Preference Service has helped reduce this problem. The Regulations provide even more control over the receipt of unsolicited marketing communications sent by facsimile transmission, public telephone or electronic mail.

Regulation 20 applies to facsimile transmission and states that no person may transmit or instigate the transmission of unsolicited communications for the purposes of direct marketing where the called line is that of:

(a) an individual subscriber (unless he or she has notified the caller of his or her consent for the time being);

(b) a corporate subscriber who has previously notified the caller that such communications should not be sent on that line; or

(c) the subscriber and the number allocated to that line is listed in the opt-out register kept by OFCOM for such purposes.

In respect of (c), a 28-day period of grace is allowed after listing. Also, any subscriber listing a line under (c) may notify a caller that he or she does not object for the time being to receiving unsolicited marketing communications, though why anyone would want to do this is not clear. In any case, this can be withdrawn at any time. Regulation 20 is without prejudice to regulation 19 on automated call forwarding.

Regulation 21 applies to unsolicited marketing by means of public electronic communications services and a person must neither use nor instigate the use of such a service for the purposes of making unsolicited calls for direct marketing purposes where the called line is that of a subscriber who has previously notified the caller that such calls should not for the time being be made on that line or the number allocated to a subscriber in respect of the called line is listed in the opt-out register kept by OFCOM in respect of such communications under regulation 26. This register was originally not available to corporate subscribers but the Privacy and Electronic Communications (EC Directive) (Amendment) Regulations 2004 opened the register to also corporate subscribers. As with regulation 20, no person is to permit the use of his or her line in contravention of the basic provisions and, again, a 28-day period of grace is permitted.

Any subscriber listing a line on the opt-out register may notify a caller that he or she does not object for the time being to receiving unsolicited marketing communications. This consent can be withdrawn at any time.

"Spam" or unsolicited electronic mail is a serious nuisance. Regulation 22 attempts to prevent or minimise this problem by prohibiting the transmission or instigation of the transmission of unsolicited communications for the purposes of direct marketing by means of email unless consent has previously been notified to the sender. There is a major exception and this is where the sender has obtained the recipient's contact details in the course of the sale or negotiations for the sale of a product or service to the recipient and the direct marketing is in respect of the sender's similar products and services only and the recipient has been given a simple means of refusing, free of charge (except for the cost of transmission refusal).

Direct marketing by email where the identity of the sender is disguised or concealed or the valid address enabling the recipient to request the cessation of such communications has not been provided is prohibited under regulation 23.

Where a public electronic communications service is used for transmitting direct marketing communications (whether by automated calling systems, facsimile transmission, public telephone or email), certain information must be provided under regulation 24. This is the name of the person sending the communication and either the address of that person or a telephone number on which he can be reached free of charge.

EXEMPTIONS

Regulation 28 provides exemption to the extent that the exemption from the Regulations is required for the purpose of safeguarding national security. The exemption closely mirrors the equivalent exemption under section 28 of the Data Protection Act 1998. A certificate to that effect signed by a Minister of the Crown is conclusive evidence that the exemption is required for this purpose. The certificate may identify the circumstances in which it applies in general terms and may be expressed to have prospective effect. Any person affected may appeal to the Information Tribunal. Other relevant provisions of the 1998 Act have effect for the purposes of the Regulations.

Regulation 29 contains exemptions relating to legal requirements and law enforcement, etc. and states that nothing in the Regulations shall require a communications provider to do, or refrain from doing anything, including processing data, if compliance with the regulation in question would be inconsistent with any requirement imposed by or under any enactment or court order or if it would be likely to prejudice the prevention and detection of crime or the apprehension or prosecution of offenders. The exemption also applies in respect of legal proceedings including prospective legal proceedings, if necessary to obtain legal advice or if it is otherwise necessary for the purposes of establishing, exercising or defending legal rights.

Apart from these cases, there are no other exemptions except as stated earlier in respect of specific provisions.

COMPENSATION, ETC.

A person who suffers damage as a result of any contravention of the Regulations by any other person may bring proceedings for compensation for that damage under regulation 30. It is a defence to show that such care had been taken as was in all the circumstances reasonably required to comply with the relevant requirement. This is without prejudice to the extension of some of the enforcement provisions of the Data Protection Act 1998 to these

Regulations. It is notable that there is no provision for compensation for distress, whether or not there is associated damage.

Under regulation 31, where there is an allegation of any contravention of the Regulations, either OFCOM or a person aggrieved may ask the Information Commissioner to exercise his enforcement powers. However, these powers may be exercised in the absence of any such request. The Information Commissioner, in connection with his enforcement powers, may seek the advice of OFCOM on technical and similar matters relating to electronic communications and OFCOM shall comply with any such reasonable request.

OTHER PROVISIONS

To the extent that any term between a subscriber to and the provider of a public electronic communications service or between such a provider and the provider of an electronic communications network is inconsistent with a requirement of the Regulations, that term is void to that extent; regulation 27.

The enforcement provisions under the Data Protection Act 1998 are modified appropriately for the purposes of the Regulations. For example, the provisions relating to special information notices and determinations of the Information Commissioner under sections 44 to 46 have no relevance to the privacy and electronic communications Regulations. However, normal enforcement notices do apply, *mutatis mutandis*.

There are a number of transitional provisions reflecting the changes brought about by the privacy and electronic communications Regulations in comparison with the previous Regulations.

APPENDIX

DIRECTIVE 95/46/EC OF THE EUROPEAN PARLIAMENT AND OF THE COUNCIL OF 24 OCTOBER 1995 ON THE PROTECTION OF INDIVIDUALS WITH REGARD TO THE PROCESSING OF PERSONAL DATA AND ON THE FREE MOVEMENT OF SUCH DATA

This is an unofficial text. For the authoritative text of the Directive, reference should be made to the Official Journal of the European Communities of 23 November 1995 No L. 281 p. 31.

Contents

Recitals

CHAPTER I GENERAL PROVISIONS

Article 1 Object of the Directive

Article 2 Definitions

Article 3 Scope

Article 4 National law applicable

CHAPTER II – GENERAL RULES ON THE LAWFULNESS

Article 5

SECTION I – PRINCIPLES RELATING TO DATA QUALITY

Article 6

SECTION II – CRITERIA FOR MAKING DATA PROCESSING LEGITIMATE

Article 7

SECTION III – SPECIAL CATEGORIES OF PROCESSING

Article 8 The processing of special categories of data

Article 9 Processing of personal data and freedom of expression

SECTION IV – INFORMATION TO BE GIVEN TO THE DATA SUBJECT

Article 10 Information in cases of collection of data from the data subject

Article 11 Information where the data have not been obtained from the data subject

SECTION V – THE DATA SUBJECT'S RIGHT OF ACCESS TO DATA

Article 12 Right of access

SECTION VI – EXEMPTIONS AND RESTRICTIONS

Article 13

SECTION VII – THE DATA SUBJECT'S RIGHT TO OBJECT

Article 14 The data subject's right to object

Article 15 Automated individual decisions

SECTION VIII – CONFIDENTIALITY AND SECURITY OF PROCESSING

Article 16 Confidentiality of processing

Article 17 Security of processing

SECTION IX – NOTIFICATION

Article 18 – Obligation to notify the supervisory authority

Article 19 – Contents of notification

Article 20 – Prior checking

Article 21 – Publicizing of processing operations

CHAPTER III – JUDICIAL REMEDIES, LIABILITY AND SANCTIONS

Article 22 Remedies

Article 23 Liability

Article 24 Sanctions

CHAPTER IV – TRANSFER OF PERSONAL DATA TO THIRD COUNTRIES

Article 25 Principles

Article 26 Derogations

CHAPTER V – CODES OF CONDUCT

Article 27

CHAPTER VI – SUPERVISORY AUTHORITY

Article 28 Supervisory authority

Article 29 Working Party on the Protection of Individuals

Article 30

CHAPTER VII – COMMUNITY IMPLEMENTING MEASURES

Article 31 – The Committee

FINAL PROVISIONS

Article 32

Article 33

Article 34

Recitals

THE EUROPEAN PARLIAMENT AND THE COUNCIL OF THE EUROPEAN UNION,

Having regard to the Treaty establishing the European Community, and inparticular Article 100 a thereof,

Having regard to the proposal from the Commission, Having regard to the opinion of the Economic and Social Committee, Acting in accordance with the procedure referred to in Article 189 b of the Treaty.

(1) Whereas the objectives of the Community, as laid down in the Treaty, as amended by the Treaty on European Union, include creating an ever closer union among the peoples of Europe, fostering closer relations between the States belonging to the Community, ensuring economic and social progress by common action to eliminate the barriers which divide Europe, encouraging the constant improvement of the living conditions of its peoples, preserving and strengthening peace and liberty and promoting democracy on the basis of the fundamental rights recognized in the constitution and laws of the Member States and in the European Convention for the Protection of Human Rights and Fundamental Freedoms;

(2) Whereas data-processing systems are designed to serve man; whereas they must, whatever the nationality or residence of natural persons, respect their fundamental rights and freedoms, notably the right to privacy, and contribute to economic and social progress, trade expansion and the well-being of individuals;

(3) Whereas the establishment and functioning of an internal market in which, in accordance with Article 7 a of the Treaty, the free movement of goods, persons, services and capital is ensured require not only that personal data should be able to flow freely from one Member State to another, but also that the fundamental rights of individuals should be safeguarded;

(4) Whereas increasingly frequent recourse is being had in the Community to the processing of personal data in the various spheres of economic and social activity; whereas the progress made in information technology is making the processing and exchange of such data considerably easier;

(5) Whereas the economic and social integration resulting from the establishment and functioning of the internal market within the meaning of Article 7 a of the Treaty will necessarily lead to a substantial increase in cross-border flows of personal data between all those involved in a private or public capacity in economic and social activity in the Member States; whereas the

exchange of personal data between undertakings in different Member States is set to increase; whereas the national authorities in the various Member States are being called upon by virtue of Community law to collaborate and exchange personal data so as to be able to perform their duties or carry out tasks on behalf of an authority in another Member State within the context of the area without internal frontiers as constituted by the internal market;

(6) Whereas, furthermore, the increase in scientific and technical co-operation and the co-ordinated introduction of new telecommunications networks in the Community necessitate and facilitate cross-border flows of personal data;

(7) Whereas the difference in levels of protection of the rights and freedoms of individuals, notably the right to privacy, with regard to the processing of personal data afforded in the Member States may prevent the transmission of such data from the territory of one Member State to that of another Member State; whereas this difference may therefore constitute an obstacle to the pursuit of a number of economic activities at Community level, distort competition and impede authorities in the discharge of their responsibilities under Community law; whereas this difference in levels of protection is due to the existence of a wide variety of national laws, regulations and administrative provisions;

(8) Whereas, in order to remove the obstacles to flows of personal data, the level of protection of the rights and freedoms of individuals with regard to the processing of such data must be equivalent in all Member States; whereas this objective is vital to the internal market but cannot be achieved by the Member States alone, especially in view of the scale of the divergences which currently exist between the relevant laws in the Member States and the need to coordinate the laws of the Member States so as to ensure that the cross-border flow of personal data is regulated in a consistent manner that is in keeping with the objective of the internal market as provided for in Article 7a of the Treaty; whereas Community action to approximate those laws is therefore needed;

(9) Whereas, given the equivalent protection resulting from the approximation of national laws, the Member States will no longer be able to inhibit the free movement between them of personal data on grounds relating to protection of the rights and freedoms of individuals, and in particular the right to privacy; whereas Member States will be left a margin for manoeuvre, which may, in the context of implementation of the Directive, also be exercised by the business and social partners; whereas Member States will therefore be able to specify in their national law the general conditions governing the lawfulness of data processing; whereas in doing so the Member States shall strive to improve the protection currently provided by their legislation; whereas, within the limits of this margin for manoeuvre and in accor-

dance with Community law, disparities could arise in the implementation of the Directive, and this could have an effect on the movement of data within a Member State as well as within the Community;

(10) Whereas the object of the national laws on the processing of personal data is to protect fundamental rights and freedoms, notably the right to privacy, which is recognized both in Article 8 of the European Convention for the Protection of Human Rights and Fundamental Freedoms and in the general principles of Community law; whereas, for that reason, the approximation of those laws must not result in any lessening of the protection they afford but must, on the contrary, seek to ensure a high level of protection in the Community;

(11) Whereas the principles of the protection of the rights and freedoms of individuals, notably the right to privacy, which are contained in this Directive, give substance to and amplify those contained in the Council of Europe Convention of 28 January 1981 for the Protection of Individuals with regard to Automatic Processing of Personal Data;

(12) Whereas the protection principles must apply to all processing of personal data by any person whose activities are governed by Community law; whereas there should be excluded the processing of data carried out by a natural person in the exercise of activities which are exclusively personal or domestic, such as correspondence and the holding of records of addresses;

(13) Whereas the activities referred to in Titles V and VI of the Treaty on the European Union regarding public safety, defence, State security or the activities of the State in the area of criminal laws fall outside the scope of Community law, without prejudice to the obligations incumbent upon Member States under Article 56 (2), Article 57 or Article 100 a of the Treaty establishing the European Community; whereas the processing of personal data that is necessary to safeguard the economic well-being of the State does not fall within the scope of this Directive where such processing relates to State security matters;

(14) Whereas, given the importance of the developments under way, in the framework of the information society, of the techniques used to capture, transmit, manipulate, record, store or communicate sound and image data relating to natural persons, this Directive should be applicable to processing involving such data;

(15) Whereas the processing of such data is covered by this Directive only if it is automated or if the data processed are contained or are intended to be contained in a filing system structured according to specific criteria relating to individuals, so as to permit easy access to the personal data in question;

(16) Whereas the processing of sound and image data, such as in cases of video surveillance, does not come within the scope of this Directive if it is carried out for the purposes of public security, defence, national security or in the course of State activities relating to the area of criminal law or of other activities which do not come within the scope of Community law;

(17) Whereas, as far as the processing of sound and image data carried out for purposes of journalism or the purposes of literary or artistic expression is concerned, in particular in the audiovisual field, the principles of the Directive are to apply in a restricted manner according to the provisions laid down in Article 9;

(18) Whereas, in order to ensure that individuals are not deprived of the protection to which they are entitled under this Directive, any processing of personal data in the Community must be carried out in accordance with the law of one of the Member States; whereas, in this connection, processing carried out under the responsibility of a controller who is established in a Member State should be governed by the law of that State;

(19) Whereas establishment on the territory of a Member State implies the effective and real exercise of activity through stable arrangements; whereas the legal form of such an establishment, whether simply branch or a subsidiary with a legal personality, is not the determining factor in this respect; whereas, when a single controller is established on the territory of several Member States, particularly by means of subsidiaries, he must ensure, in order to avoid any circumvention of national rules, that each of the establishments fulfils the obligations imposed by the national law applicable to its activities;

(20) Whereas the fact that the processing of data is carried out by a person established in a third country must not stand in the way of the protection of individuals provided for in this Directive; whereas in these cases, the processing should be governed by the law of the Member State in which the means used are located, and there should be guarantees to ensure that the rights and obligations provided for in this Directive are respected in practice;

(21) Whereas this Directive is without prejudice to the rules of territoriality applicable in criminal matters;

(22) Whereas Member States shall more precisely define in the laws they enact or when bringing into force the measures taken under this Directive the general circumstances in which processing is lawful; whereas in particular Article 5, in conjunction with Articles 7 and 8, allows Member States, independently of general rules, to provide for special processing conditions for specific sectors and for the various categories of data covered by Article 8;

(23) Whereas Member States are empowered to ensure the implementation of the protection of individuals both by means of a general law on the protection of individuals as regards the processing of personal data and by sectorial laws such as those relating, for example, to statistical institutes;

(24) Whereas the legislation concerning the protection of legal persons with regard to the processing data which concerns them is not affected by this Directive;

(25) Whereas the principles of protection must be reflected, on the one hand, in the obligations imposed on persons, public authorities, enterprises, agencies or other bodies responsible for processing, in particular regarding data quality, technical security, notification to the supervisory authority, and the circumstances under which processing can be carried out, and, on the other hand, in the right conferred on individuals, the data on whom are the subject of processing, to be informed that processing is taking place, to consult the data, to request corrections and even to object to processing in certain circumstances;

(26) Whereas the principles of protection must apply to any information concerning an identified or identifiable person; whereas, to determine whether a person is identifiable, account should be taken of all the means likely reasonably to be used either by the controller or by any other person to identify the said person; whereas the principles of protection shall not apply to data rendered anonymous in such a way that the data subject is no longer identifiable; whereas codes of conduct within the meaning of Article 27 may be a useful instrument for providing guidance as to the ways in which data may be rendered anonymous and retained in a form in which identification of the data subject is no longer possible;

(27) Whereas the protection of individuals must apply as much to automatic processing of data as to manual processing; whereas the scope of this protection must not in effect depend on the techniques used, otherwise this would create a serious risk of circumvention; whereas, none the less, as regards manual processing, this Directive covers only filing systems, not unstructured files; whereas, in particular, the content of a filing system must be structured according to specific criteria relating to individuals allowing easy access to the personal data; whereas, in line with the definition in Article 2 (c), the different criteria for determining the constituents of a structured set of personal data, and the different criteria governing access to such a set, may be laid down by each Member State; whereas files or sets of files as well as their cover pages, which are not structured according to specific criteria, shall under no circumstances fall within the scope of this Directive;

(28) Whereas any processing of personal data must be lawful and fair to the individuals concerned; whereas, in particular, the data must be adequate,

relevant and not excessive in relation to the purposes for which they are processed; whereas such purposes must be explicit and legitimate and must be determined at the time of collection of the data; whereas the purposes of processing further to collection shall not be incompatible with the purposes as they were originally specified;

(29) Whereas the further processing of personal data for historical, statistical or scientific purposes is not generally to be considered incompatible with the purposes for which the data have previously been collected provided that Member States furnish suitable safeguards; whereas these safeguards must in particular rule out the use of the data in support of measures or decisions regarding any particular individual;

(30) Whereas, in order to be lawful, the processing of personal data must in addition be carried out with the consent of the data subject or be necessary for the conclusion or performance of a contract binding on the data subject, or as a legal requirement, or for the performance of a task carried out in the public interest or in the exercise of official authority, or in the legitimate interests of a natural or legal person, provided that the interests or the rights and freedoms of the data subject are not overriding; whereas, in particular, in order to maintain a balance between the interests involved while guaranteeing effective competition, Member States may determine the circumstances in which personal data may be used or disclosed to a third party in the context of the legitimate ordinary business activities of companies and other bodies; whereas Member States may similarly specify the conditions under which personal data may be disclosed to a third party for the purposes of marketing whether carried out commercially or by a charitable organization or by any other association or foundation, of a political nature for example, subject to the provisions allowing a data subject to object to the processing of data regarding him, at no cost and without having to state his reasons;

(31) Whereas the processing of personal data must equally be regarded as lawful where it is carried out in order to protect an interest which is essential for the data subject's life;

(32) Whereas it is for national legislation to determine whether the controller performing a task carried out in the public interest or in the exercise of official authority should be a public administration or another natural or legal person governed by public law, or by private law such as a professional association;

(33) Whereas data which are capable by their nature of infringing fundamental freedoms or privacy should not be processed unless the data subject gives his explicit consent; whereas, however, derogations from this prohibition must be explicitly provided for in respect of specific needs, in particular

where the processing of these data is carried out for certain health-related purposes by persons subject to a legal obligation of professional secrecy or in the course of legitimate activities by certain associations or foundations the purpose of which is to permit the exercise of fundamental freedoms;

(34) Whereas Member States must also be authorized, when justified by grounds of important public interest, to derogate from the prohibition on processing sensitive categories of data where important reasons of public interest so justify in areas such as public health and social protection – especially in order to ensure the quality and cost-effectiveness of the procedures used for settling claims for benefits and services in the health insurance system – scientific research and government statistics; whereas it is incumbent on them, however, to provide specific and suitable safeguards so as to protect the fundamental rights and the privacy of individuals;

(35) Whereas, moreover, the processing of personal data by official authorities for achieving aims, laid down in constitutional law or international public law, of officially recognized religious associations is carried out on important grounds of public interest;

(36) Whereas where, in the course of electoral activities, the operation of the democratic system requires in certain Member States that political parties compile data on people's political opinion, the processing of such data may be permitted for reasons of important public interest, provided that appropriate safeguards are established;

(37) Whereas the processing of personal data for purposes of journalism or for purposes of literary of artistic expression, in particular in the audiovisual field, should qualify for exemption from the requirements of certain provisions of this Directive in so far as this is necessary to reconcile the fundamental rights of individuals with freedom of information and notably the right to receive and impart information, as guaranteed in particular in Article 10 of the European Convention for the Protection of Human Rights and Fundamental Freedoms; whereas Member States should therefore lay down exemptions and derogations necessary for the purpose of balance between fundamental rights as regards general measures on the legitimacy of data processing, measures on the transfer of data to third countries and the power of the supervisory authority; whereas this should not, however, lead Member States to lay down exemptions from the measures to ensure security of processing; whereas at least the supervisory authority responsible for this sector should also be provided with certain ex-post powers, e. g. to publish a regular report or to refer matters to the judicial authorities;

(38) Whereas, if the processing of data is to be fair, the data subject must be in a position to learn of the existence of a processing operation and, where data

are collected from him, must be given accurate and full information, bearing in mind the circumstances of the collection;

(39) Whereas certain processing operations involve data which the controller has not collected directly from the data subject; whereas, furthermore, data can be legitimately disclosed to a third party, even if the disclosure was not anticipated at the time the data were collected from the data subject; whereas, in all these cases, the data subject should be informed when the data are recorded or at the latest when the data are first disclosed to a third party;

(40) Whereas, however, it is not necessary to impose this obligation of the data subject already has the information; whereas, moreover, there will be no such obligation if the recording or disclosure are expressly provided for by law or if the provision of information to the data subject proves impossible or would involve disproportionate efforts, which could be the case where processing is for historical, statistical or scientific purposes; whereas, in this regard, the number of data subjects, the age of the data, and any compensatory measures adopted may be taken into consideration;

(41) Whereas any person must be able to exercise the right of access to data relating to him which are being processed, in order to verify in particular the accuracy of the data and the lawfulness of the processing; whereas, for the same reasons, every data subject must also have the right to know the logic involved in the automatic processing of data concerning him, at least in the case of the automated decisions referred to in Article 15 (1); whereas this right must not adversely affect trade secrets or intellectual property and in particular the copyright protecting the software; whereas these considerations must not, however, result in the data subject being refused all information;

(42) Whereas Member States may, in the interest of the data subject or so as to protect the rights and freedoms of others, restrict rights of access and information; whereas they may, for example, specify that access to medical data may be obtained only through a health professional;

(43) Whereas restrictions on the rights of access and information and on certain obligations of the controller may similarly be imposed by Member States in so far as they are necessary to safeguard, for example, national security, defence, public safety, or important economic or financial interests of a Member State or the Union, as well as criminal investigations and prosecutions and action in respect of breaches of ethics in the regulated professions; whereas the list of exeptions and limitations should include the tasks of monitoring, inspection or regulation necessary in the three last-mentioned areas concerning public security, economic or financial interests and crime prevention; whereas the listing of tasks in these three areas does not affect the legitimacy of exceptions or restrictions for reasons of State security or defence;

(44) Whereas Member States may also be led, by virtue of the provisions of Community law, to derogate from the provisions of this Directive concerning the right access, the obligation to inform individuals, and the quality of data, in order to secure certain of the purposes referred to above;

(45) Whereas, in cases where data might lawfully be processed on grounds of public interest, official authority or the legitimate interests of a natural or legal person, any data subject should nevertheless be entitled, on legitimate and compelling grounds relating to his particular situation, to object to the processing of any data relating to himself; whereas Member States may nevertheless lay down national provisions to the contrary;

(46) Whereas the protection of the rights and freedoms of data subjects with regard to the processing of personal data requires that appropriate technical and organizational measures be taken, both at the time of the design of the processing system and at the time of the processing itself, particularly in order to maintain security and thereby to prevent any unauthorized processing; whereas it is incumbent on the Member States to ensure that controllers comply with these measures; whereas these measures must ensure an appropriate level of security, taking into account the state of the art and the costs of their implementation in relation to the risks inherent in the processing and the nature of the data to be protected;

(47) Whereas where a message containing personal data is transmitted by means of a telecommunications or electronic mail service, the sole purpose of which is the transmission of such messages, the controller in respect of the personal data contained in the message will normally be considered to be the person from whom the message originates, rather than the person offering the transmission services; whereas, nevertheless, those offering such services will normally be considered controllers in respect of the processing of the additional personal data necessary for the operation of the service;

(48) Whereas the procedures for notifying the supervisory authority are designed to ensure disclosure of the purposes and main features of any processing operation for the purpose of verification that the operation is in accordance with the national measures taken under this Directive;

(49) Whereas, in order to avoid unsuitable administrative formalities, exemptions from the obligation to notify and simplification of the notification required may be provided for by Member States in cases where processing is unlikely adversely to affect the rights and freedoms of data subjects, provided that it is in accordance with a measure taken by a Member State specifying its limits; whereas exemption or simplification may similarly be provided for by Member States where a person appointed by the controller ensures that the processing carried out is not likely adversely to affect the rights and freedoms

of data subjects; whereas such a data protection official, whether or not an employee of the controller, must be in a position to exercise his functions in complete independence;

(50) Whereas exemption or simplification could be provided for in cases of processing operations whose sole purpose is the keeping of a register intended, according to national law, to provide information to the public and open to consultation by the public or by any person demonstrating a legitimate interest;

(51) Whereas, nevertheless, simplification or exemption from the obligation to notify shall not release the controller from any of the other obligations resulting from this Directive;

(52) Whereas, in this context, ex post facto verification by the competent authorities must in general be considered a sufficient measure;

(53) Whereas, however, certain processing operations are likely to pose specific risks to the rights and freedoms of data subjects by virtue of their nature, their scope or their purposes, such as that of excluding individuals from a right, benefit or a contract, or by virtue of the specific use of new technologies; whereas it is for Member States, if they so wish, to specify such risks in their legislation;

(54) Whereas with regard to all the processing undertaken in society, the amount posing such specific risks should be very limited; whereas Member States must provide that the supervisory authority, or the data protection official in co-operation with the authority, check such processing prior to it being carried out; whereas following this prior check, the supervisory authority may, according to its national law, give an opinion or an authorization regarding the processing; whereas such checking may equally take place in the course of the preparation either of a measure of the national parliament or of a measure based on such a legislative measure, which defines the nature of the processing and lays down appropriate safeguards;

(55) Whereas, if the controller fails to respect the rights of data subjects, national legislation must provide for a judicial remedy; whereas any damage which a person may suffer as a result of unlawful processing must be compensated for by the controller, who may be exempted from liability if he proves that he is not responsible for the damage, in particular in cases where he establishes fault on the part of the data subject or in case of force majeure; whereas sanctions must be imposed on any person, whether governed by private of public law, who fails to comply with the national measures taken under this Directive;

(56) Whereas cross-border flows of personal data are necessary to the expansion of international trade; whereas the protection of individuals guar-

anteed in the Community by this Directive does not stand in the way of transfers of personal data to third countries which ensure an adequate level of protection; whereas the adequacy of the level of protection afforded by a third country must be assessed in the light of all the circumstances surrounding the transfer operation or set of transfer operations;

(57) Whereas, on the other hand, the transfer of personal data to a third country which does not ensure an adequate level of protection must be prohibited;

(58) Whereas provisions should be made for exemptions from this prohibition in certain circumstances where the data subject has given his consent, where the transfer is necessary in relation to a contract or a legal claim, where protection of an important public interest so requires, for example in cases of international transfers of data between tax or customs administrations or between services competent for social security matters, or where the transfer is made from a register established by law and intended for consultation by the public or persons having a legitimate interest; whereas in this case such a transfer should not involve the entirety of the data or entire categories of the data contained in the register and, when the register is intended for consultation by persons having a legitimate interest, the transfer should be made only at the request of those persons or if they are to be the recipients;

(59) Whereas particular measures may be taken to compensate for the lack of protection in a third country in cases where the controller offers appropriate safeguards; whereas, moreover, provision must be made for procedures for negotiations between the Community and such third countries;

(60) Whereas, in any event, transfers to third countries may be effected only in full compliance with the provisions adopted by the Member States pursuant to this Directive, and in particular Article 8 thereof;

(61) Whereas Member States and the Commission, in their respective spheres of competence, must encourage the trade associations and other representative organizations concerned to draw up codes of conduct so as to facilitate the application of this Directive, taking account of the specific characteristics of the processing carried out in certain sectors, and respecting the national provisions adopted for its implementation;

(62) Whereas the establishment in Member States of supervisory authorities, exercising their functions with complete independence, is an essential component of the protection of individuals with regard to the processing of personal data;

(63) Whereas such authorities must have the necessary means to perform their duties, including powers of investigation and intervention, particularly in

cases of complaints from individuals, and powers to engage in legal proceedings; whereas such authorities must help to ensure transparency of processing in the Member States within whose jurisdiction they fall;

(64) Whereas the authorities in the different Member States will need to assist one another in performing their duties so as to ensure that the rules of protection are properly respected throughout the European Union;

(65) Whereas, at Community level, a Working Party on the Protection of Individuals with regard to the Processing of Personal Data must be set up and be completely independent in the performance of its functions; whereas, having regard to its specific nature, it must advise the Commission and, in particular, contribute to the uniform application of the national rules adopted pursuant to this Directive;

(66) Whereas, with regard to the transfer of data to third countries, the application of this Directive calls for the conferment of powers of implementation on the Commission and the establishment of a procedure as laid down in Council Decision 87/373/EEC;

(67) Whereas an agreement on a modus vivendi between the European Parliament, the Council and the Commission concerning the implementing measures for acts adopted in accordance with the procedure laid down in Article 189 b of the EC Treaty was reached on 20 December 1994;

(68) Whereas the principles set out in this Directive regarding the protection of the rights and freedoms of individuals, notably their right to privacy, with regard to the processing of personal data may be supplemented or clarified, in particular as far as certain sectors are concerned, by specific rules based on those principles;

(69) Whereas Member States should be allowed a period of not more than three years from the entry into force of the national measures transposing this Directive in which to apply such new national rules progressively to all processing operations already under way; whereas, in order to facilitate their cost-effective implementation, a further period expiring 12 years after the date on which this Directive is adopted will be allowed to Member States to ensure the conformity of existing manual filing systems with certain of the Directive's provisions; whereas, where data contained in such filing systems are manually processed during this extended transition period, those systems must be brought into conformity with these provisions at the time of such processing;

(70) Whereas it is not necessary for the data subject to give his consent again so as to allow the controller to continue to process, after the national provi-

sions taken pursuant to this Directive enter into force, any sensitive data necessary for the performance of a contract concluded on the basis of free and informed consent before the entry into force of these provisions;

(71) Whereas this Directive does not stand in the way of a Member State's regulating marketing activities aimed at consumers residing in territory in so far as such regulation does not concern the protection of individuals with regard to the processing of personal data;

(72) Whereas this Directive allows the principle of public access to official documents to be taken into account when implementing the principles set out in this Directive,

HAVE ADOPTED THIS DIRECTIVE:

CHAPTER I GENERAL PROVISIONS

Article 1 Object of the Directive

(1) In accordance with this Directive, Member States shall protect the fundamental rights and freedoms of natural persons, and in particular their right to privacy with respect to the processing of personal data.

(2) Member States shall neither restrict nor prohibit the free flow of personal data between Member States for reasons connected with the protection afforded under paragraph 1.

Article 2 Definitions

For the purposes of this Directive:

a) 'personal data' shall mean any information relating to an identified or identifiable natural person ('data subject'); an identifiable person is one who can be identified, directly or indirectly, in particular by reference to an identification number or to one or more factors specific to his physical, physiological, mental, economic, cultural or social identity;

b) 'processing of personal data' ('processing') shall mean any operation or set of operations which is performed upon personal data, whether or not by automatic means, such as collection, recording, organization, storage, adaptation or alteration, retrieval, consultation, use, disclosure by transmission, dissemination or otherwise making available, alignment or combination, blocking, erasure or destruction;

c) 'personal data filing system' ('filing system') shall mean any structured set of personal data which are accessible according to specific criteria, whether centralized, decentralized or dispersed on a functional or geographical basis;

d) 'controller' shall mean the natural or legal person, public authority, agency or any other body which alone or jointly with others determines the purposes and means of the processing of personal data; where the purposes and means of processing are determined by national or Community laws or regulations, the controller or the specific criteria for his nomination may be designated by national or Community law;

e) 'processor' shall mean a natural or legal person, public authority, agency or any other body which processes personal data on behalf of the controller;

f) 'third party' shall mean any natural or legal person, public authority, agency or any other body other than the data subject, the controller, the processor and the persons who, under the direct authority of the controller or the processor, are authorized to process the data;

g) 'recipient' shall mean a natural or legal person, public authority, agency or any other body to whom data are disclosed, whether a third party or not; however, authorities which may receive data in the framework of a particular inquiry shall not be regarded as recipients;

h) 'the data subject's consent' shall mean any freely given specific and informed indication of his wishes by which the data subject signifies his agreement to personal data relating to him being processed.

Article 3 Scope

(1) This Directive shall apply to the processing of personal data wholly or partly by automatic means, and to the processing otherwise than by automatic means of personal data which form part of a filing system or are intended to form part of a filing system.

(2) This Directive shall not apply to the processing of personal data:

- in the course of an activity which falls outside the scope of Community law, such as those provided for by Titles V and VI of the Treaty on European Union and in any case to processing operations concerning public security, defence, State security (including the economic well-being of the State when the processing operation relates to State security matters) and the activities of the State in areas of criminal law,

- by a natural person in the course of a purely personal or household activity.

Article 4 National law applicable

(1) Each Member State shall apply the national provisions it adopts pursuant to this Directive to the processing of personal data where:

a) the processing is carried out in the context of the activities of an establishment of the controller on the territory of the Member State; when the same controller is established on the territory of several Member States, he must take the necessary measures to ensure that each of these establishments complies with the obligations laid down by the national law applicable;

b) the controller is not established on the Member State's territory, but in a place where its national law applies by virtue of international public law;

c) the controller is not established on Community territory and, for purposes of processing personal data makes use of equipment, automated or otherwise, situated on the territory of the said Member State, unless such equipment is used only for purposes of transit through the territory of the Community.

(2) In the circumstances referred to in paragraph 1 (c), the controller must designate a representative established in the territory of that Member State, without prejudice to legal actions which could be initiated against the controller himself.

CHAPTER II – GENERAL RULES ON THE LAWFULNESS OF THE PROCESSING OF PERSONAL DATA

Article 5

Member States shall, within the limits of the provisions of this Chapter, determine more precisely the conditions under which the processing of personal data is lawful.

SECTION I – PRINCIPLES RELATING TO DATA QUALITY

Article 6

(1) Member States shall provide that personal data must be:

a) processed fairly and lawfully;

b) collected for specified, explicit and legitimate purposes and not further processed in a way incompatible with those purposes. Further processing of data for historical, statistical or scientific purposes shall not be considered as incompatible provided that Member States provide appropriate safeguards;

c) adequate, relevant and not excessive in relation to the purposes for which they are collected and/or further processed;

d) accurate and, where necessary, kept up to date; every reasonable step must be taken to ensure that data which are inaccurate or incomplete, having regard to the purposes for which they were collected or for which they are further processed, are erased or rectified;

e) kept in a form which permits identification of data subjects for no longer than is necessary for the purposes for which the data were collected or for which they are further processed. Member States shall lay down appropriate safeguards for personal data stored for longer periods for historical, statistical or scientific use.

(2) It shall be for the controller to ensure that paragraph 1 is complied with.

SECTION II – CRITERIA FOR MAKING DATA PROCESSING LEGITIMATE

Article 7

Member States shall provide that personal data may be processed only if:

a) the data subject has unambiguously given his consent; or

b) processing is necessary for the performance of a contract to which the data subject is party or in order to take steps at the request of the data subject prior to entering into a contract; or

c) processing is necessary for compliance with a legal obligation to which the controller is subject; or

d) processing is necessary in order to protect the vital interests of the data subject; or

e) processing is necessary for the performance of a task carried out in the public interest or in the exercise of official authority vested in the controller or in a third party to whom the data are disclosed; or

f) processing is necessary for the purposes of the legitimate interests pursued by the

controller or by the third party or parties to whom the data are disclosed, except where such interests are overridden by the interests for fundamental rights and freedoms of the data subject which require protection under Article 1 (1).

SECTION III – SPECIAL CATEGORIES OF PROCESSING

Article 8 The processing of special categories of data

(1) Member States shall prohibit the processing of personal data revealing racial or ethnic origin, political opinions, religious or philosophical beliefs, trade-union membership, and the processing of data concerning health or sex life.

(2) Paragraph 1 shall not apply where:

a) the data subject has given his explicit consent to the processing of those data, except where the laws of the Member State provide that the prohibition referred to in paragraph 1 may not be lifted by the data subject's giving his consent; or

b) processing is necessary for the purposes of carrying out the obligations and specific rights of the controller in the field of employment law in so far as it is authorized by national law providing for adequate safeguards; or

c) processing is necessary to protect the vital interests of the data subject or of another person where the data subject is physically or legally incapable of giving his consent; or

d) processing is carried out in the course of its legitimate activities with appropriate guarantees by a foundation, association or any other non-profit-seeking body with a political, philosophical, religious or trade-union aim and on condition that the processing relates solely to the members of the body or to persons who have regular contact with it in connection with its purposes and that the data are not disclosed to a third party without the consent of the data subjects; or

e) the processing relates to data which are manifestly made public by the data subject or is necessary for the establishment, exercise or defence of legal claims.

(3) Paragraph 1 shall not apply where processing of the data is required for the purposes of preventive medicine, medical diagnosis, the provision of care or treatment or the management of health-care services, and where those data are processed by a health professional subject under national law or rules established by national competent bodies to the obligation of professional secrecy or by another person also subject to an equivalent obligation of secrecy.

(4) Subject to the provision of suitable safeguards, Member States may, for reasons of substantial public interest, lay down exemptions in addition to

308 DATA PROTECTION LAW

those laid down in paragraph 2 either by national law or by decision of the supervisory authority.

(5) Processing of data relating to offences, criminal convictions or security measures may be carried out only under the control of official authority, or if suitable specific safeguards are provided under national law, subject to derogations which may be granted by the Member State under national provisions providing suitable specific safeguards. However, a complete register of criminal convictions may be kept only under the control of official authority. Member States may provide that data relating to administrative sanctions or judgements in civil cases shall also be processed under the control of official authority.

(6) Derogations from paragraph I provided for in paragraphs 4 and 5 shall be notified to the Commission.

(7) Member States shall determine the conditions under which a national identification number or any other identifier of general application may be processed.

Article 9 Processing of personal data and freedom of expression

Member States shall provide for exemptions or derogations from the provisions of this Chapter, Chapter IV and Chapter VI for the processing of personal data carried out solely for journalistic purposes or the purpose of artistic or literary expression only if they are necessary to reconcile the right to privacy with the rules governing freedom of expression.

SECTION IV – INFORMATION TO BE GIVEN TO THE DATA SUBJECT

Article 10 Information in cases of collection of data from the data subject

Member States shall provide that the controller or his representative must provide a data subject from whom data relating to himself are collected with at least the following information, except where he already has it:

a) the identity of the controller and of his representative, if any;

b) the purposes of the processing for which the data are intended;

c) any further information such as

- the recipients or categories of recipients of the data,
- whether replies to the questions are obligatory or voluntary, as well as the possible consequences of failure to reply,

- the existence of the right of access to and the right to rectify the data concerning him in so far as such further information is necessary, having regard to the specific circumstances in which the data are collected, to guarantee fair processing in respect of the data subject.

Article 11 Information where the data have not been obtained from the data subject

(1) Where the data have not been obtained from the data subject, Member States shall provide that the controller or his representative must at the time of undertaking the recording of personal data or if a disclosure to a third party is envisaged, no later than the time when the data are first disclosed provide the data subject with at least the following information, except where he already has it:

a) the identity of the controller and of his representative, if any;

b) the purposes of the processing;

c) any further information such as

- the categories of data concerned,
- the recipients or categories of recipients,
- the existence of the right of access to and the right to rectify the data concerning him

in so far as such further information is necessary, having regard to the specific circumstances in which the data are processed, to guarantee fair processing in respect of the data subject.

(2) Paragraph 1 shall not apply where, in particular for processing for statistical purposes or for the purposes of historical or scientific research, the provision of such information proves impossible or would involve a disproportionate effort or if recording or disclosure is expressly laid down by law. In these cases Member States shall provide appropriate safeguards.

SECTION V – THE DATA SUBJECT'S RIGHT OF ACCESS TO DATA

Article 12 Right of access

Member States shall guarantee every data right to obtain from the controller:

a) without constraint at reasonable intervals and without excessive delay or expense:

- confirmation as to whether or not data relating to him are being processed and information at least as to the purposes of the processing, the categories of data concerned, and the recipients or categories of recipients to whom the data are disclosed,

- communication to him in an intelligible form of the data undergoing processing and of any available information as to their source,

- knowledge of the logic involved in any automatic processing of data concerning him at least in the case of the automated decisions referred to in Article 15 (1);

b) as appropriate the rectification, erasure or blocking of data the processing of which does not comply with the provisions of this Directive, in particular because of the incomplete or inaccurate nature of the data;

c) notification to third parties to whom the data have been disclosed of any rectification, erasure or blocking carried out in compliance with (b), unless this proves impossible or involves a disproportionate effort.

SECTION VI – EXEMPTIONS AND RESTRICTIONS

Article 13

(1) Member States may adopt legislative measures to restrict the scope of the obligations and rights provided for in Articles 6 (1), 10, 11 (1), 12 and 21 when such a restriction constitutes a necessary measures to safeguard:

a) national security;

b) defence;

c) public security;

d) the prevention, investigation, detection and prosecution of criminal offences, or of breaches of ethics for regulated professions;

e) an important economic or financial interest of a Member State or of the European Union, including monetary, budgetary and taxation matters;

f) a monitoring, inspection or regulatory function connected, even occasionally, with the exercise of official authority in cases referred to in (c), (d) and (e);

g) the protection of the data subject or of the rights and freedoms of others.

(2) Subject to adequate legal safeguards, in particular that the data are not used for taking measures or decisions regarding any particular individual, Member States may, where there is clearly no risk of breaching the privacy of the data subject, restrict by a legislative measure the rights provided for in Article 12 when data are processed solely for purposes of scientific research or are kept in personal form for a period which does not exceed the period necessary for the sole purpose of creating statistics.

SECTION VII – THE DATA SUBJECT'S RIGHT TO OBJECT

Article 14 The data subject's right to object

Member States shall grant the data subject the right:

a) at least in the cases referred to in Article 7 (e) and (f), to object at any time on compelling legitimate grounds relating to his particular situation to the processing of data relating to him, save where otherwise provided by national legislation. Where there is a justified objection, the processing instigated by the controller may no longer involve those data;

b) to object, on request and free of charge, to the processing of personal data relating to him which the controller anticipates being processed for the purposes of direct marketing, or to be informed before personal data are disclosed for the first time to third parties or used on their behalf for the purposes of direct marketing, and to be expressly offered the right to object free of charge to such disclosures or uses.

Member States shall take the necessary measures to ensure that data subjects are aware of the existence of the right referred to in the first subparagraph of (b).

Article 15 Automated individual decisions

(1) Member States shall grant the right to every person not to be subject to a decision which produces legal effects concerning him or significantly affects him and which is based solely on automated processing of data intended to evaluate certain personal aspects relating to him, such as his performance at work, credit-worthiness, reliability, conduct, etc.

(2) Subject to the other Articles of this Directive, Member States shall provide that a person may be subjected to a decision of the kind referred to in paragraph 1 if that decision:

a) is taken in the course of the entering into or performance of a contract, provided the request for the entering into or the performance of the contract, lodged by the data subject, has been satisfied or that there are suitable measures to safeguard his legitimate interests, such as arrangements allowing him to put his point of view; or

b) is authorized by a law which also lays down measures to safeguard the data subject's legitimate interests.

SECTION VIII – CONFIDENTIALITY AND SECURITY OF PROCESSING

Article 16 Confidentiality of processing

Any person acting under the authority of the controller or of the processor, including the processor himself, who has access to personal data must not process them except on instructions from the controller, unless he is required to do so by law.

Article 17 Security of processing

(1) Member States shall provide that the controller must implement appropriate technical and organizational measures to protect personal data against accidental or unlawful destruction or accidental loss, alteration, unauthorized disclosure or access, in particular where the processing involves the transmission of data over a network, and against all other unlawful forms of processing.

Having regard to the state of the art and the cost of their implementation, such measures shall ensure a level of security appropriate to the risks represented by the processing and the nature of the data to be protected.

(2) The Member States shall provide that the controller must, where processing is carried out on his behalf, choose a processor providing sufficient guarantees in respect of the technical security measures and organizational measures governing the processing to be carried out, and must ensure compliance with those measures.

(3) The carrying out of processing by way of a processor must be governed by a contract or legal act binding the processor to the controller and stipulating in particular that:

– the processor shall act only on instructions from the controller,

– the obligations set out in paragraph 1, as defined by the law of the Member State in which the processor is established, shall also be incumbent on the processor.

(4) For the purposes of keeping proof, the parts of the contract or the legal act relating to data protection and the requirements relating to the measures referred to in paragraph 1 shall be in writing or in another equivalent form.

SECTION IX – NOTIFICATION

Article 18 – Obligation to notify the supervisory authority

(1) Member States shall provide that the controller or his representative, if any, must notify the supervisory authority referred to in Article 28 before carrying out any wholly or partly automatic processing operation or set of such operations intended to serve a single purpose or several related purposes.

(2) Member States may provide for the simplification of or exemption from notification only in the following cases and under the following conditions:

– where, for categories of processing operations which are unlikely, taking account of the data to be processed, to affect adversely the rights and freedoms of data subjects, they specify the purposes of the processing, the data or categories of data undergoing processing, the category or categories of data subject, the recipients or categories of recipient to whom the data are to be disclosed and the length of time the data are to be stored, and/or

– where the controller, in compliance with the national law which governs him, appoints a personal data protection official, responsible in particular:

– for ensuring in an independent manner the internal application of the national provisions taken pursuant to this Directive

– for keeping the register of processing operations carried out by the controller, containing the items of information referred to in Article 21 (2),

thereby ensuring that the rights and freedoms of the data subjects are unlikely to be adversely affected by the processing operations.

(3) Member States may provide that paragraph 1 does not apply to processing whose sole purpose is the keeping of a register which according to laws or regulations is intended to provide information to the public and which is open to consultation either by the public in general or by any person demonstrating a legitimate interest.

(4) Member States may provide for an exemption from the obligation to notify or a simplification of the notification in the case of processing operations referred to in Article 8 (2) (d).

(5) Member States may stipulate that certain or all non-automatic processing operations involving personal data shall be notified, or provide for these processing operations to be subject to simplified notification.

Article 19 – Contents of notification

(1) Member States shall specify the information to be given in the notification. It shall include at least:

a) the name and address of the controller and of his representative, if any;

b) the purpose or purposes of the processing;

c) a description of the category or categories of data subject and of the data or categories of data relating to them;

d) the recipients or categories of recipient to whom the data might be disclosed;

e) proposed transfers of data to third countries;

f) a general description allowing a preliminary assessment to be made of the appropriateness of the measures taken pursuant to Article 17 to ensure security of processing.

(2) Member States shall specify the procedures under which any change affecting the information referred to in paragraph I must be notified to the supervisory authority.

Article 20 Prior checking

(1) Member States shall determine the processing operations likely to present specific risks to the rights and freedoms of data subjects and shall check that these processing operations are examined prior to the start thereof.

(2) Such prior checks shall be carried out by the supervisory authority following receipt of a notification from the controller or by the data protection official, who, in cases of doubt, must consult the supervisory authority.

(3) Member States may also carry out such checks in the context of preparation either of a measure of the national parliament or of a measure based on such a legislative measure, which define the nature of the processing and lay down appropriate safeguards.

Article 21 – Publicizing of processing operations

(1) Member States shall take measures to ensure that processing operations are publicized.

(2) Member States shall provide that a register of processing operations notified in accordance with Article 18 shall be kept by the supervisory authority.

The register shall contain at least the information listed in Article 19 (1) (a) to (e).

The register may be inspected by any person.

(3) Member States shall provide, in relation to processing operations not subject to notification, that controllers or another body appointed by the Member States make available at least the information referred to in Article 19 (1) (a) to (e) in an appropriate form to any person on request.

Member States may provide that this provision does not apply to processing whose sole purpose is the keeping of a register which according to laws or regulations is intended to provide information to the public and which is open to consultation either by the public in general or by any person who can provide of a legitimate interest.

CHAPTER III – JUDICIAL REMEDIES, LIABILITY AND SANCTIONS

Article 22 Remedies

Without prejudice to any administrative remedy for which provision may be made, inter alia before the supervisory authority referred to in Article 28, prior to referral to the judicial authority, Member States shall provide for the right of every person to a judicial remedy for any breach of the rights guaranteed him by the national law applicable to the processing in question.

Article 23 Liability

(1) Member States shall provide that any person who has suffered damage as a result of an unlawful processing operation or of any act incompatible with the national provisions adopted pursuant to this Directive is entitled to receive compensation from the controller for the damage suffered.

(2) The controller may be exempted from this liability, in whole or in part, if he proves that he is not responsible for the event giving rise to the damage.

Article 24 Sanctions

The Member States shall adopt suitable measures to ensure the full implementation of the provisions of this Directive and shall in particular lay down the sanctions to be imposed in case of infringement of the provisions adopted pursuant to this Directive.

CHAPTER IV – TRANSFER OF PERSONAL DATA TO THIRD COUNTRIES

Article 25 Principles

(1) The Member States shall provide that the transfer to a third country of personal data which are undergoing processing or are intended for processing after transfer may take place only if, without prejudice to compliance with the national provisions adopted pursuant to the other provisions of this Directive, the third country in question ensures an adequate level of protection,

(2) The adequacy of the level of protection afforded by a third country shall be assessed in the light of all the circumstances surrounding a data transfer operation or set of data transfer operations; particular consideration shall be given to the nature of the data, the purpose and duration of the proposed processing operation or operations, the country of origin and country of final destination, the rules of law, both general and sectoral, in force in the third country in question and the professional rules and security measures which are complied with in that country.

(3) The Member States and the Commission shall inform each other of cases where they consider that a third country does not ensure an adequate level of protection within the meaning of paragraph 2.

(4) Where the Commission finds, under the procedure provided for in Article 31 (2), that a third country does not ensure an adequate level of protection within the meaning of paragraph 2 of this Article, Member States shall take the measures necessary to prevent any transfer of data of the same type to the third country in question.

(5) At the appropriate time, the Commission shall enter into negotiations with a view to remedying the situation resulting from the finding made pursuant to paragraph 4.

(6) The Commission may find, in accordance with the procedure referred to in Article 31 (2), that a third country ensures an adequate level of protection within the meaning of paragraph 2 of this Article, by reason of its domestic law or of the international commitments it has entered into, particularly upon conclusion of the negotiations referred to in paragraph 5, for the protection of the private lives and basic freedoms and rights of individuals.

Member States shall take the measures necessary to comply with the Commission's decision.

Article 26 Derogations

(1) By way of derogation from Article 25 and save where otherwise provided by domestic law governing particular cases, Member States shall provide that a transfer or a set of transfers of personal data to a third country which does not ensure an adequate level of protection within the meaning of Article 25 (2) may take place on condition that:

a) the data subject has given his consent unambiguously to the proposed transfer; or

b) the transfer is necessary for the performance of a contract between the data subject and the controller or the implementation of precontractual measures taken in response to the data subject's request; or

c) the transfer is necessary for the conclusion or performance of a contract concluded in the interest of the data subject between the controller and a third party; or

d) the transfer is necessary or legally required on important public interest grounds, or for the establishment, exercise or defence of legal claims; or

e) the transfer is necessary in order to protect the vital interests of the data subject; or

f) the transfer is made from a register which according to laws or regulations is intended to provide information to the public and which is open to consultation either by the public in general or by any person who can demonstrate legitimate interest, to the extent that the conditions laid down in law for consultation are fulfilled in the particular case.

(2) Without prejudice to paragraph 1, a Member State may authorize a transfer or a set of transfers of personal data to a third country which does not ensure an adequate level of protection within the meaning of Article 25 (2), where the controller adduces adequate safeguards with respect to the protection of the privacy and fundamental rights and freedoms of individuals and as regards the exercise of the corresponding rights; such safeguards may in particular result from appropriate contractual clauses.

(3) The Member State shall inform the Commission and the other Member States of the authorizations it grants pursuant to paragraph 2.

If a Member State or the Commission objects on justified grounds involving the protection of the privacy and fundamental rights and freedoms of individuals, the Commission shall take appropriate measures in accordance with the procedure laid down in Article 31 (2).

Member States shall take the necessary to comply with the Commission's decision. (4) Where the Commission decides, in accordance with the procedure referred to in Article 31 (2), that certain standard contractual clauses offer sufficient safeguards as required by paragraph 2, Member States shall take the necessary measures to comply with the Commission's decision.

CHAPTER V – CODES OF CONDUCT

Article 27

(1) The Member States and the Commission shall encourage the drawing up of codes of conduct intended to contribute to the proper implementation of the national provisions adopted by the Member States pursuant to this Directive, taking account of the specific features of the various sectors.

(2) Member States shall make provision for trade associations and other bodies representing other categories of controllers which have drawn up draft national codes or which have the intention of amending or extending existing national codes to be able to submit them to the opinion of the national authority. Member States shall make provision for this authority to ascertain, among other things, whether the drafts submitted to it are in accordance with the national provisions adopted pursuant to this Directive. If it sees fit, the authority shall seek the views of data subjects or their representatives.

(3) Draft Community codes, and amendments or extensions to existing Community codes, may be submitted to the Working Party referred to in Article 29. This Working Party shall determine, among other things, whether the drafts submitted to it are in accordance with the national provisions adopted pursuant to this Directive. If it sees fit, the authority shall seek the views of data subjects or their representatives. The Commission may ensure appropriate publicity for the codes which have been approved by the Working Party.

CHAPTER VI – SUPERVISORY AUTHORITY AND WORKING PARTY ON THE PROTECTION OF INDIVIDUALS WITH REGARD TO THE PROCESSING OF PERSONAL DATA

Article 28 Supervisory authority

(1) Each Member State shall provide that one or more public authorities are responsible for monitoring the application within its territory of the provisions adopted by the Member States pursuant to this Directive.

These authorities shall act with complete independence in exercising the functions entrusted to them.

(2) Each Member State shall provide that the supervisory authorities are consulted when drawing up administrative measures or regulations relating to the protection of individuals' rights and freedoms with regard to the processing of personal data.

(3) Each authority shall in particular be endowed with:

- investigative powers, such as powers of access to data forming the subject-matter of processing operations and powers to collect all the information necessary for the performance of its supervisory duties,

- effective powers of intervention, such as, for example, that of delivering opinions before processing operations are carried out, in accordance with Article 20, and ensuring appropriate publication of such opinions, of ordering the blocking, erasure or destruction of data, of imposing a temporary or definitive ban on processing, of warning or admonishing the controller, or that of referring the matter to national parliaments or other political institutions,

- the power to engage in legal proceedings where the national provisions adopted pursuant to this Directive have been violated or to bring these violations to the attention of the judicial authorities.

Decisions by the supervisory authority which give rise to complaints may be appealed against through the courts.

(4) Each supervisory authority shall hear claims lodged by any person, or by an association representing that person, concerning the protection of his rights and freedoms in regard to the processing of personal data. The person concerned shall be informed of the outcome of the claim.

Each supervisory authority shall, in particular, hear claims for checks on the lawfulness of data processing lodged by any person when the national provisions adopted pursuant to Article 13 of this Directive apply. The person shall at any rate be informed that a check has taken place.

(5) Each supervisory authority shall draw up a report on its activities at regular intervals. The report shall be made public.

(6) Each supervisory authority is competent, whatever the national law applicable to the processing in question, to exercise, on the territory of its own Member State, the powers conferred on it in accordance with paragraph 3.

Each authority may be requested to exercise its powers by an authority of another Member State.

The supervisory authorities shall cooperate with one another to the extent necessary for the performance of their duties, in particular by exchanging all useful information.

(7) Member States shall provide that the members and staff of the supervisory authority, even after their employment has ended, are to be subject to a duty of professional secrecy with regard to confidential information to which they have access.

Article 29 – Working Party on the Protection of Individuals with regard to the Processing of Personal Data

(1) A Working Party on the Protection of Individuals with regard to the Processing of Personal Data, hereinafter referred to as 'the Working Party', is hereby set up.

It shall have advisory status and act independently.

(2) The Working Party shall be composed of a representative of the supervisory authority or authorities designated by each Member State and of a representative of the authority or authorities established for the Community institutions and bodies, and of a representative of the Commission.

Each member of the Working Party shall be designated by the institution, authority or authorities which he represents. Where a Member State has designated more than one supervisory authority, they shall nominate a joint representative. The same shall apply to the authorities established for Community institutions and bodies.

(3) The Working Party shall take decisions by a simple majority of the representatives of the supervisory authorities.

(4) The Working Party shall elect its chairman. The chairman's term of office shall be two years. His appointment shall be renewable.

(5) The Working Party's secretariat shall be provided by the Commission.

(6) The Working Party shall adopt its own rules of procedure.

(7) The Working Party shall consider items placed on its agenda by its chairman, either on his own initiative or at the request of a representative of the supervisory authorities or at the Commission's request.

Article 30

(1) The Working Party shall:

a) examine any question covering the application of the national measures adopted under this Directive in order to contribute to the uniform application of such measures;

b) give the Commission an opinion on the level of protection in the Community and in third countries;

c) advise the Commission on any proposed amendment of this Directive, on any additional or specific measures to safeguard the rights and freedoms of natural persons with regard to the processing of personal data and on any other proposed Community measures affecting such rights and freedoms;

d) give an opinion on codes of conduct drawn up at Community level.

(2) If the Working Party finds that divergences likely to affect the equivalence of protection for persons with regard to the processing of personal data in the Community are arising between the laws or practices of Member States, it shall inform the Commission accordingly.

(3) The Working Party may, on its own initiative, make recommendations on all matters relating to the protection of persons with regard to the processing of personal data in the Community.

(4) The Working Party's opinions and recommendations shall be forwarded to the Commission and to the committee referred to in Article 31.

(5) The Commission shall inform the Working Party of the action it has taken in response to its opinions and recommendations. It shall do so in a report which shall also be forwarded to the European Parliament and the Council. The report shall be made public.

(6) The Working Party shall draw up an annual report on the situation regarding the protection of natural persons with regard to the processing of personal data in the Community and in third countries, which it shall transmit to the Commission, the European Parliament and the Council. The report shall be made public.

CHAPTER VII – COMMUNITY IMPLEMENTING MEASURES

Article 31 – The Committee

(1) The Commission shall be assisted by a committee composed of the representatives of the Member States and chaired by the representative of the Commission.

(2) The representative of the Commission shall submit to the committee a draft of the measures to be taken. The committee shall deliver its opinion on the draft within a time limit which the chairman may lay down according to the urgency of the matter.

The opinion shall be delivered by the majority laid down in Article 148 (2) of the Treaty. The votes of the representatives of the Member States within the committee shall be weighted in the manner set out in that Article. The chairman shall not vote.

The Commission shall adopt measures which shall apply immediately. However, if these measures are not in accordance with the opinion of the committee, they shall be communicated by the Commission to the Council forthwith. In that event:

–   the Commission shall defer application of the measures which it has decided for a period of three months from the date of communication,

–   the Council, acting by a qualified majority, may take a different decision within the time limit referred to in the first indent.

FINAL PROVISIONS

Article 32

(1) Member States shall bring into force the laws, regulations and administrative provisions necessary to comply with this Directive at the latest at the end of a period of three years from the date of its adoption.

When Member States adopt these measures, they shall contain a reference to this Directive or be accompanied by such reference on the occasion of their official publication. The methods of making such reference shall be laid down by the Member States.

(2) Member States shall ensure that processing already under way on the date the national provisions adopted pursuant to this Directive enter into force, is brought into conformity with these provisions within three years of this date.

By way of derogation from the preceding subparagraph, Member States may provide that the processing of data already held in manual filing systems on the date of entry into force of the national provisions adopted in implementation of this Directive shall be brought into conformity with Articles 6, 7 and 8 of this Directive within 12 years of the date on which it is adopted. Member States shall, however, grant the data subject the right to obtain, at his request and in particular at the time of exercising his right of access, the rectification, erasure or blocking of data which are incomplete, inaccurate or stored in a way incompatible with the legitimate purposes pursued by the controller.

(3) By way of derogation from paragraph 2, Member States may provide, subject to suitable safeguards, that data kept for the sole purpose of historical research need not be brought into conformity with Articles 6, 7 and 8 of this Directive.

(4) Member States shall communicate to the Commission the text of the provisions of domestic law which they adopt in the field covered by this Directive.

Article 33

The Commission shall report to the Council and the European Parliament at regular intervals, starting not later than three years after the date referred to in Article 32 (1), on the implementation of this Directive, attaching to its report, if necessary, suitable proposals for amendments. The report shall be made public.

The Commission shall examine, in particular, the application of this Directive to the data processing of sound and image data relating to natural persons and shall submit any appropriate proposals which prove to be necessary, taking account of developments in information technology and in the light of the state of progress in the information society.

Article 34

This Directive is addressed to the Member States.

Done at Luxembourg, 24 October 1995

INDEX

Access rights, 26, 86, 127
  As discovery, 10
  Charges, 26, 31, 130, 142
Accessible records, 45
Assessment requests, 213
Accounts, 80, 82
Accuracy, 64
Actors, 55
Adoption records, 39, 164
Advertising and marketing, 80, 81–82
Alignment of records, 53
Alteration of records, 52
Anonymised data, 103
Appeals, notices, 212
  Information Tribunal, 243–251
Applicable law, 16
Application of the Act, 57
Armed forces, 164, 191–192
Assessable processing, 83, 206
Automatic call forwarding, 282
Automated calling systems, 284
Automated data exemptions, 200
Automatic processing, 27, 131
  Control by subject, 149
Awareness of rights, 34

Banking, fraud protection, 7
Breach of confidence, 7, 8, 103, 117

CCTV, 1
  And see Surveillance
Caller identification, 280
Codes of conduct, Directive, 21
Combat effectiveness, 38
Combination of records, 53
Compensation, right of subjects, 61, 154
  Inaccurate data, 65, 156
Competition law, 8
Computer bureaux, 34
  See also Data processors

Computer technology, role of, 1
Conditions for processing, 88, 89–104
  Exemptions, 88
Confidential references, 29, 190–191
Confidential services, 105
Confidentiality, 19
  Electronic communications, 278
Consent, 16, 26, 33, 90, 103, 152
  Implicit, 90,103
Constraints on processing, 88–115
  Conditions for processing, 88, 89–104
Consultation of records, 52
Contract, performance of, 91
Control, concept of, 118, 143–159
Controller *see* Data controller
Corporate finance, 38, 164, 193–195
Counselling, 105
Credit rating, 2, 131
Credit reference agencies, 31, 131,
    138–140
Crime
  Exemptions, 29, 162, 164–166
  Prevention, 104, 105
Criminal convictions, 1,50
Crown appointment, 164, 192–193

Data, definition, 40
Data controller, 15, 25, 27–30, 55
  Access requests, 86
  Obligation to inform subject, 27
Data matching, 117
Data processor, 15, 34–36, 56
  Security obligations, 25, 35
Data Protection Act 1998, 24–39
  Application, 57
  Changes summarised, 37
  Definitions, 40–59
  Electronic communications, 277
  Exemptions, 38, 160–206
  Implementation, 24

Mechanism, 25
Transitional provisions, 58, 198–206
Data Protection Directive, 12–23
  Implemention, First Report of
      Commission, 256–262
    Applicable law, 259
    Disparities in implementation, 258
    Electronic communications, 277˙
    Image data, 261
    Online Survey, 257
    Sound data, 261
    Transfer to third countries, 260
Data protection law
  Application, 10
  Costs of, 6
  Defects, 6
  Development of, 3
  Enforcement, 207–226
  Harmonisation, 28
  Mechanism, 25
  Offences, 214
  Terminology, 9
Data protection principles, 60–71
Data Protection Registrar, 4,32
  See also Information Commissioner
Data security, 14
Data subjects, 16, 18, 23, 25, 30–34, 56
  Access requests, 31, 66, 127
    Enforced, 32, 140–142
    Fees, 130, 142
  Awareness of rights, 34
  Complaints, levels, 32
  Compensation, right to, 61, 154
  Concerns, 31
  Consent, 16, 26, 33, 90, 103, 152
    Implicit, 90, 103
  Control, 143
  Manual files, 33
  Obligation to inform, 31, 119
    Disproportionate effort, 124
    Exceptions, 119
    Exposing another individual, 133
    Where data from third party, 124
  Rights, 116–159
    Automated processing, 149
    Consent, 152
    Subject access, 127
    To object to processing, 27, 31
Data protection supervisors, 85
  EU, 269
Data user, 15, 34
  See Data controllers
Defamation, 145
Destruction of records, 53, 226

Direct marketing and see Advertising and
    marketing
  Control of processing, 147
  Electronic communications, 284
  Opting out, 11, 147
Directors' liability, data protection law, 222
Disclosure of records, 52, 163, 187–189
  Offences, 218
Discovery, 10
Domestic purposes, 164, 189–190
Driving convictions, 2

EEA see European Economic Area
EU Institutions, data processing, 263–275
Education, 38, 45, 170–184
Eighth data protection principle, 69
Electronic communications, privacy and,
    276–287
  Automated calling systems, 284
  Automatic call forwarding, 282
  Caller identification, 280
  Compensation, 286
  Confidentiality, 278
  Direct marketing, 284
  Directories, 283
  Emergency calls, 282
  Location data, 281
  Nuisance calls, 282
  Security, 278
  Spam, 285
  Traffic data, 278
Electoral register, 148
E-mail see Electronic communications
Emergency calls, 282
Employee liability, data protection law, 222
Employee records, 80
Employees' access to data, 67
Enforced subject access, 32, 140–142
  Offences, 219
Enforcement, 207–226
  Notices, 208–213
    Appeals, 212
    Restrictions, 212
Erasure of records, 53, 226
Ethnic origins, 6, 104
European Economic Area, 14, 111
European Union Institutions, data
    processing 263–275
Examination marks and scripts, 38, 164,
    195–197
Excessive data, 64
Exemptions, 38, 160–206
  Adoption records, 39, 164
  Armed forces, 164, 191–192

Combat effectiveness, 38
Confidential references, 29, 38, 164
Corporate finance, 38, 164, 193–195
Crime, 29, 162, 164–166
Crown appointment, 164, 192–193
Disclosures, 163, 187–189
Domestic purposes, 164, 189–190
Education, 38, 162, 170–184
Examination marks and scripts, 38,
    164, 195–197
Health and social work, 38, 162,
    170–184
History, 163, 184–185, 204–205
Honours, 164
Human fertilisation and embryology,
    39, 164
Journalism, literature and art, 88, 144,
    163
Judicial appointments, 164, 192
Management forecasts, 29, 38, 164, 193
Manual data, public, 163, 185–186
National security, 88, 105, 162,
    164–166, 286
Negotiations, 38, 164, 195
Privilege, legal profession, 164, 197
Public information, 186
Publication and freedom of expression,
    38
References, 190–191
Regulatory activity, 163
Research, 38, 163, 184–185
Self-incrimination, 164, 197
Social work, 162, 170–184
Statistics, 163, 184–185
Statutory functions, 29
Taxation, 29, 162, 164–166

Failure to notify,
    Criminal offence, 25, 72
Fair processing, 62
Fax, 284
Filing system, relevant, 42
Fifth data protection principle, 66
First data protection principle, 62
Forfeiture, 226
Fourth data protection principle, 64
Free movement of data, 3, 11
    Data Protection Directive, 12
Freedom of expression, 1, 7, 18
Freedom of information, 8

Genetic data, 117
    And see Health
Good practice, information processing, 29

Health and social work, 38, 45, 95, 101,
    130, 133–135, 162, 170–184
    Transfer of data from third country,
        113
Historical purposes, processing, 14, 163,
    184–185, 204–205
Holding data, 35
Honours, 164
Household activity, 16
Human fertilisation and embryology, 39,
    164
Human rights, 1, 116
    Respect for private and family life, 2, 7

Images
    As data, 129, 261
    Deceased persons, 147
    Manipulation, 146
Implicit consent, 90
Inaccurate data, 65, 156
Information Commissioner, 25, 227–240
    Assessment of processing, 233
    Codes of Practice, 231
        Parliament, 234
    Functions, 230
    International co-operation, 235
    International transfer, 232
    Notification, 73
    Office, 228
    Overseas information systems,
        inspection, 239
    Powers, 25
    Powers of entry and inspection, 221,
        223–226
    Processing of notification, 10
    Special purposes processing, assisting,
        234
Information notice, 210
Information Tribunal, 227, 240–255
    Appeals, 243–251
        National Security, 251–255
    Constitution, 241
    Costs, 250
    Determination, 250
    Hearing, 248
    Jurisdiction, 242
    Procedure, 243
Insurance, 105
Internet, 20,110

Journalism, literature and art,
    exemptions, 88, 144, 163
Judicial appointments, 164, 192
Judicial remedies, 19

Jurisdiction and procedure, 158
Justice, administration of, 93

Keeping data updated, 64

Lawful purposes, 63, 94
Legal obligations, 91
Lifestyle data, 117
Location data, 281

Management forecasts, exemption, 29,
    193
Manual files, 11, 15
  Data subjects' rights, 33
  Pre-existing, 23, 29
  Public authority, 163, 185–186
  Transitional provisions, 200
Medical records, 1, 95, 130
Mode of trial, offences, 222

National security, 88, 162, 164–166
  Appeals, 251–255
Negotiations, 38, 195
Non-profit organisations, 80, 100, 101
Notices, 208–213
  Enforcement, 209
  Offences, 21
  Restrictions, 212
Notification, 25, 28, 29, 72–87
  Assessable processing, 83, 206
  Changes to entries, 77
    Duty to inform, 78
  Exemptions, 80
  Fees, 77
  Offences, 215–217
  Particulars required, 74
  Register, 79
  Security measures required, 76
Nuisance calls, 282

Obtaining records, 52
  Offences, 218
Offences, 214–226
Officers' liability, data protection law,
    222
Organisation of records, 52
Overseas information systems see
    Transfer of data to third countries

Passing off, 145
Penalties, 222
Pensions, 105
Personal activity, 16
Personal data, 46

Collection, informing subjects, 11, 18
Processing, 2
  Community Institutions, 263–275
  Damage of distress, 11
Protection, 2, 3
  Legal, 7
Sensitive see Sensitive personal data
Transfer, in EU, 271
Police checks, 140
Police national computer, 2
Political information, 50, 106
Privacy, 1, 34
  Computers, as threat to, 116
  Data Protection Directive, 12, 18
  Electronic communications, 276–287
Private investigators, 117, 133
Privilege, legal profession, 164, 197
Processing, 2, 51
  Alignment, 53
  Alteration, 52
  Automatic see Automatic processing
  Combination, 53
  Constraints, 88–115
    Consent, 90
    Contract, performance of, 91
    Justice, administration of, 93
    Legal obligation, 91
    Legitimate interests of data
        controller, 94
    Sensitive personal data, 97–101, 104
    Transfers to other countries, 105
    Vital interest of data subject, 92, 100
  Control, by subject, 143
  Consultation, 52
  Damage or distress, 11
  Destruction, 53
  Direct marketing, 147
  Disclosure, 52
  Erasure, 53
  Good practice, 29
  Lawfulness, 16
  Need to be necessary, 17
  Obtaining, 52
  Organisation, 52
  Recording and holding, 52
  Retrieval, 52
  Security, 19
  Sensitive data, conditions, 97–106
  Special purposes, 54
  Systems,
    Data Protection Directive, 12
  Transparency, 118
Procuring data, offences, 218
Proportionality, 136

Public records, 45
Public interest, 104
Publication and freedom of expression, 38

Race, collection of data, 6, 50
Recipient, 56
Recording and holding data, 52
Recruitment, 141
Rectification, right of, 23, 33
Register of persons notifying, 79
Regulatory activity, 163
Relevant filing system, 42
Relevant particulars, 86
Religious beliefs, 50
Requests for assessment, 213
Research, 38, 66, 163, 184–185
Respect for private and family life, 2
Retention, excessive, 66
Retrieval of records, 52

Safe harbours, 115
Scientific purposes, processing, 14
Second data protection principle, 63
Security of processing, 19, 66
    Notification and, 76
Self-incrimination, 164, 197
Selling data, offences, 218
Sensitive personal data, 17, 26, 33, 50–51,
    Conditions on processing, 97–106
Seventh data protection principle, 66
Sexual life, 50
Sixth data protection principle, 66
Social services records, 3 and see Health
Sound data, 261
Spam, 285
Special information notice, 211
Special purposes, 54, 212
    Information Commissioner and, 234
Staff administration, 80, 82

Statistical purposes, processing, 14, 163, 184–185
Statutory functions, 29
Storage, 35
Structured manual files see Manual files
Subject access, 127
Supervisors, 85
Supervisory authorities, Directive, 21
Surveillance, 117

Taxation, 29, 162, 164–166
Telephony see Electronic communications
Third data protection principle, 64
Third party disclosure, 36, 56
Time, excessive retention, 66
Trade union, 50
Traffic data, electronic, 278
Transfer of data to third countries, 11, 14, 19, 69, 106–115
    Consent required, 26, 153
    Data Protection Directive, report on, 260
    EU, within, 271
    Health, 113
    Information Commissioner, 232, 235
        Powers to inspect system, 239
    Internet, 20, 110
    Offences, 219
    US safe harbours, 115
Transparency, concept of, 118

Unauthorised processing, 67
Unnecessary data, 64
Unsolicited mail, 148

Vital interest of data subject, 92, 100

Warrant, grant,223
Working Party, Directive, role, 21

X-rays, 130

Printed in the United Kingdom
by Lightning Source UK Ltd.
105589UKS00001B/37-114